CW00614006

THE GENESIS OF LACHMANN'S METHOD

The Genesis of Lachmann's Method

SEBASTIANO TIMPANARO

Edited and translated by Glenn W. Most

The University of Chicago Press

CHICAGO AND LONDON

SEBASTIANO TIMPANARO (1923–2000) was an Italian scholar in classics and politics. He was a member of the British Academy and the Accademia dei Lincei and the author of *On Materialism.*

GLENN W. MOST is professor of ancient Greek at the Scuola Normale Superiore in Pisa and teaches at the University of Chicago in the Committee on Social Thought and in the classics and comparative literature departments.

The University of Chicago Press, Chicago 60637
The University of Chicago Press, Ltd., London
© 2005 by The University of Chicago
All rights reserved. Published 2005
Printed in the United States of America

14 13 12 11 10 09 08 07 06 05   1 2 3 4 5

ISBN: 0-226-80405-4 (cloth)

Italian edition published by Liviana Editrice, 1981.

Library of Congress Cataloging-in-Publication Data

Timpanaro, Sebastiano.
[Genesi del metodo del Lachmann. English]
    The genesis of Lachmann's method / Sebastiano Timpanaro ; edited and translated
    by Glenn W. Most.
        p.   cm.
    Includes bibliographical references and index.
    ISBN 0-226-80405-4 (cloth : alk. paper) — ISBN 0-226-80406-2 (pbk. : alk. paper)
    1. Lachmann, Karl, 1793–1851. 2. German philology. 3. Classical philology.
    I. Most, Glenn W. II. Title.

PD64.L3T5613 2005
430'.9'092—dc22   2005015897

♾ The paper used in this publication meets the minimum requirements of the American National Standard for Information Sciences—Permanence of Paper for Printed Library Materials, ANSI Z39.48-1992.

IN MEMORY OF EUGENIO GRASSI

Contents

Editor's Introduction

Sebastiano Timpanaro (1923–2000) was one of the most important Italian intellectuals of his generation and a major figure in twentieth-century Classics, history, and Marxist and Freudian theory. He is not as well known in England and America as he deserves to be, however, in part because of the seeming disparity of his interests, in part because of the very unconventionality and originality of his views, and in part because traditionally it has been from other European countries, especially France and Germany, that thinkers have more often been translated into English (if only because traditional academic Italian, a language in which Timpanaro fortunately did not write, is singularly resistant to attempts at rendering into English). I hope the present edition will serve not only to facilitate study of those crucial aspects of the history of Classics and of the theory and practice of textual editions that his book presents so clearly, but also to introduce to a somewhat wider audience the thought of a quirkily brilliant, soberly passionate, and profoundly serious European intellectual.

*   *   *

Sebastiano Timpanaro was born into a family that combined a deep dedication to intellectual pursuits, especially to the history of science, with a no less deep commitment to leftist politics. His father, Sebastiano Timpanaro Sr. (1888–1949), was born in the small town of Tortorici, near Messina in Sicily, but then went north to study physics at the universities of Naples and then Bologna. His promising career as an assistant in experimental physics at the University of Parma was cut short in 1929 by his categorical refusal to take the oath of allegiance that the Fascist government required of all Italian state employees; he found work first in a private school in Florence, where he taught mathematics and physics for a number of years, and then—in the meantime he had been obliged to swear the loyalty oath after all—at the Domus Galilaeana, a research institute in the history of science in Pisa, which he directed from 1942 until his death. Sebastiano Timpanaro's mother, Maria Cardini (1890–1978), was born in Arezzo and took a degree in Greek literature at the University of Naples; in 1914 she studied briefly in Berlin with two of the greatest Hellenists of the past centuries, Ulrich von Wilamowitz-Moellendorff and Hermann Diels. After a brief period as a Dadaist poet (for several years she corresponded frequently with Tristan Tzara), around 1920 she abandoned poetry forever and returned to her Greek studies. She acquired considerable recognition, not only in Italy, for her editions, translations, and studies of ancient Greek philosophy and science, especially on the topic of the Pythagoreans, but she remained for her whole career a teacher in junior high schools, first in Parma (where she met Sebastiano Timpanaro Sr.), then at the same private school in Florence as her husband, finally in Pisa. After the end of the Second World War, she became actively involved in local politics in Pisa for the Italian Socialist Party, campaigning especially for the establishment of non-Church nursery schools in the city.

Sebastiano Timpanaro was much attached to his parents, even by Italian standards—he published a selection of his father's papers with a preface by himself in 1952 (Timpanaro Sr. 1952), and the very last essay he wrote was the lengthy introduction to a collection of his mother's works that he edited, which was published after his death (Cardini 2001). From them he inherited interests and characteristics that marked all his work and his whole life: an uncompromising commitment to intellectual honesty and moral rigor; an unswerving dedication to an ideal of rationality, as it is expressed for example in the progress of the natural sciences, with at the same time a painful recognition of the brutal irrationality of much of human history, especially in national and international politics; an exceptionally broad multidisciplinary and multilingual culture, with a particular fascination for French and German literature and intellectual history; a systematic preference for discussing current intellectual issues in terms not of the contemporary epigones who set the passing fashions but of the seminal thinkers who first set the fundamental questions; a constitutional inability to compromise; an almost morbid tendency to exacerbate disagreement to the point of irreparable rupture; an unmistakable tone in all his writings, above all strictly clear and precise, often austere, occasionally severe, but with a sprinkling of colloquialisms and, rarely, metaphors, unabashedly and sometimes rather ponderously didactic, free of any false rhetorical pathos and of even the slightest trace of wit or humor for their own sake.

Timpanaro was born in Parma and moved with his parents to Florence. In the university of that city he had the good fortune to be able to study Classics with Giorgio Pasquali (1885–1952), the greatest Italian Classicist of the twentieth century and a crucial figure in the sometimes difficult mediation between the German and the Italian national traditions of scholarship during that period. In Pisa Pasquali also taught at the elite Scuola Normale Superiore, and once Timpanaro's family moved there he was introduced into the intense intellectual atmosphere of that unique institution of scholarly research and teaching and into the diminutive, provincial, but culturally and politically very animated town in which it is located. It was also at Pisa that Timpanaro studied with Eduard Fraenkel, one of the greatest German Classicists of the century, who came to teach at the Scuola Normale regularly for a number of years after Pasquali's death. Under their guidance Timpanaro laid the scholarly foundations for his later work on Classical literature, especially on Latin poetry (above all in the highly technical disciplines of textual criticism and of microexegetical and lexical studies) and on the history of scholarship on Latin poetry during antiquity. In both of these fields, Timpanaro made numerous significant and lasting contributions (collected in Timpanaro 1978, 1986, 1994a, and 2001a), though he always preferred the form of the small, astonishingly erudite, highly condensed philological note to that of the expansive literary monograph and though he never himself undertook the full-scale editions of such authors as Ennius and Virgil that his teachers had hoped he would do.

On the basis of these studies, Timpanaro was widely regarded, at home and abroad, as one of the very few most highly esteemed Italian Classical scholars of his time. Yet he never became a regular professor at any Italian university (toward the very end of his life, he taught a few times at the University of Florence as a visiting professor): after some years of teaching in secondary schools near Pisa, he worked from 1960 until his retirement in 1983 as a proofreader at a Florentine publishing house, La Nuova Italia. What exactly the reason (or, likelier, the complex set of partial reasons) was for this seeming anomaly—an anomaly that was perhaps less extraordinary in Italy, where intellectual life has never been confined to the universities, than it would have seemed in some other countries—was always far from clear, even to those who knew him best. Some have suggested that the imperfect Italian university system was not capable of recognizing, or of accepting, his merits, or alternatively that he himself was not willing to compromise himself by entering into its institutional ambiguities. It should also be borne in mind that, in remaining aloof from direct participation in the university (though many of his closest friends were university professors), he was able to continue a family tradition set (though for different reasons) by his parents, to devote his free time entirely to scholarly research and publication without becoming embroiled in university administration and examinations, and to direct his pedagogical activity to friends and to anonymous readers rather than to the physically present, always unpredictable, sometimes rather unruly students who often seemed to inspire in him a degree of diffidence bordering on dread.

Timpanaro's focus on the most technical aspects of Classical scholarship and his confidence that Classics was a scientific discipline comparable, at least in certain regards, to the natural sciences did not mislead him into supposing that we might be capable of having a direct, unmediated relation to antiquity or into neglecting the history of Classical scholarship as though it were nothing more than an accumulation of superseded errors. On the contrary, from the beginning of his studies he paired the scrupulous investigation of ancient literary texts with the no less scrupulous investigation of those scholars who had investigated them before him, both in antiquity and in modern times: the interpretative variations of a single text along the line of the history of its reception helped enrich it with unexpected and not always absurd new meanings; the relative stability of that text provided a fixed point that permitted the historical variety of its attested understandings to be ordered and rendered meaningful. Timpanaro's first book, dedicated to his parents, was a study of Giacomo Leopardi's contributions to Classical studies (Timpanaro 1955, 1977a, 1997a): in it he demonstrated once and for all that Leopardi, so far from being nothing more than a self-absorbed Romantic poet obsessed only with his personal tribulations, was a Classical scholar of European rank who was not only deeply inspired by his reading of Greek and Latin texts but also capable of interpreting and emending them along with the very best of his contemporaries. This first book, which has remained the standard work on the subject, was followed by an edition of Leopardi's philological writings (Leopardi 1969) and by a number of other studies in modern literary and intellectual history, mostly devoted to nineteenth-century Italian writers (collected in Timpanaro 1965, 1969, 1980a, 1982, 1984a, 1994b). Although Timpanaro modestly defined himself once as nothing more than "a scholar of nineteenth-century cultural history who comes from Classical philology" (Bruscagli and Tellini 1996: 15), in fact his contribution to the way in which Italians understand their own intellectual history has been extremely influential. In particular, Timpanaro's insistence on the Classical component of much early nineteenth-century Italian writing has brought to prominence the continuities between a liberal strain of eighteenth-century Enlightenment thinking and a number of nineteenth-century writers who had previously been superficially pigeonholed as Romantic and were often discounted as conservatives or anti-nationalists. In so doing, he has helped reestablish an important link of continuity in European cultural history between the eighteenth and nineteenth centuries.

Timpanaro's concentration on nineteenth-century figures should not mislead: it was rather with certain aspects of the eighteenth century, especially with those that seemed to him to point to positive future developments or that had been unjustly neglected, that he himself evidently felt his deepest affinity. In particular, Timpanaro developed a sophisticated yet highly personal philosophical position that reached back to such ancient precursors as Epicurus and, above all, Lucretius but that would have been most at home in the eighteenth century. It is no accident that he chose to embody his views not only in the form of a collection of essays titled *On Materialism* (Timpanaro 1970, 1975a, 1997b; English translation, Timpanaro 1975b, 1980b, 1996) but also in that of a translation of P. Thiry d'Holbach's 1772 treatise *Le bon sens* (Good sense; d'Holbach 1985), to which he appended Voltaire's observations on the text and also provided an extensive introduction of his own, which explored the text in both historical and systematic perspectives. At the cost of a certain degree of oversimplification, we may summarize Timpanaro's philosophy under the headings of materialism, hedonism, atheism, and pessimism. As a materialist, Timpanaro was firmly opposed to any Idealistic idolatry of the supposed autonomy and freedom of the human agent. Instead he insisted on the total physical and biological determination of all human phenomena, severely criticizing on this account, among many others, the later Freud (Timpanaro 1974, 1975c, 1992; English translation, Timpanaro 1976a), almost all twentieth-century Marxists, and even Marx himself, whom he accused of lapsing frequently into Idealistic humanism and to whom he preferred Engels. Against the various forms of Idealism that, in such figures as Benedetto Croce (1866–1952), dominated Italian philosophy through most of the twentieth century, Timpanaro leaped back to Leopardi as the model for an enlightened materialism—and also for an enlightened pessimism with which it was intimately linked. For, in this view, an essential part of the biological apparatus that makes up human beings as well as all other organisms is the unremitting search for pleasure. But given that there is no God (a conclusion he derived from the failure of all attempted theodicies), it is certain that nature has not been constructed with a view toward us, so as to fulfill our ends, and hence the hedonistic desire for the satisfaction of our desires must inevitably be often frustrated—systematically, painfully, irremediably. Those who knew Timpanaro well—the oscillations in his moods between irony and despair; his intermittent bursts of intense joy at the pleasures of friendship or of scholarship; his unfailing, angular courtesy—never doubted that his pessimism was not only a well considered and carefully argued philosophical position but also a deeply ingrained way of life.

Nonetheless, Timpanaro was also for his whole life a passionately engaged militant on the far left wing of Italian politics. He began, soon after the end of the Second World War, as a member of the PSI (Partito Socialista Italiano, or the Italian Socialist Party), like both his parents; he shared with them a lifelong hostility to both the Christian Democrats, who, overtly Catholic and with the support of the Catholic Church, governed Italy uninterruptedly for the first two decades after the war, and the Italian Communist Party, which he regarded as covertly theological in structure, ideology, and appeal—opium for the masses. But it has never been easy, in Italy or elsewhere, to be both left wing and principled, and at the same time to wish to attain actual political power. When the Italian Socialists decided in 1964 to abandon the opposition and to join the government in a coalition with the Christian Democrats, Timpanaro and his mother, like many other Socialists who reacted against what they considered a betrayal of their founding principles, became active members in the newly founded PSIUP (Partito Socialista Italiano di Unità Proletaria, the original name of the PSI), which splintered off from the left wing of the PSI. The PSIUP dissolved when it failed dismally in the general elections of 1972, and Timpanaro joined a successor party, the PDUP (Partito di Unità Proletaria); but the PDUP, despite coalescing with other small left-wing groups, was crushed in its turn in the elections of 1976. Timpanaro resigned from the PDUP in that year and never again joined any other political party on offer in Italy's alphabet soup of left-wing acronyms. But until the end of his life he continued to write frequently in newspapers, journals, and private letters about specific political issues and about the tensions and contradictions in the Italian left—an ample, indeed an inexhaustible subject for reflection, which, in his last years, he seasoned with a cautious rapprochement with environmentalist positions (Timpanaro 2001b). Timpanaro's gaunt, well-dressed figure, with his high forehead and piercing eyes, was a familiar sight not only at scholarly conferences and seminars, where he was received by colleagues and students with a respect bordering on deference, but also at political demonstrations, where a vague sense of his scholarly renown and institutional marginality surrounded him with an aura of ascetic purity, indeed almost of saintliness. He must have been a formidable political opponent, erudite, eloquent, drastically and unrelentingly polemical, limited only by an intransigent incapacity to compromise and perhaps a certain remoteness from the lived realities (as opposed to the theoretical study) of politics and economics.

Oddly, the only books of Timpanaro's that have been translated into English before now are his collection of essays *On Materialism,* in which he attacks European Marxism for having betrayed the legacy of genuine materialism bequeathed by Engels, and French Structuralism for having misunderstood and misapplied the linguistic theories of Saussure (Timpanaro 1975b, 1980b, 1996), and *The Freudian Slip,* his sustained polemic against the later Freud and Freudian psychoanalysis in general for having abandoned the materialist insights of Freud's early writings, and against the psychoanalytic explanation of so-called Freudian slips in particular, which in most cases, based on his conception of materialism and his experience of textual criticism (and proofreading), he attributes instead to exactly the same kinds of mechanical processes as result so often in mistakes in transcribing manuscripts (Timpanaro 1976a). A few articles, mostly on related themes, have also been translated (Timpanaro 1976b, 1977b, 1979, 1984b, 1988). The result is that Timpanaro is known in the English-speaking world above all as a materialist philosopher, Leftist theoretician, and critic of psychoanalysis. These are, of course, important aspects of his vast and diverse production—but it can be argued that they are the ones of least permanent value, in part because they were tied closely to what appear now to have been largely ephemeral modes of Leftist politics and thought (already in the 1990s Timpanaro ruefully confessed that *On Materialism* had come to seem to him like "a fossil"; Timpanaro 1994b: xi), in part because philosophy was in fact not Timpanaro's greatest strength. Instead it is his historical and philological studies that seem to me to represent his most lasting contribution to Western culture. The present translation of *The Genesis of Lachmann's Method* will give a wider circle of readers the opportunity to enrich their understanding of this profound and enigmatic figure.

∗   ∗   ∗

Timpanaro's book examines the historical development and the systematic limits of a particularly significant moment—the attempt during the nineteenth century to increase the degree of rationalization, standardization, and professionalization, within the evolution of a process that for millennia has been central to human culture—the transmission of written texts. It is only if his argument is placed within this larger horizon that its full import can be understood.

A written record has this advantage over an oral utterance—that it lasts in time beyond the moment of expression, in a physical form independent of the speaker's and listeners' memories. Yet this physical form too has its limitations, for it is restricted to a single spatial location and must be entrusted to an ultimately perishable medium to bear it. For the one reason or the other—either because the existing copy no longer suffices for the new, spatially dispersed uses to which it is now to be put (usually, new readers), or because it has become damaged over time (by overuse, inadequate materials, or simple old age)—it may become desirable to produce new copies of written texts. Before the age of photographs, photocopies, and scanners, which copy texts by purely mechanical processes simply on the basis of the contrast between lighter areas and darker ones, the only way to produce new copies was to transcribe them from old ones, element for element, most often semantic unit for semantic unit. If greater accuracy of transmission was required, this could be done visually, by a scribe copying onto one new medium the text he saw before his eyes (but the disadvantage was the smaller number of copies that could thereby be produced at the same time from a single exemplar). If on the other hand a large number of copies was sought after, an acoustic procedure could be preferred whereby the exemplar was read out before a group of scribes, who listened to it and copied down, each onto his own medium, what they thought they had heard (at the cost of greater inaccuracy, due to homonyms, distraction, noise, and other forms of interference). It is only a guess, but probably a good one, that for most of the history of human culture the normal situation was one that began with a single exemplar to be copied (the source text) and ended up, as result and usually as purpose, with more than one copy of the text (the source text plus the target text, or multiple target texts): transmission normally entailed multiplication. And given that the procedure was performed neither by machines nor by gods but by humans, and that humans err, transmission always entailed error, and multiplication of copies usually entailed proliferation of errors.

To have only a single source greatly simplified the copyist's task: he (it was of course usually a he) could attempt to transcribe it as faithfully as he or his supervisors wished, intervening into the text as he saw fit, so as to correct obvious errors or to effect what he considered to be improvements of various sorts. But what was he to do when he had available two source texts? Given the proliferation of errors, these were bound to differ from one another in their readings, at least occasionally, if they were of any considerable length. On what basis was he to choose which reading to put into the target text? However rarely such a situation occurred—and presumably for many centuries it did not occur frequently except in the largest scriptoria, monasteries, and libraries—it must have happened regularly enough for a certain set of rule-of-thumb criteria of choice to develop: whichever seemed to be the grammatically or semantically or logically better reading would be preferred from case to case, or both readings could be imported into the target text with or without an expression of greater authorization for one of them. The next step methodologically will have been to give a general preference to the one source text over the other available one whenever possible, either suppressing apparently equipollent readings in the latter or indicating them as inferior alternatives. This will have simplified the copyist's work, freeing him from the obligation to use his brain to choose among variants from case to case and, in effect, reducing once again the number of source texts. But at this point a new question arose: on what basis was the copyist to choose which one of the available sources he was to prefer? Over the centuries, various contradictory criteria were developed, each with its own partial and specious justification: the oldest manuscript; the most legible manuscript; the one that appeared to have the most good readings; the one that had the fewest corrections; the one that had the most corrections; the one that derived from an authoritative provenance; the one that was closest to hand; and so forth. And of course even then the copyist (or his corrector) was still free as he saw fit to make whatever he thought were corrections and other improvements.

The advent of printing in the fifteenth century altered various parameters of the process of textual transmission but at first had no effect whatsoever on these methodological issues. Printing vastly multiplied the number of target texts that could be made on the basis of a single source text and created a greater degree of textual identity (though, especially at first, by no means complete identity) among those target texts. But printing did not in itself require people to change fundamentally the methods of textual transmission, and indeed for several centuries printers, correctors, and editors continued to use most of the same rule-of-thumb criteria that their predecessors, the ancient and medieval copyists, had developed. What changed matters most was instead the concatenation of three factors during the period from the fifteenth to the nineteenth centuries: the vast increase in the number of manuscripts, Greek and Latin, that became available throughout Europe during and after the Renaissance; the gradual concentration of the holdings of libraries no longer in a large number of small collections (each of which might have one manuscript of Cicero) but, more and more, in a small number of large collections (each of which might have dozens); and the general increase in the ease of communication and travel over the course of the early modern period. The result was that eventually there was no longer a scarcity of potentially available source texts from which further copies could be derived but an impressive, indeed intimidating overabundance—Montfaucon's *Palaeographia graeca* (1708) already lists more than 11,000 Greek manuscripts. Since the fifteenth century, printers and editors had tended by force of inertia to copy their own texts from those printed by their predecessors, correcting them by the lights of their ingenuity where they seemed in error or adducing for comparison some one manuscript (or a very few manuscripts), almost always one (or ones) that had the advantage of proximity or the appearance of old age. As the number of available manuscripts proliferated, further criteria for preferring one reading over another were developed—the better reading was the one to be found in the most manuscripts, or in the oldest ones, or in the oldest one of all—but a rational justification for such criteria was neither provided nor available. At least from the lofty perspective of a nineteenth-century Classical philology anxious to establish its credentials as a serious science, this was obviously an unsatisfactory state of affairs.

The first attempt to provide a thoroughly mechanical and systematic procedure for rationalizing and standardizing the choice among manuscripts, and hence among readings, was developed during the nineteenth century

and since the beginning of the twentieth century has been known as Lachmann's method because of its association with Karl Lachmann (1793–
1851), a German Classicist who produced celebrated editions of texts in
Latin, Greek, and medieval and modern German. Lachmann's method is genealogical and mechanical in nature and aims at providing a standardized,
rational procedure for editing texts on the basis of multiple manuscripts
without requiring that the editor use his personal judgment in order to
choose among variant readings. Its goal is to determine the filiation of manuscripts, that is, to ascertain which ones have been copied from which other
ones: given that every act of transcription is likely to introduce new errors,
a manuscript B, if it has been copied mechanically from a manuscript A, will
have all the errors that A had (if it does not have all of them, then it has
probably corrected some of them during the transcription and hence is likely
not to have been copied mechanically after all), and it is also likely to have
at least one new error of its own. If this can be shown to be the case, then B
can be discarded for the purposes of the constitution of the text it shares
with A, since B, compared with A, brings no new information that is not erroneous. Lachmann's method is mechanical, both in the sense that it must
presuppose the unthinking transcription of manuscripts if it is to be applied
to them and in the sense that the determination of relations of filiation is
achieved on the basis of simple rules and calculations of probability. Ideally,
choices of manuscripts and of readings based on this method will be rational
in that they will depend not on the taste of the individual scholar but on objective evidence that can be mathematized and evaluated; hence they will be
capable of becoming standardized, because any scholar, young or old, inexperienced or expert, should on principle come up with exactly the same
results if he is given the same information. We may interpret Lachmann's
method as a defensive reaction to the proliferation of possible source texts,
intended to reduce them to a more manageable number, and can identify it
as one important element in the professionalization of Classics during the
nineteenth century, since it established rules that all who wished to be recognized as full members of the discipline could be expected to follow so as
to produce uniform and hence generally acceptable results.

Timpanaro's book examines Lachmann's method in three regards:
(1) What was its origin, and, in particular, did Lachmann invent it? (2) What
was its subsequent development and outcome? and (3) How valid is it? These
three questions determine the structure of his book.

(1) In chapters 1 to 7 and Appendix A, Timpanaro considers the development of the methods of textual edition from the fifteenth century through
the middle of the nineteenth century and inquires into the origin of the various features that go to make up Lachmann's method. Part of the genius of
Timpanaro's study is that he applies the very same technique of genealogi-

cal investigation to Lachmann's method that characterizes the method itself. The aims of Timpanaro's analysis are set out with exemplary clarity in the second paragraph of his introduction, and its results are summarized tersely and lucidly in chapter 7. These conclusions are the following: that many of the techniques and presuppositions associated with the method were well established either among the Renaissance Humanists or during the following centuries, especially among the New Testament scholars of the eighteenth century; that the particular formulation of the method associated with Lachmann's celebrated edition of Lucretius (Lachmann 1850) was anticipated in most of its essentials by such other scholars as Orelli, Zumpt, Ritschl, and Madvig in the decades before the publication of this work, and in particular almost in its entirety in Bernays's work on Lucretius of 1847 (and to a lesser extent in Purmann's of 1846); and that Lachmann's own application of the method, not only in his earlier editions but even in his great Lucretius edition, was generally inconsistent and was marked by fundamental errors. In short, Timpanaro demonstrated, once and for all, both that "Lachmann's method" was not in fact Lachmann's method (for he did not invent it) and that Lachmann's method was not in fact "Lachmann's method" (for he did not apply it consistently). Since the first publication of Timpanaro's study, scholars who use the term "Lachmann's method" without quotation marks have done so at their peril.

(2) In chapter 8, Timpanaro sketches a brief history of the decline of Lachmann's method between the second half of the nineteenth and the beginning of the twentieth century. His focus is on the analogies that were perceived during that period between the developments in Classical textual editing on the one hand and those in comparative historical linguistics on the other: a first period in the middle of the nineteenth century in which a version of Lachmann's method was applied, with euphoric hopes for success, to the search for genealogical relations within the Indo-European family of languages was followed in the last decades of that century by a wave of disillusionment and skepticism in both disciplines. The discovery that the method was fully applicable only in a relatively small number of cases led some textual critics to misapply it by artificially reducing the number of witnesses they took into consideration and hypothesizing filiations on the basis of inadequate evidence or none at all, and others to emphasize instead the importance of those many situations in which the method could not be applied safely because target texts had not been copied mechanically and exclusively from single sources. By the beginning of the twentieth century, the general reaction against Positivism in all the human sciences had led to a widespread distrust of Lachmann's method in such Classicists as Pasquali, to whom the closing section of the chapter is dedicated.

(3) What then is the lasting value of Lachmann's method, and what are

the limits of its validity? It is to these questions that chapter 8 is partly and Appendices B and C are fully addressed (as is also the posthumous essay, which I have titled "Final Remarks on Bipartite Stemmas" and which appears here for the first time). They largely take the form of a long drawn-out argument with Paul Maas (1880–1964), who provided the most authoritative statement of the principles of Lachmann's method in his lapidary *Textkritik* (Maas 1958 [1927]). Against Maas's almost mathematical formulation of the principles of mechanical textual edition, Timpanaro insists on the infinite diversity of human error and in particular on three well-attested and universally recognized ways in which manuscripts can come to differ from one another without the differences being explicable in terms of mechanical copying: contamination (when scribes make use of more than one source text and on the basis of their own judgment mix readings from the one with readings from the other); scribal conjecture (when copyists deliberately make corrections of their own in the text they are copying because, for one reason or another, they are dissatisfied with the source text's readings); and polygenesis (when the same errors are produced entirely independently in different transmission processes, either by chance or because under certain circumstances certain kinds of errors occur with greater probability).

As Timpanaro's investigation of the limits of Lachmann's method proceeds, it becomes more and more focused on one highly technical but very important issue: why is it that so many textual traditions seem to take a bipartite form, dividing neatly into two and only two branches or families of witnesses? The problem was first posed by the French medievalist Joseph Bédier (1913, 1928); his suggestion that the explanation for this striking prevalence was to be sought not in the intrinsic nature of textual transmission itself but in the faulty methods of textual editors provoked an intense discussion among many scholars, including Pasquali and Maas. Where Pasquali denied the truth of Bédier's observation, arguing that bipartite stemmas were far less frequent than Bédier thought, Timpanaro agreed with Bédier about the fact of their overwhelming dominance; and where Maas accepted that apparent fact but attempted to provide a statistical explanation for it in terms of the possible outcomes of various scenarios involving the copying of manuscripts, Timpanaro attacked both Maas's statistics and his whole methodology. Timpanaro himself seeks a cautious middle way, accepting the predominance of bipartite stemmas as an objective fact due to the modes of textual propagation in the Middle Ages, but suggesting that certain erroneous editorial techniques increase the number of apparent cases of bipartitism beyond what ought to be the case. His own arguments (including most recently another posthumous text, Timpanaro 2001c) did not conclude the discussion once and for all, but gave rise to a series of contributions by other scholars, particularly Michael Reeve (especially Reeve

1986). As is indicated by Timpanaro's posthumous paper published here, he himself believed that Reeve had definitively proven him wrong in several important points (though not in all), and this judgment of his, though perhaps too harsh, seems substantially correct.

But the issues at stake are of great enough interest from a methodological point of view that the value of Timpanaro's arguments is not thereby simply vitiated: anyone interested in questions of textual transmission can learn from the debate as a whole. And beyond the specific question of bipartite stemmas, the disagreement between Maas and Timpanaro retains a permanent significance. For Maas's concluding aphorism, "No specific has yet been discovered against contamination" (Maas 1958 [1927]: 49), in setting narrow limits to the scope of rationality in textual edition, had seemed to assign everything outside them to the sway of caprice and blind chance: Timpanaro's sustained effort was directed not only to extending those limits as far as he could, but also to demonstrating that even inside of them matters were not at all so geometric and predictable as Maas seemed to suggest. Ultimately, what was at stake in the debate between them were different views of what was to count as rationality in textual edition—for Maas, only pure algorithms; for Timpanaro, statistical probabilities and stochastic procedures as well. If only for this reason, the disagreement between them, which reflected not only their personalities but also larger differences in the conditions of the sciences when the two men were being educated, could never have known a final winner. This makes their debate not less interesting and significant but all the more so.

Timpanaro's demonstration in the present study is compact, pointed, stringent, and, especially for the first of its three goals, entirely convincing. Yet it is remarkable not only for these strengths, which it shares with other great works of scholarship, but also in three other regards, in which it is unusual, indeed anomalous.

First, when it was first published, in the form of two articles that appeared in 1959 and 1960 (Timpanaro 1959, 1960), it was the work of an astonishingly young man: Timpanaro was only thirty-six years old at the time, yet he was already prodigiously learned, assured in his judgments, mature in his formulations, authoritative in his tone.

Second, even more strikingly, at the time he wrote these articles Timpanaro had never himself performed a critical edition of any text, ancient or modern. He was best known in this period for his work on Leopardi's philological writings, yet he had not edited these and did not do so until a decade later, and then in collaboration with Giuseppe Pacella (Leopardi 1969). To be sure, Timpanaro had already published a number of articles that demonstrated his interest and competence in questions of textual criticism of Latin poetry, especially a series of three articles presented as preparatory toward a new edition of the fragments of Ennius (Timpanaro 1946, 1947, 1948–49). But that edition of Ennius had not yet appeared at the time, ten years later, and in fact it never did appear. Indeed, by the end of his life the only editions that Timpanaro published were of writings by modern Italian authors which he prepared, almost always in collaboration with friends, on the basis of autograph manuscripts or early editions (e.g., Ascoli 1959; Bartoletti-Bornmann-Manfredi-Timpanaro 1961, 1970; Leopardi 1969; Pasquali 1986a, 1986b), and two popular editions of foreign texts with Italian translation (d'Holbach 1985; Cicero 1988, 1998, the latter indeed quite remarkable, but for its extraordinarily rich commentary, not for its text). Thus Timpanaro never published during his entire lifetime a single critical edition of an ancient author on the basis of the very procedures of collation, recension, and emendation of manuscripts that he had analyzed with such expertise and penetration in this book. He also planned for many years to write a handbook of textual criticism, but nothing ever came of this project. We should bear this in mind when we read what are almost the closing words of the body of this book: "And the practical exigency remains, that certain critical editions not be postponed forever for the sake of studying the history of the tradition in all its smallest details, that scholars not bury themselves so deeply in the study of medieval and Humanist culture that they forget to return to textual criticism" (below, p. 138).

Third, *The Genesis of Lachmann's Method* is in a certain sense a book without a genre. Those who work on the modern study of ancient Greek and Latin literature tend in general to produce one or another of various kinds of sharply differentiated studies of its techniques. There have been (1) numerous histories of Classical scholarship, such as Bursian 1885, Sandys 1908–21 (1903–8) and 1915, Gudemann 1909 (1907), Kroll 1919 (1908), Wilamowitz 1982 (1921), or, more recently, Pfeiffer 1968 and 1976, Reynolds-Wilson 1991 (1968), Kenney 1974, and Briggs and Calder 1990; (2) many manuals of textual criticism, of which the best-known ones of the twentieth century are Havet 1911, Kantorowicz 1921, Maas 1958 (1927), Dain 1975 (1949), van Groningen 1963, and more recently West 1973; (3) various biographical studies of individual scholars, which have attempted to set their work in the context of their personal lives and historical periods, such as Bernays 1855 on Scaliger, Mähly 1864 on Politian, Jebb 1882 on Bentley, Pattison 1892 on Casaubon, Clarke 1937 on Porson, and Grafton 1983–93 on Scaliger; and finally (4) a few introductory textbooks discussing methods in an individual scholarly discipline as a whole, which have included important technical histories of that discipline, most notably Wachsmuth 1895 on ancient history and Traube 1965 (1909–20): 1.1–80 on paleography. The differences between these various kinds of works could not be more evident. The histories of Classical scholarship tend to be diachronic in sequence, biographical in format, and sometimes unmistakably hagiographic in tone: along the line of a more or less simple temporal axis they string together the biographies of the great scholars of the past, indicating their personal vicissitudes, strengths, and foibles, listing their great works, and inviting the student to admire their contributions to scholarship, to try to understand them, and to imitate them as best he can. The manuals of textual criticism are usually systematic in orientation, synchronic in structure, entirely unbiographical in format, and usually cool and reasoned in tone: they attempt to construct a series of rules to explain how errors come about and to indicate to the future editor what techniques and lines of reasoning he should apply in order to construct the best possible edition out of the materials at his disposal. The biographies of individual scholars are usually closely focused on the life and works of the particular person who forms their object, often employ archival material, and are usually more interested in synchronic and local, rather than in diachronic and large-scale contextualization. Finally the introductory manuals are most often encyclopedic in character within the terms of the specific discipline that is being presented; only rarely do they succeed in combining perceptive analysis of individual figures with the larger development of the field and of cultural history as a whole. What unites all these kinds of studies is that with very few exceptions indeed, their author is legitimated in the eyes of his readers by the first-class work he does in separate publications as an editor of Classical texts—an apparent generic requirement of such studies that makes the fact that Timpanaro never did edit a Classical text himself seem even more anomalous.

The Genesis of Lachmann's Method, on the contrary, is an attempt to historicize the techniques of textual criticism and edition such as had not really ever been ventured before. It fits into none of the categories of scholarship on the history of Classical scholarship we have just distinguished. (1) Timpanaro is indeed writing a history and for that purpose does make use of biography as one of the important strategies with which he organizes his material, but he employs the accounts of individual lives only tactically, instrumentally, in order to explain and make these historical developments concrete, never as an end in itself. Besides, he makes no claim to present a survey of the whole of Classical scholarship in the period he considers, but only a single technique, Lachmann's method. (2) Moreover, he considers editorial procedures not as a timeless set of universally valid rules that were always waiting to be discovered and, once revealed, could now be formalized once and for all in a permanent and perfectly systematic arrangement, but rather as the product of specific human needs as these developed over the course of centuries in frequent contact with other cultural domains.

(3) His book does bear Lachmann's name in its title, and it provides a penetrating analysis of many of Lachmann's works, yet it does not really fit into the category of biographical studies: its historical focus is far too wide (for it considers the history of a method from ancient times to the present), while its thematic focus is far too narrow (for it ignores many aspects of Lachmann's life and works and concentrates only on the question of Lachmann's method). (4) And finally, Timpanaro's work displays similarities in certain respects to Traube's history of paleography, which Pasquali and Timpanaro much admired, and Traube's analysis of Jean Mabillon's *De re diplomatica libri VI* (Traube 1965 [1909–20]: 1.20–30) is perhaps the closest analogue within Classical studies to Timpanaro's account of Lachmann; yet Timpanaro's monograph is certainly not a study of the history of any discipline in its entirety, and Timpanaro himself is careful to emphasize that its object is not even textual criticism as a whole (below, p. 37), but only a single and very specific editorial procedure.

How are we to explain the oddities of this book? No doubt some are due to the individual peculiarities of its author, and doubtless no set of explanations will ever suffice to clear up altogether, or perhaps even to reduce significantly, its mysteries. Nonetheless it would be unfair to Timpanaro not to attempt to subject his own book on Lachmann's method to the very same kind of genealogical analysis that he applied with such success to that very method. We may therefore rephrase the above question as follows: What are the personal influences and scholarly traditions within which it makes most sense to situate *The Genesis of Lachmann's Method*?

The most obvious answer is of course Giorgio Pasquali, Timpanaro's teacher at Florence and Pisa. Pasquali had responded to the eighteen highly condensed and abstract pages of Maas's *Textkritik* (Maas 1958 [1927]) with a detailed and highly critical review that filled more than twice as many pages in the most prestigious German disciplinary organ (Pasquali 1929); five years later appeared the first edition of a lengthy monograph, ten times longer, which presented a full version of his views, *Storia della tradizione e critica del testo* (History of the tradition and textual criticism; Pasquali 1952 [1934]). Where Maas had striven to formulate in its most essential form an extreme version of Lachmann's method, formalizing a mechanical set of rules for determining relations of filiation among manuscripts in order to permit mere copies to be discarded for the sake of textual constitution, Pasquali insisted on all the factors that set limits to the validity of any such method, reminding scholars that copyists could be not only fallible machines but also creative and intelligent readers and writers, that medieval variants might well go back in certain cases to a plurality of ancient editions, and above all that medieval and Renaissance manuscript copies were not only dispensable witnesses to ancient texts, for the reconstitution of which they could be sacrificed without loss, but also a precious testimony to later understandings of earlier writings, documents of reception that had not only a hermeneutic value but also a cultural and historical dignity of their own.

It is evident that Pasquali's book provided the stimulus and the model for Timpanaro's—indeed, Timpanaro himself acknowledges as much when he writes in the preface to the first edition that his book is "an investigation born, one might say, in the margins of Pasquali 1952 (1934), of which it presupposes the reader's familiarity and to which it constantly refers" (below, p. 37). Pasquali posed many of the basic questions for which Timpanaro's study went on to try to provide more detailed and satisfactory answers. Moreover, the very structure of Pasquali's book bears a striking affinity to Timpanaro's: both books begin with a historical examination of the origins of Lachmann's method and of Lachmann's own use of it, and then go on to assess the limitations of its validity, though of course the proportions between the two parts are completely inverted in the two cases. Indeed, Pasquali's text has even influenced a number of the verbal formulations in Timpanaro's—for example, compare the following text of Timpanaro:

> Later—in the nineteenth century, as we shall see, and unfortunately even today—this procedure, which has received the technical name of *eliminatio codicum descriptorum* [elimination of derivative manuscripts], has often become a convenient expedient for saving the Classical philologist time and trouble: insufficient evidence, or even the simple observation that there is a mass of *recentiores* [more recent witnesses] alongside a manuscript of considerable antiquity, has too easily suggested that the more recent ones derived from the older one. (Below, p. 47)

with that of Pasquali:

> And one must answer that every time there was an ancient manuscript on the one side and a certain number of recent ones with the same contents on the other, that generation tended to derive these latter ones from that former one, and did not hesitate unscrupulously to abuse technical means of proof, or, to speak more clearly, was satisfied with demonstrations devoid of any value. (Pasquali 1952 [1934]: 26)

It is only if this relation of openly professed dependence is borne in mind that we can fully understand the justice of Timpanaro's decision to conclude the final chapter of his book with a lengthy evaluation of Pasquali's scholarship, which, first published less than a decade after his master's death, moves well beyond the limits that considerations of mere argumentative relevance might have imposed in order to assume the dimensions and character of a formal eulogy.

Yet the evident similarities and filiation between the two books should not mislead us into mistaking the fundamental difference in their orientations. It is not accidental that Pasquali's investigation into the origins and development of Lachmann's method occupies only the first, brief chapter of his book (Pasquali 1952 [1934]: 3–12), for his principal object is not so much the historical evolution of a set of procedures as rather what he considers to be the facts of the transmission of a large number of mostly ancient texts, which he takes to be such that those procedures cannot be applied to them appropriately and successfully. Ultimately, Pasquali's is a manual of editorial technique, addressed above all to this question: given the true nature of textual transmission, how best are we to edit texts? Its principal difference from other such manuals is that, so far from setting itself the task of promulgating rules that are to be applied more or less mechanically, it insists on the many factors that set narrow limits to the validity of all such rules; the extraordinary richness of its documentation ends up performing a deconstruction of traditional manuals of textual criticism, but from within the genre. Even Pasquali's introductory chapter on Lachmann's method is intended not so much to provide a dispassionate investigation of its history as rather to deprive it of the authority that, for so many scholars, derived from the prestige of his name. Timpanaro's book, by contrast, is the history of the gradual discovery of a particular scholarly method over the course of centuries; the considerations of that method's degree of validity, which occupy the final sections of his book, are appended to that historical investigation and are not at all indispensable to its argument. Ultimately, Timpanaro's is a history of Classical scholarship, differing most strikingly from traditional examples of that genre in being organized not as a series of biographies but rather in terms of a single and highly specific scholarly method, to whose discovery a large number of individuals contributed in varying ways and degrees over the course of hundreds of years.

In a larger sense, the closest parallels to Timpanaro's study of Lachmann's method are to be found not in the field of Classical scholarship after all, not in histories of the discipline nor in manuals of textual criticism nor in biographies of scholars nor in introductory textbooks on method, but instead in the history of science: for Timpanaro's investigation into the development of a single method, the most striking analogies are the sorts of studies of the development of an individual scientific technique or concept—the integral calculus, the heliocentric theory, the theory of relativity, and the like—which have been standard fare in the history of science since the nineteenth century. These were the kinds of studies that filled a considerable part of the libraries and minds of Timpanaro's parents during his childhood and youth, and they have left an evident trace on all of his own work. Sebastiano Timpanaro Sr. had already been passionately engaged in the history of science even before he was compelled to abandon his active participation in research in experimental physics, and afterward he devoted his considerable energies and intelligence to this field above all: he always regarded the history of science as a crucial link between science and civil society, a link that had to be vigorously nourished and strengthened in order to prevent a potentially quite dangerous cultural fragmentation, particularly in a country with a strong humanistic tradition like Italy. And Timpanaro's mother devoted her work on ancient Greek philosophy above all to the connections between philosophical and scientific thought in the period from the pre-Socratics through Aristotle, for example, in the case of the Pythagoreans, insisting against many of her colleagues on those elements in their doctrines that were more mathematical and naturalistic, less mystical and shamanistic.

Timpanaro himself cultivated an active interest in the discipline of the history of science, for example, maintaining a fairly close personal relation with the prominent Italian Communist philosopher of science Ludovico Geymonat (despite the absolute incompatibility of their political views), collecting, reading, and annotating his books and publishing two important reviews of his works (Timpanaro 1973, 1977c). And his quasi-professional familiarity with the scientific discipline of historical linguistics is evident on many pages of the present book. For this presence of a strong scientific component in Timpanaro's scholarship, it seems evident that his parents are an important explanatory factor. To those who have studied their works (edited expertly by Timpanaro himself), much in the present study will have a familiar ring. Thus Timpanaro takes care here to link the historiography of science with that of society as a whole—but already his mother had written, "the historian of science is a scientist with a critic's and a historian's mentality, who feels the need to illuminate scientific creation and to insert it into the process of scientific thought and of the general vision of the world of its period, with which it stands in a relation of such intimate necessity that if it is abstracted from it that vision ends up not only being distorted, but also falsified" (Cardini 1951). We can see throughout these pages how fruitful a cautious use of biography can be for the history of science, given that there is no science without scientists—but already his father and mother had written the history of science in precisely the same way, in terms of individuals like Leonardo and Galileo, Alcmaeon and Melissus, and his father had declared programmatically, "the history of science . . . must present to us the physicists, the chemists, the naturalists, the mathematicians, the astronomers, living and working, in such a way that they become as familiar to us as we are ourselves. We must live their triumphs, their investigations, their hypotheses in all their details, in all their nuances, in all their energy" (Timpanaro Sr. 1952: 13).

Between this very narrow context provided by Pasquali and Timpanaro's parents, on the one hand, and the very broad context supplied by the history of science on the other, it is very difficult indeed to identify a specific, middle-range institutional context within Classical studies proper that can adequately explain the genesis of *The Genesis of Lachmann's Method*. Indeed, Timpanaro's book is not really very much at all like any of the standard forms of the history of Classical scholarship that preceded it. Yet there is one field of scholarship that flourished in Italy in the 1940s and 1950s, and with which Timpanaro was demonstrably familiar, in which the kinds of questions he raised here and the kinds of strategies he deployed in trying to answer them did have an important place: the study of the scholarly practices of Renaissance Humanism. Of course, the Italian Humanists have long been a favorite object for study by their modern compatriots, but such study has usually not been focused on the kinds of precise technical issues that are so characteristic of Timpanaro's book but on other kinds of questions: biographical, political, literary, archival. Yet already in the 1920s Remigio Sabbadini had examined, acutely if only briefly, "the method of the Humanists" (Sabbadini 1922), and even before the Second World War so too did a few other scholars, most notably Berthold L. Ullman and P. O. Kristeller, who were not themselves Italian but were closely associated with Italian scholars and institutions (thus Kristeller taught German at the Scuola Normale Superiore di Pisa from 1935 to 1938, before the Fascist racial laws forced him to emigrate to America). But it was not until after 1945 that these studies of philological method really took off, especially in Italy and England, perhaps in part as a sober and dignified reaction against the excesses of the rhetorical culture of Fascism. These were the years of such pathbreaking studies as those by José Ruysschaert on Lipsius and Tacitus (Ruysschaert 1949), by Giuseppe Billanovich on Petrarch (Billanovich 1951), and by Carlo Dionisotti on Filetico and Virgil (Dionisotti 1958), to mention only a few particularly remarkable examples. For Timpanaro, the crucial figure in this scholarly movement was certainly Alessandro Perosa (1910–98), who studied at the Scuola Normale Superiore di Pisa from 1928 to 1932 and then was the administrative secretary there (a post also involving teaching duties) from 1933 to 1953, and was professor at the University of Florence from 1959 to 1980. Much influenced by his teacher Pasquali, Perosa turned away in the 1940s from the study of Greek and Latin literature themselves and devoted himself henceforth to research into the Italian Renaissance Humanists—research conducted with the learning and interests of a trained Classical scholar. He investigated above all Politian as a Humanist philologist and demonstrated convincingly the range and brilliance

of his Classical scholarship and the almost inextricable mixture of tradition-
ality and originality in his methodology (his papers are collected in Perosa
2000). Perosa's catalogue of the 1954 exhibit on Politian at the Laurentian
Library in Florence (Perosa 1954) provided one extraordinary example of
how the methods of a long-dead scholar could be analyzed tersely, techni-
cally, and nonetheless quite interestingly; and Perosa's seminars at Pisa must
have supplied many more—Timpanaro himself refers to them with un-
mixed admiration (below, p. 46). And some of Timpanaro's own earliest
and already most polished work belongs very clearly to this line of research
(e.g., Timpanaro 1951).

In the 1950s, when Timpanaro's *Genesis of Lachmann's Method* was in
the course of gestation, Classical studies in Italy had not yet fully recovered
from Pasquali's death and were languishing to a certain extent. But in those
same years Humanist studies were burgeoning there, and it does not seem
at all unlikely that it was from this lively, fresh, and challenging field that
Timpanaro derived some of his deepest inspiration and at least some of the
models and standards for his own highly personal brand of scholarship.
This might well help to explain why his book on Lachmann begins, perhaps
somewhat oddly, not with the ancient grammarians who first invented some
of the philological practices that Timpanaro investigates, nor with the great
eighteenth-century biblical scholars who first explicitly formulated them,
nor with the nineteenth-century German Classicists who were Lachmann's
most immediate predecessors, but rather with the Humanists of the Italian
Renaissance, and above all with Politian. And it represents a point of some
difference between Timpanaro and Pasquali, for the latter, for all his love
and knowledge of Italian literature and of the history of the reception of the
Classics, never quite achieved a degree of familiarity with the Renaissance
Humanists comparable to that of his student Timpanaro, preferring instead
to concentrate on such traditionally literary Italian Classics as Dante, Petrarch, and Boccaccio.

Finally, it is not entirely impossible that some role in shaping the young
Timpanaro's sense of the history of scholarship—the nature and importance of the field, the kinds of questions to ask, the strategies available for
answering them—was also played by the historian Arnaldo Momigliano
(1908–87). Momigliano had left Italy for England in 1939, but after the
war he reestablished intense contacts with Italian colleagues, especially
younger ones; in 1964 he accepted a position at the Scuola Normale Superiore di Pisa, while retaining his chair at the University of London. A close
intellectual and personal friendship developed between the older historian
and the younger Classicist during the 1950s and lasted until Momigliano's
death; it is documented both in the books and articles of each to be found
in the personal libraries of the other (now both part of the library of the

Scuola Normale Superiore di Pisa) and in the letters exchanged by the two
scholars over the course of more than three decades, scores of which have
been preserved and will be published shortly by Riccardo Di Donato (Di
Donato 2005). To be sure, in this book itself Timpanaro only mentions Momigliano three times, tangentially, in bibliographical footnotes added in
later editions (chap. 6, n. 6; chap. 8, nn. 37, 38); moreover, nothing in the
surviving correspondence between the two goes beyond discussions of specific scholarly and political issues, and expressions of intellectual affinity and
personal cordiality, to prove that Timpanaro consciously took Momigliano
as the model for his own work in the latter part of the 1950s. Nonetheless,
it is difficult to imagine that he might have conceived his own work without
any reference to Momigliano's whatsoever. Timpanaro studied closely the
first volume of Momigliano's *Contributi*, published in 1955 (Momigliano
1955), which contained a number of pathbreaking and now classic articles
on such topics as the relation between ancient history and antiquarian research (67–106), the development of historiography on the Roman Empire
from the seventeenth to nineteenth centuries (107–64), the genesis and
function of the concept of Hellenism (165–94), and such important individual figures of eighteenth- and nineteenth-century historiography as Gib-
bon (195–211), Grote (213–31), Creuzer (233–48), Niebuhr (249–62),
and Droysen (263–74). In all these essays, and in the later ones he was writing during the same time as Timpanaro was formulating the first version of
his own study, and in the following years, when their contact became ever
more intense, Momigliano focused on questions of scholarly method and
endeavored not only to unravel the complicated genesis of concepts and procedures, deploying for this purpose a subtle dialectical interchange between
individual biography and larger social contexts, but also to determine the
extent to which these concepts and procedures could renew the methods
that historians use even today. And given the extraordinary importance of
German Classical scholarship in the first half of the nineteenth century, it is
not surprising that Momigliano kept returning to the period and country
that Timpanaro studied most closely in this book—though it is also not surprising, given that Momigliano was much more concerned with historical
questions than with philological ones, that he only rarely touched on Lachmann himself in his own work.

It would be tempting to suggest that in *The Genesis of Lachmann's
Method* Timpanaro provided a Momiglianian answer to a Pasqualian question, but to do so would be a drastic oversimplification. Much separated the
two men, and not only their ages and academic disciplines: beyond their
evident and mutually acknowledged political differences, Momigliano still
retained a certain measure of commitment to a version of the Crocean
Idealism that was anathema to Timpanaro. Above all it is extremely odd, if

Momigliano did indeed influence Timpanaro in any significant way, that the latter never acknowledged this in his writings, given his tendency scrupulously to record all his intellectual debts—even Timpanaro's keen awareness of his disagreements with Momigliano in other matters would scarcely have prevented him from recognizing such a debt to him in this one. Viewed from above and outside, the fundamental affinities in method between the two scholars are unmistakable, and Momigliano is probably the most important Italian, or indeed European, intellectual figure active in the field of the history of Classical scholarship in the late 1950s who could have exerted any degree of formative influence on Timpanaro. But the likeliest proximate explanatory context for Timpanaro's work remains not Classical scholarship at all in the narrow sense but the history of Italian Humanism.

In any case it should cause no surprise that Timpanaro's work on the history of Classical scholarship is here associated so closely with the history of science, for it is only in a narrow and historically provincial view of the history of science that this discipline can be thought to be restricted to the study of the physical and biological sciences. "Science" and its equivalents in many languages designate any disciplined and institutionalized effort to apply the sustained exercise of reason to the study of man and his world, and precisely this was certainly Timpanaro's deeply felt and often asserted understanding of the nature of Classical philology. Of course there are many other components to the professional activity of the Classical scholar (as, for that matter, of the natural scientist as well) besides purely rational ones—taste, intuition, empathy, experience, to name only these. But in the present book Timpanaro concentrates as far as possible on some of the technical procedures of Classical scholarship that are most clearly an expression of rationality and considers their sources and scope. After all, there can be no doubt that the method of examining the filiation of manuscripts is a triumph of reason, for it is quite irrational to accept the readings found in a manuscript merely because it happens to be near to hand or is old or because other scholars have accepted it in the past.

Thus the story Timpanaro tells in this book is that of the gradual triumph of reason over the forces of habit, laziness, religious intolerance, and stupidity. For all his materialism, Timpanaro seems to acknowledge a teleological force that certainly does not operate in the wider field of human history as a whole but at least seems to a certain extent to do so in this narrower, technical domain, driving his story forward as a kind of motor and endowing it with a forceful internal dynamic. This may be why he emphasizes that some figures, such as Gottfried Hermann, lag behind the point at which others have already arrived, and why he always takes pains to isolate as clearly as possible the individual steps forward made by this scholar or that one, be it Le Clerc or Madvig or many others. An expectation, if not of the inevitability, then at least of the strong probability of rational progress within the limited confines of a particular science seems to underlie his account and makes it difficult for Timpanaro to account satisfactorily for two kinds of exceptions to this progress, which he nonetheless takes care insistently and repeatedly to point out: that progress is not continuous but encounters relapses and regressions, as in Germany at the beginning of the nineteenth century; and that scholars' theoretical precepts often do not square fully with their actual practice (for example, in the cases of Bentley, Ernesti, and Orelli).

But the story Timpanaro tells is not a purely internal one, in the sense of involving nothing more than increasing degrees of rationalization of scientific procedures, determined only by strictly scientific considerations. It is also external, for the process he describes is partly impeded, but also partly supported and encouraged by the fact that the techniques of text edition do not exist in isolation from the other regions in the larger culture around them but are instead profoundly influenced by them. After all, one of the texts whose edition was at issue in this period was the New Testament, and questions of which reading to choose in that text could easily acquire not only a scholarly weight but also a doctrinal one. Timpanaro takes care, following Pasquali, to point to the importance of the division between Catholics and Protestants, and within Protestantism to the influence of heretical currents, for the field of textual criticism of the New Testament in the seventeenth and eighteenth centuries (although both scholars were oddly uninterested in the no-less-important role of Old Testament criticism during the same period). So too, Timpanaro explores at length the relations between Classical textual criticism and Indo-European linguistics, and points to the impact of the general rise of irrationalist tendencies at the end of the nineteenth century on the value attributed to Lachmann's method. Despite the narrowness of his focus, Timpanaro is careful to situate his theme as broadly as possible: his story is one that moves from the fifteenth century to the twentieth, from Italy to France to Holland to England to Germany and back once more to Italy and France, from Humanists to theologians to Classical scholars.

In his scholarship as in his politics, Timpanaro may have been a progressivist, but he was very far from being triumphalistic—quite the contrary. He saw rationality as difficult to achieve and as always endangered by the threatening forces of various kinds of irrationality—in this regard his study of Lachmann's method is at one with his political and environmentalist writings. It is after all quite rational to apply Lachmann's method to those cases in which it is appropriate to do so—where there is one archetype, mechanical transmission, and no contamination—and it would be quite irrational not to do so: there are indeed such cases, and it is a triumph

of human reason, not perhaps the greatest one but certainly worthy of admiration and investigation, to have discovered this method and to have
learned to apply it. Yet the success of a method inevitably leads some people
to attempt irrationally to overextend it and to abuse it by applying it to cases
to which it is not in fact applicable—so already Cobet, perhaps the true vil-
lain of Timpanaro's story, and so too Maas—and in so doing to cast discredit irrationally on a method that, applied appropriately, would have led
to entirely acceptable results.

In a certain sense, then, one underlying purpose of Timpanaro's study is
to rescue Lachmann's method against Lachmann's own errors and against
his teacher Pasquali's overstated polemics. Pasquali had suggested that that
method was not Lachmann's, but only in order to discredit it further by driving a wedge between it and his celebrated name. Timpanaro proves that the
method is not Lachmann's, but so as to demonstrate that it was not merely
the invention of a single person, however gifted, but rather a culmination of
many centuries of philological insights and hard work. What this book
shows is that Lachmann's method was a shared discovery in which many
scholars of different generations, countries, disciplines, and interests all had
a hand. It was not inevitable that it should have been discovered—quite the
contrary—and once it was discovered, its limits and value were not always
assessed correctly—again, quite the contrary. All the more reason that the
story of its discovery, as it is recounted here, however austerely, has its own
deeply human fascination and rather melancholy pathos.

*   *   *

Timpanaro was as scrupulous in his scholarship as he was intransigent in
his politics. One result was that this study was constantly revised, corrected,
and updated over the course of almost four decades: it began its life in the
form of two lengthy articles (Timpanaro 1959, 1960) and went through
three editions as a book in Italian (1963, 1981, 1985) and one in German
translation (1971). Each time it was republished, the originally lithe and
austere line of argumentation became more and more enriched (or should
one say encrusted?) by further references to and discussion of the secondary
literature that had appeared since the preceding publication. For Timpanaro's work was widely discussed and broadly influential. In general it may
be said that recent scholarship has never fundamentally contradicted the find-
ings of the historical portion of the book but only confirmed and deepened
them, whereas the positions Timpanaro adopted in the systematic sections
concerning the limits of the validity of Lachmann's method have sparked
considerable discussion, controversy, and disagreement.

Another result was that after a certain point, sometime around 1986,

Timpanaro, always a perfectionist, but now aged, fatigued, and depressed, finally abandoned the attempt to revise his book yet again. A moving testimony to this decision is the hitherto unpublished essay, a rejoinder to Michael Reeve, one of his critics, which was presumably written around 1986 and appears posthumously in this edition in Additional Materials A, "[Final Remarks on Bipartite Stemmas]"—and no less moving testimony is provided by the fact that Timpanaro chose not to publish it. The reader of this volume should be aware that in the years after 1986, Timpanaro refused repeatedly to allow his book to be translated into English, claiming that it was by now obsolete and that he no longer had the energy required to update it. It is translated now by the generous permission of his wife and literary executor, Maria Augusta Timpanaro Morelli. My own view is that the historical portion of this work remains almost entirely valid, that the systematic sections can be enormously stimulating to students and scholars engaged in the problems of textual edition, and that the fact that Timpanaro himself no longer felt able to correct and revise his work as he wished to should not prevent it from being made available to the many readers who will be able to benefit from it—and who will be able to decide on their own whether he was right, or whether I was.

The basis for this translation was the last Italian edition published during Timpanaro's lifetime; I was able to make use of his personal copy, with a number of marginal annotations in his hand. Considering the importance of this book and its evolution through a series of different versions, it has seemed appropriate to indicate that development as tactfully but as clearly as possible. Hence while the numbered footnotes are all Timpanaro's own, the notes signaled by letters have been inserted by myself in order to indicate textual divergences between the final Italian edition and the earlier Italian and German ones; these divergences are presented in a genetic critical apparatus in Additional Materials B, "Differences among the Various Editions." All divergences in the text that are not merely stylistic have been indicated; on the other hand, no divergences in the notes have been indicated, as this would have swollen the apparatus beyond any degree of usefulness. The reader who chooses to ignore these notes can be confident that the text he reads represents the fully considered views of Timpanaro toward the end of his life, but whoever dips into their riches will be able to trace out in detail the development of his thought over a span of more than four decades and to admire all the more his scrupulous honesty and generosity of spirit.

Timpanaro was generally quite careful in his citations of primary and secondary sources, but the method of citation he used, although well established in Italy, may seem haphazard to American readers. I have systematized his references in the following way: author's surname (with first initial or other indication in case of homonyms); the year of publication of the edition or translation of reference, followed in parentheses by the original year of publication of the work; colon; volume and page number, separated by a period, if the work comprises more than one volume, otherwise only the page number. The full bibliographical details can be found in the bibliography of works referred to by Timpanaro.

I have also added a selective bibliography of scholarly works on the various topics treated by Timpanaro that have appeared since 1986, the date of the last Italian edition of this book. This bibliography is of course far from complete, but I hope it provides at least a starting point for readers who wish to deepen their acquaintance with these topics and to find out how Timpanaro's views are regarded today.

ACKNOWLEDGMENTS

At the conclusion of what has been an intense and very agreeable labor, it is a great pleasure to thank all those who have made it possible.

First of all I thank Timpanaro's wife and literary executor, Maria Augusta Timpanaro Morelli, who has supported this project from the beginning, for giving me permission to translate this book and for making available to me Timpanaro's own copy of the 1986 edition and the unpublished text that is included in an appendix. Her hope, and mine, is that with this translation her late husband will continue to find and inspire readers not only in Italy but throughout the world.

I am also very grateful to Mario Telò, an advanced student at the Scuola Normale Superiore di Pisa, who has assisted this publication in many ways. In particular, he collated the various editions of the work and thereby furnished the materials indispensable for the genetic critical apparatus; he systematized and checked all of Timpanaro's references and prepared the bibliography of works cited by Timpanaro; he helped me to put together the bibliography of items that have appeared since 1986 (Additional Materials C, "Recent Bibliography"); he prepared a first transcript of the very difficult, and at times illegible, manuscript of Timpanaro's unpublished essay; and he checked and corrected my English translation with care and elegance. It is a source of great satisfaction to me, and would certainly have been to Timpanaro as well, to know that Italy is still producing young Classical scholars of the very highest quality.

Riccardo Di Donato (Pisa) has improved this edition by his suggestions for the introduction and by his generosity in making available to me a preliminary transcription of the correspondence between Momigliano and Timpanaro, which he has edited and which will appear in 2005. Antonio Carlini (Pisa) helped with the decipherment of Timpanaro's unpublished essay.

At a conference on Sebastiano Timpanaro and his parents that took place on 22–23 August 2003 in Tortorici, in the province of Messina in Sicily, I learned much about Timpanaro and his family and presented a first version of part of the introduction to this volume. My thanks to the organizers, Michele Feo, Vincenzo Fera, Giacomo Ferraù, and Silvia Rizzo, and to the Centro Interdipartimentale di Studi Umanistici, Facoltà di Lettere e Filosofia, Università degli Studi di Messina, for inviting me to this conference, and to all those who participated in the lively discussion after my lecture.

Michael Reeve (Cambridge) had the generosity and kindness not only to lend his support to this project at an early stage but also to subject the first version of the translation of the opening chapters to a searching criticism from which, I hope, it has emerged much improved. J. E. G. Zetzel (Columbia) read through the whole translation in its penultimate form and made many suggestions for its improvement.

Franz Martin Scherer (Heidelberg), Jan-Dirk Mueller (Munich), and Antje Wessels (Berlin) were very helpful in tracking down Timpanaro's references to German works of scholarship that could not be traced in Tuscany.

The penultimate version of the whole introduction was read by Giuseppe Cambiano (Pisa), Antonio Carlini, Carlo Ginzburg (UCLA), Filippomaria Pontani (Pisa), Lucia Prauscello (Pisa), Mario Telò, Claudia Wassmann (Chicago), and Isabelle Wienand (Fribourg) and has benefited greatly from their observations and criticisms. Above all, Anthony Grafton (Princeton) subjected it to an incisive, erudite, and deeply generous critique, which has enormously improved it.

My editors at the University of Chicago Press, Alan Thomas and Susan Bielstein, were always supportive, imaginative, resourceful, and (what is even rarer) patient.

My heartfelt thanks to all.

Glenn W. Most
Baratti-Florence-Pisa
June 2004

BIBLIOGRAPHY

Ascoli 1959: G. I. Ascoli, "Note letterario-artistiche minori durante il viaggio nella Venezia, nella Lombardia, nel Piemonte, nella Liguria, nel Parmigiano, Modenese e Pontificio. Maggio-Giugno 1852," ed. S. Timpanaro, *Annali della Scuola Normale Superiore di Pisa*, ser. 2, 28: 151–91.

Bartoletti-Bornmann-Manfredi-Timpanaro 1961: V. Bartoletti, F. Bornmann, M. Manfredi, and S. Timpanaro, eds., "Inediti di Eugenio Grassi," *Atene e Roma*, ser. 5, 6: 129–65.

Bartoletti-Bornmann-Manfredi-Timpanaro 1970: V. Bartoletti, F. Bornmann, M. Manfredi, and S. Timpanaro, eds., "Inediti di Eugenio Grassi," *Atene e Roma,* ser. 5, 15: 20–24.

Bédier 1913: J. Bédier, preface to J. Renart, *Le lai de l'Ombre,* xxv–xliv. Paris, 1913.

Bédier 1928: J. Bédier, "La tradition manuscrite du *Lai de l'Ombre,*" *Romania* 54 (1928): 161–96.

Bernays 1855: J. Bernays, *Joseph Justus Scaliger.* Berlin, 1855.

Billanovich 1951: G. Billanovich, "Petrarch and the Textual Tradition of Livy," *Journal of the Warburg and Courtauld Institutes* 14: 137–208.

Briggs and Calder 1990: W. W. Briggs and W. M. Calder III, eds., *Classical Scholarship: A Biographical Encyclopedia.* New York and London, 1990.

Bruscagli and Tellini 1996: R. Bruscagli and G. Tellini, eds., *Bibliografia degli scritti di Lanfranco Caretti.* Rome, 1996.

Bursian 1885: C. Bursian, *Geschichte der classischen Philologie in Deutschland: Von den Anfängen bis zur Gegenwart.* Munich, 1885 (reprint: New York, 1965).

Cardini 1951: Maria Timpanaro Cardini, "La storia della scienza," *L'Eco della Scuola Nuova* (Turin), Suppl. 3, 20 March 1951.

Cardini 2001: Maria Timpanaro Cardini, *Tra antichità classica e impegno civile,* ed. Sebastiano Timpanaro. Pisa, 2001.

Cicero 1988: Marco Tullio Cicerone, *Della divinazione,* ed. S. Timpanaro. Milan, 1988.

Cicero 1998: Marco Tullio Cicerone, *Della divinazione,* 4th rev. and updated ed., ed. S. Timpanaro. Milan, 1998.

Clarke 1937: M. L. Clarke, *Richard Porson: A Biographical Essay.* Cambridge, 1937.

Dain 1975 (1949): A. Dain, *Les manuscrits.* Paris, 1975 (1st ed. Paris, 1949).

d'Holbach 1985: P. Thiry d'Holbach, *Il buon senso,* ed. and trans. S. Timpanaro. Milan, 1985.

Di Donato 2005: R. Di Donato, ed., *Arnaldo Momigliano–Sebastiano Timpanaro: Carteggio.* Pisa, 2005.

Dionisotti 1958: C. Dionisotti, "'Lavinia venit litora': Polemica virgiliana di M. Filetico," *Italia Medioevale e Umanistica* 1: 283–315.

Grafton 1983–93: A. Grafton, *Joseph Scaliger: A Study in the History of Classical Scholarship,* 2 vols. Oxford, 1983–93.

Gudemann 1909 (1907): A. Gudemann, *Grundriss der Geschichte der klassischen Philologie,* 2nd ed. enlarged. Leipzig and Berlin, 1909 (1st ed., 1907).

Havet 1911: L. Havet, *Manuel de critique verbale.* Paris, 1911.

Jebb 1882: R. C. Jebb, *Bentley.* New York, 1882.

Kantorowicz 1921: H. Kantorowicz, *Einführung in die Textkritik.* Leipzig, 1921.

Kenney 1974: E. J. Kenney, *The Classical Text: Aspects of Editing in the Age of the Printed Book.* Berkeley, Los Angeles, and London, 1974.

Kroll 1919 (1908): W. Kroll, *Geschichte der klassischen Philologie,* 2nd improved ed. Berlin and Leipzig, 1919 (1st ed., 1908).

Lachmann 1850: K. Lachmann, Lucretii *De rerum natura libri VI,* trans. and ed. C. Lachmannus. Berlin, 1850.

Leopardi 1969: G. Leopardi, *Scritti filologici (1817–1832),* ed. G. Pacella and S. Timpanaro. Florence, 1969.

Maas 1958 (1927): P. Maas, *Textual Criticism,* trans. from the German by B. Flower. Oxford, 1958 (= *Textkritik,* 3rd ed. Leipzig, 1957; 1st ed. Leipzig, 1927).

Mähly 1864: J. Mähly, *Angelus Politianus: Ein Culturbild aus der Renaissance*. Leipzig, 1864.

Momigliano 1955: A. Momigliano, *Contributo alla storia degli studi classici*. Rome, 1955.

Pasquali 1929: G. Pasquali, review of P. Maas, *Textkritik* (Leipzig and Berlin, 1927), *Gnomon* 5 (1929): 417–35, 498–521.

Pasquali 1952 (1934): G. Pasquali, *Storia della tradizione e critica del testo*. Florence, 1952 (1st ed. Florence, 1934).

Pasquali 1986a: G. Pasquali, *Scritti filologici,* ed. F. Bornmann, G. Pascucci, and S. Timpanaro. Florence, 1986.

Pasquali 1986b: G. Pasquali, *Rapsodia sul classico: Contributi all'Enciclopedia italiana,* ed. F. Bornmann, G. Pascucci, and S. Timpanaro. Rome, 1986.

Pattison 1892: M. Pattison, *Isaac Casaubon, 1559–1614*. Oxford, 1892 (reprint: Geneva, 1970).

Perosa 1954: A. Perosa, ed., *Mostra del Poliziano nella Biblioteca Medicea Laurenziana: Manoscritti, libri rari, autografi e documenti: Firenze, 23 settembre–30 novembre 1954*. Florence, 1954.

Perosa 2000: A. Perosa, *Studi di filologia umanistica*, 3 vols., ed. P. Viti. Rome, 2000.

Pfeiffer 1968: R. Pfeiffer, *History of Classical Scholarship from the Beginning to the End of the Hellenistic Age*. Oxford, 1968.

Pfeiffer 1976: R. Pfeiffer, *History of Classical Scholarship from 1300 to 1850*. Oxford, 1976.

Reeve 1986: M. D. Reeve, "Stemmatic Method: 'Qualcosa che non funziona?'" in *The Role of the Book in Medieval Culture: Proceedings of the Oxford International Symposium, 26 September–10 October*, ed. P. Ganz, *Bibliologia* 3: 57–69.

Reynolds-Wilson 1991 (1968) : L. D. Reynolds and N. G. Wilson, *Scribes and Scholars*. Oxford, 1991 (1st ed. Oxford, 1968).

Ruysschaert 1949: J. Ruysschaert, *Juste Lipse et les Annales de Tacite: Une méthode de critique textuelle au XVIe siècle*. Turnhout, 1949.

Sabbadini 1922: R. Sabbadini, *Il metodo degli umanisti*. Florence, 1922.

Sandys 1908–21 (1903–8): J. E. Sandys, *A History of Classical Scholarship*, 3 vols. Cambridge, 1908–21 (1st ed., 1903–8).

Sandys 1915: J. E. Sandys, *A Short History of Classical Scholarship from the Sixth Century B.C. to the Present Day*. Cambridge, 1915.

Timpanaro 1946: S. Timpanaro, "Per una nuova edizione critica di Ennio," *Studi Italiani di Filologia Classica*, n. s., 21: 41–81.

Timpanaro 1947: S. Timpanaro, "Per una nuova edizione critica di Ennio," *Studi Italiani di Filologia Classica*, n. s., 22: 33–77, 179–207.

Timpanaro 1948–49: S. Timpanaro, "Per una nuova edizione critica di Ennio," *Studi Italiani di Filologia Classica,* n. s., 23: 5–58, 235.

Timpanaro 1951: S. Timpanaro, "*Atlas cum compare gibbo* (Marziale VI 77)," *Rinascimento* 2: 311–18 (reprinted in Timpanaro 1978: 333–43).

Timpanaro 1955: S. Timpanaro, *La filologia di Giacomo Leopardi*. Florence, 1955.

Timpanaro 1959: S. Timpanaro, "La genesi del metodo del Lachmann, pt. 1," *Studi Italiani di Filologia Classica* 31 (1959): 182–228.

Timpanaro 1960: S. Timpanaro, "La genesi del metodo del Lachmann, pt. 2," *Studi Italiani di Filologia Classica* 32 (1960): 38–63.

Timpanaro 1965: S. Timpanaro, *Classicismo e illuminismo nell'Ottocento italiano*. Pisa, 1965.

Timpanaro 1969: S. Timpanaro, *Classicismo e illuminismo nell'Ottocento italiano*, 2nd ed. enlarged. Pisa, 1969.

Timpanaro 1970: S. Timpanaro, *Sul materialismo*. Pisa, 1970.

Timpanaro 1973: S. Timpanaro, review of L. Geymonat, *Storia del pensiero filosofico e scientifico*, vols. 1–6 (Milan, 1970–72), *Belfagor* 28: 371–78.

Timpanaro 1974: S. Timpanaro, *Il lapsus freudiano: Psicanalisi e critica testuale*. Florence, 1974.

Timpanaro 1975a: S. Timpanaro, *Sul materialismo*, 2nd ed. rev. and enlarged. Pisa, 1975.

Timpanaro 1975b: S. Timpanaro, *On Materialism*, trans. L. Garner. London, 1975.

Timpanaro 1975c: S. Timpanaro, *Il lapsus freudiano: Psicanalisi e critica testuale*, 2nd ed. rev. Florence, 1975.

Timpanaro 1976a: S. Timpanaro, *The Freudian Slip: Psychoanalysis and Textual Criticism*, trans. K. Soper. London, 1976.

Timpanaro 1976b: S. Timpanaro, "Freudian Slips and Slips of the Freudians," *New Left Review* 95: 45–54.

Timpanaro 1977a: S. Timpanaro, *La filologia di Giacomo Leopardi*, 2nd ed. rev. and enlarged. Rome and Bari, 1977.

Timpanaro 1977b: S. Timpanaro, "Friedrich Schlegel and the Beginnings of Indo-European Linguistics in Germany," trans. J. P. Maher, in *Über die Sprache und die Weisheit der Indier: Ein Beitrag zur Begründung der Altertumskunde*, by F. Schlegel, ed. E. F. K. Koerner. Amsterdam, 1977.

Timpanaro 1977c: S. Timpanaro, review of L. Geymonat, *Storia del pensiero filosofico e scientifico*, vol. 7 (Milan, 1976), *Belfagor* 32: 723–25.

Timpanaro 1978: S. Timpanaro, *Contributi di filologia e di storia della lingua latina*. Rome, 1978.

Timpanaro 1979: S. Timpanaro, "The Pessimistic Materialism of Giacomo Leopardi," *New Left Review* 116: 29–50.

Timpanaro 1980a: S. Timpanaro, *Aspetti e figure della cultura ottocentesca*. Pisa, 1980.

Timpanaro 1980b: S. Timpanaro, *On Materialism*, trans. L. Garner, 2nd ed. enlarged. London, 1980.

Timpanaro 1982: S. Timpanaro, *Antileopardiani e neomoderati nella sinistra italiana*. Pisa, 1982.

Timpanaro 1984a: S. Timpanaro, *Il socialismo di Edmondo De Amicis: Lettura del "Primo maggio."* Verona, 1984.

Timpanaro 1984b: S. Timpanaro, "Freud's 'Roman Phobia,'" trans. K. Soper and M. H. Ryle, *New Left Review* 147: 4–31.

Timpanaro 1986: S. Timpanaro, *Per la storia della filologia virgiliana antica*. Rome, 1986.

Timpanaro 1988: S. Timpanaro, "Otto Skutsch's Ennius," trans. N. M. Horsfall, in *Vir bonus discendi peritus: Studies in Celebration of Otto Skutsch's Eightieth Birthday*, ed. N. M. Horsfall, 1–5. London, 1988.

Timpanaro 1992: S. Timpanaro, *La "fobia romana" e altri scritti su Freud e Meringer*. Pisa, 1992.

Timpanaro 1994a: S. Timpanaro, *Nuovi contributi di filologia e storia della lingua latina*. Bologna, 1994.

Timparano 1994b: S. Timpanaro, *Nuovi studi sul nostro Ottocento.* Pisa, 1994.

Timparano 1996: S. Timpanaro, *On Materialism,* trans. L. Garner, 3rd ed. London, 1996.

Timparano 1997a: S. Timpanaro, *La filologia di Giacomo Leopardi,* 3rd ed. rev. and with addenda. Bari, 1997.

Timparano 1997b: S. Timpanaro, *Sul materialismo,* 3rd ed. rev. and enlarged. Milan, 1997.

Timparano 2001a: S. Timpanaro, *Virgilianisti antichi e tradizione indiretta.* Florence, 2001.

Timparano 2001b: S. Timpanaro, *Il Verde e il Rosso: Scritti militanti, 1966–2000,* ed. L. Cortesi. Rome, 2001.

Timparano 2001c: S. Timpanaro, "Stemmi tripartite e lapsus (antichi e moderni)," ed. G. Magnaldi, *Il Ponte* 57, nos. 10–11 (October–November 2001): 323–30.

Timpanaro Sr. 1952: Seb. Timpanaro [Sr.], *Scritti di storia e critica della scienza,* [ed. Sebastiano Timpanaro]. Florence, 1952.

Traube 1965 (1909–20): L. Traube, *Vorlesungen und Abhandlungen,* 3 vols., ed. F. Boll. Vol. 1: *Zur Paläographie und Handschriftenkunde,* ed. P. Lehmann. Munich, 1965.

van Groningen 1963: B. A. van Groningen, *Traité d'histoire et de critique des textes grecs.* Amsterdam, 1963.

Wachsmuth 1895: C. Wachsmuth, *Einleitung in das Studium der alten Geschichte.* Leipzig, 1895.

West 1973: M. L. West, *Textual Criticism and Editorial Technique.* Stuttgart, 1973.

Wilamowitz 1982 (1921): U. von Wilamowitz-Moellendorff, *History of Classical Scholarship,* trans. from the German by A. Harris, ed. with an introduction and notes by H. Lloyd-Jones. London, 1982 (= *Geschichte der Philologie,* Leipzig and Berlin, 1921; rev. ed., 1927).

Editor's Note to the Reader

There are two separate systems of annotation in the present edition:

1. Notes indicated by superscript numbers or asterisks formed part of the original Italian edition of Timpanaro's work and are keyed to footnotes at the bottom of the page.
2. Notes indicated by superscript letters have been added by the present editor in order to mark differences among the various editions of the Italian original and are keyed to Additional Materials B, "Differences among the Various Editions," on pages 216–33 below.

THE GENESIS OF LACHMANN'S METHOD

Preface to the First Edition

A first version of this study appeared earlier as Timpanaro 1959, 1960. That it can now reappear in a revised and enlarged form is due to my friend Gianfranco Folena and to the director of the Bibliotechina del Saggiatore, Prof. Bruno Migliorini. To both of them I express my deep gratitude.

The modifications and additions have been more numerous than I anticipated. Nonetheless, the aims and limits of my work remain the same ones as are indicated in its brief introduction. This is not a history of textual criticism—that would demand a much greater breadth of treatment—but merely an investigation that aims to clarify the gradual formation and then the crisis of that "genealogical method" that goes under Lachmann's name: an investigation born, one might say, in the margins of Pasquali 1952a (1934), of which it presupposes the reader's familiarity and to which it constantly refers. And because many of the methodological problems faced by Lachmann, his contemporaries, and his followers are still unresolved, it seemed to me that it might be useful if I made some contribution to the discussion concerning them: see in particular chapters 6 and 8 and the second and third appendices [appendices B and C].

In the course of revising this essay, I received valuable contributions from Konrad Müller (a textual critic who knows the history of his discipline as few others do), Fritz Bornmann, and E. J. Kenney. Thanks to them, chapter 5 and the first two appendices appear here in a more complete and correct version. The third appendix, which is published here for the first time, owes much to the friendly collaboration of Vincenzo di Benedetto and Alfredo Stussi. I have also taken account of suggestions and criticisms by Eduard Fraenkel, Antonio Carlini, Antonio La Penna, Manfredo Manfredi, and Jean Panvini.

What Eugenio Grassi's friendship meant to me I cannot express adequately. An incomparable expert on Greek language and style, animated by the aspiration to submit all hypotheses to rigorous verification and to clear the field of the many ambitious and arbitrary constructions in which Classical philology abounds, he was a unique guide and judge, for me as for his other friends: now that we can no longer avail ourselves of his illuminating criticism, our work has become all the more difficult and uncertain. Besides the interpretation of ancient texts (the activity for which he was best fitted by nature), he also made extremely acute contributions to the methodology of textual criticism: among the posthumous writings published in Grassi 1961, see his observations on the concept of an archetype and the difficulties it presents. It is to be hoped that those observations, together with others he has left us, will be reconsidered and further developed by future scholars.

S.T.

Preface to the Second Edition

The first edition of this little volume, which appeared in 1963 (= Timpanaro 1963a), has been out of print for many years. In 1971 a German edition, *Die Entstehung der Lachmannschen Methode,* appeared in Hamburg, published by Helmut Buske (= Timpanaro 1971), with additions and corrections due in part to myself, in part to my friend the translator, Dieter Irmer, who is also an important scholar on Demosthenes and the Greek medical writers, and to his colleague Volkmar Schmidt. But this second Italian edition is not simply a retranslation of that German edition into the Italian language. From 1971 until now I have felt the need to deepen and broaden my research on various points, even without aiming at a degree of completeness that would be impossible anyway. Moreover, two important works have appeared that, more than all others, have induced me to add corrections and additions to my work: Rizzo 1973 (an exemplary book, whose wealth of historical sense and interpretative acumen is far fuller than the title would suggest) and Kenney 1974, of which a revised and enlarged Italian edition will appear shortly. Kenney's book, notable for its lucidity of exposition and sureness of judgment, is a history of textual criticism from the Renaissance to the present—something never even attempted until now (this fact was neglected by certain reviewers, learned and acute, but too sarcastic and inclined to criticize before reading attentively), comprising a much broader range of material than the present study. As is only obvious, Kenney has reconsidered many of the arguments and problems I had already discussed, and has often done so in greater depth. Hence I have derived great profit for this new edition from his book, as from Rizzo's.

It would take too long to list here other recent works that I have found useful for this new edition: the reader will find them cited in the course of the volume. One danger I ran, paradoxically, was to take *too much* account of all these new contributions—not that they did not deserve it, but I did not wish my little book, even if corrected and enlarged, to become "bloated" just in order to repeat badly everything that Kenney and other future scholars had said and will say so well: it was supposed to stay within the limits of its specific subject matter, which were already explained clearly in the preface to the first edition, reprinted above; and the first two chapters in particular were supposed to retain their introductory character. It was not easy for me, in those first two chapters, to reconcile the need to be "streamlined" with the need to be not too incompletely informative: I hope that I have not succeeded too badly. Upon certain figures and problems of seventeenth- and eighteenth-century philology, about which interest has been particularly lively in recent years, I did linger, perhaps a bit too much with respect to the general economy of the book, even if too little with respect to their importance: I would like to return to deal with them elsewhere soon, although I recognize that the history of the philology of that period is indissolubly linked to the history of the movements of religious reform, a field in which it will not be easy for me to acquire an adequate preparation.

To counterbalance my many revisions and additions, I have performed only a few little cuts in comparison with the German edition. Both my friends Irmer and Schmidt, whom I have already mentioned, but especially the former, had inserted into that edition some notes briefly indicating the results of their own research on particular problems of textual criticism. Although these notes were very interesting in themselves, they ran the danger of remaining somewhat extraneous to the continuity of my exposition; and anyway, Irmer and Schmidt themselves later developed those ideas in separate works and will go on, I believe, to develop them further. For that reason I have left out some of their contributions and condensed others into a few words. To Irmer I have a further debt of gratitude: he was the first to mention to me, and then to supply, Lutz-Hensel 1975.

Appendix C, on the other hand, has been much reworked to take account of recent studies. Among the many reasons that lead to disproportionately increasing the number of bipartite stemmata, I have now emphasized more forcefully the one that from the very beginning had seemed to me the most important one, and I have tried to explain its mechanism better. I wish I could have been briefer: I do not believe that exclusively and abstractly stemmatological problems should be overvalued in textual criticism, but, precisely in order to reduce them to their correct dimensions, it was necessary to examine in a bit more depth certain arguments and to unmask certain specious sophisms.

Whoever has seen in this work of mine a desire to diminish the figure of Lachmann has misinterpreted my intentions. I wanted instead to show how "Lachmann's method" was the result of a collective effort in which other excellent philologists besides Lachmann participated, each one with his own intellectual character. What mattered to me was to define each one's role, to clarify the influences and relations of collaboration and antithesis, to show how the "crisis" of the method (a crisis that has deprived it of its absolute validity but has not at all vitiated its usefulness) was manifested not only in the period after Lachmann, which I discuss in my last chapter, but was already found *in nuce* in philologists' studies long before Lachmann, and even in Lachmann himself in certain oscillations and contradictions beneath his invariably self-confident and peremptory tone. I had no desire to make litigious and antihistorical claims for priority, to hunt for "precursors"—even though it is not without interest to determine from whom Lachmann derived certain ideas and even certain technical terms, and to present, even if only in brief hints, an image of "the man Lachmann" that is free not only of moralistic censure but also of that hagiography of which some of his overly zealous disciples made him the object. In my view, it is not at all useless, even in the history of a rigorously technical discipline, to take account of biographical elements, to seek to "make the characters come alive," without of course making any concessions to an episodic and gossipy biographism.

My revision and enlargement of this work have been greatly assisted not only by works published in these last years but also by personal or epistolary exchanges of ideas with various scholars. Here too I have preferred to declare my debts as I go along, in the course of my exposition. But here I wish to mention in particular Giovan Battista Alberti, Severino Caprioli, Antonio La Penna, Scevola Mariotti, Dante Nardo, Antonio Enzo Quaglio, Wolfgang Schmid, Alfonso Traina, and Gian Piero Zarri. To Dante Nardo I am deeply grateful not only for suggestions of considerable importance, derived from his experience as a textual critic and student of the history of philology (the essays that he will publish soon on Giulio Pontedera and Pietro Canal will show these two Latinists, who are not known well enough, under an almost entirely new light*), but also for the friendship he showed me by supporting the publication of this edition of my work with the Liviana publishing house. And an expression of thanks just as warm and affectionate is due to the director of the series, Sergio Romagnoli, for accepting this little book.

Twenty years have passed since an early and cruel death extinguished at only thirty-three years the man to whose memory this work was dedicated, and is still dedicated. But the memory of his lucid intellect and of his melancholy, concealed under irony, still remains present in his friends, as do ad-

---

* On Pontedera see now Nardo 1981; on Pietro Canal, a distinguished Venetian philologist of the nineteenth century, whom the character of his studies excludes from the scope of this little volume, important studies edited by Nardo and his students have already been published and others will follow.[a]

miration for what he achieved in such a brief time and mourning for what he was not destined to accomplish.

S.T.

*   *   *

This edition has sold out in a short time; I have prepared only a corrected reprint. I have rectified typographical errors and my own mistakes in the text (I am grateful to G. B. Alberti, R. Führer, A. Golzio, M. D. Reeve, A. Rotondò, and A. Stussi for pointing out several to me); I have made a *minimum* of additions at the back of the volume, but I have left the treatment substantially unchanged without subjecting it to further revisions that would have ended up deforming it and destroying its original physiognomy. I believe that this little book can still serve generally to orient readers and that it remains valid in many essential points. In others it is outdated; but perhaps it has contributed toward stimulating new ideas and new research in a field of studies in which much work still remains to be done in depth. But other scholars will continue that work better than I can, bringing fresh energy and new ideas to it.[b]

Introduction

Of the two parts into which Lachmann divided textual criticism—*recensio* [recension] and *emendatio* [emendation]—the second had been practiced since antiquity. In the seventeenth and eighteenth centuries it had also been the object of good methodological discussions, to the degree that this was possible considering that by its nature it is an "art" rather than a "science." [1] In the nineteenth century, methods of emendation were refined further (this was especially due to progress in the study of the language and style of the various epochs and authors),[a] but they were not transformed in a revolutionary way; nor can one say that, as far as divinatory talent is[b] concerned, even the best conjectural critics of that century were superior to a Turnebus or a Bentley[c] or a Reiske.

Instead, the great novelty of nineteenth-century textual criticism was the scientific foundation of *recensio*. But how this was attained; how much of "Lachmann's method" should really be attributed to Lachmann, and how much should be claimed for his predecessors and contemporaries instead; through what phases Lachmann himself passed in the course of developing his method—all this still remains to be clarified. The histories of Classical scholarship say almost nothing about it. Valuable hints concerning these

---

1. Among these discussions of the art of conjecture before the nineteenth century, the two best are the *Ars critica* of Le Clerc 1730 (1697) and Morel 1766 (= Quantin 1846: 969–1116). The work of Le Clerc also treats some questions that today we would assign to *recensio*. On this see below, pp. 61–63, 68n29. On Morel, see Kenney 1974: 44–46. Robortello 1557, a short treatise, is worth recalling without too much anachronistic severity, since it represents the first attempt at this kind of discussion (although obviously the attempt is imperfect, in certain aspects it anticipates the future); on this see Carlini 1967: 65–70; Kenney 1974: 29–36. But the Middle Ages (twelfth century) had already possessed in Nicola Maniacutia of Rome an isolated scholar—in several respects an interesting one—who enunciated certain theoretical principles of textual criticism. He is the subject of a series of studies that are valuable (although occasionally tending toward exaggeration): Peri 1967 and 1977.

historical matters can be found in some discussions of textual criticism: Quentin 1926: 27–38 and *passim;* Dain 1975 (1949): 160–86; Giarratano 1951: 106–23; and above all, Pasquali 1952a (1934), in which, as in all his writings, philology and the history of philology are closely united (see especially chap. 1, "Lachmann's Method," which has already appeared separately as Pasquali 1931).[2] Nonetheless the need is felt for a broader study, such as Joseph Bédier called for as early as 1928.[3] I wished to make an attempt; others, after me, will do better. I only want to warn readers that the first two chapters have a purely introductory character; they do not aim at all[d] to trace out a history of textual criticism from the Humanists until the end of the eighteenth century, but only to isolate some historical presuppositions and partial anticipations of "Lachmann's method."

2. In the following pages other writings by Pasquali are cited. Kenney 1974 has recently dealt with the subject more fully. The biography of Lachmann (Hertz 1851) offers very little on the questions that interest us here.

3. Bédier 1928. As is well known, the ideas Bédier proposed in this article are highly debatable (see below, chap. 3, n. 23), but he was right to deplore the lack of a study on the genesis of "Lachmann's method" (1928: 163n2).

Emendatio ope codicum from the Humanists to Bentley

In the vast majority of cases, the *editiones principes* [first printed editions] made by the Humanists were based on recent manuscripts, since these were easier to get hold of and more comfortable for the typesetters to read.[1] Hence these editions for the most part reproduced a text that had been adjusted and "prettified" by copyist-interpolators. This text, propagated from one edition to another, constituted the "vulgate."

In order to improve and correct the vulgate where it did not seem satisfactory, one could have recourse either to conjectures or to collation of manuscripts considered more authoritative. Classical philologists followed both these paths from the Humanist period until the end of the eighteenth century, some expressing their preference for the one, some for the other. The two approaches are described by Ruhnken at the beginning of his famous *Elogium Tiberii Hemsterhusii* [Eulogy for Tiberius Hemsterhuis]:[2] "Therefore scholars embarked upon one method of doing Criticism or the other, depending on the differences among their native talents. Some rashly uprooted things that were solidly established and should not have been disturbed at all, and harassed things that were certain by means of uncertain conjectures; others did nothing more than gather together the materials provided by manuscripts." It is easy to see that Ruhnken is indicating the harmful exaggerations of the two approaches here rather than their positive aspects: evaluating his hero's achievement in a way that was certainly exaggerated,[a] he wanted to show that Hemsterhuis had been the first scholar to harmonize the two requirements and to establish the true, balanced *ars cri-*

---

1. Cf. Dain 1975 (1949): 160–61, who points out very well the close affinity between Humanist manuscripts and the first printed editions, in both external appearance and editorial technique; Pasquali 1952a (1934): 49–50, 78, and most of chap. 4; Kenney 1974: 4–5; Rizzo 1973: 69–75.

2. Ruhnken 1875 (1789): 1.

tica [art of textual criticism]. But what must be particularly emphasized is that even the champions of the manuscripts tended not to use as a constant basis for their editions the very manuscripts they considered superior; instead, they kept the vulgate as the basis, and only had recourse to the manuscripts where the vulgate was not satisfactory. Thus what they practiced was not *recensio* and *emendatio,* but rather, according to their own conception and terminology, two different types of *emendatio* of the vulgate: *emendatio ope codicum* [emendation with the help of manuscripts] and *emendatio ope ingenii* [emendation with the help of native wit] or *coniecturae* [of conjecture].[3]

In the Humanist period, Politian was the most rigorous proponent of *emendatio ope codicum.*[4] He has recourse quite rarely to conjecture in his first and second[b] *Miscellanea* (nor are his conjectures comparable in brilliance to Valla's in Livy or Marullo's in Lucretius): for the most part he contrasts the corrupt[c] reading of the *exemplaria quae sunt in manibus* [avail-

3. As is well known, ancient grammarians already used the term *emendare* in the general sense of "to correct," also including in it therefore corrections made as a consequence of (for the most part occasional) collation of manuscripts: cf. the words *emendatio* and *emendare* in the *Thesaurus,* and Pascal 1918; further bibliographical references in Rizzo 1973: 250n1. So too, the corresponding Greek term διορθοῦν and other analogous ones (μεταγράφειν, μετατιθέναι, etc.) were used in the same ambiguous sense: cf. Ludwich 1885: 93, 104–5. Among Italianists, even ones of high standing in textual criticism, the wide sense of *emendatio* has lasted until recent times: cf. Pasquali 1942: 226 (= Pasquali 1968: 2.159), in which a passage of Michele Barbi is translated, as it were, into the modern terminology of Classical philology. The distinction between the two types of *emendatio* is often enunciated in Vettori 1569 (e.g., 30.22, tit.: "A passage corrected [. . .] in part with the help of an old manuscript, in part by conjecture"; 36.6; etc.); when he simply says *emendare* or *corrigere* without any addition, the context shows that he generally means correcting *ope codicum,* in conformity with his conservative tendency, to which we shall refer in a moment. Among the many other passages from Classical philologists of the fifteenth to eighteenth centuries that could be cited, see also N. Heinsius in the preface to his edition of the works of Ovid (Heinsius 1661: without page numeration): "which I have already emended in many passages, in part on the authority of old manuscripts, in part by relying upon the guidance of my native wit alone." Sabbadini 1920: 56–60 is still useful for providing a preliminary orientation on the champions of conjectures and of manuscripts in the Humanist period; some more detailed observations now in Kenney 1974: 26–27 and chap. 2 passim.

4. During the last ten years, studies on Politian and editions of his unpublished writings have flourished intensely; this tendency is still in full swing. This is not the right place for a full bibliography; I therefore limit myself to referring to the lively synthesis of Grafton 1977a (with an up-to-date bibliography, and rich in references to earlier and contemporary Humanists). I also wish to recall with undiminished gratitude the seminars of Alessandro Perosa at Pisa on the first *Miscellanea,* which I had the good fortune to attend at the beginning of the 1950s. In what follows I shall cite other scholarly contributions.

able copies]—recent manuscripts or printed editions—with the genuine reading of a *codex pervetustus* [very ancient manuscript] that he has found in the Laurentian Library or to which some other Humanist has drawn his attention.

Up to this point there is nothing substantially new in comparison with the ancient grammarians: for example, controversies regarding textual criticism in Aulus Gellius's *Noctes Atticae* (which constitute the principal model of the *Miscellanea* in their compositional structure[d] too) are often resolved by recourse to manuscripts of venerable antiquity (sometimes too venerable to be believable!).[e,5] But Politian often goes on to add a consideration of a genealogical nature in order to reinforce his preference for the older manuscript: recent manuscripts are copies of the older one; hence they do not have the value of an independent tradition.[6]

Later—in the nineteenth century, as we shall see, and unfortunately even today—this procedure, which has received the technical name of *eliminatio codicum descriptorum* [elimination of derivative manuscripts], has often become a convenient expedient for saving the Classical philologist time and trouble: insufficient evidence, or even the simple observation that there is a mass of *recentiores* [more recent witnesses] alongside a manuscript of considerable antiquity, has too easily suggested that the more recent ones derived from the older one. Did Politian too sometimes work in this way? In the first edition of this book I suggested that he had done so, and even now I cannot bring myself to exclude this possibility altogether. And yet even then I cited a well-known example of an *eliminatio* that Politian based on solid evidence; and now I am inclined to believe, though with some reservations, that Rizzo is right (1973: 315n2) to maintain that such cases make up if not the totality, at least the great majority.[f] In chapter 25 of his first *Miscellanea*, Politian demonstrates that the Laurentian manuscript 49,7 of Cicero's *Epistulae familiares*, which had one quire out of order by an error

5. Cf., e.g., Aulus Gellius 1.7; 1.21.2; 2.3.5; 9.14; 12.10.6; 13.21.16; 18.5.11. More generally on the use of manuscripts by Greek and Latin grammarians, cf. Lehrs 1882: 344–49. Oscillations between age and large numbers of manuscripts as a criterion for judging were not lacking; on Galen's ideas on this subject cf., e.g., Bröcker 1885: 417.

6. E.g., *Misc.*, chap. 5 ("an extremely old manuscript of the *Argonautica* of Valerius Flaccus [. . .] from which I think all the other available ones are derived"; cf. the passage of the second *Miscellanea* cited below, n. 8), 25 (to which we shall refer shortly), 41, 89, 93, 95. Cf. the famous *subscriptio* to the incunable containing the *Silvae* of Statius *inter alia*: "I have come upon a text of the *Silvae* of Statius [. . .] from which alone all the other available manuscripts seem to have emanated, though it is full of errors and corrupt and, what is more, as I think, reduced to half its original extent" (cf. Perosa 1955: 15, and below, n. 9; this is not the place to linger on the very controversial problem of just which manuscript Politian saw); and the analogous *subscriptio* to Apicius (Rizzo 1973: 315n2).

of binding, is the ancestor of a group of more recent Laurentian manuscripts
in which the same disturbance in the order of the letters is found without
this being explicable by a displacement of the quires.[7] He eliminated the
apographs of an old manuscript of Valerius Flaccus by analogous reasoning, as the second *Miscellanea* now prove.[g,8] Thus Politian not only venerates[h] the oldest manuscripts in general: he also has the beginnings of a historical understanding of manuscript traditions. He is also aware that when
a conjecture is necessary, it must find its starting point in the oldest stage
of the tradition that we can reach, not in the deceptive patchings-up that
corruptions have undergone in the more recent manuscripts (*Misc.* chap. 57,
cf. chap. 20)—a criterion that will not be fully recognized until the age of
Lachmann.

What is more, Politian already understood that the manuscripts (at least
the oldest and most valuable ones) had to be collated not occasionally but
systematically, registering all the readings that diverged from the vulgate
text, including those that were certainly erroneous but that might turn out
to be useful for restoring the text. This is the criterion he asserted in the *sub-
scriptiones* to the writers *De re rustica,* to Pliny, Statius, Pelagonius, and
Terence; he had a full and justified awareness of its methodological novelty,
even if earlier Humanists and, probably, medieval scribes had already begun
to apply it.[9] In this regard he was a precursor of Ernesti and Wolf (see below, pp. 71–74) and was already beginning to overcome the erroneous concept of *emendatio ope codicum,* which implies that collations are made not
constantly but only occasionally.[i]

Politian's orientation toward conservative textual criticism, his polemic
against the copyist-interpolators,[j] and his tendency to belittle[k] recent manuscripts as copies of a *vetustissimus* still preserved recur in Pier Vettori, with
greater support from arguments and examples.[10] Always disinclined to make
conjectures, he is especially hesitant when the old manuscripts unanimously
attest a reading: "I scarcely think that all the old manuscripts can be subject
to the same error." [11] This was a legitimate hesitation until scholars attained

7. In turn Laur. 49, 7 derives from Laur. 49, 9 of the ninth century. Politian noticed
this too (see the beginning of the same chap. 25), but he did not take the time to supply
the evidence: "The fact that this one is copied from that one is clear from many proofs
which I shall omit now." The whole question is well clarified by Kirner 1901: 400–406.

8. Politian 1972: 4.6–7 (chap. 2); cf. 1.23 and n. 45; Branca 1973: 347–52.

9. Cf. the passages cited by Perosa 1955: 15, 22, 26, 38, 66.

10. Among the many passages that could be cited, see his preface to the *Epistulae familiares* of Cicero (Vettori 1586 [1558]: 69–70). Vettori writes *inter alia:* "These perverse
correctors have inflicted upon them [sc. writers] wounds no fewer than those dealt them
by time itself and the ignorance of earlier centuries."

11. Vettori 1540: 524.

with clarity[1] the concept of an archetype, which explains the corruptions shared by a whole tradition. In fact, despite certain professions of an extremely conservative creed ("I prefer to be in error with old manuscripts rather than out of excessive fondness for my own ideas"),[12] Vettori is anything but uncritical in his actual philological practice: his defense of the manuscript tradition is almost always the result of a deeper interpretation, a better understanding of the writer's style. This is true especially of Cicero, the author whom Vettori knew best; it is somewhat less true of the Greek texts he published, in which he sometimes really did fall into excesses of conservatism.[13]

But, even if only in passing, Erasmus had already arrived at the use of[m] the concept of archetype for the purposes of *emendatio*. In his *Adagia*[14] he proposed a correction to a proverbial expression cited in Aristotle's *Metaphysics*,[15] and observed, "The agreement of the manuscripts will not seem at all astonishing to those who have even a modicum of experience in assessing and collating manuscripts. For it very often happens that an error of one archetype, so long as it has some specious appearance of the truth, goes on to propagate itself in all the books that form as it were its descendants, 'and the children of its children and those who are born later.'"[16]

We must linger for a moment on this passage, which I discussed inadequately in the first edition of this work, in part because of a banal error of interpretation (corrected by Rizzo 1973: 316). Scholars used to think that

12. Vettori 1571: 166. Cf. 71: "Since by nature I was always shy about changing anything rashly in someone else's writings."

13. On his edition of the *Agamemnon*, cf. Fraenkel 1950: 1.34–35. On Vettori's personality in general, which even now is not sufficiently known (some indications in Grafton 1975: 162–79), we expect much new information from Lucia Cesarini Martinelli's research. On a group of important students and followers of Vettori, who distinguished themselves *inter alia* in *eliminationes descriptorum* following in the footsteps of Politian, see Grafton 1977b: 175–76; and, with particular reference to the *Corpus iuris*, before and after Vettori, Caprioli 1969 (Caprioli's fundamental study extends into the sixteenth century as well), and Troje 1971.

14. Erasmus 1538 (1500): 209 (Chilias I, century VI, adage 36). In the first edition (Paris, 1500) this adage is not yet to be found; it appears for the first time in the Venice edition of 1508, as N. G. Wilson informs me.

15. *Metaph.* α 993b5: Τίς ἂν θύρας ἁμάρτοι; i.e., "Who would err trying to hit (a target as big as) a door?" The expression, Alexander of Aphrodisias explains, εἴληπται ἀπὸ τῶν τοξοτῶν τῶν ἐπὶ σκοπὸν τοξευόντων. Erasmus wanted to correct θύρας to θήρας, wrongly: cf. Leutsch 1851: 678.

16. So (or else, certainly erroneously, καίτοι) the editions of the *Adagia* available to me. The Homeric text (*Il.* 20.308) has καὶ παίδων παῖδες, τοί κεν, etc. The accusative παῖδας is an adaptation required by the context in Erasmus; the other changes will have been errors of citation from memory.

the Humanists (like the ancients before them: cf. Cicero, *Ad Att.* 16.3.1) meant by the term *archetypum* or *codex archetypus* only the "official text" checked by the author and intended to be published afterward in further copies. A wider and deeper examination (Rizzo 1973: 308–17) has made it clear that alongside that meaning (perhaps the prevailing one) the term also has many other usages in the Humanist age, among them the one that will go on to prevail later, namely, that of a manuscript—even if it is later than the author by many centuries, even if it has been preserved by chance and is devoid of any "official" quality or authority, even if it is disfigured by errors or lacunas—from which all the others are derived. It is in this sense that Merula, in the preface of his Plautus edition of 1472, applies the term *archetypum* to the lost *unus liber* [single book] from which the copies still extant of the Plautine comedies are derived (Rizzo 1973: 314), even if he introduces the word with a *velut* [as it were], which gives it an almost metaphorical meaning; and Politian uses the same term in his commentary on Statius's *Silvae* for Poggio's manuscript, which he had seen and judged *mendosus* [full of errors] and *dimidiatus* [reduced to half its original extent].[17] What is still lacking, it seems to me, before we arrive at the "Lachmannian" usage of *archetypum* (or of the adjective *archetypus*), is the *limitation* of the term to lost ancestors alone and, what is more, to ones distinct from the original or official text. Politian himself applies the term *archetype* more than once to the Pandects first preserved in Pisa, then in Florence, that is, to a manuscript that was still extant and that he thought was one of the official texts Justinian circulated to various cities.[18]

In any case, the importance of the passage of Erasmus we have cited consists not in his application of the term *archetypum* to a lost common copy—as we have seen, at least Merula had preceded Erasmus in giving this meaning to the term, even if with a somewhat cautious wording; and probably Erasmus too considered legitimate the other meanings commonly given it in the Humanist period—but rather in his energetic affirmation of the right to correct a reading that appears erroneous without allowing oneself to be intimidated by the *consensus codicum* [consensus of the manuscripts] (as, even after Erasmus, Pier Vettori allowed himself to be, as we saw just now): it was not the case that each and every copyist committed the same error independently of the others, by an improbable phenomenon of polygenesis spreading through the whole tradition; instead, it was a single copyist who was responsible for the error, and subsequent copyists repeated it because it

17. Politian 1978: 33.16; cf. 10.13–17; and above, n. 6.
18. See the passages cited by Rizzo 1973: 313 and 313n2; and, for other Humanists who were in contact with Politian or underwent his influence, Caprioli 1969: 393–404 and passim.

was an insidious error, one with an appearance of truth (*fucus*), so that it did not occur to them to correct it. Erasmus was certainly thinking of an *ancient* archetype in that passage from the *Adagia,* since he is not embarrassed by the fact (which he notes expressly) that Alexander of Aphrodisias had already read the presumed error θύρας in his copy of Aristotle. But, in general, he shows that he believes it to be impossible for "crude" errors such as meaningless expressions or lacunas to spread through the entire manuscript tradition: subsequent copyists would have noticed these and would have tried to heal them. Erasmus's conception of textual transmission was almost too unmechanical—it was appropriate only for certain traditions.[n]

The great French Classical philologists of the sixteenth century, from Turnebus to Lambinus, to Daniel, to Pithou, all felt the requirement to seek out old manuscripts and to use them for their editions, but Joseph Scaliger felt it more than anyone else. A conjectural critic much less gifted and spontaneous than Turnebus, hostile to collections of occasional *adversaria,* tending to compose organic works already in the first period of his activity,[19] animated by a historical spirit far more than by a taste for the interpretation of individual passages, he was the first to set himself the problem of reconstructing a medieval archetype (even if he did not use the term *archetype* to designate it). In his *Castigationes in Catullum* he believed that on the basis of the corruptions in the apographs he could establish that their ancestor was written in pre-Caroline minuscule.[20] His demonstration must be considered a failure,[21] but in any case the very attempt is quite interesting. Scaliger too, following in the footsteps of Politian and Vettori, took issue with fifteenth-

19. See his letter to Janus Dousa of 1594 (Scaliger 1627: 52): "We have made many observations on authors in both languages, which could give birth to a monstrous progeny of Variants, Old Readings, Miscellanies and other things of this type, with which the ambition of Philologists is nowadays wont to run riot. . . . But in order for our sleepless nights to bear fruit, we undertook to interpret and purify authors as wholes." This demand for wholeness was later developed fully in the great historical and chronological works of his more mature years. Cf. Bernays 1855: 46–47.

20. Scaliger 1582 (1577): 4 of the *Castigationes:* "Moreover, I suspect that that Gallic copy was written in Langobardian letters, since the errors that have been disseminated in later manuscripts by inexperienced scribes seem to have arisen precisely from those crabby characters, as we shall indicate carefully in the proper place." By "Langobardian letters" we must understand here pre-Caroline minuscule and not Beneventan script, as is made clear by the fact that on pp. 23 and 73 Scaliger hypothesizes errors due to the confusion between *a* and *u:* "because there is no difference between these letters in the Langobardian script" (p. 23); "*u* and *a* are the same in Langobardian characters" (p. 73). On the rather broad usage of the term *Langobardian letters* in the Humanist period, cf. Casamassima 1964: 566–67; Rizzo 1973: 122–23. For other confusions of letters that Scaliger considered significant, cf. below, Appendix B, n. 3.

21. See again Appendix B, n. 3.

century interpolators, who gave particular offense to this enemy of stylistic allurements and lover of the austerities of archaic Latin;[22] but he understood that the old manuscripts too were contaminated by corruptions that had to be healed by conjecture: "Just as more recent editions must be weighed against old copies, like gold at an assay, so too the manuscripts must be correctly weighed in the scales of judgment."[23] And on the basis of the perfectly legitimate hypothesis of an archetype in rather bad shape, he felt himself all too authorized to transpose sections of poems, especially of Tibullus, so as to provide them with a logical order.[24] Caution in *recensio*, excessive boldness in *emendatio:* we shall find the same contrast once again in Lachmann.[o,*]

From his Italian predecessors and contemporaries, especially from Vettori, Scaliger derived and developed further the demand for a complete collation of the manuscripts in his edition of Catullus and in the edition of Valerius Flaccus he scarcely sketched out; later, in his edition of Manilius, he returned to the practice of merely occasional collations.[q,25]

---

22. See, e.g., the *Castigationes* (Scaliger 1582 [1577]: 105). For Scaliger's fondness for archaism one may recall his Latin version of the Orphic hymns and his famous judgment on Ennius (quoted by Bernays 1855: 282).

23. In the *Prolegomena* to Scaliger 1600 (1579): 8.

24. Heyne 1817 (1755): xviii–xix protested against these transpositions even before Haupt 1875–76: 3.30–41 did.

* On Scaliger, A. T. Grafton (of whom I cited a preparatory work, Grafton 1975) has now published volume 1 of a large-scale complete study: Grafton 1983 (important for Scaliger's precursors too). The second volume is eagerly awaited. To the disagreement that I had expressed in n. 25 below, Grafton replies courteously, repeating his thesis (1983: 320), and points out to me that the chronological computations Scaliger had to perform for the great works of his second period of activity demanded just as much patience and attention of him as had been required for doing complete collations of manuscripts. This is quite true; but that patience and attention were a *conditio sine qua non* for the great chronological works to which Scaliger devoted himself, whereas a critical edition could also be prepared by relying solely upon conjectural criticism and neglecting to do a systematic *recensio* first, even despite an awareness of the risks to which such a procedure would give rise (see below, p. 75). It is beyond doubt that Scaliger's relations with Vettori and his followers were ruined both by personal reasons and by Vettori's conservatism as a textual critic (cf. Grafton 1983: 184–86), but it continues to seem improbable to me that *this was the reason* why Scaliger regressed methodologically and became convinced that systematic collations of the manuscripts were superfluous (to the contrary of what he had believed when he had edited Catullus). To be sure, as far as I know he never provided a theoretical justification for this regression. Cf. also what I point out in chap. 2, nn. 39 and 47, concerning Ernesti and Wolf. Neither of them repudiated the principles they had expounded with such lucidity, yet they did not have the self-consistency to apply them in all their editions. Cf. also Jocelyn 1984: 60.[p]

25. For Catullus, cf. Grafton 1975: 158–61; for Valerius Flaccus, Waszink 1979: 81 and n. 21; for Manilius, Grafton 1975: 174–76. To me it seems implausible to attribute

Knowledge about manuscript material was greatly increased by the work of the Dutch Classical philologists of the seventeenth century, in particular by Nicolaas Heinsius, who, as is well known, examined an enormous number of manuscripts during his travels throughout Europe and made collations that even today are admired for their exactitude.[26] He was also able to indicate the best manuscripts for many texts; and not only did he have a clear concept of what a medieval archetype was, as Scaliger already did, but he was also able to distinguish two families of manuscripts in the manuscript traditions of Curtius Rufus and Prudentius, though the method he applied in doing so was not entirely rigorous. Yet the fact that, as Kenney has observed, he took as the basis for his own editions of Ovid the text that his father, Daniel Heinsius, had prepared for his edition of 1629, indicates that his point of view was somewhat obsolete.[r,27] And his love for facile and elegant Latin versification, more Ovidian than Ovid himself, led him not only often to propose conjectures for the sole purpose of beautifying the text but also more than once to prefer brilliant but specious readings found in recent manuscripts. Later he worked with a much more cautious methodology on the text of Petronius: he understood that many "anomalies" were due not to corruptions but to that author's unique style.[28] But here we find a limiting case: no one could have dreamed of "Ciceronianizing" the Latin of the *Satyricon,* so enormous was its difference from so-called Classical Latin, and not just in the *Cena.* Probably the scholarly disagreements about N. Heinsius and the divergent assessments of him for all the general recognition of his greatness, now as in the past, derive from the fact that he was a transitional figure, perhaps more conspicuously than others—half a Humanist in the restrictive sense of the term, half a Classical philologist aware of new requirements.[s,29] The defects of Heinsius the "Humanist" were magnified in

---

the reason for this methodological regression to the worsening of relations between Scaliger and Italian Classical philologists, as Grafton suggests. On the other hand, it is true that Scaliger's taste for textual criticism had not weakened at the time of his Manilius edition (Grafton 1975: 175; and already Housman in a letter cited by Grafton, ibid., n. 71). Instead, I would think of a decrease in the patience and powers of concentration necessary for complete collations, which can become weaker even when a scholar is still very interested in problems of textual criticism.

26. Cf., e.g., Munari 1950 and 1957; further bibliography in Kenney 1974: 59n51; the article by M. D. Reeve announced by Kenney has appeared, Reeve 1974; cf. Reeve 1976.

27. Kenney 1974: 62–63. Cf. the objections of Grafton 1977b: 173, and the reply of Kenney 1980. See also the formulation, directed substantially toward the past and not the future, which we cited above, n. 3, from Heinsius's preface to his Ovid edition.

28. Cf. Blok 1949: 246–53, esp. 247–52.

29. Such contradictions are well brought out by Kenney 1974: 57–63 (and they are repeated in Kenney 1980). The characterization of N. Heinsius given by L. Müller 1869:

other Dutchmen, for example, in Jan van Broekhuizen (Broukhusius). And in general in the seventeenth century, and to some extent still in the eighteenth, it was more in breadth than in depth that the examination of manuscripts made progress. An extreme example of this tendency is the Jesuit Girolamo Lagomarsini, a pure and simple collector of variants drawn from innumerable manuscripts and printed editions[t] of Cicero[30] (whereas another Italian student of Cicero, Gaspare Garatoni, was later to demonstrate a much superior natural talent for Classical philology). With only a few exceptions, which the progress of research may well reveal to have been more numerous,[u] the hints at a history of the manuscript tradition which we have noted in Politian, Erasmus, and above all Scaliger, were not developed very much.[31]

Richard Bentley, the most brilliant Classical philologist between the end of the seventeenth century and the first decades of the eighteenth, and one of the most brilliant Classical philologists of all times,[w] possessed a great capacity for evaluating manuscripts (even if not for reconstructing their genealogy) and for distinguishing genuine readings from interpolated ones. "No one who knows Bentley well will doubt that a new editor of Horace, once he has eliminated most of Bentley's conjectures (what in fact is not difficult), will find that after him he has almost nothing left to do for the con-

---

51–54 is incomplete, but charming for its liveliness and perceptiveness, and hence still worth reading. Blok 1949 is fundamental for its richness of documentation and for having brought to light new aspects of Heinsius's personality; the title, *N. Heinsius in Dienst van Christina van Zweden,* is infelicitous inasmuch as it suggests primarily a biography of Heinsius as a diplomat; the book is written in Dutch, so my consultation of it was laborious and incomplete. The main results of Blok's book are summarized by Waszink 1979: 72–73, 82–83, and are shared by Grafton 1977b. I cannot get rid of my impression that its tendency is excessively apologetic, even if in any case, I repeat, Heinsius's greatness is not in question.

30. Nardo 1970: 147–48, 154–58 demonstrated that the majority of the so-called Lagomarsinian manuscripts are in reality old printed editions, for the most part derived in turn from inferior manuscripts.

31. One of these exceptions, pointed out to me by Dante Nardo (cf. now Nardo 1981[v]), is constituted by Giulio Pontedera, a distinguished botanist of Vicenza who dedicated himself to the study of antiquity and made excellent contributions to the texts of the Latin agricultural writers (Cato, Varro, Columella, Palladius), for the most part defending the readings of the manuscripts against the vulgate and thereby developing further that line of research, which had been inaugurated by Politian and Pier Vettori, and in these very same authors. The importance of Pontedera's studies (see esp. Pontedera 1740) was noticed by Johann Gottlob Schneider, who in his edition of the *Scriptores rei rusticae* also reproduced his posthumous *Epistulae ac dissertationes* (Schneider 1794–96: 4.2, cf. 1.vii–viii); many of his contributions, mediated by Schneider, have been accepted by more recent editors, but until now historians of classical scholarship have neglected him.

stitution of the text": this judgment of Lachmann's, repeated by other first-rate scholars,[x,32] is substantially true, even if it runs the risk of giving too simplistic a picture of Bentley's mode of operation, in which the recourse to manuscripts (in the case of Horace, often *recentiores*) and the work of conjectural emendation did not follow first the one and then the other, but were interconnected, and indeed for the most part the latter preceded the former.[y,33] But Bentley's healthy distrust for the vulgate was illuminated almost a hundred years after his death by none other than Lachmann, who discovered it by starting out from the field in which it was most visible, New Testament criticism (see below, pp. 63f., 85f.). For the most part, this aspect of Bentley's activity as a textual critic remained concealed from the Classical philologists who were his contemporaries or immediate successors by another, more conspicuous one: his conjectural criticism, extraordinarily ingenious (just think of his emendations to Callimachus and Manilius),[z] but often rash.[34] He himself contributed to this impression with some of his vigorous[aa] pronouncements, like the celebrated "For us, reason and the facts are worth more than a hundred manuscripts,"[35] or like the perhaps even more characteristic passage in the preface to his edition of Horace in which he maintains that conjecture, precisely because in it the Classical philologist's personal responsibility is entirely at stake, ends up yielding more secure results than accepting the transmitted reading or choosing between variants does.[bb,36] Against a lazy and uncritical adherence to the vulgate or

32. Lachmann 1876: 2.253n1 (= Lachmann 1830: 820n1). Cf. Wilamowitz 1982 (1921): 81; Kenney 1974: 72.

33. On this point cf. now, with great precision, Brink 1978: 1141–48, esp. 1147–48. But I believe that Brink exaggerates in trying to rehabilitate Bentley's Horatian conjectures and in maintaining, in the footsteps of Paul Maas, that the transmitted text of Horace is extensively corrupt (see also below, n. 37). Besides, it is not true that Wilamowitz (as Brink reports 1978: 1144) said that the text of Horace "has no need" of conjectures but rather that it has "very little need" ("verschwindend wenig": cf. Wilamowitz 1927: 36): the difference (due perhaps to the Italian translator of Brink's English text?) is not negligible.

34. On Callimachus, cf. Pfeiffer 1976: 153, and Pfeiffer 1949–53: 2.xliv–xlvi (see also Hemmerdinger 1977: 490–92). On Manilius, Housman 1937 (1903): xvi–xix. This is not the place to linger on the splendid conjectural contributions of Bentley to these authors and to many others.

35. In his edition of Horace (Bentley 1711), note on *Carm.* 3.27.15 (for analogous pronouncements by other Classical philologists, cf. Kenney 1974: 42n2, 99). In point of fact, to those words Bentley added, "especially with the further vote of the old Vatican manuscript." But in any case the *vetat* he supported against the *vetet* of the better tradition is mistaken.

36. Bentley 1711: 2 (preface): "In these Horatian labors, then, we offer more readings by means of conjecture than with the aid of manuscripts, and, unless I am entirely mistaken, for the most part more certain ones: for when there are variant readings, authority

to the first reading offered by just any manuscript, this argument had a certain degree of truth (cf. Kenney 1974: 72–73); but it tended to set up as the goal of a critical edition not the historically most probable text but the best text that the editor's taste and mentality could imagine. I do not believe that, as some have said, Bentley's edition of Milton's *Paradise Lost,* which is full of arbitrary conjectures, is evidence of his senile decline or of his lesser familiarity with English poetry than with Latin and Greek poetry (even though there may well be some truth in this latter explanation); instead, I think we should seriously consider Brink's somewhat paradoxical suggestion (Brink 1978: 1161–64) that Bentley's Miltonic conjectures, misguided on the level of textual criticism, were an indirect form of literary criticism, opposing a different taste to Milton's and to the corresponding poetic language. But, in my opinion, something similar also happens in Bentley's edition of Horace, even if to a lesser degree: in the overwhelming majority of cases, Bentley's hundreds of conjectures on Horace are "corrections" not of the transmitted reading but of the poet; and many of them betray a lack of understanding of that element irreducible to pure rationality in the strict sense, which is inherent in any poetic language, in quite different forms and degrees.[cc,37]

---

itself often deludes people, and encourages the deplorable itch to emend; but when conjectures are proposed against the testimony of all the manuscripts, not only do fear and a sense of shame tweak one's ear, but reason alone and the clarity of the meanings and necessity itself dominate. Furthermore, if you produce a variant reading from one manuscript or another, you achieve nothing by claiming authority for one or two witnesses against a hundred, unless you bolster it with enough arguments to settle the matter on their own almost without the testimony of a manuscript. So don't worship scribes alone: no, venture your own wisdom, so that it is only when you have tested on their own the individual points against the general drift of the discourse and the character of the language that you pronounce your opinion and deliver your verdict." On the value assumed in the Enlightenment by Horace's *sapere aude,* see Venturi 1959; but the pious Bentley, a ferocious adversary not only of atheists but also of deists (see below, p. 63f.), limited his own "Enlightenment" to textual criticism.

37. I have lingered a bit on this point because some writings about Bentley (Goold 1963; Shackleton Bailey 1963; Brink 1978: 1087–1164) that add new points of view and very intelligent considerations nonetheless tend toward an indiscriminate exaltation of all of Bentley, as though his greatness would be diminished by any recognition of the limits possessed by every scholar, even the greatest. This is particularly noticeable in the essay by Brink, who in another respect is the very one who has dug most deeply into Bentley's personality. Many critics of Bentley's conjectural boldness can be accused of a myopic conservatism, but it would be difficult to nullify the observations of a Housman in this way: but see what he says in the already cited preface to his edition of Manilius (Housman 1937 [1903]: xvi *infra*–xvii) concerning the "faults" of Bentley's Manilius, which are "the faults of Bentley's other critical works"; and he repeats analogous reservations in the preface to his edition of Lucan, Housman 1927 (1926): xxxii–xxxiii. Bentley gave his worst perfor-

The English Classical philologists of the second half of the eighteenth century and the first half of the nineteenth who were inferior to Bentley in talent and breadth of horizon but nevertheless followed his powerful example in textual criticism (Musgrave, Porson, Dobree, Elmsley) were above all conjectural critics, endowed with a refined knowledge of linguistic and metrical usage, especially regarding the recitative parts of Greek tragedy and comedy. But they also felt the need to check the manuscripts. If Porson "was conditioned by the fact that he never stirred from England, where only *recentiores* manuscripts" of Euripides [38] and the other tragedians existed, before him Samuel Musgrave ventured as far as Paris and collated two important manuscripts of Euripides there, and after him Peter Elmsley went to Italy, studied the Laurentian manuscript of Sophocles (he was the first to recognize clearly its superiority),[39] and collated and evaluated Vatican manuscripts of Euripides, for the most part correctly.[40] To Elmsley we also owe the suggestion that all the manuscripts of Aeschylus derive "from the same copy, which appears to have survived alone the general wreck of ancient literature."[41] We already know that the concept of an archetype goes back three centuries before Elmsley. All the same, his strictly "medieval" conception of the archetype of Aeschylus, as the sole manuscript to have escaped a "shipwreck" that befell civilization, is interesting because it anticipates Madvig's and Lachmann's formulations. It is altogether another matter that one can no longer think today of an archetype of this kind for the text of Aeschylus.

But my wish not to separate his English followers from Bentley has led me to jump too far ahead in my story. We must now take a step back, in order to show how New Testament philology gave rise to great progress in the methodology of textual criticism.[dd]

---

mance as a conjectural critic not with the text of Horace but with the tragedies of Seneca; if one skims the apparatus criticus of the Paravian edition of Moricca 1946–47, one will find only very few conjectures of Bentley's worthy of attention and innumerable other ones that are entirely useless, "violent," even tasteless. One almost fails to recognize the brilliant emender of Callimachus.

38. Di Benedetto 1965: 10.

39. Cf. Jebb 1900 (1886): liv.

40. Di Benedetto 1965: 11–12.

41. Elmsley 1810: 219. The passage is cited by Dindorf 1876: 405. Its correct interpretation (derivation of the surviving manuscripts from an archetype lost today, not from the Medicean manuscript, as Dindorf had understood it) is due to Wilamowitz 1914: xxiii.

The Need for a Systematic *Recensio* in the Eighteenth Century

As we have suggested, it was above all the study of the Greek New Testament that made the technique of *recensio* progress beyond the point it had reached with Scaliger. This was observed by Giorgio Pasquali 1952a (1934): 8: "with regard to *recensio, philologia profana* [. . .] is still, without knowing it, a tributary of *philologia sacra*"; he also indicated the reasons for it. The New Testament has an extremely rich manuscript tradition; conjectural criticism can achieve little or nothing: hence the problems of choosing among the innumerable variants and assessing the different degrees of authority of the manuscripts moved to the forefront. And here every question of textual criticism aroused a particularly lively interest, since it went beyond pure philology and implied, or at least could imply, questions of theology.

The *editio princeps* of the Greek New Testament, edited by Erasmus, was one of that great Humanist's least successful editions, for he prepared it in haste and based it on Byzantine manuscripts of little value.[1] But here too that phenomenon occurred that we described at the beginning of chapter 1: most of the subsequent editions reproduced the text of the *editio princeps,* with some contamination. One of these editions, the so-called *textus receptus,* published by Elzevier of Leiden (1624, 1633), had an enormous diffusion and was adopted by the Protestant churches.[2,*] From then on it was

1. Waszink 1979: 75–77 has observed that for the most part Erasmus's original contributions to textual criticism should not be sought in his editions of Classical texts, prepared hastily for the printers' use, but must be gleaned from his Latin translations of Greek texts.

2. Gregory 1900–1909: 2.937–42 (still fundamental). There is a more concise but very clear exposition in Hundhausen in Wetzer-Welte 1882–1903: 2.608–9. Metzger 1968 (1964): chapters 3 and 4 (see also the addenda at the end of the second edition) are rich in information and very up to date, but the author does not characterize the individual personalities of the New Testament critics of the eighteenth century distinctly enough, and, as chapters 6 and 7 demonstrate, he does not always have a clear understanding of the principles and methods of more recent textual criticism; to a certain extent his historical exposition is thereby also impaired.

* On the *textus receptus,* de Jonge 1978 is fundamental. But I cannot agree with the same scholar's recent defense of Erasmus's edition: de Jonge 1984. According to de Jonge,

indeed permitted to amass variants at the foot of the page—John Mill collected more of them in his Oxford edition of 1707 than anyone else did—but every attempt to introduce modifications into the text, even if on the authority of the oldest manuscripts, encountered the theologians' fierce opposition: "If someone [. . .] would dare to change even a little word or a single letter or one stroke of a letter by the application of critical judgment, then at once with their cries of protest they tear him apart as impious, and with great fierceness they accuse him of heresy," wrote Wettstein (1730: 158)—and he himself had had firsthand experience of these theological furors.

Such intolerance was stronger in Protestant countries than in Catholic ones: "For the Reformation, in contrast to Catholicism, Sacred Scripture is the only source of truth, and at the same time, quite otherwise than in Catholicism, it is the only book that the whole populace reads. What will happen if that first certainty, from which all others well forth, becomes uncertain?"[3] All the same we must add that a similar error, which allowed the *textus receptus* to be venerated as *the tradition* and made a return to the ancient manuscripts seem a rash innovation, was not limited to theologians alone but was widely diffused among Classical philologists as well. It derived from that error of method we have already described, namely, to take the vulgate as the basis and emend it afterward by recourse to manuscripts and conjectures: in this way recurring to manuscripts seemed to be a break with tradition rather than a return to it. Exceptionally fierce struggles were necessary in the field of New Testament studies to defeat this illogical form of conservatism; but so too in Classical philology Ernesti, Reiske, and Ruhnken had to work hard[4]—just like, in Dante studies, Bartolomeo Perazzini,[5]

---

what mattered to Erasmus was making a Latin translation of the New Testament, not an edition of the Greek text. Even if this were true (and it is not, at least not entirely: many of de Jonge's arguments are strained), the fact remains that in that case Erasmus ought to have published only the Latin translation: whoever publishes the Greek text as well (and this was the first printed Greek text!), and publishes it as extraordinarily badly as Erasmus did, cannot be excused by his lack of interest in this work. It is not even fair to accuse Wettstein of being a detractor of Erasmus: Wettstein passes a severe judgment on the Greek text published and republished by Erasmus, but he also defended it generously, in the first and especially in the second *Prolegomena,* against attacks by intolerant theologians. More generally, let me say that R. Pfeiffer and Dutch scholars have contributed to the development of a "cult" of Erasmus, a defensive attitude regarding every aspect of his personality, of which that great man has no need.[a]

3. Pasquali 1952a (1934): 9; and see all of his fine tribute to Wettstein, which concludes: "Even in a field as technical as textual criticism, the greatest discoveries are for the most part the work of men of noble spirit."

4. For Reiske and Ernesti, see below, pp. 70–73. For Ruhnken, cf. Ruhnken 1875 (1789): 21.

5. See below, n. 43.

a remarkable philologist from Verona who remained almost completely isolated,[b] so that in Italy that[c] prejudice lasted even into the nineteenth century:
many of the readings in Plautus that Tommaso Vallauri defended were vulgate readings of very little or no documentary authority, or even quite recent
conjectures, to which Ritschl often opposed not his own conjectures but
readings from the Ambrosian palimpsest (Milan, Biblioteca Ambrosiana
G82 sup.).[6] The most stubborn defenders of the *receptus* were Protestants,
but the very spirit of the Reformation encouraged[d] the textual criticism of
the New Testament and consequently that of Classical texts too. Wettstein
always appealed against his persecutors to the principles that had inspired
the Reformation.[7] He understood that those principles remained alive not
in the restrictive dogmatism of the great Protestant churches (Lutheran,
Calvinist, Anglican) in the countries where they had won the victory and
been recognized by the political powers or were even identified with them,
but rather within the "heretical" currents of Protestantism itself, in developments that were rationalistic or, often, simultaneously rationalistic and
mystical, but of a mysticism that was not contemplative and inert but subversive. It was to such currents that the principal New Testament critics belonged. Jean Le Clerc was an Arminian, as were already two other men
whose characters were stronger than his and whose interests were wider,
Gerhard Johannes Vossius and Grotius, who both found the time to make
distinguished contributions to various kinds of philology, including Classical philology (but this was especially true of Grotius, despite his dedication
to law, to theology, to active politics); Wettstein was a Socinian, or at least
was suspected of Socinianism; Semler was strongly rationalistic; even the
more timorous Lutheran Bengel was a Pietist and adhered to millenarian
tendencies in his commentary on the *Apocalypse,* exerting an influence in
this direction on the English Methodists.[e] In comparison,[f] the Catholics,
except for one distinguished heterodox, Richard Simon,[g] contributed very
little to the criticism of the Greek New Testament in the seventeenth and
eighteenth centuries; and textual studies of the Latin Vulgata as well ceased
almost entirely once the Sistine and Clementine editions had established a
text with eclectic criteria.[8]

6. Cf. Vitelli 1962: 130–31.

7. Wettstein 1730: 158, and esp. 1734: 220.

8. On the Sistine and Clementine editions, see Quentin 1926: 18–20. On attempts un-
dertaken in Catholic milieus to base editions of Patristic texts upon systematic collations
of manuscripts, cf. Petitmengin 1966 (accurate and intelligent, but with some apologetic
exaggerations). Rudolf Pfeiffer's Catholic viewpoint prevented this distinguished and much
lamented scholar not only from understanding the development of New Testament textual
criticism, but even from narrating it, even after its importance for the history of Classical
philology had been pointed out: in Pfeiffer 1976, Bengel, Semler, and Griesbach are not

We have named Richard Simon and Jean Le Clerc. Strictly speaking, neither one still belongs to the history of attempts to edit the New Testament. Simon worked especially on problems of authenticity, stratification, and the historical criticism of the Old and New Testaments (as did, for the Old Testament, Baruch Spinoza, a contemporary of Simon's, another "heretic" greater than all those we have named so far, hated equally by Jewish theologians and by Christian ones), but he only provided a few illuminating hints concerning textual criticism in the strict sense.[9] Le Clerc worked on these very same problems, with a strongly rationalistic criticism like that of Simon, but dissenting from him in many points. As a philologist he dealt with "profane" Latin and Greek texts and prepared a number of editions of them, none of them excellent. But his methodological treatise, the *Ars critica,* which we mentioned at the beginning of this study (Introduction, n. 1), demonstrates that it was his heterodox theology that provided the impulse to his philology. He applies his principles in the same way to Latin, Greek, and Hebrew philology. From the second to the fourth edition of his work, he adds after its two volumes a third one, *Epistolae criticae et ecclesiasticae, in quibus ostenditur usus artis criticae, cujus possunt haberi volumen tertium* [Critical and ecclesiastical epistles, in which is demonstrated the use of the critical art, of which they can be considered the third volume]; and in the *Ars critica* he often has recourse to examples from the Old Testament, and even more from the New Testament. His *Epistola de editione Milliana* [Epistle on Mill's edition] is directed even more exclusively to the textual criticism of the New Testament; it is found (without page numeration) after the preface of Ludolf Küster's edition of the *Novum Testamentum Graecum* (Küster 1710). Here Le Clerc asserts a restriction on the criterion of the *lec-*

---

even named, while Wettstein is merely alluded to once, insignificantly, and Le Clerc is in a certain sense restored to the mainstream of Catholicism thanks to his edition of the works of Erasmus (137).

9. See, e.g., below, n. 28. After so much neglect of Simon as a textual critic of the New Testament, it is pleasant to read the claims made for him by Reynolds-Wilson 1991 (1968): 188; yet, with regard to the methodology of textual criticism in the strict sense, they go too far. Chapters 29–32 of Simon 1689: 336–416 contain not so much innovative methodological criteria as rather important individual observations (e.g., 250 on the value of the so-called *codex Bezae* of Cambridge) combined with other assertions that are still quite old-fashioned: e.g., Simon—who had indeed observed the process of banalization in the transmission of texts, as we shall see in a passage cited later—declares that he prefers the "simpler" reading compared to the one that "contains an expression that seems more forceful" (277: that is, he prefers the *lectio facilior*), and he still believes in the criterion of the majority of manuscripts (ibid.). It is intolerable to claim that Bentley's *Proposals* (below, p. 63f.) "scarcely mark any advance" beyond the work of Simon (Reynolds-Wilson 1991 [1968] 187)!

tio brevior [shorter reading], which we will quote shortly (p. 69n30) and assigns great importance to the indirect tradition (which Mill had largely neglected), though he does not overestimate its value and distinguishes passages in which the divergences of the indirect tradition are due to errors of citation by memory from ones that instead probably preserve better readings. This must be taken into account if we are to arrive at a fair evaluation of his philological personality—not a great one, to be sure, but still quite a notable one. Certainly, if he is judged only on the basis of his notorious polemic with Bentley about the fragments of Menander and Philemon, it is easy to arrive at a dismissive judgment of him: Le Clerc's knowledge of Greek meter was below the average of his time, Bentley's was well in advance of his age; Bentley's victory was clear. But this does not authorize us to speak of "the mental aberration of a vain and vainglorious man" (Brink 1978: 1140), as though that unhappy outcome indicated *everything* about Le Clerc, as though there were no *Ars critica*. The conservative approach that Le Clerc advocates more than once in this work, his polemic against conjectures "invented so that the writer, who had not expressed his meaning so badly after all, would only speak more elegantly or wittily," [10] is aimed against Scaliger, whom Le Clerc sometimes also cites explicitly, and certainly against most Dutch Classical philologists too (perhaps not yet at Bentley). But it would be mistaken to see here merely a mediocre scholar, incapable of making conjectures, venting his spleen against the great emenders of texts. In the age and environment in which Le Clerc was operating, his polemic was justified. Le Clerc knows well that the ancient texts are corrupt in many places; he knows that many corruptions are not medieval but ancient, and he proves this with a rich documentation (1730 [1697]: 2.12–27); perhaps he even assigns too little importance to so-called paleographical corruptions, upon which later scholars will insist too much, and he pays intelligent attention to psychological corruptions, from more mechanical ones such as what will later be called "saut du même au même" [leap from the same to the same] (1730 [1697]: 2.48–56, though his examples are inconclusive) and similar errors due to vernacular pronunciation (1730 [1697]: 2.56–78), to substitutions of synonyms and analogous phenomena (1730 [1697]: 2.5 and elsewhere). He notices, and here too he is ahead of his times, that most errors arise from the fact that copyists transcribe not

10. Le Clerc 1730 (1697): 2.269. Le Clerc adds: "For what writer has ever polished sentences so perfectly that the subject matter can never be expressed better?" Wilamowitz 1982 (1921): 173–74 will make an analogous observation; he regards this as an achievement of recent textual criticism, which has overcome the "demand for absolute perfection implicit in the canonical authority of antiquity." Cf. also Le Clerc 1730 (1697): 2.10–11, 259, and elsewhere.

word for word, but "whole phrases, or in order to save time they even read whole sentences and only write them down afterward" (1730 [1697]: 2.5). He requires that a conjecture be able to explain the genesis of the corruption (1730 [1697]: 2.277), but he does not establish this as an absolute requirement ("if it can be done"); indeed, he admits (1730 [1697]: 2.278 and esp. 9) the existence of "inexplicable" corruptions, since the copyist or, what amounts to the same thing, the person who reads aloud to him may even have substituted for the text of the model completely different words referring to thoughts that occupied his mind at that moment—we are not far from the "Freudian slip," indeed, we have gone too far beyond it in a certain respect, since such a substitution would not have been facilitated by similarities of sound or sense, by what Freud will call *Begünstigungen* [favoring conditions]. He has no interest in the genealogy of manuscripts but limits himself in general to preferring the oldest manuscripts (1730 [1697]: 2.290); but we should not forget that it was only later that the rehabilitation of the *recentiores* became justified and fruitful, and that the first, necessary stage had to be one of distrust for the all-too-often interpolated manuscripts of the Humanist age. We shall refer shortly to Le Clerc's contributions regarding other editorial criteria (*usus scribendi* [the author's habitual style], *lectio difficilior* [the more difficult reading]): in this way we shall see even more clearly how the *Ars critica* (which, let us recall, had many editions and hence a broad diffusion) paved the way in large measure for the immediately subsequent development of New Testament textual criticism.[h]

But history follows winding roads, even the history of a limited problem; and so the first project of editing the New Testament which overcame the general conception of the *textus receptus* was due not to one of the religious reformers to whom we have referred and to whom we shall return later, but to Richard Bentley, a man as brilliant and bold in philology as he was orthodox in matters of religion. And it was, precisely, a religiously orthodox aim that inspired him, besides the philological problem itself: he wished to defend the authority of the biblical text against the "free thinkers" (in reality not atheists but deists) led by Anthony Collins. For free thinkers, the existence of so many variants in the New Testament manuscript tradition, such as had been amassed by Mill in his edition of 1707, already mentioned (above, p. 59), was an argument against the Gospels' authenticity and truth; for Protestant theologians of strict observance, it was a reason to fear a similar polemical use of the text's "uncertainty" and hence to refuse to part company with the *receptus;* for Bentley, it was an incentive to establish the text more solidly and thereby to defeat skepticism.[11] So he planned an edition

---

11. See the polemic against Collins in Bentley 1713 = Bentley 1836–38: 3.287–368 (esp. 347–61).

based on a comparison of the oldest Greek manuscripts with the Latin Vulgata and the citations in the Patristic texts, which ought to have restored for us the state of the tradition as it had been at the time of the Council of Nicaea.[12] He recognized that *recensio* had to take precedence before conjectural criticism in a textual tradition that was so rich and ancient (Bentley 1836–38: 3.488). But even though, as we have seen, his project was dictated by intentions that were anything but subversive in religious matters, it nonetheless encountered the theologians' opposition. And so Bentley ended up giving up this plan, also because of his commitment to other projects and because of the very difficulty of completing so enormous a task.[i,13]

There were certainly more practicable ways to improve the *receptus*. One could draw upon Mill's apparatus and introduce more reliable individual readings into the text; in certain cases, one could also have recourse to conjectures. The first procedure was already followed in 1709–19, that is, before Bentley's *Proposals,* by the theologian and mathematician Edward Wells;[14] the first and second ones together, by the Presbyterian Daniel Mace.[15] Both improved the *receptus* very notably; they performed a courageous and philologically valuable deed. Nonetheless this was still just occasional corrections, *ope codicum* and, more rarely, *ingenii.* Bentley's project was methodologically more innovative, because he intended to set aside the *receptus* altogether and to refer constantly to the manuscripts. It was along this path that Johann Albrecht Bengel and Johann Jacob Wettstein, the two greatest New Testament critics of the eighteenth century (whom we have already mentioned for their religious positions), moved and made further progress. More cautious than Wells or Mace regarding interventions into the text (not least because in continental, Calvinist and Lutheran Europe,

---

12. Bentley 1721 = Bentley 1836–38: 3.477–86. Cf. Gregory 1900–1909: 2.949–50; Fox 1954: 105–8; Metzger 1968 (1964): 109–10; Kenney 1974: 100 (quoting the essential part of a letter written by Bentley in 1716 to Archbishop William Wake, which contains the fundamental outlines of the project); Brink 1978: 1150–52 (he rightly emphasizes the methodological awareness implied in Bentley's refusal to try to go back to an epoch before the Council of Nicaea). For the "geographical criterion" already adumbrated by Bentley in the *Remarks* cited above, see below, p. 85f.

13. Part of the material he left unpublished, now preserved in the library of Trinity College, Cambridge, was later published by Ellis 1862.

14. Metzger 1968 (1964): 109 and n. 1. I have not been able to inspect the edition of Wells.

15. [Mace] 1729. Cf. Gregory 1900–1909: 2.950–51 (and 3.1360); McLachlan 1938–39 (this article, which cannot be found in Italy, was made available to me by E. J. Kenney); Metzger 1968 (1964): 110–12. On other English New Testament critics of the second half of the eighteenth century, see Metzger 1968 (1964): 115–17.

this was much riskier than in Anglican England), they were more acute regarding theoretical questions.[j]

Each felt[k] needs unknown to the other: hence their polemics and their mutual incomprehension. Bengel has the merit of having been the first to try to determine the relations of kinship among manuscripts: "Manuscripts are closely related to one another if they have the same ancient arrangements of text on the page, subscriptions, and other subsidiary features."[16] Besides these kinds of evidence he also argued on the basis of shared readings,[17] though he did not yet go so far as to distinguish between shared corruptions, the only truly probative evidence, and shared correct readings. He imagined that in the distant future the whole history of the New Testament tradition could be summarized in a *tabula genealogica,* that is, in what will later come to be called a *stemma codicum.*[18] What is more, Bengel also saw lucidly that such a genealogical classification would furnish a secure criterion for choosing among the variants, thereby allowing editors to overcome the old and

---

16. Bengel 1763a (1734): 18. The 1763 volume also contains (pp. 625–952) Bengel's other writings on New Testament textual criticism, including the *Prodromus Novi Testamenti Graeci recte cauteque adornandi* (already published at the beginning of Bengel 1725). Bengel also edited Cicero's *Epistulae familiares* and some Patristic texts besides the one just cited. On him cf. Nestle 1893 (useful, despite the irritatingly apologetic tone); Nolte 1913; and now Mälzer 1970, an ample monograph that, however, discusses Bengel as a theologian much more fully than as a textual critic (in any case see chap. 6, useful for various epistolary testimonia). On the expression *apparatus criticus* (used by Bengel, perhaps for the first time) and on his use of symbols (Greek letters, which however indicate not manuscripts but "degrees of value" of the various readings), cf. Kenney 1974: 156 and n. 4; for the symbols, also Metzger 1968 (1964): 113 and Mälzer 1970: 162. Wettstein will be the first one who uses symbols to indicate the manuscripts (capital letters for MSS in uncials, Arabic numerals for the MSS in minuscules): cf. Metzger 1968 (1964): 114 and, for a precursor in this usage (Savile 1612), Kenney 1974: 157 *infra*. In general, on the development of the technique of critical editions, see Kenney 1974: 152–57. But see also, for the Humanist age, Rizzo 1973: 301–23 and the passages listed in the index (p. 390) under "sigle per indicare mss."

17. Bengel 1763a (1734): 18: "but if the readings themselves are collated, they tend to go together"; he goes on to cite various groupings of manuscripts.

18. Bengel 1763a (1734): 20. I will not cite the whole passage, already quoted by Gregory 1900–1909: 2.908 and by Pasquali 1952a (1934): 9. Bengel added: "Magnam coniectanea nostra silvam habent: sed manum de tabula, ne risuum periculo exponatur veritas" [Our conjectures are based on a lot of material: but hands off, lest the truth be exposed to the risk of laughter]. Hence he believed that the attempt had to be postponed to better times. *Manum de tabula,* with *aufer* understood, is a well-known proverbial expression in Latin to say "Stop!" "Enough!"; Bengel uses it with the traditional meaning, but at the same time he alludes jokingly to the *tabula genealogica* of which he has just spoken.

deceitful criterion of the majority of manuscripts. "Two or more groups, often agreeing, are worth the same as one: two or more manuscripts of a single group are worth the same as one when they agree with one another. But when they disagree with one another, a group or a manuscript agreeing with many does away with the present error of its comrades (i.e., with the error of its present comrades)":[19] hence the important thing is not that a reading be attested by the majority of the manuscripts but by the majority of the families; only within each family does the majority of the manuscripts have a value for reconstructing its ancestor's reading. This is already the procedure that Lachmann will later develop, and that Paul Maas (1958 [1927]: p. 6, sec. 8) will call *eliminatio lectionum singularium* [elimination of unique readings]—an infelicitous expression, but we too will use it for lack of a better one:[l] a procedure to follow whenever the tradition is not too contaminated. Further on Bengel repeats even more explicitly that it is the consensus of manuscripts *belonging to different families* that guarantees the antiquity of a reading.[20] Obviously, in a tradition as contaminated as that of the New Testament Bengel could not apply these criteria immediately (nor could more recent scholars do so); they became fruitful only when they were applied to simpler and more mechanical traditions. What is more, Bengel's fear of controversy (which in fact broke out immediately)[m] and persecution led him to refuse to accept into the text "even one syllable that had not already been

19. Bengel 1763a (1734): 21: "the present error of its comrades" must mean a difference of reading that is found in a group of manuscripts *existing now* but that was not found in their model.

20. Bengel 1763a (1734): 65: "But a difference among the witnesses closest to the source, the first hand, and most distant from one another, does have value; in this way they reveal the genuine reading by their agreement." Ibid., 68: "If that agreement embraces a diversity of manuscripts, all doubt will be annulled." It is apparent from the whole context that Bengel understands this "distance" or "diversity" more in the sense of belonging to different families than as geographical distance. So too later, Griesbach 1796 (1774): 1.lxxii: "And yet if those witnesses which can really be considered different agree with one another in a friendly way, that should finally be considered an agreement which lends authority to them." Nonetheless, since Bengel distinguished a *natio Asiatica* and a *natio Africana* in the New Testament manuscript tradition, the "distance" came to assume a geographical meaning as well, as already in a reference by Bentley and later, more explicitly, in Lachmann: see below, p. 85f. The geographical meaning becomes more explicit in a later writing of Bengel's, Bengel 1763b (1742): sec. viii, regula v: "But these manuscripts were diffused through the churches of all the ages *and climates (et climatum)*, and in spite of the multitude of variants they come so close to the original text that they show the genuine reading *all together*." Here *clima*, as already in post-Classical Latin, can only mean "zone," "region."

accepted by some earlier editor":[21] so his edition turned out to be much inferior to the methodological principles he expounded in the *Apparatus*.

Wettstein, a scholar of a much more combative character, pursued the polemic against the *receptus* initiated by Bentley and other Englishmen;[n,22] and he had no trouble demolishing the arguments that Bengel had adduced to justify his own prudence.[23] So too, Wettstein attacked the apparently reasonable criterion, followed by some, of retaining the *receptus* where there were no reasons to abandon it, for he saw clearly that in this way the *receptus* rather than the manuscripts continued to serve as the basis of the edition, and that editors were thereby led to accept a large number of banalizations, if not of outright corruptions (1730: 167). In the edition he completed shortly before his death, in general he too ended up limiting himself to expounding his own disagreements with the *receptus* in the notes, but we can explain this if we think of the persecutions he had had to undergo (accusations that he was aiming to deny the divinity of Christ by altering the text of the Gospels; removal from his office as pastor; exile from Basel until he found refuge in Amsterdam).[o] But Wettstein showed no interest in the criteria of the genealogical classification of the manuscripts which Bengel had formulated with such intelligence; instead he remained attached to the criterion of majority rule, and he never understood the arguments with which Bengel had demonstrated its fallaciousness.[24,**]

21. Bengel 1763a (1734): 607. The only largely new edition he made was of the *Apocalypse*.

22. Wettstein 1730: 166–67. On the relations between Bentley and Wettstein, cf. Jebb 1889: 159; Bertheau 1908: 199.

23. Wettstein 1734: 218–31, and 1751–52: 1.156–70.

24. Wettstein 1730: 195, and even more 1734: 226–28; Wettstein 1751–52: 1.166–67. Even before Wettstein, the criterion of the majority of manuscripts had been codified by Mastricht 1711: 13. Wettstein had no particular faith in the oldest manuscripts, agreeing with Bengel in this point (see below, n. 33); this was the principal reason for his gradual separation from Bentley.

** On Wettstein there is only one point I am anxious to emphasize here. As is well known, the edition of 1751–52 represents a refusal (perhaps a forced refusal) to insert into the text the readings differing from the *receptus*, which Wettstein considered better. But the *Prolegomena* of that edition are, so to speak, felicitously inconsistent with that refusal: the attack on the *receptus* is repeated and developed there, the polemic against Bengel's timidity is repeated with a forceful, sometimes even excessive, tone, the accusations of "impiety" are rejected with undiminished energy. My citation on this page at n. 23 already indicated this, but did so too hastily. On Wettstein's precursors regarding the formulation of internal criteria for the selection of variants, editorial technique (the use of signs), and many other methodological principles, Armando Golzio has collected a considerable amount of

Nonetheless, Wettstein's *Prolegomena* of 1730, which represent the most interesting phase of his thought, assigned the first place in the choice of readings to internal criteria: *usus scribendi* and *lectio difficilior*. He and Bengel were in agreement on this question. It is only when two readings are equivalent in themselves, declares Bengel, "that the decision is referred to a more accurate examination of the manuscripts":[25] a position opposed to that of Lachmann, who will recur to *iudicium* [judgment] only when two readings have the same external authority.

One of these internal criteria, the *usus scribendi,* was already well known to the ancient grammarians;[26] the philologists of the fifteenth to seventeenth centuries then made ample use of it, even if they employed it perhaps more for conjectural *emendatio* than for choice among variants.[27] Sporadic anticipations of the criterion of the *lectio difficilior* can also be found from antiquity until the seventeenth century;[28] as far as I know, the first to formulate it precisely was Jean Le Clerc.[29] Thus Wettstein and Bengel found the

---

material and has evaluated it intelligently: I hope that the results of his researches will be published soon. Another field in which Golzio has enriched, modified, and also corrected many of the matters discussed in this work of mine is the conceptual and methodological contribution made by Orelli and Madvig, which now turns out to be more significant than what I had indicated (see below, pp. 90f., 97f., 102f.), even if the importance assigned to Madvig was a point to which I was particularly committed.p

25. Bengel 1763a (1734): 18. This position is now reaffirmed by Waszink 1979: 87, with good reason.

26. Especially to Aristarchus: Lehrs 1882: 354–56; Pasquali 1952a (1934): 233, 240–41; Pfeiffer 1968: 227–28 (but one might still have expected to find something more here). Aristarchus certainly applied the idea of *usus scribendi* excessively, hyper-analogically.

27. It is asserted as a criterion for conjectural emendations, e.g., by Le Clerc 1730 (1697): 2.270–82.

28. E.g., in Galen, *Medici Graeci,* ed. Kühn, 18.1.1005; 17.2.98, 101, 110 ("this was the ancient reading, but it was altered by many interpreters in order to make it clearer"). But Galen uses this internal criterion only so as to confirm the authority of the oldest manuscripts, which remain the fundamental principle for him. Some further details on Galen's procedure are furnished by D. Irmer in the German edition of my book, Timpanaro 1971: 19. Probus (in Servius auctus on Virgil, *Aeneid* 12.605) followed the criterion of the most archaic reading (which is a special case of the *lectio difficilior*) in order to prefer *floros* to *flauos* in one passage of Virgil. I cannot bring myself to believe that this is an archaism that Probus arbitrarily introduced; I hope to discuss this passage in more detail elsewhere. In the Middle Ages a reference to the *lectio difficilior* is found in Irnerius: cf. Kantorowicz 1921: 31. In the seventeenth century, Simon 1689: 375–76 too observed that copyists tend to banalize, but he did not deduce from this observation an explicit criterion for choice among variants.

29. Le Clerc 1730 (1697): 2.293: "If one of them [sc. the readings] is more obscure and the others clearer, then the more obscure one is likely to be true, the others glosses." The only defect of this formulation is the too restrictive character of the concept *lectio facilior*

terrain already prepared for them; but it was left to them, and particularly to Wettstein, to develop more fully the theoretical assertion and practical application of these two norms.[30] It was only later that Wettstein, preoccupied by accusations of subjectivism in the choice among variants, ended up adhering above all to the criterion of the majority of manuscripts, but without ever repudiating internal criteria.[q,31]

In the second half of the eighteenth century another New Testament critic, Johann Salomo Semler, distinguished between *äusserliches* and *innerliches Alter* [external age and internal age], that is, between the antiquity of a manuscript and the antiquity of the readings attested by it: a manuscript that is more recent than another one can preserve readings that are more ancient.[32] Bengel had already noticed this, as others had even earlier, but not

---

or *clarior*, which for Le Clerc always had its origin in a marginal gloss that had intruded into the text and substituted for the original reading, or at least in *conscious* banalizations; yet at least as often, if not more often, the origin is an unconscious banalization.

30. Bengel 1763a (1734): 17: "Where the one [sc. reading] is more easy, the other less so, the one that is old, weighty, brief, is preferred; the one that charms us by its greater perspicacity and fullness, as though it had been introduced deliberately, is generally set aside." A fuller discussion is in Wettstein 1730: 179, 184 (on *lectio difficilior*) and 188 (on *usus scribendi*, from which he rightly distinguishes the repetition of a passage with identical words, which is suspected of leveling and is therefore to be rejected in favor of the "varied" expression). I shall not cite in their entirety the passages of Wettstein, which are already quoted by Pasquali 1952a (1934): 10–12. It should be noted that already in Bengel, and then in Wettstein and Griesbach, and even in recent manuals, the *lectio brevior* appears as a subspecies of the *lectio difficilior*—but in fact the *lectio brevior* is a *much* more uncertain criterion, since if the fuller reading can derive from the desire to make the text clearer or from interpolations of various kinds, the briefer reading can be caused by omissions (Dain 1975 [1949]: 20), especially by unconscious elimination of words not strictly necessary to the context yet still present in the authentic text: cf. Timpanaro 1976: 35–40; other examples in Rizzo 1977: 104–5. In this point, Le Clerc proved himself to be more cautious, for in the epistle inserted into Küster's edition (cf. above, p. 61) he had maintained the authenticity of two words that are not strictly necessary in part of the tradition of Matt. 3:11 and that are absent in other witnesses, "for there was no reason why these words should have been added, for they are obscure and add nothing to clarify the meaning of the passage: on the contrary, for these very reasons they could have been eliminated as obscure and useless." As already in the case of the *lectio facilior*, Le Clerc speaks of an intentional alteration, which is not the most frequent case; but in itself his argumentation is entirely correct and demonstrates that the *lectio longior* can even be the *lectio difficilior*.

31. The *Animadversiones et cautiones* for choice among variants are no longer to be found in the much fuller *Prolegomena* to Wettstein 1751–52, but they are republished separately at the back of the edition.

32. Semler 1765: 88–89. Semler 1765: 396 also polemicizes against the criterion of the majority of manuscripts but does so only very briefly. In this regard he makes no progress beyond Bengel, but a little later Ernesti will go another step in the criticism of "pro-

with such clarity.[r,33] In the end Johann Jacob Griesbach summarized the results of earlier criticism in a didactically perfect form in the *Prolegomena* to his second edition,[34] but although by now he fully recognized the inconsistency of the *receptus,* he too did not free himself from it courageously enough.[s,35,***]

*   *   *

In the meantime, Classical philologists had noticed that they had fallen behind the theologians in textual criticism. In 1730 Wettstein (1730: 166)

---

fane texts" (cf. below, n. 43). On the classification of manuscripts proposed by Semler, developing Bengel's classification, see below, chap. 4, n. 5.

33. The fact that recent manuscripts could have good readings had been observed, e.g., by Nicolaas Heinsius (1661: 2.195: "in the Arundel manuscript, though it is recent, but nonetheless offering very correct readings"), but without wondering whether this might be due to felicitous conjectures. As for Bengel, he had limited himself to observing that "almost the whole variety of readings was created a long time before the Greek manuscripts extant today" (1763a [1734]: 12) and that therefore ancient manuscripts are already not less corrupt than more recent ones: a claim that is doubtless exaggerated (though shared also by Wettstein), although it is true that the variants and corruptions of greatest importance often go back to very ancient times, as Le Clerc had noticed.

34. Griesbach 1796 (1774). As for methodological criteria, there is nothing in Griesbach that is not already found in his predecessors, and hence it is mistaken to place him at the beginning of the "modern critical period" of New Testament textual criticism, as Metzger 1968 (1964): 119 does: he honorably concluded one important period, but he did not begin a new one. So too, the criterion of the *lectio media* (Griesbach 1796 [1774]: lxiii), to which Pasquali (1952a [1934]: 11) points as a novelty, had already been formulated by Bengel 1763a (1734): 17 ("Where there are not only two readings, but many readings, the *middle* one is the best. For from this one, as though from a center, the others dispersed"): this is what has been called "diffraction" in our times by Contini 1955: 134, and then elsewhere. Nonetheless, Griesbach's formulations are clearer and more elegant than his predecessors'.

35. Nonetheless he introduced into his own text some readings that diverged from the *receptus.*

*** In the 1981 edition I modified certain details of this first part of chapter 2 concerning the great New Testament critics of the eighteenth century; but it would need a more drastic revision than any of the others, even though only a few years have passed (and even recalling that chaps. 1 and 2 have a merely introductory character). I learned much that I had not known previously by taking part in the seminar on Wettstein conducted by my friend Antonio Rotondò at the Istituto di Storia of the Facoltà di Lettere (1983–85); I am profoundly grateful to Rotondò and his students for this experience. One fruit of this seminar will be the edition with commentary of Wettstein's *Prolegomena* (1730 and 1751–52) prepared by Cecilia Asso, a student of Rotondò. On Wettstein the "heretic," who is linked with Wettstein the textual critic even more closely than is usually thought, we await a book by Rotondò himself, which will be innovative and rich in unpublished documents.[t]

could still point to the critics of profane texts as an example that students of the New Testament should follow; but by 1770 the roles had been reversed after the works of Wettstein himself, Bengel, and Semler, and Johann Jacob Reiske wrote, "We should not treat profane authors with less scrupulous veneration than the New Testament. For the very same reason that we carefully collate manuscripts of the New Testament, it is only fair that we inspect the manuscripts of Demosthenes and all the other ancient authors too and dig out and publish their readings. For this is the only way to demonstrate the historical truth of any text, be it sacred or profane, on the basis of the consensus of many ancient manuscripts of approved reliability." [36]

In fact, Reiske did more for the text of the Attic orators and of Atticists like Libanius[u] with his splendid conjectures than by investigating the manuscript tradition (many of his conjectures were later confirmed by manuscripts of which he had no knowledge).[37] But the need to use the manuscripts as the text's *constant* foundation instead of only making occasional collations was reaffirmed a little later with great clarity by Ernesti in the preface to his edition of Tacitus, and once again by Friedrich August Wolf at the beginning of his *Prolegomena ad Homerum*.[38] Each of these scholars observed correctly that to follow the old method of having recourse to the manuscripts only where the vulgate was not satisfactory resulted in leaving in the text a large number of small corruptions and *lectiones faciliores* that, for better or worse, made some sense and hence did not arouse suspicion. Wolf writes: "A true, continuous, and systematic recension differs greatly from this frivolous and desultory method. In the latter we want only to cure indiscriminately the wounds that are conspicuous or are revealed by some manuscript or other. We pass over more [readings] which are good and passable as regards sense, but no better than the worst as regards authority. But a true recension, attended by the full complement of useful instruments, seeks out the author's true handiwork at every point. It examines in or-

---

36. Reiske 1770: lxxvi.

37. Nonetheless, as Dieter Irmer has pointed out to me, Reiske had the merit of being the first to recognize the value for the manuscript tradition of Demosthenes of manuscript A (Augustanus, now Monacensis 485) and to make use of it. In his own edition of Demosthenes (H. Wolf 1572), Hieronymus Wolf had already cited some readings of this manuscript, communicated to him by Simon Fabricius, but he had not introduced them into his text (cf. Voemel 1857: 183, 193–94; I also owe to D. Irmer my knowledge of this work).

38. Ernesti 1801 (1772): vi. F. A. Wolf 1985 (1795): 43–55. Wolf was not only clearly influenced by Ernesti but also probably by Semler; on the intimate friendship between Wolf and Semler, cf. Koerte 1833: 1.129 (brought to my attention by Konrad Müller, who also points out to me Wolf's reference, in the preface to his Homer edition [F. A. Wolf 1804: 1 = F. W. Wolf 1869: 1.252], to Griesbach, "eminent founder of Sacred criticism," with regard to the various degrees of external and internal probability of transmitted readings).

der the witnesses for every reading, not only for those that are suspect. It changes, only for the most serious reasons, readings that all of these approve. It accepts, only when they are supported by witnesses, others that are worthy in themselves of the author and accurate and elegant in their form. Not uncommonly, then, when the witnesses require it, a true recension replaces attractive readings with less attractive ones. It takes off bandages and lays bare the sores. Finally, it cures not only manifest ills, as bad doctors do, but hidden ones too." [39] Only a procedure of this sort deserves the name of *recensio* and not of mere *recognitio* (F. A. Wolf 1985 [1795]: 45); and only after a systematic *recensio* will one be able to go on to conjectural *emendatio,* for which Wolf did not feel much sympathy anyway.[40] Thus it was that the old concept of *emendatio ope codicum* was completely overcome.

But Wolf's recognition of the need for a systematic *recensio* and for a repudiation of the vulgate is not accompanied by a too exclusive faith in the most ancient manuscripts. It will have been Semler[41] who positively influenced him in this recognition of *recentiores non deteriores* [the more recent

39. F. A. Wolf 1985 (1795): 43–44. Cf. also Wolf's preface to his edition of Plato's *Symposium* (F. A. Wolf 1782: v–vi = F. A. Wolf 1869: 1.135–36): "But this cannot happen if manuscripts and old editions are only checked and compared occasionally, for individual obscure or apparently erroneous passages." But so already Ernesti 1801 (1772): vi: "In previous ages, those who set about to edit ancient writers thought it was enough to check manuscripts and printed editions in those passages where they got stuck [. . .]. In this way [. . .] they ended up leaving many things untouched that could have been emended from those same manuscripts and printed editions. And yet no one is so sharp-eyed that he can see all the faults of the vulgate reading on his own, and not sometimes approve corruptions as though they were correct." In Ernesti, however, these fine theoretical pronouncements almost never found any practical application: both his edition of Tacitus and his (better) edition of Cicero are based in substance upon preceding editions, not upon manuscripts, as C. G. Zumpt 1831: 1.xxiv–xxviii rightly observed regarding Cicero. From this point of view, his edition of Callimachus (Ernesti 1761) is better; in the preface (fol. 5b) Ernesti asserts that all the noninterpolated manuscripts of the *Hymns* are derived from a single lost model, on the basis of their agreement "in lacunas and in readings" (cf. Pfeiffer 1949–53: 2.lv).

40. "A pleasant pastime" is what he calls it at the beginning of the *Prolegomena;* F. A. Wolf 1985 (1795): 45 (cf. 44; and F. A. Wolf 1869: 1.242). All the same, Wolf is not an uncritical conservative: echoing Bentley's famous phrase (above, p. 55), he admits that one must prefer "talent" to "treasure chests full of parchment" (1795: vi), but he maintains that emendation should not precede recension nor, even less, take its place; and, like Ernesti, he insists on the importance of emendation for healing "latent errors" (see above). But we should bear in mind that although Wolf is speaking in general terms in the *Prolegomena,* he is thinking above all of the Homeric text, one of the very few from antiquity that have no need of conjectural criticism (except for the problem of the interpolated verses). He will later judge emendation more favorably, in F. A. Wolf 1807: 40 (= F. A. Wolf 1869: 2.832).

41. See above, p. 69, and n. 38 for the relations between Wolf and Semler.

manuscripts [are] not the worse ones], which, as we know, is in itself not new, but it is worth the trouble to quote Wolf's own formulation (F. A. Wolf 1985 [1795]: 46): "For newness in manuscripts is no more a vice than youth in men. In this case, too, old age does not always bring wisdom. Insofar as each follows an old and good authority well, it is a good witness." The comparison between a manuscript's "youth" and a human being's is little more than a graceful witticism, but the final phrase explains well why a *recentior* can on principle be not at all a *deterior:* the recent copyist may have copied an ancient and good manuscript *well* (and, Wolf seems to imply, directly).[42,v]

So too, during the last three decades of the eighteenth century, the need for a genealogical study of the manuscripts, which we have seen Bengel assert in the field of New Testament studies, gradually spread among Classical philologists. Ernesti clarified even better than Bengel had done the principle that several manuscripts deriving from the same ancestor had the same value as only one;[43] Christian Gottlob Heyne and the Alsatian Jean Schweig-

---

42. Cf. Kantorowicz 1921: 21–22; Pasquali 1952a (1934): 46. Their arguments are formulated more clearly and fully than Wolf's but are not substantially different from his.

43. Ernesti 1801 (1772): xxviii: "When manuscripts are involved, one should make sure that we have not as many in number as possible, but as many of those that possess as it were the legal right to give an opinion. . . . For if you have a hundred manuscripts of the same book, but it is certain that they are derived from a single apograph, then all together they only have the right and force of a single book." Griesbach 1796 (1774): 1.lxxi will express this concept with very similar words. But although Italy was a philologically quite "depressed" milieu (in which, nonetheless, Verona constituted an exception), Domenico Vallarsi had already enunciated this principle there in the preface to his edition of Saint Jerome (Vallarsi 1766 [1734], reprinted in Migne 1845: p. xxxix, para. 35): manuscripts that agree in errors or in arbitrary changes (*criticorum ausis*) are worth "not more than one manuscript": evidently Vallarsi wrongly neglected the possibility of contamination when he considered the arbitrary acts of *critici*. And above all, textual criticism of Dante in the second half of the eighteenth century possessed at Verona itself a philologist of European standing in the figure of Bartolomeo Perazzini (Perazzini 1775), to whom Folena 1965: 67–69 has justly called our attention. Perazzini, besides repeating the aforementioned genealogical principle (probably under Vallarsi's influence), also wrote passionate polemics against the defenders of the vulgate that have much in common with those of the New Testament philologists who were his contemporaries or a little earlier than he. This similarity is increased by the fact that the *Divina Commedia* was considered a "sacred text" too for a complicated series of religious and artistic reasons, though to a much lesser degree than the New Testament. Perazzini speaks explicitly of a "prejudice of a sacred text" (1775: 56), and he repeats: "nor should any text be *sacred,* unless it has first been perfectly emended"; and again: "Hence it is not I who should be called an innovator, but rather those who altered the text which was once received" (i.e., in this case, not the *receptus* in the sense of the New Testament, but the oldest stage of the tradition, the *antiqua lectio,* as he says immediately before).

häuser tried to reconstruct genealogies, the former for the manuscripts of
Tibullus, the latter for the *Manual* of Epictetus.[44] To be sure, these scholars'
attempts turned out quite imperfectly, not only because of their inexperi-
ence and incomplete knowledge of the manuscript material but above all for
the objective reason that even today makes it impossible in so many cases
to trace a *stemma codicum:* contamination. Heyne—a philologist whose
greatest originality certainly did not consist in textual criticism but who
even as a textual critic is more valuable than is generally said[45]—was well
aware of this phenomenon of contamination; for the New Testament, Griesbach was too.[46]

So too, the manuscript tradition of Homer was too contaminated to permit the fulfillment of Wolf's proposal that the manuscripts be organized
"into classes and families."[47] But thanks to his use of the Venetian scholia
discovered by Villoison, Wolf was able to achieve something else in his *Prolegomena:* the history of a text in antiquity.[48] In this way he prepared the
way not for Lachmann, but rather for Jahn's and Wilamowitz's concept of
Textgeschichte [history of a text] and for all the nineteenth- and twentieth-
century studies on "ancient variants and ancient editions" (to repeat the
title of one of Pasquali's chapters). For Wolf, the Homeric question itself was
nothing more than the first phase, oral and popular, of the history of the text
of the *Iliad* and *Odyssey:* in the *Prolegomena* it is only discussed in these
terms and not as a problem in literary history.[49]

44. Heyne 1817 (1755): xiii–lxxviii: but what Heyne provides is in the first instance
a genealogy of the *editions* of Tibullus, and only secondarily one of the manuscripts.
Schweighäuser 1798: preface: to classify the manuscripts, Schweighäuser relied on shared
corruptions less than on the reciprocal arrangement of the text of Epictetus's *Manual* and
of Simplicius's commentary on it (cf. Timpanaro 1955: 70). Schweighäuser had more merits in the *eliminatio codicum descriptorum:* see below, p. 99.

45. Heyne 1817 (1755): xv, xxxvi (where he speaks of "apographs, perhaps prepared
with others, or made out of them"). Heyne's fame as a textual critic, and as a Classical
philologist in general, was impaired by the scornful tone adopted toward him by his students Wolf and Lachmann (and, in a less technical field, Friedrich Schlegel), in great measure unjustly; for Lachmann in particular, see Lachmann 1876: 2.106.

46. Griesbach 1796 (1774): lxxviii: "The readings of the one recension have been introduced into the manuscripts of the other family," etc. Already Semler (1765) had often observed that in different passages the very same manuscript belongs to different "recensions."

47. F. A. Wolf 1985 (1795): 44. In his editions of other authors (Plato, Cicero, etc.),
which in certain cases would have allowed an application of the genealogical method,
Wolf limited himself to hasty *recognitiones* in contrast with his principles.

48. Simon 1689 had already arrived at this concept of a "history of the text," but he
had had no followers among Classical philologists. Cf., for now, Pfeiffer 1976: 130.

49. On this point cf. Timpanaro 1980: 125 and n. 28.

3

The First Phase of Lachmann's
Activity as a Textual Critic

After the considerable progress achieved by the method of textual criticism during the eighteenth century, we witness a return to old positions in the first fifteen years of the nineteenth century. Gottfried Hermann and Immanuel Bekker, the two greatest textual critics of the generation after Wolf, differed greatly from one another in many ways, but both remained quite unaffected by the need for a systematic *recensio* as it had been adumbrated by the great New Testament critics and by Ernesti and Wolf. Hermann was an admirable expert on Greek language and style and supplied contributions of decisive importance to the study of meter, but he had no interest in manuscript tradition: his editions are based not on manuscripts but on preceding editions, and the improvements he contributed to the text of the Greek poets are the fruits of conjecture or, when he does choose between variants, are based solely on internal criteria. To be sure, he succeeded very often in resolving once and for all textual difficulties that had remained unsolved until then: for after all, a thorough knowledge of an author's language and style always remains the first and essential condition for restoring his text. And yet his complete indifference with regard to the documentary foundation of the classical texts represents not only one aspect of his lack of understanding for the new Classical philology of Wolf and Boeckh but also a step backward compared to the textual criticism of the eighteenth century.[1,a]

Bekker, on the other hand, was an indefatigable explorer of manuscripts:

---

1. Cf. Jahn 1849: 20. Sauppe 1841: 5 = Sauppe 1896: 82 writes, "Whoever wishes to perform the art of criticism properly must first of all examine the manuscripts and seek out and investigate their characteristics as carefully as possible. I recall that you [i.e., G. Hermann] gave this advice very often." It remains uncertain whether Sauppe *captandae benevolentiae causa* is attributing here to his teacher something that the latter had in reality never said, or whether Hermann really did give this advice to his students without going on to apply it himself; we have already noticed a similar contrast between theory and practice in Ernesti and in Wolf himself; cf. chap. 2, nn. 39, 47. Cf. the addendum to this chapter.

we are indebted to him for the rediscovery or appreciation of first-rate textual sources such as the Urbinas of Isocrates (Vatican, Urbin. gr. 111), the Parisinus manuscripts of Demosthenes (Paris. gr. 2934) and of Theognis (Paris. suppl. gr. 288), the Ravennas of Aristophanes (Raven. gr. 429), and many manuscripts of Plato. Yet despite the fact that Bekker was Wolf's favorite pupil, not even he ever thought of doing a systematic *recensio:* as Wilamowitz rightly notes, "in his choice of manuscripts and readings Bekker essentially relied upon his sense of language and style,"[2] which, for Attic prose, was certainly very experienced.

This step backward in the methodology of textual criticism at the beginning of the nineteenth century[3] helps to explain the impression of great originality that Lachmann's first works make even when they do nothing more than reaffirm, sometimes with less refinement and caution,[b] principles that were well known to the Classical philology of the eighteenth century.

In the field of the criticism of Classical texts (we shall refer to Germanic texts shortly), Lachmann began his activity with an edition of Propertius in 1816, followed by editions of Catullus and Tibullus and an *editio minor* of Propertius (all 1829). His review of Gottfried Hermann's edition of Sophocles' *Ajax*[4] and two reviews concerning Tibullus[5] are also important.

In this first phase of his thought, Lachmann claims, polemically and paradoxically, that the most urgent task is to supply rigorously diplomatic editions reproducing the manuscript tradition in the most ancient form we can attain, "without taking into the least consideration meaning or grammatical rules."[6] Hence not only is conjectural criticism postponed until later; so too is even interpretation itself. Until that time, most critical editions had been simultaneously exegetical, even if some scholars like Heyne accorded the first rank to exegesis, others like Hermann to textual criticism; and all the Romantic theorists of Classical philology, from Friedrich Schlegel to Ast, to Schleiermacher, to Boeckh, had insisted, or would do so a little later, on the "critical and hermeneutic circle."[c] Lachmann, instead, produces editions that are purely critical: in the preface to his Propertius (1816: iv) he

2. Wilamowitz 1894: 42.

3. Other examples could be cited. For example, Friedrich Ast, one of the leaders of the new historical approach to Classical philology, took the Aldine edition of 1513 as the basis for his own edition of Plato (Ast 1819: iii) and set himself the goal of adhering to it as closely as possible! For Elmsley as a partial exception in England, see above, p. 57.

4. Lachmann 1818 = Lachmann 1876: 2.1–17.

5. Lachmann 1826 = Lachmann 1876: 2.102–45; Lachmann 1836 = Lachmann 1876: 2.145–60.

6. Lachmann 1876: 2.2. Cf. Lachmann 1876: 2.145–46: "In my edition of the Roman elegists I had the modest aim of presenting the authentic transmission completely, excluding as far as possible all later vagaries."

refers the reader for everything regarding interpretation to the commentary on the poet that J. G. Huschke was planning to publish, just as in the preface to his Lucretius (1850a: 15) he will refer to the future exegetical works of Steinhart and Reisacker.[7] The critical apparatus, which in his first edition of Propertius is still "selective," becomes "scant" in his editions of Catullus and Tibullus and in his second edition of Propertius.

With regard to the manuscript tradition, Lachmann insists above all on the distinction between interpolated manuscripts and uninterpolated ones. Manuscripts that contain Humanist interpolations must be set aside: you are in trouble if you yield to the attraction of their specious readings! In this polemic favoring *truth* over *elegance*, which assumes a tone of particular vehemence in his preface to Propertius,[8] in this distrust of the *docti Italiani* [learned Italians],[9] Lachmann feels himself particularly close to Scaliger but has harsh words for most of the Dutch Classical philologists.[10] Lachmann's language, like Scaliger's, reveals not only the pure requirement of documentary truth but also a motivation typical of aesthetic criticism: anyone capable of judging can tell that the original reading is more beautiful than the interpolated one; Classical harshness is preferable to Classicist tinsel.

Lachmann sympathizes more with Bekker than with Gottfried Hermann among the Classical philologists nearest to him in age, and this is only natural.[11] It is strange that he does not name Wolf; yet it was Wolf who had demanded editions based on a solid diplomatic foundation (see above, p. 71f.), even more than Bekker; and Lachmann, who studied the Homeric question and created an analogous "Nibelungen question," knew Wolf's *Prolegomena ad Homerum* better than anyone else.[12]

But once the interpolated manuscripts have been excluded, how is the text to be constituted in those passages in which the uninterpolated ones differ from one another? Lachmann answers that the original reading can be

7. He alludes to Steinhart without naming him ("a certain illustrious man"): cf. G. Müller 1958: 253n1.

8. See esp. Lachmann 1816: xvii–xviii.

9. Lachmann 1816: xii: here and in what follows *codices interpolati* and *codices Italici* are synonyms for Lachmann.

10. Lachmann 1816: xvii (where aside from Scaliger the only scholar praised is Livineius, i.e., Jean Lievens, 1546–99); Lachmann 1829: iii.

11. Lachmann 1829: iv: "In any case, if I seem to have made progress in this art beyond Immanuel Bekker, I myself will be pleased and I hope that he will not protest." For Hermann, cf. the review cited above (n. 4).

12. Certain similarities in expression are perhaps not accidental. For example, F. A. Wolf 1985 (1795): 44: "A true recension [. . .] takes off bandages and lays bare the sores" (quoted above, pp. 71f.); Lachmann 1829: iii: "That plague breaks out which [. . .] leaves bandages and disgusting scars in place of wounds."

found in these cases only "by reason and the effort of a skilled mind," [13] so to determine the original reading he does not yet have recourse to any kind of mechanical criterion (of the sort Bengel had already enunciated). Nor can he have such recourse, since he is not yet tracing a genealogy of the manuscripts in these editions of Propertius, Catullus, and Tibullus. He does indeed refer a very few times to the fact that some manuscript "almost completely agrees" with some other one, or that some manuscripts are "derived from a single source," [14] but these references are so sporadic that they could have furnished no basis for mechanical choice among the variants. From this point of view, he is still very far behind Heyne's and Schweighäuser's genealogical attempts, imperfect as these were. His distinction between sincere manuscripts and interpolated ones refers only to their value, not to their origin: unlike Politian and other Classical philologists who followed him,[d] Lachmann eliminates interpolated manuscripts not because they are copies of extant manuscripts but simply because they are untrustworthy.[15] And in part because of the difficulty of procuring collations of manuscripts preserved in distant libraries,[16] in part out of a haughty disdain for anything that looked to him like a useless aggregation of erudition,[17] he always ended up basing

13. Lachmann 1816: xvi: "Since in the case of good manuscripts that present different readings and in other cases as well the correct and original reading can be restored only by means of reason and the effort of a skilled mind." The phrase "in other cases" refers, I think, to cases in which all the manuscripts present a corrupt reading and the editor must heal it by conjecture.

14. Lachmann 1816: xii; 1829: vi.

15. Pasquali 1952a (1934): 5, 25 justly observes that Lachmann never practiced *eliminatio codicum descriptorum*. But his formulation suggests that this operation was not performed until the generation that followed Lachmann; yet we have seen (pp. 47–49) that it was already practiced by Politian and Vettori, and we shall see that it had continued to be practiced by Boivin and Schweighäuser, and then during Lachmann's lifetime by Sauppe, with a particularly rigorous method (p. 100). Another correction: according to Pasquali 1952a (1934): 4n1, Lachmann refused to trust the *recentiores* only in the case of "texts which during the Middle Ages were read hardly or not at all." But in fact the testimony of Haupt that he cites (Belger 1879: 121) refers to *recentiores* in general: "He thought that it was almost never at all useful to distinguish those manuscripts quite devoid of authority into groups and classes with the same meticulousness [sc. as ancient manuscripts]."

16. Pasquali 1952a (1934): 4–5 emphasizes this difficulty. To be sure, scholars such as Heinsius and Bekker had managed to inspect an enormous number of manuscripts; but they had had the opportunity of traveling throughout Europe, whereas Lachmann never left Germany except during the war against Napoleon of 1815. Nonetheless the basic reason remains the second one: see the following note.

17. See, e.g., Lachmann 1816: viii: "Since so many manuscripts from this worthless group have been collated that we are already thoroughly glutted with their readings to the point of nausea." Lachmann 1829: vi: "Anyway, whoever wants to waste his time use-

his editions on an extremely limited number of manuscripts, selected some-times rather arbitrarily:[18] for Catullus he used only two manuscripts, and in this case it is quite obvious that the choice among variants could only be based on internal criteria, since mechanical criteria require at least three wit-nesses. Yet in that very same edition of Catullus he thought he could recon-struct the pages of the lost ancestor, whose numbers he indicated in its mar-gins—a failed attempt, despite Moriz Haupt's attempt to defend it.[19] As we shall see, in the case of Lucretius Lachmann will have far more success with an analogous attempt.

At the same time as he was publishing his editions of Propertius, Catul-lus, and Tibullus, Lachmann was also extremely active as a textual critic in the field of medieval German poetry. To the flowering of Germanic studies during those years in response to the stimulus of Romanticism (it is not nec-essary to recall the names of Wackenroder, Tieck, Uhland, Arnim and Bren-tano, and the brothers Grimm), he contributed a rigorously philological method that he had learned from the Classical philologists; in this way he made a significant contribution to the birth of a scientific approach out of what had originally been a "return to the Middle Ages" espoused by pop-ulist[e] and reactionary literary figures.[20] In the period 1816–29, which we discussed earlier with regard to his Classical philology, Lachmann published editions of the *Nibelungen* (1826), Hartmann von Aue's *Iwein* (1827), and the poems of Walther von der Vogelweide (1827), alongside a large num-ber of articles and reviews concerning Germanic philology. In the same field his editions of Wolfram von Eschenbach (1833), Hartmann von Aue's *Gre-gorius* (1838), Ulrich von Lichtenstein (1841), and various articles and re-editions will follow later.[21]

---

lessly will be able with little trouble to pile up monstrous errors and scholars' innumerable interpretations."

18. For Propertius he used the Neapolitanus (now in Wolfenbüttel: Gud. lat. 224), rightly, but he was mistaken to consider it inferior to the Groninganus (Groningen: Bibl. Universitatis 159). For Tibullus, the only really important manuscript among the ones he used (disregarding the *fragmentum Cuiacianum*) is the Eboracensis, lost but collated by N. Heinsius (Berlin, Diez. B. Sant. 55 d, pp. 15–24). For Catullus his choice was even less felicitous (cf. Pasquali 1952a [1934]: 5n2).

19. Haupt 1836: 1–2 = Haupt 1875–76: 1.1–2. Cf. Ellis 1878: xxxv–xxxvi; Wi-lamowitz 1982 (1921): 130, 141.

20. On the relations between Lachmann and German Romanticism, see Leo 1893: 6–7, 17–18 = Leo 1960: 2.418–19, 430–31. I have not had access to Sparnaay 1948 (brought to my attention by D. Irmer). On Lutz-Hensel 1975, cf. below, p. 144n11.

21. For more detailed bibliographical references, see Hertz 1851: 100–119 and xxiv–xxxii in the appendix. The Germanistic articles and reviews are republished in Lachmann 1876: 1. I have not been able to see Lachmann's edition of *Iwein* myself.

Obviously, it is not up to me to judge this part of Lachmann's activity, given my ignorance of Germanic studies. Nonetheless, I might perhaps venture to say something regarding the pure and simple technique of *recensio* as he applied it in this field. It seems to me that the Lachmann recognizable in these works is indeed fundamentally the same one as the Classical philologist who wrote the prefaces to the Latin poets,[22] but nevertheless it is noticeable that as a Germanist Lachmann devotes greater care to seeking out the manuscript material (as the mere list of the manuscripts he collated already makes clear) and greater effort to investigating the kinship relations among the manuscripts or at least to distinguishing among different redactions of the same work. I think that this slight difference in method can be explained partly by the greater accessibility of the manuscripts (which are almost all found in Germany or Austria), partly by the fact that here Lachmann's polemical target was different: in the case of Classical texts he felt above all the necessity of eliminating the worthless excess variants that had been accumulated in the editions of the seventeenth and eighteenth centuries, and this ended up leading him to excessive simplification; in the case of medieval texts, on the other hand, he had to refute the opposite prejudice, that the edition had to be based on a single manuscript (as a rule, the oldest one),[23] and this induced him to collate other manuscripts and to enlarge the documentary basis for his edition. So we see Lachmann the Germanist asserting that to restore a text to its original form, at least four or five manuscripts are necessary;[24] that even if a recent manuscript contains linguis-

---

22. For example, in his preface to Wolfram von Eschenbach (Lachmann 1879 [1833]: xviii) he refuses with typical impatience to study the genealogy of the manuscripts in greater depth ("But why should one extend the investigation to the smallest details?") and declares that he has constantly followed one class of manuscripts, however much this "might impair the truth as a whole."

23. Among Medievalists this prejudice lasted for a long time: in Italy it was defended in the second half of the nineteenth century by Ernesto Monaci and attacked by Rajna and Barbi (cf. Pasquali 1942: 224 = Pasquali 1968: 2.157–58). In our century Bédier sought to revive it (Bédier 1928); against his attempt see Pasquali 1932a: 130–31 and 1942: 232–33 (= Pasquali 1968: 2.163–64); Dain 1975 (1949): 142; cf. also below, Appendix C, n. 3, and Avalle 1972: 28–29 (who bases his argument in part on the methodological observations of Contini 1942: 129–32). As these scholars have observed and as Barbi already understood, the only case in which Bédier's criterion is somewhat justified occurs when every manuscript (or group of manuscripts) represents an independent redaction, in a certain sense an autonomous work, as often happens in texts of popular tradition (or in literary texts revised by the author): if practical considerations make us abandon as impossible the idea of publishing all the different redactions separately, it is indeed better to select only one of them rather than to compile a contaminated text that does not correspond to any redaction that has ever really existed.

24. Lachmann 1876 : 1.89, and cf. 161, 285–86 (= Lachmann 1817).

tic and orthographic modernizations, it can still preserve readings that are more genuine than an older manuscript;[25] that the only manuscripts that can really be neglected are the apographs of ones still extant[26]—all assertions that if transposed into the field of Classical philology sound almost anti-Lachmannian.[27]

Lachmann also attempted to apply a mechanical criterion of choice among variants to the criticism of Germanic texts before he tried to do so with Classical ones. Unfortunately, the rules he formulated for this purpose, in his review of F. H. von der Hagen's second edition of the *Nibelungen,* are a real brainteaser and probably contain not only several slips but also some genuine mistakes: on this see below, Appendix A. Lachmann himself ended up making no use of them in his own edition of the *Nibelungen.* Still, even this first inchoate attempt has some importance for studying the genesis of "Lachmann's method."

25. Lachmann 1876: 1.163 (= Lachmann 1820b: x).

26. Lachmann 1876: 1.89: "The only manuscripts that can easily be neglected are the copies of exemplars that are still extant."

27. On Lachmann as an editor of medieval texts, cf. Stackmann 1964, esp. 255 and n. 45. I am pleased that Stackmann, with his specific experience as a Germanist, has substantially confirmed the analysis I offered with some hesitation in the first edition of this study (and, of course, has enriched it with new observations).

Addendum to Chapter 3

In the last years of his life, did Gottfried Hermann feel the need to refer to manuscripts instead of taking the vulgate as the sole basis for a conjectural criticism? Did he recognize at least in part the justice of Lachmann's criticisms of him in his review of the *Ajax* many years before (cf. above, chap. 3, n. 4)? The answer seems certainly yes. Antonio La Penna has brought to my attention this statement by Hermann from the beginning of his essay "De hymnis Dionysii et Mesomedis" (Hermann 1842: 1 = Hermann 1827–77: 8.343): "There can be no doubt that the reliability of the written documentation must be examined first of all when an erroneous transmission is emended. Usually this is easy when we have only one exemplar of a text; it is more difficult when there are several that differ from one another; it is most difficult of all when we suspect that the true form of the text has not been transmitted but must finally be tracked down by conjecture."

Sauppe's testimony, which we quoted above and which dates from 1841, only one year before this essay of Hermann's, therefore corresponds at least in part to the truth, even if with some distortion. Indeed, as we shall see in chapter 5, by this time not only Lachmann but also Orelli, Madvig, C. G. Zumpt, and Ritschl had been repeatedly declaring for many years that it was necessary to investigate the documentary foundation of the texts, the *fides scripturae*. Hermann could not possibly have remained entirely deaf to these voices.

On the other hand, by this time he was too committed to his own version of philological practice (which indeed had produced many splendid results) and perhaps was also too old to "renew" himself completely. He never applied the new methods in a way corresponding to that statement of principle, not even in that very same article, except for a few sporadic references to manuscript readings; what is more, the statement itself is not a model of clarity and coherence.

Above all, Hermann seems to be still committed to the distinction between *emendatio ope codicum* and *ope ingenii*, rather than to the one between *recensio* and *emendatio*. Furthermore, when he enumerates the three degrees of "difficulty" in restoring the genuine text, he creates a certain confusion between different points of view. The "ease" of having a single manuscript available must apparently be understood here in the sense of "convenience": in this case one need not bury oneself in those laborious investigations of collating various manuscripts and stemmatology that Hermann continued to find a heavy burden, and sometimes a useless one (and it must be conceded that he was not entirely wrong). But although it is not necessarily a misfortune for a philologist to have only a single manuscript upon which to establish his text (on this point, cf. S. Mariotti 1971), that does not mean that the presence of more than one manuscript makes it "more difficult" to reach the authentic text, as long as one of the manuscripts preserves good readings that are lacking in the others or helps reject *lectiones singulares* by agreeing with other manuscripts. To be sure, it is more "difficult" to work on more than one manuscript, not only because of the greater toil involved but also because of the often arduous problems of choice among variants; but it can also be "easier" for the purpose of arriving at the correct reading. To take a banal example at random, if only a single representative of the Palatine redaction of Plautus (and not even one of the better ones) had survived, and we possessed neither the other Palatine manuscripts nor, worse still, the Ambrosian palimpsest, then the work of editors of Plautus would in a certain sense be "easier," but it would be far more difficult to make a good edition. And finally, it is true that *emendatio* is the most difficult task that the textual critic confronts, at least in very many cases; but *emendatio* is not a "third degree" of difficulty with regard to a first degree constituted by the existence of a single manuscript. The comparison is not one between homogeneous entities: a single manuscript may be swarming with errors and stand all the more in need of conjectural criticism.

Perhaps these are pedantic and overlong criticisms of a passage written by a great Classical philologist whose greatness lies elsewhere, namely, in that kind of conjectural criticism (or in that intelligent defense of the transmitted reading) which he always considered the loftiest kind of philological labor, as this very passage demonstrates with all its incoherence.[a]

4

Lachmann as an Editor of
the New Testament

From Germanic studies let us return to Greek and Latin texts. We can distinguish two parallel lines in Lachmann's activity as a textual critic during the fifteen years from 1830 to 1845. On the one hand he edited a series of texts transmitted in only one manuscript or *editio princeps*, for which it was naturally not *recensio* that posed problems but only *emendatio:* Genesius (1834); Terentianus Maurus (1836); Gaius (1841), an edition begun by J. F. L. Goeschen and completed by Lachmann;[a] and Babrius (1845).[1] On the other hand he edited the New Testament: the *editio minor* appeared in 1831, the first volume of the *editio maior* in 1842.[2]

The last important edition of the New Testament had been Griesbach's (see above, p. 70). Lachmann severely criticized Griesbach's persistent acquiescence in[b] the *textus receptus* (Lachmann 1876: 2.151), and he finally achieved what Bentley had planned: an edition founded solely upon the ancient manuscripts and Saint Jerome's Vulgata. Not even Lachmann was spared unpleasant accusations by narrow-minded theologians,[3] but times had changed and[c] the authority of the *receptus* was no longer able to reassert itself.

1. Shortly after his edition of Babrius, in the same year, 1845, Lachmann published a little edition of Avianus in Berlin. In this case there were many manuscripts, but Lachmann pushed his desire for simplification to an extreme and hence did not even indicate them, instead using in the critical apparatus vague terms like "very many," "few," "two very ancient ones," "a very ancient one." The only value to this edition consists in some good conjectures. The first scholar to undertake a true *recensio* of Avianus was Fröhner in 1862; cf. Fröhner 1862: xii.

2. Lachmann 1831, without a preface or critical apparatus (but Lachmann explained the criteria he had followed in Lachmann 1830 = Lachmann 1876: 2.250–72, which I cite); Lachmann 1842–50.

3. Lachmann 1876: 2.151; Lachmann 1842–50: 1.xxx–xxxiii and *passim;* Hertz 1851: 160, 165–67.

Alongside Bentley's example, it was Bengel who influenced Lachmann.[4] The two families, Eastern and Western, which Lachmann distinguished within the tradition of the New Testament, correspond in substance to Bengel's two *nationes,* Asian and African;[5] and above all, the mechanical method of choosing the variants derives from Bengel. Lachmann writes in his *Rechenschaft* of 1830: "Every reading shared by both families, whether it is the only reading attested or both families vary in the same way, thereby proves itself to have been widespread [*verbreitet*] and is worth accepting into the text; a reading of the one family and a different one of the other family have equal authority for me; a reading attested only by one part of one of the two families is to be eliminated (even if perhaps it is the only genuine one)."[6] This formulation is more detailed than Bengel's, which we quoted earlier (pp. 65f.); but Lachmann's debt to Bengel is clear, especially if we compare this passage of the *Rechenschaft* to the extremely confused rules Lachmann enunciated in his review of von der Hagen (see pp. 81, 139ff.), when in all probability he was still unacquainted with Bengel's work.

Of the three cases that Lachmann distinguishes in his *Rechenschaft,* he divides the first one into four in the preface to his *editio maior* of 1842, so that the rules become six.[7] The third one introduces a geographic consideration and is particularly interesting. the agreement of some manuscripts of one family with some of the other has greater value if the manuscripts come from places very distant from one another. In fact, distance is a guarantee against "horizontal transmission," against contamination.[8] Already Bentley

4. Lachmann states in the preface to his *editio maior,* "these men alone [sc. Bentley and Bengel] understood what it is that I call editing [*recensere*]" (Lachmann 1842–50: 1.xxxi).

5. Already before Lachmann, Semler (in the preface to Semler 1765) had designated the two families as "the Eastern" and "the Western" ones; he called them *recensiones,* a term that suggests he conceived them as "ancient editions," "redactions," rather than as mere genealogical groupings.

6. Lachmann 1876: 2.257; his qualification "even if perhaps it is the only genuine one" precedes the distinction between *leçon vraie* [true reading] and *leçon authentique* [authentic reading] established much later by Havet 1911:425–27. But, as Lachmann himself declares (pp. 258, 269), in general he followed the "Eastern" family in the *editio minor,* even where the other one offered readings that he himself recognized to be superior. He remedied this incoherence in his *editio maior,* but this too was based on a manuscript material that was too incomplete to allow him to really reconstruct the original readings of the two families (which as it turns out are more than two and all contaminated): cf. Tischendorf-Gebhardt 1897: 2.758–61; Gregory 1900–1909: 2.966–82; Metzger 1968 (1964): chaps. 2, 6, 8 (chap. 6 must be used with caution).

7. Lachmann 1842–50: 1.viii; Quentin 1926: 34–35 gives a paraphrase of the six rules.

8. Lachmann 1842–50: 1.viii: "Furthermore, the confirmation in the agreement of witnesses brought together from different regions is greater than the danger arising from some

had made an observation of this sort, but he connected it with the reliability of the New Testament tradition as a whole, not with the choice among variants: "'Tis a good providence and a great blessing, that so many manuscripts of the New Testament are still amongst us; some procured from Egypt, others from Asia, others found in the Western churches. For the very distances of places as well as numbers of the books demonstrate, that there could be no collusion, no altering nor interpolating one copy by another, nor all by any of them."[9] And we have seen (chap. 2, n. 20) that Bengel included[d] a geographic consideration among his rules as well.

Pasquali insisted on the importance of this geographical criterion, emphasizing its analogy with the criterion of lateral areas used by "neolinguists."[10] Shortly before, while Pasquali was studying the manuscript tra-

---

manuscripts from the same countries which differ from them either through carelessness or almost by intention." A few pages earlier Lachmann had expressed himself more simply: "Above all we shall take account of the most ancient [sc. witnesses], and among these of such ones as derive from the most widely separated places" (p. vi). Cf. also: "Where manuscripts from distant regions agree with one another, this is likely to have been propagated from very ancient sources into the various places: on the other hand, we must suspect that unique readings of individual exemplars were born at home and are not derived from a common source" (p. vii). But in this last passage what is opposed to agreement among "distant" manuscripts is not agreement among "near" manuscripts, as being less decisive, but rather the readings of individual manuscripts: unless we understand *exemplar* in the sense of "subarchetype," there is a certain contamination between the "geographical criterion" and *eliminatio lectionum singularium*.

9. Bentley 1836–38: 3.350 (from his *Remarks upon a Late Discourse of Free-Thinking*; see also above, p. 63f.): Lachmann had this passage in mind and expresses himself in a similar way on p. ix of his preface. Less convincing is Lachmann's attempt (p. vii) to find an anticipation of the geographical criterion in S. Jerome, *Ep. Ad Damasum*, in Migne 1846: 559.

10. Pasquali 1952a (1934): xvii–xviii, 7–8, 159–60, 224n 3; cf. also Pasquali 1951a: 217 = Pasquali 1968: 2.440 on a similar idea already expressed in 1891 by Michele Barbi. On the value Pasquali attributed to this criterion, cf. also Pasquali 1952a (1934): 345: "indeed, this is one of the ideas that prompted me to write this book." Pasquali himself cites Bartoli 1925: 6–23. See also the conclusion of Bartoli 1943: 76. Neolinguistics (also called area or spatial linguistics) was a school originating from the teaching of Hugo Schuchardt and Jules Gilliéron which aimed above all to reconstruct the relative chronology of linguistic facts on the basis of their geographical distribution. The "neolinguists" were opposed to the "neogrammarians" and were influenced by the idealism of Benedetto Croce and Karl Vossler; this influence appears to be stronger in Giulio Bertoni, much less so in Matteo Bartoli, in whom it had to struggle against a prejudicial distrust of any philosophy of language (or, as he used to say ironically, "glottosophy"). This brief indication is intended for any non-Italian readers who may not have heard of neolinguistics.

dition of Gregory of Nyssa, he had encountered a case in which a genuine reading was preserved by two manuscripts that came from "marginal" zones.[11] It is understandable that when he read this passage from Lachmann's preface to the New Testament he was pleased by the coincidence and thought he could detect in that preface a less mechanical, less Lachmannian, more Pasqualian Lachmann than the better-known Lachmann of the Lucretius commentary.

But it seems to me that Lachmann's preface to the New Testament, reread with greater detachment, is substantially in line with the whole development of his textual criticism, except for the few indications of a more complex conception of manuscript tradition that can be found in Lachmann's work as a Germanist, as I indicated in the preceding chapter. It should be noted that the criterion of lateral areas can be understood in two different ways in both linguistics and textual criticism, one "mechanical" (without giving this term any pejorative meaning) and one sociocultural.[e] In the former case, what is involved is an elementary calculation of probability: if two witnesses at a great distance from one another agree with one another with little or no[f] possibility of communication, and if the agreement is such that it can hardly be attributed to chance (that is, to polygenesis of innovations),[g] then it must be concluded that they preserve a genuine tradition. This is how Lachmann (and already Bentley and Bengel, as we have seen) understood the geographical criterion; so too Giacomo Leopardi and Wilhelm von Humboldt, who applied it to certain agreements between Latin and Sanskrit against Greek, in unpublished writings that Lachmann could not have known.[12] On the other hand, while the neolinguists' and Pasquali's formulation does not entirely neglect this "mechanical" aspect, it emphasizes instead a sociocultural fact: the "province" is more backward, more conservative than the "center": "victorious innovations," as Pasquali writes (1952a [1934]: 7), "usually radiate outward from a center toward the periphery, and they do not always manage to reach it." Here the word "center" is not to be understood in a purely spatial sense, and what guarantees the greater degree of archaism of facts attested in the lateral areas is not the lack of communication between such areas but the lesser dynamism and cultural prestige of their inhabitants—so much so that, according to neolinguistics and

11. Pasquali 1959 (1925): xliv; cf. Pasquali 1952a (1934): 158–62.

12. Leopardi, *Zibaldone*, pp. 2351–54 of the autograph (= Flora 1937: 1417–19); cf. Timpanaro 1997 (1955): 162–63. More fleetingly, Humboldt 1903–20: 6.1.253. The passage from Leopardi dates from 1822, the one from Humboldt from 1827–29, but both were not published until long after Lachmann's death.

Pasquali, even facts attested in *only one* marginal area are probably more ancient.[13]

In any case, the fact that Lachmann is rigidly Lachmannian as an editor of the New Testament too is demonstrated by the very beginning of his preface (p. v), in which he not only distinguishes between *recensio* and *emendatio* more clearly than in his earlier writings but also repeats quite drastically the difference between *recensio* and interpretation: "We both can and must edit [*recensere*] without interpreting"—the very principle against which Pasquali always protested. Lachmann had already objected against Griesbach in his *Rechenschaft* of 1830 that internal criteria for the choice among variants "by their nature almost all cancel each other out,"[14] and this disdain for internal criticism is also why he unjustly disparaged Wettstein.[15] Without a doubt, there are cases in which internal criteria cancel each other out: sometimes a reading is *difficilior* in one respect, *facilior* in another; sometimes the criterion of the *lectio difficilior* runs afoul of the *usus scribendi,* especially if it is applied with scholastic rigor.[16] But *recensere sine interpretatione* was never anything more than empty boasting, even on Lachmann's part, not only because he had at the very least to understand the readings of the manuscripts in order to be able to classify them, but also because after the *eliminatio lectionum singularium* there still remained a large mass of variants of equal documentary authority from among which he too had to choose on the basis of internal criteria.[17] More recently, Quentin's

13. Pasquali 1952a (1934): 160 n. 1. Bartoli 1925: "The earlier phase tends to be preserved in the more isolated area" (p. 4); "If of two linguistic phases one is found in lateral areas and the other in an area in the middle, the phase in the lateral area is normally the earlier one, *as long as the area in the middle is not the more isolated area*" (p. 7, my italics). The element we have called "sociocultural" appears in the writings of other students of geolinguistics (e.g., Terracini, Bertoldi, Devoto) even more than in Bartoli, who usually preferred to limit himself to statistical observations. On the criterion of the marginal areas in textual criticism, cf. Corti 1961 and Santoli 1961: 116 and n. 9.

14. Lachmann 1876: 2.252.

15. Lachmann names Wettstein only rarely, unlike Bentley and Bengel, and not favorably; e.g., in the preface to Lachmann 1842–50: xxiii.

16. This kind of contrast not only corresponds to the one between the grammatical theories of analogy (= *usus scribendi*) and anomaly (= *lectio difficilior*), even if what is involved is neither a mechanical correspondence nor an irreconcilable opposition; the two contrasts are also connected historically, starting from the philology of Alexandria, as I shall try to explain elsewhere. For a partially similar repercussion of these two grammatical theories upon textual criticism, cf. Kenney 1974: 114.

17. It will be recalled that according to Lachmann's division, which is still generally followed, *recensio* also includes the choice among variants of equal external authority, i.e., what Paul Maas calls *selectio*.

method was an attempt to really achieve *recensio sine interpretatione,* but it very quickly revealed its sterility.[18]

18. Pasquali 1932a: 131 writes justly: "Already Lachmann did not trust *iudicium* enough; Quentin exaggerates this distrust in a somewhat too Catholic, monkish way." Dain 1949: 162–64 demolishes Quentin's "ecdotic" theory with affectionate irony in a paragraph titled "La grande illusion" [The grand illusion] (the title reproduces that of Renoir's famous film and is already ironic); Dain's criticism of Quentin in the corresponding paragraph of later editions of his work is more perfunctory and less effective. More recently, Balduino 1979: 232–34 has raised calm but radical objections to Quentin. The Quentinian method has been revived by theoreticians of the automation of textual criticism (Froger 1968; Zarri 1969, 1979, and other works of Zarri's which I do not cite for lack of space). I have had the benefit of exchanging ideas with my friend Zarri, and I am convinced that new methods can yield great advantages, and already have done so, for unraveling to a certain extent manuscript traditions that are very complex and richer in variants than in real corruptions. More than ever I find mistaken and reactionary any hostility against the methods of automation which is based on rhetorical claims for the uniqueness of the "human spirit." But one fact remains: Quentin's method is powerless in the face of the objection that only coincidence in error can indicate the kinship between two manuscripts; coincidence in the correct reading proves *nothing,* since it is a fact of conservation that can also occur in manuscripts unrelated to one another. The recourse to Quentin's method on the part of theoreticians of automation is a "sad necessity," since a computer is not capable of distinguishing a correct reading from a corruption: for that, we would need an "artificial philologist," something we do not yet possess.

5

Contributions of Lachmann's Contemporaries

In the meantime, during the 1830s, other philologists had made contributions of enormous importance to the method of textual criticism, especially regarding the genealogy of the manuscript tradition.

"The families and as it were lines of descent, both of manuscripts and of editions, must be established": this was the plan Johann Caspar Orelli proclaimed in the preface to the first volume of his edition of Cicero, which appeared in 1826.[1] He himself only succeeded in fulfilling that plan to a very small extent: a whole lifetime would not have sufficed for a truly critical edition of all the works of Cicero, especially at that time, when manuscript collations were so difficult to obtain; and the interests of Orelli, an attractive figure as scholar and religious and political reformer and an intelligent follower of Pestalozzi's ideas,[a] were too various to allow him to dedicate himself entirely to this project. For that reason his edition, which was completed in only six years, from 1826 to 1831, ended up being in large part a hurried revision[b] of the preceding editions.[2] Once again we find the same contrast between editorial theory and practice that we have already noted, for example, in Ernesti. But Orelli had the merit of at least reviving the programmatic demand for the investigation of the genealogical relations between the manuscripts in a period in which it had fallen into neglect after having been asserted with such energy at the end of the eighteenth century (see above, pp. 75f.). And just as his brief reference to the manuscript tradition of Lucretius provided a starting point for Johan Nicolai Madvig and other scholars before the publication of Lachmann's Lucretius (see the following chapter, pp. 102ff.), so too his edition of Cicero stimulated Madvig to give a first,

1. Orelli 1826–38: 1.xiii.

2. It was only for the manuscript traditions of Cicero's letters that he was able to do an accurate and partly original job: see the preface to Orelli 1826–38.

substantially correct genealogical outline of the tradition of Cicero's Verrine orations in his *Epistola ad Orellium* [Epistle to Orelli].[3]

This was the first exchange in a fruitful dialogue between the Classical philologist of Zurich and his younger colleague from Denmark, which continued in the following years and can be followed in the inaugural dissertations and editions of individual works of Cicero's which were published by the one scholar or the other.[4] This was a genuine dialogue in which, even if from the very beginning Madvig displayed a more vigorous and original philological personality, Orelli too made contributions that were far from negligible and demonstrated that he knew how to study certain problems in depth which he had barely touched on in his Cicero edition.

And soon the dialogue was enriched by the addition of a third interlocutor, Carl Gottlob Zumpt from Berlin. A student of Wolf's, Zumpt had learned from him to disdain eclecticism and to demand a text based constantly on the best manuscripts. He put these precepts into practice, first in an edition of Quintus Curtius Rufus, then in an edition of Cicero's Verrine orations that appeared in 1831.[5] This latter edition bears the traces of toilsome revision: Zumpt had to begin his work on the basis of old printed editions because of the difficulty of obtaining reliable collations; only later was he able to go back to the manuscripts, and he did not feel up to eliminating completely the old and by now quite superfluous hodgepodge from the preface and critical apparatus.[6] All in all, his genealogical reconstruction makes little progress beyond Madvig's much more concise one, which Zumpt read only when his own work was almost finished.[7] But the *stemma codicum* that Zumpt drew up as a conclusion and summary of his investigation (1831: 1.xxxviii) was a very important technical innovation:

3. Madvig 1828: 7–10. Cf. Klotz 1923: viii.

4. For Orelli see esp. Orelli-Beier 1830, preceded by an *Epistola critica ad Io. Nic. Madvigium*; Orelli 1832, 1835, 1837. For Madvig see the prefaces and dissertations collected in Madvig 1834 and 1842. On Madvig see also below, p. 97. As is well known, Orelli undertook a new edition of Cicero in collaboration with Baiter in 1845; after his death it was continued by Baiter and Karl Halm.

5. C. G. Zumpt 1826: esp. xvi; later, in 1849, Zumpt published an *editio maior* of the same author, cf. K. Müller 1954: 798. C. G. Zumpt 1831. On his relations with Wolf see A. W. Zumpt 1851: 17, 31–34. Zumpt's preface to the *Verrines* reveals Wolf's influence in its very terminology, for example, in the distinction between *recensio* and *recognitio*: "Thus, employing a recent, but useful, distinction, it will be truer to say that he published a revision (*recognovisse*) of Gruter's text than a critical edition (*recensuisse*) of Cicero" (C. G. Zumpt 1831: 1.xxv–xxvi); cf. above, p. 71f.

6. He himself explains this in his preface, C. G. Zumpt 1831: 1.xxxiv.

7. C. G. Zumpt 1831: 1.xxxv–xxxvi.

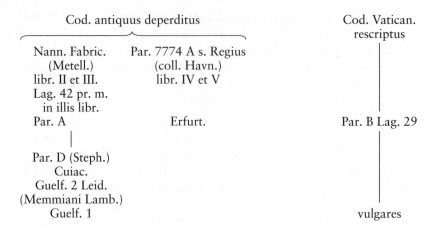

Is this the first *stemma codicum* that was ever actually drawn up, and not only planned like Bengel's *tabula genealogica?* No. In the first version of my study (Timpanaro 1959: 213), I attributed the innovation to Ritschl (see below, p. 93f.), though I added, "I know well how cautious one must be in such assertions of priority." My caution was all too justified! When this study was first published as a book (Timpanaro 1963a: 46 and n. 1), I was able to backdate the first stemma from Ritschl to Zumpt, thanks to a kind reference by Konrad Müller. But, a little later, a Swedish scholar, Gösta Holm, demonstrated that Carl Johan Schlyter had drawn up a stemma of a type more "modern" than Zumpt's in the first volume of an edition of ancient Swedish legal texts published in 1827 (and thus four years before Zumpt's edition of Cicero), in a field very remote not only from Classical philology but also from the study of Germanic literary texts as Lachmann had practiced it, and furthermore that already at an extremely early date he was quite aware of certain causes of disturbance in a purely "vertical" transmission (not so much contamination as rather the conjectural activity of individual copyists).[8] Given the subject matter of Schlyter's publication, it is not surprising that it escaped the notice of Classical philologists: it is almost certain that Zumpt drew up his stemma without knowing that he had such an acute predecessor in Schlyter.[c]

8. Collins-Schlyter 1827. Cf. Holm 1972: 74–80, 53 (reproduction of Schlyter's stemma), 77–79 (comparison with other, slightly later stemmas). Perhaps Holm overestimates somewhat Schlyter's contribution regarding the reconstruction of the text of the ancestor (Holm 1972: 60–64): as far as I can tell (but it must be borne in mind that I only have access to the passages that Holm translates or summarizes), Schlyter oscillated between the criteria of the "best manuscript" and of the majority of the witnesses; thus in this regard he still lagged behind Madvig (see below, pp. 97f.) and Lachmann.

In the field of Latin texts, in 1809 and 1813, even before Schlyter, Johann August Goerenz[d] had summarized in the form of a *tabula* [table] or *tabella* [small table] his subdivision of the manuscripts of Cicero's *De legibus* and *De finibus* into two classes.[9] But Goerenz's classification still referred to the value of the manuscripts (on the one side the *codices potiores* [superior manuscripts], on the other the *deteriores* [inferior ones]), not to their relations of derivation; and his *tabulae* were simple lists of the manuscripts of both categories, not genealogical trees. Zumpt, on the other hand, already indicates the manuscripts' derivation, even if somewhat less precisely than Schlyter;[e] and so far as we know,[f] he is also the first to introduce the term *stemma* (that is, precisely, "genealogical tree"), which will end up prevailing over other synonyms.[10]

The young Ritschl is also connected with Wolf, even if he did not study directly with him. Typically Wolfian is his interest in the history of the text (understood in a very broad sense, as the history of Alexandrian and Byzantine philological culture), which he showed starting with his edition of Thomas Magister's Ἐκλογὴ ὀνομάτων καὶ ῥημάτων Ἀττικῶν [Selection of Attic nouns and verbs].[11] If I am not mistaken, the very term *history of the text* comes to Ritschl from Wolf.[12] But within this broad perspective he also

9. Goerenz 1809–13: 1.ix–x, xxxi–xxxii, 3.vii, xxix. On Goerenz, see Kämmel 1879.

10. He presents his stemma with the words, "Thus is produced more or less this stemma of the manuscripts" (C. G. Zumpt 1831: 1.xxxviii n1). The term *stemma* reappears later in Schneidewin's preface to Martial (1842: cxxxi; see below, pp. 101f.), in Bernays's dissertation on Lucretius (1847; see below, chap. 6, n. 8), and in Ritschl's edition of Plautus (Ritschl 1849–54: 1.xxxvii). Earlier, Ritschl had used other expressions: in his edition of Thomas Magister he writes, "The connection of both relations can be displayed in a single diagram in this form" (1832: xxx), and in his articles on Dionysius of Halicarnassus of 1838 and 1847 (see below, n. 13) he speaks of *artificium* [device]. But, as Konrad Müller points out to me, the notes Ritschl took in Italy in 1837 already contain the German expression corresponding to *stemma*: "a formal genealogical tree ('einen förmlichen genealogischen Stammbaum') for the descent and relation of all the fathers, brothers, cousins, and nephews in the great family of Plautus manuscripts" (cf. Ribbeck 1879: 1.201). Madvig speaks of *tabula* in his 1833 dissertation (see below, p. 97), as Bengel already had a century earlier (cf. above, p. 65); Schlyter (cf. n. 8) used the expression *schema cognationis Codicum manusc(riptorum)* [scheme of the kinship relations among the manuscripts], cf. Holm 1972: 53.

11. Ritschl 1832. We must also recall Ritschl's studies, only a little later, on Orus and Orion, and on the Alexandrian libraries, which demonstrate his interest in the history of ancient philology.

12. Ritschl writes, "in order to see clearly the history of the text, if I may use a recent term" (1832: xxix); cf. also below, n. 14: "the history of the text (as we now say) . . . " And Wolf had spoken of the *Geschichte des Textes* [history of the text], for example, in his preface to Plato's *Symposium* (F. A. Wolf 1869: 1.143).

sets himself the task of reconstructing the precise genealogical relations between the manuscripts: on page xxx of the prolegomena to his edition of
Thomas Magister we find a stemma of the manuscripts and first printed editions, in which lost manuscripts are indicated with Greek letters, according
to what will become the customary usage:

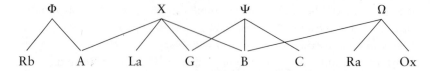

Clearly this is not a genealogy *a primo fonte deducta* [derived from the
earliest source]: Ritschl does not explain the relation among the four ancestors ΦΧΨΩ, which, as his words and a brief examination of the critical apparatus suggest, is not a pure and simple direct derivation of all four from
an archetype or Byzantine edition. Indeed, as we have seen, not even the
stemma of the manuscripts of the Verrine orations which Zumpt traced one
year earlier started out from a single ancestor for the whole tradition—from
this point of view, once again, Schlyter's stemma is more similar to the ones
that became customary later.[g] Ritschl makes another step forward beyond
Zumpt by specifying the position of each and every manuscript within the
stemma: Zumpt had been satisfied with indicating some groups of related
manuscripts. But the greater specification means greater complexity: Ritschl
was facing a very contaminated tradition—as was only natural, given that
this was a Byzantine anthology widely used in medieval schools—and was
obliged to indicate a double derivation for many witnesses. With all those
intersecting lines, his stemma already resembles the ones that are found more
and more often in recent critical editions and that aim to give some idea of
the manuscript tradition in all its disarray, without convenient but arbitrary
simplifications. But when the disarray is excessive, it is better to give up on
the stemma![h]

Some years later Ritschl investigated the manuscript traditions of Dionysius of Halicarnassus and Plautus by the same method.[13] For Dionysius, he
based his genealogical reconstruction only on internal data, on shared cor-

13. On Dionysius of Halicarnassus, see esp. Ritschl 1838 (incomplete reprint in Ritschl
1866–68: 1.471–515) and Ritschl 1847 (= Ritschl 1866–68: 1.516–40). On Plautus, after some works completed in 1834–35, esp. Ritschl 1835: 153–216, 486–570 (reprinted
with additions in Ritschl 1866–68: 2.1–165), see the extensive prolegomena to his edition, Ritschl 1849–54. Of course we are setting aside here Ritschl's studies on Plautine
prosody and metrics, contained above all in Ritschl 1845.

ruptions and lacunas; for Plautus he was obliged from the very beginning to make use above all of external indications, but he confirmed them later by an internal inquiry.[14] In both cases he summarized his results in a *stemma codicum*.

But despite Ritschl's outstanding ability to reconstruct the history of a text, he did not feel a corresponding need to use the stemma in order to determine the archetype's readings: even where it would have been possible, he never had recourse to mechanical rules for the *eliminatio lectionum singularium* as they had been indicated by Bengel and, even better, by Lachmann in the *Rechenschaft* to his *editio minor* of the New Testament. In his dissertation on Dionysius of Halicarnassus (Ritschl 1838: 26) he traced out this stemma:

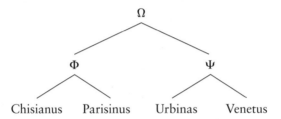

This is a typical case of a "mechanical recension."[i] But once Ritschl had reached the point where he could have announced the criteria for reconstructing Ω, instead he merely suggested "that we should side with the Chisianus as long as possible, but on the other hand should not fear to take refuge in the Urbinas whenever reason itself demands this or sometimes only counsels it." Thus he did not even hint that the reading of Ω could be reconstructed with certainty every time one of the two apographs of Φ agreed with the two apographs of Ψ, or one of the apographs of Φ and one of Ψ agreed with one another against singular readings of each of the other two. Perhaps he did not know the rules Lachmann had formulated; or perhaps (and this is more likely) those rules seemed to him to have no practical usefulness in the case of Dionysius. For he was convinced that the Parisinus (Paris, Bibliothèque Nationale: Coisl. gr. 150) and the Venetus (Venice, Biblioteca Marciana: Marc. gr. 272) provided nothing useful for the constitu-

14. Ritschl himself distinguishes the two kinds of history of tradition, for example: "While in other cases it is possible first to investigate the history of the manuscripts and then to move on to judging their value (this happens, e.g., in the manuscripts of Plautus), we have gone in the opposite direction ourselves, first weighing the value of the individual manuscripts and then moving on to outlining the history of the text (as we now say) even without external evidence" (1838: 25). Cf. Ritschl 1849–54: i.xxxvi.

tion of the text.[15] Later, returning to this question, he concluded that they were *descripti* and hence should be eliminated: thus the choice was really between the Chigianus (Vatican, Chig. gr. 58) and the Urbinas (Vatican, Urbin. gr. 105) alone, so that it became impossible to apply any sort of mechanical criterion.[16]

Thus Ritschl and Lachmann present a striking contrast: the former was passionately attached not only to *ars critica* in the sense of Gottfried Hermann but also to the history of the tradition as such and tended to transform it into cultural history, like Wolf before him; the latter was completely intent upon the goal of freeing the text from late interpolations and restoring it to the oldest attainable form but was indifferent to the kind of genealogical inquiry that was an essential step toward reconstructing the archetype. There was also a difference in their explanatory styles: Ritschl loved didactic clarity, to the point of lapsing sometimes into a certain verbosity,[17] while Lachmann preferred an oracular style made up of sentences imparted from above and intelligible only to initiates. For the same reason, as we shall see, Lachmann did not adopt the use of *stemmata codicum* even in his very last editions, although these had rapidly became popular and were even introduced into his own school by Karl Nipperdey.[18] To use a stemma to make the history of the text more understandable would have seemed to him a narrow-minded pedantry.

15. Ritschl 1838: 25. Ritschl speaks sometimes of *Venetus,* sometimes of *Veneti,* for he was not entirely sure whether the incomplete and secondhand information available to him referred to one manuscript or to two (1838: 19–20).

16. See his stemma, quite different from the preceding one, in Ritschl 1866: 1.539, 490 (for the explanation of his symbols). In a specimen edition he published in 1846 he had already written, "Thus it is clear that for emending Dionysius it is better to weigh carefully the meaning and style of the individual words and sentences than to investigate the value of the manuscripts" (Ritschl 1866: 1.492). Karl Jacoby adhered to this criterion in his Teubner edition of Dionysius's *Antiquitates.* As far as I know, no one since Ritschl has ever reexamined the entire manuscript tradition to see whether there might indeed be manuscripts not copied from the Chigianus or the Urbinas. It would be highly advisable to do so, especially now, when historians and scholars interested in the most ancient Roman institutions have become more willing to ignore Dionysius's wordy rhetoric and to attribute a high value to his work.

17. He himself declares in his prolegomena to Plautus, "I confess that my inborn nature leads me to employ a somewhat fuller style than experienced readers might seem to need, since I bear in mind above all the needs of those who wish to learn this discipline" (Ritschl 1849–54: 1.lxix). On Ritschl as a philologist and teacher, besides Ribbeck's classic work (Ribbeck 1879), see the lively evocation in Schmid 1968: 131–37, 141–42.

18. Nipperdey 1847–56: 1.48 (I owe this indication too to Konrad Müller). Nipperdey studied first with Moriz Haupt, then with Lachmann. His prolegomena to Caesar contain no genuine methodological novelties, but his arguments are very rigorous and clear.

Now let us return for a moment to studies on Cicero, which, as we have seen, in the years around 1830 were one of the fields in which the genealogical method was tested concretely for the first time. In 1833 Madvig published the first part of his dissertation *De emendandis Ciceronis orationibus pro P. Sestio et in P. Vatinium* [On emending Cicero's speeches Pro Sestio and In Vatinium],[19] in which he drew up a *stemma codicum*, the fourth one in time after those of Schlyter (Collins-Schlyter 1827), Zumpt (1831), and Ritschl (Ritschl 1832).[j] Two important innovations are found here. First of all, Madvig derives his three families of manuscripts from a single lost medieval ancestor, already disfigured by lacunas and mechanical errors,[20] and indicates that ancestor with the expression *codex archetypus* [archetype manuscript], which thus takes on for the first time the precise and narrow technical meaning that we attribute to it even today.[21] Second, Madvig explicitly sets himself the aim of using the stemma to reconstruct the readings of the archetype: although the third family has less authority in itself since it is represented only by recent manuscripts, it serves in case of disagreement between the first two families to tip the balance in favor of the one or the other.[22] Thus Ritschl's genealogical requirement is joined here

19. Madvig 1833 (= Madvig 1834: 411–76). In the second edition, Madvig 1887: 333–407, he modified this text and suppressed some parts of the original version, because in the meantime the objections of Karl Halm had convinced him that the tradition should be divided into only two families, not three.

20. Madvig 1833: 7 (= Madvig 1834: 416). Madvig gives examples of such lacunas and errors at 1833: 8n1 (= Madvig 1834: 416n1). In an edition of some of Cicero's speeches he published in 1830, he did not yet trace out any stemmas nor use the term *archetype* but had already written that all the manuscripts of the *Pro Roscio Amerino* are "derived from one not very good manuscript and share the same errors, interpolations, and lacunas" (1834: 118). As we have seen, more and more scholars were beginning to recognize that the derivation of several witnesses from a single ancestor can only be demonstrated by coincidence in lacunas and serious corruptions, not in correct readings, and not even in innovations that can derive from contamination or polygenesis; this conviction is already clear in Madvig, even if it will only be explicitly codified later.

21. Several years later, the expression reappears in Orelli (1837: 2) in the Greek form ἀρχέτυπον; he had already used it occasionally in a more general sense. Then it was picked up by various other Classical philologists and was finally sanctioned by Lachmann (see below, p. 103).

22. Madvig 1833: 22 (= Madvig 1834: 434): "While the individuals [sc. inferior manuscripts] have absolutely no authority, it has already been demonstrated by examples that, especially when they are compared with the best manuscripts from other families, readings can be extracted from them that were found in much older and better manuscripts and in the origin of this lineage, and that when these are found they can be used to restore the authentic text and to adjudicate the disagreement of those most ancient manuscripts of the first and second family which now should rightly prevail."

with Lachmann's mechanical method. Madvig is also fully aware that medieval manuscripts already present not only mechanical corruptions but also intentional alterations to the text, though to a lesser degree than Humanist ones; he considers this fact to be "strange" but nonetheless undeniable[k]—an awareness that Lachmann always lacked.[23]

A few years later, Madvig will give a fuller application of these principles of textual criticism in his famous critical edition of Cicero's *De finibus* with commentary.[24] Here he maintains the distinction of manuscripts into *meliores* [better ones] and *deteriores* [worse ones], which Bremi and Goerenz had already made,[25] but he understands the two families genealogically and not just axiologically; he demonstrates that the manuscripts of *De finibus* are all derived from a single archetype and shows how the *deteriores* too have a function in reconstructing that archetype.[26]

A little later (1841) Hermann Sauppe published his *Epistola critica ad Godofredum Hermannum* [Critical epistle to Gottfried Hermann], in which he explains some of the principles of *recensio* and *emendatio*[l] with exemplary clarity.[27] In this case too the first impulse will probably have come from Orelli and his circle: Sauppe taught at Zurich from 1832 until 1845, in close contact with Orelli and his student and collaborator Johann Georg Baiter.[28]

---

23. Madvig 1833: 10 (= Madvig 1834: 419): "But what I have said must still be explained, namely, that the Parisinus, even if it is the oldest manuscript and as a whole the least interpolated one [. . .], nonetheless in a few passages [. . .] has clearly been interpolated by the substitution of a rash conjecture for a corrupted reading in the archetype—certainly a very strange thing to have happened in that period." In the specific case of this manuscript, the existence of "rash conjectures" is anything but proven. But the important thing is the general criterion. For Lachmann's different attitude, see below, p. 111.

24. Madvig 1869 (1839); I leave out of account the later editions. See in particular, on the concept of archetype, Madvig 1869 (1839): xx–xxi.

25. He cites them himself at Madvig 1869 (1839): xxii. Johann Heinrich Bremi, a student of Wolf's, had published an edition of *De finibus* in 1798 (Bremi 1798). For Goerenz see above, p. 93.

26. Madvig 1869 (1839): xli. But Madvig still had too little faith in the *deteriores:* cf. Schiche 1915: x–xi.

27. Sauppe 1841 = Sauppe 1896: 80–177. Besides the section on *eliminatio descriptorum,* about which I shall speak shortly, see especially the passage on the classification of manuscripts (82: Sauppe is quite aware that this must be based on "shared *errors*," but he recognizes much more clearly than Ritschl, Madvig, and Lachmann that contamination almost always makes this very difficult or impossible); the excellent criteria for using the indirect tradition (111, even if Sauppe does not evaluate some of his particular examples correctly); and the discussion about different kinds of corruptions and the rules for *emendatio* (121–77).

28. Cf. Ziebarth 1910: 148–49.

Sauppe devoted particular attention to the *eliminatio codicum descriptorum*. We have already seen (chap. 1) that excellent examples of this procedure were already produced by Politian and other scholars who followed his teaching in the sixteenth century.[m] Later, Jean Boivin (1663–1726)—a first-class paleographer and Classical philologist, who unfortunately published little in this strictly technical field and was satisfied for the most part to leave the fruits of his own researches unpublished or to supply them to other scholars, and for this reason is still neglected by the historians of philology—demonstrated convincingly in an autograph annotation at the beginning of Parisinus gr. 2036 (tenth century) that the text of Pseudo-Longinus Περὶ ὕψους contained in that manuscript was the source for all the other extant manuscripts (except for two, which contain the so-called *fragmentum Tollianum*): "for where the other manuscripts have a lacuna, whole leaves are missing in this manuscript, exactly two or four, or even more." Boivin also noticed that the apographs had been copied from the Parisinus (formerly Laurentianus) at a time when it was already in bad shape but less so than later: so that they have some usefulness for establishing the text of certain passages.[29] Almost a century later, Schweighäuser, a scholar we have already mentioned for his edition of Epictetus, demonstrated that the Venetus of Athenaeus (Marc. gr. 447, temporarily transported to Paris in the Napoleonic era) is the source of all the other surviving manuscripts: where the Venetus presents material damage, the others have omissions or obviously conjectural stopgaps.[n,30]

These *eliminationes* follow one another at long intervals of time and do not seem to form a continuous scholarly tradition: it is unattested and seems unlikely that Boivin knew the results Politian and his followers had attained, nor that Schweighäuser knew about Boivin (even if on this point more caution is perhaps necessary); and Sauppe, a conscientious and scrupulous scholar, would have mentioned his predecessors in his turn if he had known of them. It is not impossible that other cases of *eliminationes* unknown to me will be indicated in the future and that the series will become more

29. Nicolas Boileau publicized Boivin's discovery, and a little later Zacharias Pearce supplied some further details: cf. Hemmerdinger 1977: 518. Boivin's annotation, of which I have only quoted one phrase, is cited fully by some editors of the Περὶ ὕψους, e.g., Rostagni 1947: xxxix. The article on Boivin in *Nouvelle biographie générale* 1855: 5.479–80 is inadequate. On his conjectures on the *Cesti* of Julius Africanus, of which he started a translation that he did not complete, cf. Vieillefond 1970: 85, 87; on his discovery of a palimpsest, one of the first such discoveries ever, cf. Timpanaro 1980: 249–50.

30. Cf. Schweighäuser 1801–7: i.lxxxviii–ci. Kaibel 1887–90: i.vii–viii does not seem to me to assign Schweighäuser enough importance: he claims that Dindorf, in a later article (Dindorf 1870), was the first to demonstrate that all the other manuscripts are derived from the Venetus. But in fact Schweighäuser's arguments are already conclusive.

crowded, but for now I have the impression that the technique of *eliminatio* was "rediscovered" independently on several occasions—after all, in certain cases one arrives at this technique with relative ease. In any case, even if Sauppe cannot claim the priority that some have awarded him, he can claim to have fully formulated this technique, which had been entirely neglected in times close to his by Bekker, with consequent harm to his edition of the Attic orators, and had always been neglected by Lachmann, as has already been indicated.º He also gave an excellent applicationᵖ by demonstrating that Palat. Heidelberg 88 is the ancestor of all the other manuscripts of the orations of Lysias (except for the *Funeral Oration,* which has a separate tradition), since a lacuna that in the Palatinus is due to the loss of eleven pages recurs in the other manuscripts without any material damage being detectable in them.³¹ To be sure, this very same *Epistola ad Hermannum* and other writings of Sauppe's also contain rash *eliminationes* based not on indisputable evidence but on mere presuppositions;³² Sauppe got carried away with his first success and extended the procedure of *eliminatio* beyond its legitimate limits. But it should not be forgotten that, in the case of the manuscript tradition of Florus, it was he who reacted against the overestimation of the value of the Bambergensis (Bamberg Class. 31 [E.iii. 22]) taken alone.³³ A little later the Dutch scholar Carel Gabriel Cobet went on to show far less caution in his famous *Oratio,* which laid out the program of his future work: though he was a fine expert on the Greek language, he was hyper-analogist as a critic, and regarding manuscript tradition was convinced that the dependence of the *recentiores* on one or two late ancient or medieval manuscripts (which he called *archetypi,* with a usage closer to that of certain Humanists than to Madvig's and then Lachmann's) was not just *one* of the possible cases but was the most frequent (indeed was almost constant) and, what is worse, the most "desirable" one.³⁴ This was the begin-

31. Sauppe 1896: 83–84. Cf. the preface to Baiter-Sauppe 1839–43. Earlier, Bekker had considered codex C (Florence, Biblioteca Medicea Laurentiana: Laur. 57,4), one of the apographs of the Palatinus (Heidelberg, Universitätsbibliothek: Codex Palatinus gr. 88), to be superior to all the other manuscripts of Lysias.

32. Cf. Wilamowitz 1894: 42.

33. Sauppe 1870 = Sauppe 1896: 608–28. Cf. the preface to Malcovati 1938: vi. Only with Malcovati's edition has a fair evaluation of the Bambergensis been achieved; it is certainly the best manuscript (Otto Jahn emphasized it), but it does not deserve to be constantly preferred.

34. Cobet 1847: 26–27, 27n, and 102–37. See esp. 27: "And we hope with some confidence that someday either one manuscript or else very few will supply a complete basis for the recension and emendation of every single author." Similar ideas recur in various later writings of Cobet's. For criticism of this approach cf. Wilamowitz 1982 (1921): 90–91; Kenney 1974: 118–20. Hemmerdinger 1977 contains much interesting material intel-

ning of that tendency toward as it were voluntary *eliminationes,* which, as we shall see, spread in the second half of the nineteenth century and has still left conspicuous traces in Maas's *Textual Criticism.*[q,35]

In the edition of Martial that F. W. Schneidewin published in 1842, one year after Sauppe's *Epistola,* he dedicates the whole third chapter of the Prolegomena (pp. c–cx) to examining "what the kinship relations among the individual manuscripts are, what the families share, finally what the authority and value of each of the individual families is." Nor does Schneidewin stop at the bipartition of the manuscripts into *meliores* and *deteriores,* by now customary: he also distinguishes three families among the *meliores* on the basis of shared corruptions (p. cv). His claim to be the first to give a solid foundation to the textual criticism of Martial (p. c) is justified: the genealogy he established is still valid in its fundamental structure, just as his preference for the Thuaneus (Paris lat. 8071: p. cviii) remains by and large valid.[36]

I hope that my brief exposition makes it sufficiently clear that the scholars I have mentioned did not limit themselves to applying a method that Lachmann had already established but that they must be considered among the founders of that method, alongside of Lachmann and sometimes before him. This is especially true of Ritschl, Madvig, and Sauppe; and we shall see that with regard to Lucretius it is also true of Jacob Bernays.[⁎⁎]

---

ligently discussed, also concerning earlier cases of *eliminatio* (Boivin, Schweighäuser), which I had not noticed; but all in all this essay is too apologetic with regard to Cobet. Kramer 1844–52: 1.liv–lv had warned against too hasty *eliminationes* but was not listened to enough.

35. Cf. esp. Maas 1958 (1927): p. 4, sec. 8 (a) (to which we shall return later, p. 155) and the unsatisfactory discussion of *recentiores, non deteriores* in the "Retrospect 1956" (pp. 52–53), ending with a quotation of Cobet's motto "Comburendi, non conferendi" [They should be incinerated, not investigated]—one piece of evidence among many that Maas understood nothing of Pasquali's work.[r]

36. Cf. Citroni 1975: xxxix n. 1, with further details concerning Schneidewin's already "modern" terminology.

⁎ Cf. n. ⁎⁎ in chap. 2.[r]

Studies on the Text of Lucretius

Lachmann's last two works of textual criticism were his editions of the *Agrimensores* and Lucretius. The first volume of the *Agrimensores* appeared in 1848: Lachmann edited the text but did not provide it with a preface. The second volume did not appear until 1852, when Lachmann was already dead; the complex history of the tradition was explained in it very fully and accurately by his student Friedrich Blume, an excellent investigator of manuscripts (it should be enough to recall his *Iter Italicum*).[1]

Of all the most important Greek and Latin authors, Lucretius was perhaps[a] the most suitable one for applying the canons of the new *ars critica*: only a small number of medieval manuscripts, whose genealogical relations are easy to reconstruct; a mass of Humanist manuscripts that can certainly be neglected without detriment to the *recensio*, even if they do not derive from medieval manuscripts known to us (but today such a derivation seems highly probable).[b,2] For Lucretius too, as for Cicero, the way was indicated by Orelli and Madvig. In 1827 Orelli referred briefly to the fact that all the manuscripts of Lucretius are derived from a single ancestor;[3] in 1832 Madvig confirmed this hypothesis and noticed the particularly close relation between the *schedae Gottorpianae* and one of the two Vossiani, the one that Lachmann would later call the Quadratus.[4] But it was above all starting in 1845 that Classical philologists focused their attention and rivalry on Lucretius. In that year Lachmann began to work on his edition, which saw the

---

1. Blume-Lachmann-Rudorff 1848–52. A. Rudorff was Professor of Law at Berlin.

2. On the Humanist manuscripts, see below, pp. 108–9, 111–12.

3. Orelli 1827: 86n. Orelli suggested doubtfully that an exception needed to be made for the *fragmentum Gudianum* (i.e., the Gottorpianae, now in Copenhagen, collated in the seventeenth century by Marquard Gude: Gl. Kgl. S. 211 2°). But there was in fact no reason to make this exception, as Madvig demonstrated: cf. the following note.

4. Madvig 1832 = Madvig 1887: 248–62.

light in 1850;[5] and in that very same year, at the initiative of Ritschl, Bonn
University established a competition for a study on the text of Lucretius and
the criteria for a new edition. The winner was a student of Ritschl's, Jacob
Bernays; his dissertation was published in *Rheinisches Museum* in 1847.[6]
And in the meantime, in 1846, another young scholar, Hugo Purmann, had
dealt with the same problems; he had studied with Ambrosch and Schneider in Breslau but was influenced above all by Madvig's writings on textual
criticism.[7]

In the preface to his Lucretius, Lachmann refers to the works of Purmann and Bernays with haughty condescension: "Once Johann Nicolaus
Madvig, an extremely erudite man, had indicated the proper method, two
very well trained youths, Hugo Purmann of Silesia and Jacob Bernays of
Hamburg, [. . .] worked with great energy and some success on evaluating
the evidence for improving the text of this poem [. . .]. But although they in-
vested their labor in this subject in a way that was no doubt quite praiseworthy, nonetheless, if I may speak the truth, they did not seem to contribute anything to it as a whole for me, since some of the things they said were
ones of which I was already fully cognizant, while other things they either
left out or else mixed up with errors and thereby contaminated, since they
were young men insufficiently experienced in recognizing Lucretius's peculiar talent" (Lachmann 1850b: 4). And he absolves himself from any obligation to cite them in the rest of his work, justifying this refusal by his habitual disdain for bibliographical minutiae: "Therefore my agreement with
them in certain matters will make it easy to tell when I think they are right:
but I prefer not to indicate everything in detail so as not to burden my readers" (1850b: 4). With the same haughty tone he attributed to himself the
merit of having been the first to adopt the term *archetype* in a technical sense,
although in fact, as we have seen, this was due to Madvig, and Madvig had
already been followed by Purmann and Bernays in this usage.[c,8]

5. Lachmann 1850a, 1850b. See Hertz 1851: 139–46 on Lachmann's first idea in the
summer of 1845 and on the various phases of the development of his work.

6. Bernays 1847. On Bernays's education and earliest works, Usener 1902: 395 is still
interesting. On his personality in general, see Gomperz 1905: 106–25. The most lucid and
at the same time most passionate appreciation of Bernays is Momigliano 1975: 1.127–58.

7. Purmann 1846. Purmann recalls his teachers in his autobiography on p. 70; the influence of Madvig (not only of his study of Lucretius, Madvig 1832, but also of his preface to *De finibus*, Madvig 1869 [1839]) is evident, for example, on pp. 6–7, 15, 19.

8. On Madvig, see above, p. 97. Purmann (1846) uses the expression *codex archetypus* on p. 7 ("All the manuscripts we know of until now . . . derived from one and the
same archetype manuscript") and then many other times; Bernays 1847: 570 n. ** (in the

In fact Purmann's work and Bernays's differ in originality and completeness. Purmann proposed several shrewd conjectures but[d] did nothing more
for the classification of the manuscripts than add some further confirma-
tions (not all of them sure ones) to what Madvig had already noticed, namely,
that all the manuscripts are derived from an archetype and that the Quadratus and the Schedae are particularly closely related.[9] Purmann had no clear
idea of the importance of the other Vossianus (Lachmann's Oblongus) for
various reasons, including the lack of a reliable collation, and he even inclined to classify it among the *deteriores,* since he was misled by its real affinities with the Italici.[10] The only thing that was really new, even if it was
still expressed imprecisely, was an observation regarding the script of the archetype or pre-archetype, which Lachmann neglected.[11]

Bernays too started out from Madvig, but he studied the problem in much[e]
greater depth than Purmann did and succeeded in designing a stemma that
is basically correct:[12]

---

stemma we reproduce on p. 105). But the fact that Lachmann stated at the beginning of
his preface, "that exemplar, the ARCHETYPE of all the others (that is how I am accustomed
to call it)," made people believe in general that he had been the first person to use the word
in this sense (see, e.g., Pasquali 1952a [1934]: 3). Cf. also below, p. 113.

9. Purmann 1846: 7–23. I use Lachmann's designation *Schedae* to indicate the totality made up of the Gottorpiani, now at Copenhagen (Gl. Kgl. S. 211 2°), and Vindobonensis MS 107, which were particularly studied by Purmann 1846: 15–16 after Siebelis
1844: 788 had drawn attention to them. But it was only in 1857 that it was noticed that,
although fols. 9–14 of the Vindobonensis belong to the same manuscript from which the
Gottorpiani leaves were detached, the following fols. 15–18 derive from another manuscript (Goebel-Goebel 1857); cf. Diels 1923–24: xix, who designates the former as *V* and
the latter as *U.* In any case, I neglect this distinction here, both because it has no influence
on the *stemma codicum* (*G* + *V* and *U* both belong to the same family as *Q*) and because
it was still unknown to the philologists I am discussing (Madvig, Purmann, Bernays, Lachmann).

10. Purmann 1846: 16: "Given Haverkamp's lack of consistency in indicating variant
readings, it is not yet clear to me to which family of manuscripts Lugd. 1 [i.e., the Ob-
longus] is to be assigned, to the genuine and more sound ones or to the more recent and
inferior ones. Nonetheless, as matters now stand, I would prefer to assign it to the inferior ones."

11. See Appendix B, n. 9.

12. Bernays 1847: 570n. Lugd. 1 and 2 are the manuscripts that Lachmann will call
Oblongus and Quadratus; Memm. is Lambinus's *codex Memmianus* (which seems to be
identical to the Quadratus: Bernays 1847: 546, 550 already inclined toward this identifi-
cation); Poggianus is the ancestor of the Italici. On the Gottorpiani leaves and the Vindobonenses see above, n. 9.

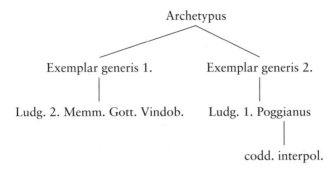

One can disagree (and, as is well known,[f] scholars still disagree) about where to assign the Poggianus, the ancestor of the Italici; and one can point out that Bernays did not demonstrate with conclusive arguments that the Quadratus and Schedae are both derived from the *exemplar generis 1* [exemplar of the first family], even if in fact it is entirely certain;[13] but everything else is unexceptionable. And unlike Purmann, Bernays fully recognized that the Lugdunensis 1 (the Oblongus) was certainly no less valuable than the Quadratus.

Bernays's article has exerted very little influence. Until the first version of this study of mine, everyone attributed[g] to Lachmann the merit of having been the first to reconstruct the genealogy of the manuscripts of Lucretius.[14] Even Usener, who appreciated Bernays's extraordinary brilliance more than

13. He relied only on the groups of verses of books 1, 2, and 5, which are lacking in their correct location in the Quadratus and Schedae and are added at the end: according to him, this was due to an error of the copyist of the subarchetype from which the Quadratus and Schedae were derived, *exemplar generis 1* (Bernays 1847: 534, 571–72). In reality, as Lachmann went on to demonstrate (see below, n. 19), *the archetype* had *already* suffered the displacement of four leaves after the Oblongus had been copied from it; hence the Quadratus and Schedae could have derived from the archetype after it had been damaged in this way. All the same, the existence of the *exemplar generis 1* is demonstrated with absolute certainty by the many corruptions shared by the Quadratus and Schedae against the Oblongus (it should be enough to cite 1.62, 104, 117; 2.217, etc.). On this point many recent editors (Bailey, Leonard and Smith, Martin, Büchner) express themselves in a very confused manner; not even Diels 1923–24: xvi is quite satisfactory. This is a methodologically interesting case, since it shows that lacunas that can derive from material damage (loss of leaves, holes, etc.) suffered later by the ancestor have no value as conjunctive errors (to use Paul Maas's terminology). As far as I know, this point is not to be found in manuals of textual criticism (cf. also below, pp. 173–74).

14. The only editor later than Lachmann who refers with due consideration to Bernays's article is Munro 1886: 1.20.

anyone else in the nineteenth century, did not think it appropriate to include his dissertation on Lucretius in the collection of Bernays's articles he edited "since it has been rendered obsolete by Lachmann."[15] Lachmann and Bernays themselves contributed to this unjust oblivion: the former by the condescending reference we have cited, which gave the impression that Bernays had only glimpsed in a confused manner what Lachmann had recognized as clear as daylight; the latter by his excessive modesty, which led him to admit fully Lachmann's superiority.[16]

It would certainly be unjustified to accuse Lachmann of plagiarism. A letter of his to Moriz Haupt makes clear that he had decided that he would read Bernays's article in its entirety only after he had finished the first draft of his preface to Lucretius to his own satisfaction,[17] and there is no reason to doubt that he did just this. But what matters here is not a dispute about chronological priority but rather a comparison between the one scholar's results and the other's; and the comparison is not entirely favorable to Lachmann. Lachmann's mistake does not consist in his having made use of Bernays's work, but rather in his not having made sufficient use of it.[h]

As a matter of fact, Lachmann went beyond Bernays in two regards: *eliminatio lectionum singularium* and reconstructing the archetype's external form. Bernays did not think of *eliminatio lectionum singularium,* just as his teacher Ritschl had not thought of it in the case of Dionysius of Halicarnassus. Although Bernays understood clearly that the Schedae were not copied from any of the surviving manuscripts, in practice he reduced *recensio* to the two Vossiani alone: "Therefore the two Lugdunenses are the basis upon which alone the textual criticism of Lucretius rests today" (Bernays 1847: 570). Lachmann, on the contrary, saw that the mechanical criterion could be applied to Lucretius, just as to the New Testament, so that the agreement of the Oblongus with the Schedae against the Quadratus and

15. Usener in Bernays 1885: v. In fact, Usener added, "and it is easily accessible for the specialist." But as we have seen, among specialists too no one has acknowledged Bernays's just merits.

16. This excessive modesty inspires Bernays's preface to his Teubner edition of Lucretius, Bernays 1852.

17. Cf. Lachmann 1892: 180; Wolfgang Schmid has drawn my attention to this passage. All the same it is not free from ambiguity: Lachmann himself says that he has given a first glance at Bernays's article. So the observations of Kenney 1974: 107 and nn. 3–4 are justified: he also recalls that Lachmann's attitude to Bernays must have been influenced by the very strong hostility between Lachmann and Ritschl, Bernays's teacher. Nonetheless, I believe that the essential point, in scholarly terms, not moral ones, is the one I make immediately below in the text.

with the Quadratus against the Schedae gives us with certainty the reading of the archetype. It is true that the lack of accurate collations of the Schedae meant that he was only able to make a very limited use of this criterion; even today, indeed, *eliminatio lectionum singularium* is not very useful in practical terms for Lucretius, both because the Schedae are lacking for a large part of the text and hence *recensio* is limited to the Oblongus and the Quadratus, and because almost all the *lectiones singulares* are obvious errors that in any case would not have misled any editors.[18] All the same, there is no doubt that from the point of view of methodology Lachmann was ahead of Bernays in this regard.

Lachmann's ability to calculate the number of lines of every page of the archetype—and consequently the number of pages too—was based on the length of certain passages that were transposed or damaged.[19] It was above all this reconstruction that impressed his contemporaries: "And where is

18. For a long time I have been hoping that some scholar would determine the real contribution of *eliminatio lectionum singularium* to constituting the text of Lucretius. Now this has been done by Alberti 1979: 60–61, and the result is just what might have been expected: "the *lectiones singulares* are made up for the most part of quite banal errors which can be eliminated without recourse to mechanical criteria." On the other hand, in about twenty cases a *lectio singularis* supplies what is certainly the right reading, and polygenesis of errors must have taken place (according to Alberti 1979: 61; but in some passages I think one must hypothesize contamination or, even more, a correct conjecture on the part of a copyist). Of course, this does not imply a devaluation of the method of *eliminatio lectionum singularium,* which has proven its practical utility for many other texts. And in the text of Lucretius itself there is one passage, not mentioned by Alberti, in which the method functions usefully: 3.1, where the agreement of the Oblongus with the Schedae serves to confirm the correctness of the initial interjection O, missing in the Quadratus (the concept of *lectio singularis* also includes what might be called "zero readings," i.e., omissions): cf. Timpanaro 1978: 135–93. In this case Lachmann accepted the bad conjecture E and thereby failed to make fruitful use of his own "method."

19. What is involved are not only the passages transposed in the Quadratus and Schedae (these alone would have no probative value, since the displacement could have occurred in the subarchetype from which the Quadratus and Schedae derive: see above, n. 13) but also the transposition of 4.323–47 before 299–322 and the mutilation of 1.1068–75 to which the lacuna after 1.1094 corresponds. This damage is found in all the manuscripts, hence it goes back to the archetype; and since it is explained on the hypothesis that each of the pages of the archetype had twenty-six lines, it follows with great probability that the transpositions of the Quadratus and Schedae too, which presuppose the same number of lines per page, go back to the archetype (from which the Oblongus had already been copied), not to the subarchetype, as Bernays had supposed; see the note cited just above. On this point too some of the recent editors (Ernout, Martin) are anything but clear.

this manuscript described with such precision? It was destroyed or lost; and yet there is not a single point in the description that is not demonstrated with almost mathematical certainty." [20] Nowadays this kind of certainty has been quite shaken: doubts have arisen regarding the exact number of the pages and the script of the archetype; above all, scholars have come to realize that they cannot use the reconstruction of the archetype for practical purposes (that is, to justify transpositions of whole passages) as hastily as Lachmann supposed.[21] All the same, the reconstruction remains valid in its essentials and is a fine proof of Lachmann's acumen.

But Lachmann's explanation regarding the actual genealogy of the manuscripts is much more confused and contradictory than Bernays's. The most important contradiction has not yet been noticed, as far as I know: it regards the place in the stemma to assign the ancestor of the Italici. As we have already suggested, this question was controversial for a long time and probably will never be finally resolved:[i] scholars have disagreed—and they will continue to disagree—about whether[j] the ancestor of the Italici constitutes a third branch of the tradition alongside the Oblongus and the shared ancestor of the Quadratus and the Schedae,[22] or whether it was derived from a subarchetype from which the Oblongus also descends,[23] or whether, as now seems almost certain,[k] it was even derived from the Oblongus.[24] But

20. Hertz 1851: 142. Cf. Haupt 1911 (1854): 534.

21. See Merrill 1913: 227–29, 234–35. Doubts about the number of pages and lines were already expressed by Chatelain 1908: vii; cf. Ernout 1948 (1920): xv–xviii, but this is barbed by nationalistic animosity. A more balanced and precise judgment can be found in Goold 1958. For the script of the archetype, see below, Appendix B.

22. This is the view of Martin 1969 (1934); Smith in Leonard-Smith 1942: 114; Bailey 1947: 1.42–43. According to Büchner 1956: 201 (= Büchner 1964. 1.121–23), the ancestor of the Italici was in fact independent of the archetype to which both the Oblongus and the shared source of the Quadratus and the Schedae go back. But his hypothesis has been contested with good arguments by Pizzani 1959: 82–87 (cf. 54–78) and, even more effectively, by Schmid 1967: 475. A similar hypothesis had already been suggested by Chiari 1924, republished with an addendum in Chiari 1961: 3.1–27. Chiari 1961: 23–24 is right to defend his article against one unfounded objection raised by Pasquali 1952a (1934): 112n4; but I think there is some validity to Pasquali's other objection, that Chiari too easily considered to be tradition what in the Humanistic manuscripts "can derive either from contamination or from conjecture," especially from conjecture (ibid.).

23. As has been seen, this was Bernays's opinion; it was taken up again by Birt 1913: 22. It is strange that it has enjoyed so little success. Whoever denies that the Italici are derived from the Oblongus must consider their descent from a shared subarchetype to be the most obvious solution, given the undeniable affinity between them. We shall see that Lachmann inclined toward this kind of solution, but incoherently.

24. This hypothesis, already maintained by Diels in his edition (Diels 1923–24: xxi–xxiii) and thereafter, more succinctly, by R. Heinze, H. Mewaldt, and U. Pizzani, has been

Lachmann does not opt for one of these solutions (as Bernays had done) or admit he was uncertain, but instead slips from the first to the second in the course of his explanation without noticing it. He begins by saying that three copies were derived from the archetype, the Oblongus, the ancestor of the Italici, and the ancestor of the Quadratus and the Schedae.[25] In this case we would have one of those tripartite stemmas that notoriously constitute a very rare piece of good luck in the criticism of ancient and medieval texts:

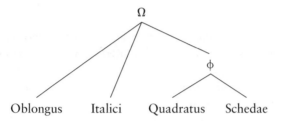

In this case the mechanical method would be quite fruitful: the agreement of two branches would give us the reading of the archetype with certainty;[26] we would only remain in doubt if each of the three branches presented a different reading, but in practice this happens only very rarely.

But just one page later, although Lachmann still speaks of three independent apographs, he characterizes the Italici in the following way: "they are extremely similar to our Oblongus in every regard and yet they are not derived from the Oblongus; for sometimes they disagree with it and go together with the Quadratus, and indeed this happens in readings that no one could have arrived at by conjecture" (1850b: 5). While the derivation of the Italici from the Oblongus is decisively excluded, no reason is given why both the Oblongus and the ancestor of the Italici could not depend on a shared subarchetype (as we have seen, Bernays's thesis was just this). The good (and, according to Lachmann, not conjectural) readings that the Italici share with the Quadratus might indeed go back directly to the archetype, but they

---

revived with new arguments by K. Müller 1973 and, even more analytically, by Cini 1976. And indeed it seems to be the most probable hypothesis. All the same, it does not seem to be possible to perform an *eliminatio descriptorum* "to a T" like those of Politian, Boivin, Schweighäuser, and Sauppe, already mentioned by us. And so it is not surprising that the hypothesis of the independence of the Italici keeps coming up again: cf. now Flores 1978: 21–37 (attractively polemical and intelligent but, I think, rather lacking in arguments).

25. Lachmann 1850b: 3: "From that [sc. archetype . . .] many have been derived from three copies, as far as we can tell." 4: "But from those three apographs," and he goes on to speak about each one.

26. Except, of course, for the cases of a disturbed tradition noted by Alberti (cf. above, n. 18).

might also have been found in a subarchetype, which the copyist of the Poggianus copied faithfully while the copyist of the Oblongus committed *errores singulares*. For the moment, Lachmann does not consider this possibility; but his reference to the extraordinary similarity (in correct readings or
only in errors?) between the Italici and the Oblongus seems to indicate that,
like Bernays, he was already inclining unconsciously toward the hypothesis
of a bipartite tradition.[l,27]

For the moment this is a vague and rather uncertain suggestion; but it becomes an explicit declaration on page 9, where Lachmann writes concerning the norms for reconstructing the readings of the archetype:[m] "It annoys
me to have to speak too much about matters of no usefulness whatsoever:
the whole tradition of the original reading must be derived from the Voss-
ian manuscripts, except that sometimes the Italici cancel out the Oblongus's
testimony, and once in a while, as I said,[28] the Schedae diminish the Quadratus's authority" (1850b: 9). Here the only function assigned to the Italici is
to eliminate the Oblongus's *errores singulares*, just as the Schedae serve in
parallel to eliminate the Quadratus's *errores singulares*. Without saying so
and, apparently, without[n] noticing it, Lachmann has slipped from the hypothesis of a tripartite tradition to that of a bipartite one, one family represented by the Oblongus and the Italici, the other by the Quadratus and the
Schedae—just as Bernays had maintained. If Lachmann had adhered firmly
to the tripartite scheme he would have had to say that the Italici "sometimes
annul the Oblongus's authority, sometimes the Quadratus's and the Schedae'," and not the Oblongus's alone.

Once again we read a little later (p. 10), "I say this. Wherever it is clear
from trustworthy testimonies compared with one another that there were
two readings in the archetype (and this is the case whenever the Oblongus
and the Quadratus disagree with one another and it is clear either from the
Schedae or from the Italici, either manuscripts or printed editions, that nei-

---

27. Canfora 1964: 612 has drawn attention to this passage. But perhaps it is an exaggeration to say that "Lachmann lacked in part the very concept of subarchetype and the
ability to identify it and make use of it in constituting the text" (even if the words "in part"
do well to lessen the force of the claim). When he wrote the final version of his preface,
Lachmann had certainly read Bernays's article with its stemma, in which the "concept of
subarchetype" was quite clear. What is instead the case (and the observations of ours that
follow will demonstrate it) is that Lachmann slipped from one stemma without subarchetypes to another one with subarchetypes without noticing it.

28. The words "as I said" refer to Lachmann 1850b: 8: "None of these Schedae, neither the Haunienses nor the Vindobonenses, have any authority of their own except when
they sometimes agree with the Oblongus."

ther of them is in error), then judgment must be used for constituting the text, nor can it be said with as much certainty which reading is older, as there can be disagreement about which one is true or closer to the truth" (Lachmann 1850b: 10). Here too Lachmann is presupposing a bipartite tradition: he says that one must have recourse to *iudicium* every time a reading attested by the Oblongus and the Italici is opposed by another reading attested by the Quadratus and the Schedae. If so, then the Oblongus and the Italici would be copies of one and the same subarchetype.

For the practical purposes of constituting the text, the problem of the Italici is not very important, even if they were independent of the Oblongus, as now seems entirely excluded:° on this point I think we must agree in any caseᴾ with Luigi Castiglioni.²⁹ But the contradiction into which Lachmann fell confirms that he was not very interested in the history of the text as such. He would probably have noticed the contradiction if he had drawn up a stemma, following the examples of Ritschl and Bernays; but we already know that he avoided such didactic expedients, and thus he remained a victim of the very obscurity he sought.³⁰

But there is another oddity in the passage cited last. Every time the two families disagreed with one another, Lachmann supposed that there was a double reading in the archetype. Thus he did not admit that the copyists of the two subarchetypes could have, I will not say voluntarily altered the text, but even fallen into psychological errors of a certain magnitude, for example, substituting one word for another similar one. As Pasquali has justly observed, this was a consequence of Lachmann's absolutely mechanical conception of the transmission of texts in the Middle Ages: "He had so low an opinion of the copyists' activity of thought and half-conscious transformation that he immediately concluded that the archetype had a double reading wherever the copies disagreed and the one reading could not be eliminated by this mechanical procedure."³¹ Later it was demonstrated that there really

---

29. Castiglioni 1937: 558, 561.

30. One might perhaps suppose that, before reading Bernays's article carefully, Lachmann had become convinced that the tradition of Lucretius was tripartite, and that reading Bernays then made him incline toward the other hypothesis. But it remains strange that he did not revise his whole exposition to make it coherent. Probably the preface to Lucretius was written hastily.

31. Pasquali 1929: 427. In the corresponding passage of Pasquali 1952a (1934): 112, he seems to change his mind. In someone who knew the German language as perfectly as Pasquali did, the stylistic harshness of the phrase "der Denk- und halbbewusst umgestaltenden Tätigkeit der Schreiber" [the copyists' activity of thought and half-conscious transformation] is strange, even if the meaning is clear (conscious and semi-conscious changes

were double readings in many archetypes, and *perhaps* in Lucretius's too, but on the basis of completely different arguments.[32]

And another peculiarity needs to be pointed out. We saw (chap. 3) that Lachmann's distrust for the *docti Italiani,* those insidious interpolators, was deeply rooted and that he tended to neglect *a priori* the manuscripts they transcribed. In the case of Lucretius, unlike that of other authors, such a distrust would have been legitimate, and indeed we have seen that it ended up prevailing. But in Lachmann it is far less strong than we might have expected. To be sure, in the course of his explanation he does "declass" the Poggianus from being a direct copy of the archetype to being a copy of a subarchetype; but he never supposes that it might be a *descriptus* (indeed, as has been seen, he excludes this possibility from the very beginning, and on this point he never belies himself), and he assigns it a function in reconstructing the archetype, even if only a subsidiary one. And even after that initial passage we have already quoted, he asserts that the Humanist manuscripts do indeed have "many [. . .] conjectural emendations" but also other passages "which are less emended, that is, which better preserve the reading of the ancient archetype" (1850b: 6). Must we suppose—but the question will have to be studied further—that Lachmann might perhaps have been influenced by Madvig's less negative attitude toward the *recentiores* of Cicero or Jahn's toward those of Persius (see below, pp. 125f.)? In constituting the text, Lachmann went on to take account almost exclusively of the Oblongus and Quadratus, as was only right; but one can say that he presents himself in his preface, paradoxically, as an almost too ardent believer in *recentiores non deteriores!*[q]

In any case, Lachmann's preface to Lucretius contains the results he arrived at in the course of studying that specific manuscript tradition and not a general methodological exposition, such as is found in contrast in Madvig's and Sauppe's writings, which have already been recalled, and to a certain extent also in Lachmann's own preface to the New Testament. On the first page of his book Pasquali has characterized perfectly the tone of detached superiority that one senses in Lachmann's preface to Lucretius; but it is not with the same degree of justice, I believe, that he then went on to say that Lachmann explained the method in this preface "in the most com-

---

introduced by copyists into the text). But a typographical error or the omission of some words is quite unlikely.

32. Pasquali 1929: 498. For Lucretius cf. Diels 1923–24: xxiv–xxvii (but almost all the cases Diels cites are anything but certain), and more recently, but quite unsuccessfully, Büchner 1964: 1.128–32 (refuted by Schmid 1967: 476–78). But "archetypes with variants" is another question that ought to be reexamined from top to bottom. Cf. below, Appendix C, n. 51.

plete way and in the most didactic form" (Pasquali 1952a [1934]: 5). The very contradictions we have noted in the course of our exposition make such a "didactic" quality very doubtful![r] And it cannot even be said that "Lachmann based his method upon the premise that always and in every case the tradition of every author goes back to a single exemplar already disfigured with errors and lacunas, what he called an archetype" (1952a [1934]: 15). Lachmann never formulated such a general theory, nor, as far as I know, did any of his contemporaries. I suppose it was the large number of texts in which all the manuscripts agree in errors and lacunas[s] that gradually convinced Classical philologists that there had been an archetype in all cases.[33]

Of course, the importance of Lachmann's commentary on Lucretius is not at all limited to the preface—on the contrary, the commentary is superior to the preface if we do not wish to assume as a criterion of judgment only the "method" but to consider instead its results.[t] In a large number of cases, Lachmann knew how to perform extremely well not only the *recensio* of the text of Lucretius but also its *emendatio*,[34] even if the *interpolator philosophus* [philosophical interpolator] he hypothesized never existed,[35] and even if Munro was not mistaken in observing that other conjecturers were superior to him in *curiosa felicitas* [success that seems intuitive but in fact is painstaking] But above all, Lachmann brought together in his commentary an extraordinary quantity of new observations on the grammar and orthography of the Latin language[36] and made an enormous contribu-

33. Blass 1892: 281 still considered the derivation of all the manuscripts from an archetype as only one of the possible cases.

34. Excellent conjectures are, for example, *alia* at 1.665, *diri* at 2.421, *parcat* at 2.660 (680), *consequë . . . redeunt* at 5.679. Lachmann also collected the indirect tradition and used it very well, except in a few cases.

35. G. Müller 1958 and 1959 have tried to revive this hypothesis. K. Müller 1975 adheres to it as well: hence his many deletions, which are always ingenious but, in my judgment, too numerous. The problem would deserve a more detailed discussion; but my own view is that, even if in many cases the hypothesis of an original text left incomplete by its author, with passages not yet definitively put into their proper location, "doublets" not yet eliminated, etc., has demonstrated itself to be little more than a convenient expedient for shirking the responsibility of constituting a reliable text, in the case of the *De rerum natura* what we know about its incompleteness and its posthumous publication makes that hypothesis still quite legitimate—without considering that it is characteristic of Lucretius's style to repeat his verses, to retrace his steps, in a certain way. This does not justify a hyperconservative mode of criticism, but it ought to counsel caution.

36. The most celebrated of these observations is "Lachmann's law" (1850b: 54, on Lucretius 1.805), according to which verbs of the type *făcio–făctus* are opposed to those of the type *ăgo–āctus,* as is made clear by their compounds (*effectus* but *exactus*): cf. Leumann 1977: 114. Starting from Mommsen's drastic negative judgment, the question

tion to our knowledge of the linguistic and prosodic peculiarities of the archaic poets: especially for Ennius and Lucilius his achievement is in a certain sense analogous, even if of smaller dimensions, than Ritschl's for Plautus in the same period.[37] In this regard Lachmann's commentary on Lucretius is still alive and valid.

---

whether Lachmann had an adequate knowledge and understanding of the thought of Epicurus and Lucretius has been much discussed: cf. Kenney 1974: 108 and n. 6. Probably he did not, and certainly his commentary does not indicate that he did. But we must consider that, with extremely rare exceptions regarding commentaries to individual books of the *De rerum natura,* until now it has been almost impossible to find a commentator or editor of Lucretius endowed in equal measure with abilities in the fields of philology and linguistics on the one hand and in philosophical interpretation on the other.

37. He also undertook an edition of Lucilius; interrupted by his death, it was completed and published by Vahlen 1876.

7

What Really Belongs to Lachmann

Let us briefly recapitulate the results we have attained.

Ordinarily, when reference is made to "Lachmann's method," what is meant is a complex of criteria for *recensio*. As we have seen, a number of different Classical philologists contributed to its formulation.

1. *The rejection of the vulgate and the requirement that the manuscripts not merely be consulted from time to time but be used as the foundation of the edition.* We have seen that this point was already clear to Bentley, and even more so to Ernesti and Wolf. Lachmann's merits consisted in his return to insisting on it after Gottfried Hermann had caused it to be almost forgotten and also in his application of it to the criticism of the New Testament, where nonscientific reasons had delayed its application, even if in that same field it had been theorized lucidly in the eighteenth century.[a]

2. *The distrust for manuscripts of the Humanist period.* The predecessor for Lachmann's distrust (much reduced, as we have seen, in the preface to Lucretius)[b] was Scaliger in particular (and earlier Politian and Vettori).

3. *The reconstruction of the history of the text and particularly of the genealogical relations that link the extant manuscripts.* This is usually considered to be an[c] essential characteristic of "Lachmann's method," yet I believe that I have demonstrated that Lachmann's original contribution in precisely this regard was very limited and uncertain.[d] The true founders of the genealogical classification of manuscripts are Schlyter (in a field different from Classical philology),[e] Zumpt, Madvig, and above all Ritschl and Bernays, who concretely fulfilled the requirement to which Bengel had given expression. In particular, for the derivation of all the manuscripts of a work from a single archetype we must go back even further, to Erasmus and Scaliger; and, for the technical term *archetype* in the specific sense of a lost medieval or late ancient[f] ancestor, to Madvig. In the procedure of *eliminatio codicum descriptorum*, the scholars who distinguished themselves were, after Politian, above all Boivin, Schweighäuser,[g] and Sauppe. The first history of a text in antiquity was attempted by Wolf in his *Prolegomena ad Homerum*.[h]

4. *The formulation of criteria permitting a mechanical determination (without recourse to* iudicium*) of which reading goes back to the archetype.* This is Lachmann's most genuine[i] contribution, even if his debt to Bengel and, nearer in time, to Madvig[j] must be acknowledged.

It might be objected that we have committed a sophism to Lachmann's detriment by analyzing the method in this way into its various components and indicating the "precursors" for each one, and that his genius consisted precisely in uniting these isolated procedures into a synthesis and making them serve the purpose of a rigorous *recensio.* This is not a negligible objection: many other discoveries and theories in various sciences have arisen from the combination of principles and techniques that were already known individually, and this "combination" has often been a creative act of high value. There is no doubt that tracing out genealogies of manuscripts, even if in a masterly way, but then not making use of them for the *recensio*, as Ritschl and Bernays had done, remains sterile for the purposes of the critical edition, even if it is fruitful for the history of the text conceived as an episode of cultural history.

And yet we must insist upon two points, not out of a narrow-minded taste for diminishing Lachmann's work but in order better to attribute to each scholar his own role:

1. The first to make use of the *stemma codicum* in order to reconstruct the archetype was not Lachmann but Madvig; and if in the case of Bengel we must speak of a mere project that was not yet fulfilled, one cannot say the same of Madvig (cf. above, pp. 97–98).
2. Perhaps more out of impatience than because of a true lack of aptitude, Lachmann himself remained strangely unable to reconstruct those genealogies of manuscripts which were the indispensable prerequisite for *eliminatio lectionum singularium:* he needed to make use of genealogies traced out by others, and his preface to Lucretius shows us how difficult this was for him, so much so that he does not notice that he contradicts himself within a few pages.[k]

But at the same time as we reduce the dimensions of Lachmann's figure and acknowledge the claims of other Classical philologists who cooperated with him or preceded him in certain fundamental points, we must explain the reasons for which his fame as a textual critic[l] has ended up obscuring that of all the others.[1] No doubt various inferior reasons contributed toward

---

1. But this process happened gradually, and there was no lack of scholars who continued to recall the merits of some of Lachmann's contemporaries, even if only incidentally: e.g., Boeckh 1886: 205 recalls Sauppe together with Lachmann; Blass 1892 (1886):

producing this result: Lachmann's oracular tone, which ended up creating around him an atmosphere of veneration and "untouchability," as later around Wilamowitz; the tendency—sincere and affectionate but too exclusive—to glorify the master on the part of certain students and friends, above all Moriz Haupt.[2] We have also recalled the impression produced upon his contemporaries by a fact whose importance is all in all only secondary—the calculation of the number of pages and lines of the archetype of Lucretius. But there were also more serious and fundamental reasons for this development. Whereas[m] editorial textual criticism was only one of many activities for a Ritschl or a Madvig—Madvig was justly celebrated above all for his conjectural emendations in the field of Latin prose, to say nothing of his innovative historical and linguistic writings; Ritschl studied all the aspects of Plautine philology, and in particular prosody and metrics—this was the activity to which Lachmann primarily dedicated himself starting from his earliest years and to which therefore his name was linked. And above all, as we have shown, Lachmann was the one who aimed in the clearest and most immediate way at the practical goal of reconstructing the archetype without wasting time on problems of the history of the tradition—a limit, as we have said, but also a strength.[n] He was a great simplifier, with all the virtues and vices this brings with it. The very one-sidedness with which he separated *recensio* from interpretation, though mistaken in itself, had a pedagogical function: it made a powerful contribution toward recalling scholars' attention to the requirement to give critical editions a solid documentary basis (a requirement that other Classical philologists had expressed in a way that was more complex and balanced, but for that very reason less harshly ef-

255–56 and Birt 1913: 16 praise Sauppe 1841; Wilamowitz 1894: 42 cites Lachmann and Madvig next to one another. See also Vitelli 1962: 11. I would say that it was Ritschl whose merits in this field scholars failed to recognize more than anyone else's; even Ribbeck, in his fine biography of Ritschl (Ribbeck 1879), does not give sufficient prominence to his importance for the methodology of textual criticism.

2. See esp. Haupt 1836 and 1911 (1854); passages from the latter were quoted by Belger 1879 before its full publication. Other somewhat too exclusive glorifiers of Lachmann were Hertz, Vahlen 1893, and Leo 1893 = Leo 1960: 2.415–31 (but Leo admitted that Haupt's words about Lachmann were never "characterizing but always purely admiring and venerating ones": Leo 1893: 4 = Leo 1960: 2.416). How much effort it cost German Classical philology to free itself from the "cult" of Lachmann is indicated by Wilamowitz 1982 (1921): 132: "The impact of his personality and speech on his hearers was so overwhelming that they were sometimes paralysed and sometimes tempted into grotesque attempts to copy him. We have to free ourselves from his leading-strings, but only by first surrendering willingly to him, as he himself prescribed." And Wilamowitz had not been a student of Lachmann's, and belonged to a generation that was already remote in time from him.

fective):° *primum recensere* [Do the *recensio* first]! Although Lachmann's natural talent as a Classical philologist was less acute and profound than that of some of his contemporaries (Gottfried Hermann, Ritschl, Boeckh, Karl Otfried Müller) and although he tended more toward a certain dogmatism than they did,ᵖ he still deserves a place of considerable prominence in the history of nineteenth-century Classical scholarship because of his salutary insistence on the problem of *recensio*. And we will be able to continue to speak of "Lachmann's method," even if we will have to use this expression as an abbreviation and, as it were, a symbol, rather than as a historically accurate expression.

Textual Criticism and Linguistics, and Their Crises at the End of the Nineteenth and in the Twentieth Century

Already on one occasion (pp. 86–88) we have pointed to a parallel between the methods of textual criticism and those of historical-comparative linguistics. Now we must linger a bit more on this subject, not for a mere ostentation of interdisciplinarity but because the comparison really can help explain the difficulties that the application of Lachmann's method soon encountered and certain hostilities in principle to the method itself.[a]

There is an undeniable affinity between the method with which the Classical philologist classifies manuscripts genealogically and reconstructs the reading of the archetype, and the method with which the linguist classifies languages and as far as possible reconstructs a lost mother language, for example, Indo-European. In both cases inherited elements must be distinguished from innovations, and the unitary anterior phase from which these have branched out must be hypothesized on the basis of the various innovations. The fact that innovations are shared by certain manuscripts of the same text, or by certain languages of the same family, demonstrates that these are connected by a particularly close kinship, that they belong to a subgroup: a textual corruption too is an *innovation* compared to the previously transmitted text, just like a linguistic innovation. On the other hand, shared "conservations" have no classificatory value: what was already found in the original text or language can be preserved even in descendants that are quite different from one another.[b]

Naturally, like all analogies, this one too is valid only within certain limits: in linguistics there is nothing corresponding to the distinction between *archetype* and *original*; and even when a corruption has spread through the whole manuscript tradition, it is still always felt to be something that disturbs the context (and hence it is felt as a real error, or as a banalization that constitutes a deterioration too,[c] not as a simple neutral "innovation"), while a linguistic innovation, once it has achieved success, ceases by that very fact to be felt as an error. But the parallel between the research methods of the two disciplines remains valid: indeed, it becomes even more evident if we think of the linguistics of someone like Schleicher, who really thought he could reconstruct the Indo-European language with the same certainty with which Lachmann had reconstructed the archetype of Lucretius (to the point that he presumed to rewrite the celebrated fable of the sheep and horses in Indo-European), and who regarded phonetic changes as a "decline" from an original state of perfection and therefore as being completely analogous to textual corruptions.[1] And just as the philologists, beginning with Schlyter, Zumpt, and Ritschl,[d] represented the genealogies of manuscript traditions graphically by means of *stemmata codicum,* so too somewhat later Schleicher introduced the use of genealogical trees into comparative linguistics.[2] If one wished, one could also compare the trust of Lachmann and his contemporaries in the oldest manuscripts, and their exaggerated depreciation of the *recentiores,* with the analogous prejudice on the part of the linguists of that period (or better, of a somewhat earlier one: Jones, F. Schlegel)[e] that Sanskrit, the language of most ancient attestation, always preserved the most ancient phase as well.

These analogies authorize us to ask whether there might have been a direct relation of influence of the one discipline upon the other. At first sight, it might seem likelier that comparative linguistics, which arose between the end of the eighteenth century and the beginning of the nineteenth, supplied Lachmann, or better still Madvig and Ritschl, with a model for the method of textual criticism.[f] Such a hypothesis might seem to be supported by the fact that the founders of that method, unlike other Classical philologists such as Gottfried Hermann, were interested in and sympathetic with the new linguistic science.[3]

However, this hypothesis does not withstand closer examination.[g] In fact, as we have seen, editorial textual criticism came about by developing *iuxta propria principia* [close to its own beginnings], and Lachmann and his contemporaries did nothing but systematize and apply coherently methods that had already been formulated by the textual critics of the eighteenth century (or, in some cases, already by the Humanists and Scaliger). Moreover, there is no reference in the writings on textual criticism of Lachmann, Ritschl,

---

1. This theory of the *Verfall* [decline] of languages in the historical period is found in all of Schleicher's writings; see esp. 1874: 35, 47–50, 64.

2. Schleicher 1874: 28, 82. See below, pp. 121–22.

3. Lachmann was a close friend and collaborator of Jacob Grimm's (Lachmann's commentary on Lucretius 3.198 also quotes Grimm's *Deutsche Grammatik:* Lachmann 1850b: 149–50). For Ritschl, see the following passage from a text of 1833: "scientific expositions of Greek literature and Latin grammar, of which the latter is quite impossible if one does not assimilate research into general comparative linguistics, which scholars still view all too timidly" (Grimm 1864–71: 5.17). Madvig was interested in comparative linguistics, and even more in general linguistics.

or Madvig to comparative linguistics. It must also be noted that in the period 1830–42—when, as we have seen, the fundamental principles of the new *ars critica* were being established—Indo-European linguistics had not yet taken on the predominantly reconstructive character that it possessed for Schleicher starting in 1850. For Friedrich Schlegel, for Rask, for Bopp, the essential purpose was still to *demonstrate* the kinship among the Indo-European languages and to go back from there to the problem of the origin of the grammatical forms; they certainly were not yet thinking of precise genealogical trees, of reconstructions of "asterisked" forms or even of texts in Indo-European. So in the 1830s and 1840s the analogy between textual criticism and linguistics was not yet as clear as it later became.

At first the inverse hypothesis, that the model of textual criticism had influenced Schleicher, seemed improbable to me as well. I thought I saw a difficulty in Schleicher's rigidly naturalistic mentality: he had already established a clear distinction between philology, a "historical discipline," and linguistics, a "natural science," toward the end of the 1850s,[4] and had studied botany starting in his youth. But Henry H. Hoenigswald[5] has had the merit of recalling a fact that was not quite unknown but had been too easily forgotten: the young Schleicher was seriously interested not only in botany but also in Classical philology, studied with Ritschl at Bonn, and even started his career as a textual philologist. So Schleicher probably derived the idea of a genealogical tree of the Indo-European languages[6] and of reconstructing their extinct mother language from Ritschl himself (one of the first

4. Schleicher 1874: 119–20: "Philology is a historical discipline [. . .]. Linguistics on the other hand is not a historical discipline but rather a natural historical one [. . .]. The object of glottic science is a natural organism." Cf. Schleicher 1863: 7n1. Maher 1966 has well demonstrated that Schleicher's naturalism is pre-Darwinian, and that even the work of his that I have just cited does not represent a real change in his thought, notwithstanding its title and its vague profession of Darwinism. We should not be misled by the adjective "natural historical" in the passage just quoted: Schleicher is referring to *historia naturalis* in its old sense, for which ἱστορίη means "description" without any diachronic implications. In any case, as is well known, Schleicher saw pure *Werden* [becoming] and even decadence in the diachronic evolution of languages (cf. above, p. 120n1), while he reserved the dignity of *Geschichte* [history] for conscious human history alone, in conformity with his early formation in Hegelianism, which lasted into his later materialism, as into Jacob Moleschott's.

5. Hoenigswald 1963: esp. 8.

6. Morpurgo Davies 1975: 636n53 has observed that there is already a genealogical table of languages in Klaproth 1823. But as far as I know, Klaproth's work no longer enjoyed great prestige or diffusion at the time of Schleicher. Hence the derivation of Schleicher from Ritschl remains probable, even if Maher 1966 and Morpurgo Davies 1975 are right to note that an image as obvious as that of a genealogical tree could have arisen independently in various diachronic disciplines.

to study the genealogy of a manuscript tradition in depth and to trace out *stemmata codicum,* as we saw in chap. 5)—even if reconstructing the archetype, the counterpart of this second linguistic operation, was practiced by Madvig and Lachmann, not by Ritschl, as we have seen and as Hoenigswald does not sufficiently emphasize.[h]

But beyond this direct connection (which, I repeat, is probable but still only hypothetical), one might think[i] that the comparativist atmosphere widespread in all of European culture at that time could have favored the rise both of comparative linguistics and of that form of *vergleichende Textkritik* [comparative textual criticism] that is "Lachmann's method." Even before linguistics, comparative anatomy had stimulated a taste for the comparative method. But the relations between comparative anatomy and linguistics too cannot be reduced to a pure and simple influence of the one upon the other, as I hope to demonstrate in studies to be published shortly.[7]

What is certain is that the similarity of their research methods ended up seeming clearer and clearer to linguists on the one hand and textual critics on the other.[j] Georg Curtius, a linguist who[k] always claimed to be a philologist too and who insisted more than once on the necessity of a rapprochement between philology and linguistics,[8] developed the comparison fully in the introduction to his *Grundzüge der griechischen Etymologie* [Fundamentals of Greek etymology]:

> The individual languages of the Indo-European trunk resemble just as many old copies of a lost original manuscript. None reproduces the original text exactly, but all are important for us inasmuch as they are old witnesses to a state of affairs of which we have no direct knowledge [. . .]. If we indicate with A the stage earlier than the differentiation of the Indo-European languages, the Greek language (C) and the Latin one (D) cannot be derived from it directly, but both go back to an apograph (B) which is lost for us, Greco-Italian,[9] which itself descended directly from A. In the same way there is a particularly close affinity between Sanskrit, which deserves the first place among all the copies of A for its legibility and correctness, and Persian, as well as between the readings of the Germanic languages on the one hand and those of the Balto-Slavic languages on the other [. . .]. To try to deal with etymological questions by limiting oneself to a single language is just as im-

7. Cf. for now Timpanaro 1972 and 1973 on the Schlegel brothers and Franz Bopp, and Timpanaro 1979: esp. 474–86, on Giacomo Lignana. But see already Maher 1966.

8. E.g., Curtius 1862.

9. Curtius still believed in a particularly close kinship between Greek and Italic, as did most of his contemporaries, for that matter: cf. Meillet-Vendryes 1963: Introduction; Devoto 1958: 1.129.

permissible as to suggest conjectures to the text of Plautus without taking account of the Ambrosian palimpsest and the *vetus codex*,[10] or to the text of Sophocles while neglecting the Laurentianus A. (Curtius 1858–62: 1.22)

As these last words indicate, Curtius intended that his comparison between the two disciplines would help convert Classical philologists to linguistics — many of them were still persisting in the footsteps of Lobeck in constructing etymologies of Greek words based only on Greek.[11]

Since then, the evolution of linguistics and that of textual criticism have continued to follow parallel lines. If the passage from Curtius that I have just quoted still displays an unshaken faith in the genealogical method, in the last decades of the nineteenth century such a faith began to falter among both textual critics and linguists. In textual criticism cases of the perfectly successful application of the genealogical method were not lacking (and they have not been lacking even in times nearer our own): it should suffice to recall Leo's preface to Venantius Fortunatus, of which Eduard Fraenkel has rightly emphasized the paradigmatic value.[12] In Romance philology too, the method has had distinguished applications; without tarrying in a field with which I am insufficiently familiar, I shall only recall two eminent names, Gaston Paris and Pio Rajna.[l]

All the same, little by little scholars came to realize that the method achieved full success only in a relatively limited number of cases. All the manuscript traditions that were "too simple" (those represented by only one or two witnesses) remained outside its range, as did all those that were "too complicated" (those in which the copyists not only transcribed but also collated or conjectured so much that the kinship relations among the manuscripts were obscured). As we have seen, even the founders of the method had some trouble before they found in Lucretius an author to whom the method was fully adapted; and even the tradition of Lucretius is absolutely clear only if we set aside the problem of the Italici and leave out of consideration certain cases of contamination among the Oblongus, Quadratus, and Schedae as well![m]

In the face of these difficulties, some scholars followed a tendency that,

---

10. The so-called *vetus codex Camerarii* is Palat. Vat. 1615, usually indicated as *B*.

11. Lobeck 1853: vii: "I have decided to discuss the language not of Ogygia but of Greece, which is more than enough work in itself." Cf. Curtius 1858–62: 1.10–11. Curtius returns to the analogy between textual criticism and linguistics on pp. 26 and 98. So too Lefmann 1891: 52; and still Kretschmer 1927: 5, even if his ideas on linguistic kinship and affinity were by now very different from those of the genealogical comparativism of the nineteenth century (cf. below, p. 126 and n. 20).

12. Fraenkel in Leo 1960: 1.xxii–xxiii.

as we have seen, had its first representative in Lachmann himself: they preferred to cut the knot rather than untie it. They tried to eliminate as many manuscripts as they could, as suspected in general of being interpolated or *descripti*.[13] Once the manuscript tradition had been reduced to one or two manuscripts, every genealogical difficulty conveniently vanished; and so, for example, Wilhelm Dindorf could prepare editions of very many (too many)[n] Greek authors with little effort, and Eyssenhardt could publish a Macrobius based arbitrarily on only two manuscripts; even a critic as prudent as Vahlen mistakenly eliminated one of the best manuscripts (the Heinsianus: Leiden B.P.L. 118) in his edition of Cicero's *De legibus* and refused to change his mind explicitly even when faced by Jordan's and C. F. W. Müller's stringent objections;[14] even Leo, whom we have already mentioned as an intelligent Lachmannian for his edition of Venantius Fortunatus and whose edition of Plautus and *Plautinische Forschungen* would much later contribute to overcoming Lachmannism, published an edition of the tragedies of Seneca in 1878 that remains important for the metrical studies contained in its first volume but is fundamentally mistaken in its prejudice that the only independent witness is the *codex Etruscus* (Florence, Laur. 37. 13).[o,15]

Other critics realized that this was not the right way: instead, it had to be recognized that many traditions were extremely complex, since contamination and the innovations introduced by copyists and ancient and medieval "editors"[p] had played a large role in them, starting from the most ancient stages we can reach; therefore the mechanical method of choice among variants adopted by Lachmann was not applicable to these (or if it was, then only with many precautions and reservations).[q] This meant a positive reassessment of the internal criteria (*lectio difficilior, usus scribendi*) which Lachmann had despised, a return to principles already maintained by Classical philologists before Lachmann or those contemporary with him (recall how Sauppe had insisted on contamination),[r] and, at the same time, an in-

13. Cf. Pasquali 1952a (1934): 25–40, and above, p. 100f., for Cobet's unhealthy influence in this direction. See also below, p. 155 and n. 22.

14. See the preface to Vahlen 1883, and now the preface to Ziegler 1950: 16.

15. As is well known, the positive revaluation of the manuscripts of the so-called family A (*ceteris paribus* less reliable than the Etruscus, but superior in very many passages) is due above all to Carlsson 1926 and his later contributions; cf. Pasquali 1952a (1934): 126–29 and now many recent studies (by Philp, Giardina, Tarrant, Zwierlein, and various others). Fraenkel in Leo 1960: 1.xviii–xxi does indeed mention the defects of Leo's edition, but out of love for his teacher tends rather to minimize them. Besides the question of the manuscripts, I do not think one can say that Leo contributed "a large number of excellent emendations": Leo was a great interpreter and historian of Latin literature and culture, a distinguished metrician, but an infelicitous conjecturer—of his conjectures on Seneca, in particular, almost none are still remembered.

creasing distance between the history of tradition and textual criticism. The history of tradition became more and more the history of ancient and medieval culture; in Wilamowitz, in Traube, in Eduard Schwartz, for example, it acquired a richness and complexity unknown to the scholars of the preceding generation, but at the same time it became less and less capable of furnishing a secure criterion for constituting the text, since in highly disturbed traditions no reading could be rejected *a priori* and in a particular passage even the most suspect manuscript might preserve the correct reading.

On the problem of the *recentiores* too, scholars retreated little by little from Lachmann's total condemnation (which is already weakened anyway in his preface to Lucretius, as we have seen)[s] to the more balanced attitude of Semler and Griesbach in the eighteenth century (cf. p. 69f.) and Madvig as late as the nineteenth century (p. 97). In fact Otto Jahn,[16] the most intelligent and least servile of Lachmann's students, had already shown his impatience with his teacher's too rigid criteria in the period of full Lachmannism. Jahn's *editio maior* of Persius, published in Leipzig in 1843, is dedicated to Lachmann, "the incomparable teacher, the incorruptible friend": but in its opening dedicatory epistle Jahn already expresses his fear that his teacher will not approve its apparatus criticus, so full of variant readings derived from Humanist manuscripts [17] And toward the end of its extensive prolegomena (which constitute a real history of the text of Persius, more in Wolf's and Ritschl's style than in Lachmann's), Jahn makes a declaration that sounds obviously critical if not of Lachmann himself then certainly of too scholastic a way of understanding his method: "In general, the nature of the manuscripts of Persius is such that one cannot constitute different classes and families to which the individual manuscripts could be assigned. Everyone understands that the manuscripts differ in age and authority (which is usually linked with age in this case) and that in different cases different ones come close to other ones in the quality of their readings; but since no manuscript is so uncorrupted that you could use it as a basis for the recension, it cannot even be observed that in particular passages certain manuscripts agree in genuine or corrupt readings. . . . Therefore I could not select certain manuscripts according to whose rule I could establish the author's words, but I always had to consider all of them" (Jahn 1843: cxciii–cxciv)—even if he

16. I have learned much about this brilliant and anticonformist scholar, whose activities extended to many fields (philology, archaeology, history of ancient and modern music), from conversations with Eduard Fraenkel. On Jahn's attachment to Lachmann's memory, see the testimony of Gomperz 1905: 29.

17. Jahn 1843: cxciv: "Although I do not know whether I will succeed in convincing you that I have done well to indicate the readings of so many recent manuscripts too." In his *editio minor* (Jahn 1851), Jahn provided a much more concise apparatus.

immediately goes on to indicate that in those "all of them" he does not include all the most recent ones. In the specific case of Persius, Jahn was exaggerating somewhat: a genealogy of the manuscripts can be traced out, even if it is not entirely rigorous and goes back not to a medieval archetype but to at least two ancient editions, and it was Jahn himself who traced out its first outline; nor should the importance of the *recentiores* be exaggerated.[18] But all the same the passage we have quoted has a considerable methodological value: it is a first rebellion (even an excessive one, let us repeat) against orthodox Lachmannism by a disciple and admirer of Lachmann.[t] As we shall see, these ideas on contamination and on the impossibility of following mechanical criteria were taken up again and developed at the end of the nineteenth and in the twentieth century.

The crisis of comparative linguistics occurred at the same time as the crisis of "Lachmann's method." The concept of an absolutely unitary mother language, from which two daughter languages branched out and then went on in turn to produce by successive differentiations the various historically attested Indo-European languages, began to seem unsatisfactory. Already in 1872 Johannes Schmidt, a student of Schleicher's, had opposed the "wave theory" to the theory of the genealogical tree.[19] His ideas were developed further by his student Paul Kretschmer, who emphasized more and more the importance of "horizontal transmission" of linguistic facts as compared with "vertical transmission," the only one that the theory of the genealogical tree had considered.[20] Hugo Schuchardt had arrived at analogous results starting out from the study of the Romance languages. More and more— and with undeniable exaggerations[u]—linguistic kinship started to become something that was not inherited but acquired by means of contacts. And more and more the "intermediate unities" between Indo-European and the historically attested languages were dissolved: after Italo-Greek was dissolved, it was Italo-Celtic's turn (later, with Devoto, came Italo-Latin's too). The original Indo-European language itself was conceived more and more as having already been rich in dialectal differentiations that could not be located geographically.

Here too the analogy with textual criticism is clear. In both disciplines the claim for the importance of "horizontal transmission" was made in the same period. Whoever wanted to have some fun writing a showpiece like Curtius's on the analogies of the Schleicherian-Lachmannian period could note that for Kretschmer the Indo-European languages, or for Schuchardt

18. Cf. Scivoletto 1961: v–vi, xiv–xv. Clausen 1956 is more inclined to trust the *recentiores*.

19. J. Schmidt 1872: esp. 15, 27–28.

20. Kretschmer 1896: see esp. chap. 4, 93–124.

the Neo-Latin ones, can be compared with highly contaminated manuscripts (for which it is therefore impossible to trace out a stemma), and that these authors conceive the original Indo-European language as an "archetype with variants."

In this period, linguistics certainly directly influenced textual criticism with regard to explaining the origin of corruptions. Schuchardt's great work, *Der Vokalismus des Vulgärlateins* [The vocalism of Vulgar Latin] showed Classical philologists that corruptions due to phonetic vulgarisms, or to psychological phenomena such as occur in the evolution of languages (assimilation and dissimilation, metatheses, etc.), are just as numerous as purely graphic corruptions, or even more so.[21] This was not an absolute novelty,[22] but in the period of Lachmannism almost all medieval corruptions had tended to be explained as graphic errors.[23]

Then Louis Havet, an eminent French scholar, demonstrated with an extraordinary richness of examples the complex character of many corruptions, which originate in graphic errors or, more often, in psychological ones, upon which clumsy attempts at correction are then superimposed; he too brought to textual criticism the experience not of a pure Classical philologist but of a linguistic philologist and expert on metrics.[24] And some of his

---

21. Schuchardt wrote, with a bit of exaggeration, "The number of genuine graphic mistakes is very limited; most of what are called *lapsus calami* [slips of the pen] are *lapsus linguae* [slips of the tongue]" (Schuchardt 1866–68: 1.17).

22. Le Clerc had attributed considerable importance to psychological corruptions and those due to the vulgar pronunciation: see above, p. 62f. Cf. also Hermann 1827–77: 6.23: "Substitutions of words which occur to the copyist at the wrong moment because they are in constant use cannot have a diplomatic explanation because their motivation is psychological."

23. This tendency is noticeable, for example, in Ribbeck 1866; it reached grotesque extremes in Hagen 1879. On the other hand, Bruhn 1887 demonstrated the frequency in the text of the Greek tragedians and Homer of psychological corruptions, including more complex ones than those investigated by Schuchardt: banalizations, substitutions of words with a basically similar sound and length, etc. Bruhn, repeating observations of Le Clerc's (cf. above, p. 62f.) in all probability unconsciously, called attention to the fact that the copyist reads relatively long passages of the original and hence when he copies them down is exposed to errors of memory and of "self-dictation," especially at the end of the sentence (or at the end of the verse in poetic texts).

24. On Havet's studies as a young man, cf. Chatelain 1925: 22; and Freté 1926: 21, who observes correctly, "He enriched the domain of philology by making his concerns as a linguist penetrate into it." Among Havet's methodological works preceding his great *Manuel de critique verbale* [Manual of verbal criticism] (Havet 1911), one of the most interesting is Havet 1884; see on p. 804 his distinction between "servile mistakes" and "critical mistakes" and his assertion that this second kind of error is more frequent. Cf. also below, pp. 129–30.

best students were linguistic philologists, like Jules Marouzeau and Alfred Ernout.

All the same, in the second half of the nineteenth century, just as in the preceding period, the analogies between linguistics and textual criticism are the result not only of undeniable direct influences but also of a shared cultural atmosphere. Just as around the 1850s and 1860s linguists and philologists (and philosophers, and scientists) had breathed a common comparativist and evolutionary air, so too at the end of the nineteenth century people began to breathe an air of reaction against positivism. As is well known, this was a reaction that combined some justified elements (an impatience with hasty schemes and generalizations, the need for greater faithfulness to the complexity and variety of historical facts) with other more dubious ones (a return to a spiritualist metaphysics far older than the old positivism, a sophistic rejection of empirical classifications in the name of the uniqueness of the individual phenomenon, irrationalist and antihistorical tendencies now named "historicism").

It is not up to me to recount how these latter aspects became stronger and stronger in linguistics, especially in Italy, during the course of the nineteenth century, and how scholars fell headlong from a conception of language that was still as historical and as rich in problems as Schuchardt's into "aesthetics as general linguistics."[25] But textual criticism too, a much more specialized and less ideologized discipline, witnessed not only justified criticisms of the excessive schematism of Lachmannism but also exaggerations in the opposite direction, caused by a desire to deny to every manuscript tradition any "mechanical" character whatsoever and to demonstrate that the history of textual transmission is essentially a "spiritual" history. For example, when the great Ludwig Traube wrote, "A conjecture does not become better because it can be explained paleographically, and certainly it does not become correct because in the best of cases it is paleographically possible,"[26] without any doubt he was right regarding the second proposition, but not at all regarding the first one; or, at least, that expression contained a certain ambiguity.[v,27] Traube's lofty concept of paleography as cultural his-

25. Many observations can be found in Nencioni 1946. On Crocean and Vosslerian linguistics and a certain kind of Structuralism as two different forms of antimaterialistic reaction (the one subjectivist, intuitionist, and aestheticizing, the other mathematizing and "Platonic"), see my observations in Timpanaro 1975: 137–39. But it cannot be denied that nonetheless Structuralism has been much more fruitful and richer in scientific discoveries than intuitionist linguistics has been.

26. Traube 1909–20: 3.113.

27. Naturally, the possibility of justifying a conjecture paleographically does not make it better from the point of view of meaning and style. But *ceteris paribus,* paleographical probability is a strong argument in favor of a conjecture.

tory in the fullest sense, which constitutes his glory, led him in this case to underestimate the strictly graphic aspect of textual transmission, which rarely is the *sole* cause of errors, but very frequently acts as one cause among others.[w] Among Traube's conjectures to the *Anthologia Salmasiana* there are some splendid ones, but others are faulty precisely by reason of their paleographical improbability;[28] and the *Anthologia Salmasiana* is one of those texts in which mechanical corruptions (graphic ones, or else ones due to the vulgar pronunciation, but not to the copyist's whims) are prevalent.[x] We must also remind ourselves that "mechanical corruption" and corruption due to confusion of graphic signs are not identical: many psychological corruptions are just as unconscious and involuntary (and hence "mechanical") as graphic corruptions are, or sometimes even more so. This is an ambiguity into whose trap many have fallen, sometimes even Pasquali (e.g., 1952a [1934]: xviii, 114–15, and 481–86 [Appendix 2, "Conjectures and Diplomatic Probability"]).[y]

So too, there can be no doubt about the extraordinary methodological value of Eduard Schwartz's "Prolegomena" to his edition of Eusebius's *Historia ecclesiastica* [Church history]; yet all the same Schwartz went too far in his distrust for genealogical classifications based on shared corruptions and in his view that horizontal transmission (not only of correct readings or of conscious innovations but also of real errors) was just as frequent as vertical transmission, or even more so.[29] It is true that prose texts have in general a much less mechanical transmission than poetic ones; it is also true, and Madvig had already noted it very exactly,[30] that mechanical corruptions are less frequent in Greek texts than in Latin ones, because the Byzantine Middle Ages had no Dark Ages comparable with those in the medieval West. But even so, a text like Eusebius's *Historia ecclesiastica* is quite an exceptional case, even among Greek prose texts, since it was linked with theological disputes and changes in political affiliation and hence was exposed all the more to conscious reworkings;[z] so it is risky to assign it a paradigmatic value.

The French school was better at avoiding dangers of this sort. As we have already suggested, Havet's *Manuel de critique verbale* (Havet 1911) does indeed represent a reaction against the Lachmannians' oversimplification regarding the genesis of corruptions and the affiliation of manuscripts;[31] and

28. Traube 1909–20: 3.51–59 Among his best conjectures may be cited those to *Anth. Lat.* 198.38 and 304.4; among the least successful ones, the one to 83.88 and his complete rewriting of poem 377.

29. Schwartz 1909: cxlvi–cxlvii. Even so, it cannot be denied that real corruptions can be transmitted horizontally, even if this happens only rarely: cf. below, Appendix C, n. 44.

30. Madvig 1871: 1.13 and n. 1.

31. "My whole book, in any case, is a continuous protest against mendacious oversimplification," declares Havet in his preface, 1911: xii. And see at 1911: 418–24 his ex-

yet Havet has no wish at all to dissolve textual criticism into a multitude of individual problems that cannot be compared with one another. On the contrary, he even aspires to turn it into a rigorous science, a "pathology and therapy of errors": the study of the genealogy of manuscripts is replaced by the study of the genesis of corruptions.[aa] As Ernout writes, "Louis Havet was an enemy of empirical conjecture, of what he called amateurs' criticism. Between two corrections of different value for the same error, I am sure that he would have chosen the inferior one—or at least the one that most scholars would consider such—if this allowed him to determine more exactly the process by which the restored word, had it been the original reading, could have given rise to the faulty reading." [32] Here, certainly, he went too far: although explaining easily the genesis of a corruption has great importance (more, I think, than Maas and Pasquali attribute to it), no genetic consideration can ever induce one to prefer the "inferior" correction.[bb] And in fact most of the too many conjectures Havet published in the *Revue de philologie,* many of which he collected in his *Manuel de critique verbale,* are unacceptable precisely because they try only to explain how the corruption was produced, not above all to find the right word for that particular context. Havet had many abilities, but he was not a great interpreter, and this harmed his activity as a textual critic too. But Marouzeau and especially Dain, his students, knew how to profit from his extraordinary experience and, together, partly to overcome his limits.

Among these new approaches to textual criticism, Giorgio Pasquali's book occupies a special position. As is well known, Paul Maas provided the occasion for inspiring this work with his *Textual Criticism;* but the contrast between the mathematical mentality of Maas (who was interested above all in the rigorousness of his formulations, without their always being rigorous in fact[cc]), and the lively sense of the uniqueness of each manuscript tradition that animates Pasquali's exposition, leaps to the eyes of every reader.[33] The true inspirers of Pasquali's book were Wilamowitz, Traube, and above all

---

cellent discussion of the "pitfalls of genealogical classification" and his observation that groups of manuscripts can be formed by "convergence," by processes of contamination, even from originally distinct branches of a tradition. Here too we must note the analogy with the linguistic concept of "affinity" between languages, as opposed to genealogical "kinship."

32. Ernout 1926: 24.

33. Cf. S. Mariotti 1952: 213–14 (this article is also important for its new observations and examples); Canfora 1968. I intend to write something myself about some other cases of lack of rigor in Maas for all his ostentation of rigor. See in the meantime below, pp. 155f., 162–70. See now Canfora 1982 and Timpanaro 1985a.[dd]

Schwartz, "the greatest textual critic of the century, the first one to overcome Lachmann in his method" (Pasquali 1952a [1934]: 471).[cc]

Other approaches that were akin to his own despite the difference in
formation and cultural background remained little known to him, especially
because of a prejudiced aversion, which went back to his youth and which
lasted for a long time, against Classical studies detached from a general
conception of *Altertumswissenschaft* [the science of antiquity], such as was
practiced in France and England from the beginning of the nineteenth century on.[34] In Pasquali's last years he did indeed manage to approach the
French school, some characteristics of which we traced out a little earlier
in summary fashion, with interest and almost with an astonished sympathy:
in his lengthy review of Alphonse Dain's *Les manuscrits* [Manuscripts][35]
he observed many points of agreement (especially regarding the genesis of
corruptions and the history of tradition conceived as cultural history rather
than as an abstract stemmatics) alongside some differences in intellectual
character (Dain's interest in text constitution, in *recensio* and *emendatio*,
was weaker than his predominant interest in codicology and the vicissitudes
of the manuscript tradition: the title of Dain's book had already indicated
this, and it was confirmed later by his mediocre edition of Sophocles).
Pasquali's death nipped in the bud what might have become a very fertile exchange of ideas and experiences between Dain and himself.

Pasquali's relations with English textual philology followed a rather different course. There really had been a period of depression in English Classical studies, more or less from 1825 (Dobree's death and, a little earlier,
Elmsley's) until the last years of the nineteenth century (when the star of
Housman rose on the horizon),[36] a depression partly, but only partly, com-
pensated for by the many good commentaries that appeared in England during that long interval. It cannot be said that Pasquali did not recognize
Housman's brilliance, but his image of Housman as a "Humanist," not a

---

34. On French philology see the conclusion of Pasquali 1964 (1920): 89–90, with its
bizarre final juxtaposition of Kant and Treitschke, a genius on the one hand and a mediocre and narrow-minded *Realpolitiker* [pragmatic politician] on the other, as the two greatest representatives of modern German culture. An important reason for Pasquali's low
opinion of French Classical philology were the all-too-numerous bad, and sometimes ter-
rible, editions published in the first years of the collection *Belles Lettres:* cf. Pasquali
1952b (1933): 242–43, 249; and esp. Pasquali 1935: 206–7 = Pasquali 1968: 1.191,
196, 379. On English Classical philology, aside from Housman and Lindsay, to whom we
shall refer shortly, cf. Pasquali 1964 (1920): 81.

35. Pasquali 1951b (in Italian, translated by Timpanaro, in Pasquali 1952a [1934]:
469–80).

36. See Brink 1978: 1196–1213.

"scientist," remained too reductive, a bit because of insufficient knowledge,[37] a bit because Housman's own aggressive character, his contempt for
all routine and mediocrity, inevitably provoked in those who did not know
him very well either irritation or a fanatical enthusiasm, but only rarely a
reasoned admiration.[38] Certainly, one notes in Pasquali a growing admiration for Housman, from the reference in *Filologia e storia* ("a scholar of
acute but uncontrolled natural talent"; 1964 [1920]: 81) to the exclamation
witnessed by Otto Skutsch, "There is only one man who knows how to
make emendations, and that is Housman!"[39] to his judgment on Housman's
edition of Lucan ("for knowledge of the poet's highly individual language
and style, for judgment, for sureness in emendation, it is a masterpiece, notwithstanding the author's well-known eccentricity"; 1952a [1934]: 432n1);
and in its spontaneity the assessment Skutsch reports is even quite exaggerated. But although Pasquali always defended the legitimacy and value of
emendatio against short-sighted Italian critics, he was more interested in *recensio;* and his lack of familiarity with Housman's edition of Manilius (in
which the genealogy of the manuscripts is traced out with a sure hand), an
evidently infelicitous hypothesis in Housman's edition of Juvenal,[40] Housman's fundamentally correct (but still somewhat too summary) liquidation
of the genealogy of the manuscripts of Lucan as being completely contaminated[41]—all this convinced Pasquali that Housman, brilliant as he was, was

37. It seems certain that Pasquali never had direct acquaintance with Housman's edition of Manilius: Pasquali 1964 (1920): 81; 1952a (1934): 392n3. This was observed simultaneously by Kenney 1974: 129n1 and Momigliano 1974: 370.

38. It must be acknowledged that, even if Housman has exerted an extraordinary positive influence on the rigor and sense of style of the English textual critics of the following
generations (it is in large part his merit, besides that of German refugees in England, if all
in all the Classical philology of this nation today enjoys an indisputable superiority over
all others), he has nonetheless also stimulated an arrogance and an exaggerated snobbism
in some English Classical philologists to which their value as scholars does not always correspond (and even when the value is there, it would be better if the arrogance were not!).
Cf. my observations in Timpanaro 1964: 790–91; Momigliano 1974: 368 on the *imita-
tio Housmani;* and now Salemme 1981: 290.

39. Skutsch 1960: 6–7. I myself can add another oral testimony: the admiration with
which during a seminar Pasquali spoke of Housman's celebrated punctuation and interpretation of Catullus 64.324, as simple as it is brilliant.

40. Housman 1931: xxxix. Pasquali's objection (1952a [1934]: 430n2) is entirely correct, as far as I understand it; but it is expressed with a polemic animosity all the more excessive as he agreed with Housman about the authenticity of that passage of Juvenal and
disagreed only about the explanation for its absence in almost all the manuscripts.

41. Housman 1927 (1926): vii. Pasquali acknowledges that Housman "judges the tradition in its totality more correctly than any of his predecessors"; but he insists that even
a contaminated tradition should be disentangled as far or as little as is possible and there-

in essence unmethodical, indeed antimethodical. Certainly, Housman had words of contempt for *Textgeschichte;* but his *emendatio* was always guided by rigorous methodical criteria, and the material on various types of corruptions and their genesis which he collected in the prefaces and notes to his editions and in many articles confirms what he himself always repeated, that the "intuitive" element which one cannot do without in conjectural activity must receive the confirmation of experience and reasoning. His syntactical, stylistic, prosodical, and metrical observations, which he always considered to be a necessary support for his conjectures (or for his defenses of transmitted readings: these too exist, and for the most part they are excellent), go in the very same direction.[42]

Wallace M. Lindsay, an English contemporary of Housman's, is cited in Pasquali's *Storia della tradizione* more often than Housman is—very often with agreement but with the conviction that Lindsay's "histories of the text" and his editions remain below the best results obtained by German Classical philology.[43] And it is certain that Lindsay was much better as an expert on Latin linguistics (his old *Latin Language,* in certain points, is still superior to Leumann's *Laut- und Formenlehre* [Phonetics and morphology]), on grammatical works and Latin glossaries, above all on paleography, than as an editor of texts (although his edition of Martial remains exemplary,[44] and his editions of Festus, Nonius, and Isidore of Seville, for all their defects, are unlikely to be replaced in the foreseeable future). But the greater accusation of neglect and forgetfulness of Lindsay must be lodged not against Pasquali and not even against the Germans, but against the English themselves.[45] It is not a question of opposing Lindsay to Housman: there is no doubt that

---

fore approves the in fact truly exemplary review of Fraenkel 1926 = Fraenkel 1964: 2.267–308. We cannot linger here on the later relations between Fraenkel and Housman, which are fascinating not only from a human perspective but also because of the difficult symbiosis between English philology and the German philology transplanted into England as a result of the Nazi persecutions; there is a brief testimony in Housman 1972: 3.1277.

42. Kenney 1974: 127–29 provides the best account of Housman's profoundly methodical character, despite his attacks against "method" as a form of routine; there are other excellent observations in Brink 1978: 1206–13.

43. It is especially in the case of Plautus that Pasquali is constantly concerned to place Lindsay below Leo and other German Classical philologists: e.g., Pasquali 1952a (1934): 331n1, 337n2, 338n4, etc.

44. I am referring both to his edition (Lindsay 1903) and to his *Ancient Editions of Martial* (Lindsay 1902); Pasquali 1952a (1934): 416–26 too gives a clearly positive judgment of both works, and he even tended to agree too much with Lindsay on the problem of authorial variants, even though he was already then more cautious than Lindsay himself. See now Citroni 1975: xli–xliv.

45. Unless I am mistaken, neither Kenney nor Brink names Lindsay even once.

Lindsay did not possess Housman's genius. It is a question of reconsidering a scholar who was certainly one of the greatest Latinists of the period between the end of the nineteenth century and the first decades of the twentieth, and who did not follow in others' footsteps but almost always worked in fields that had not been sufficiently explored hitherto.[ff]

Let us return to Pasquali.[gg] His defense of the *recentiores* against prejudiced and hasty condemnations,[hh] and his insistence on the importance of contamination in rich traditions and on the nonmechanical character of very many corruptions are in keeping with the Wilamowitzian and Schwartzian inspiration of his work.[ii] Pasquali was oriented in this direction not only by the teachers we have mentioned but also by his own direct experience as a textual critic (the letters of Gregory of Nyssa, which he edited, have a very rich and very contaminated and interpolated tradition) and his growing interest in medieval and modern philology and particularly in Italian texts, especially following the fruitful exchanges of ideas and experiences between himself and Vittorio Rossi, Giuseppe Vandelli, and above all Michele Barbi.[jj] This last aspect is especially evident in the last chapter of his *Storia della tradizione,* dedicated to authorial variants: here the rich documentation offered by the texts of Petrarch, Boccaccio, and Manzoni provides a starting point for going back to analogous phenomena in antiquity whose attestation is far more infrequent and uncertain.

Pasquali was one of the Classical philologists most interested in linguistics, not old-style Indo-European linguistics—and, what is more, not Structuralism either[kk]—but the history of the Greek and Latin languages, and, in his last years, that of Italian. That is why the analogy of method between linguistics and textual criticism, to which we pointed earlier, is far more explicit in his book than in the writings of his predecessors.[46] The very tendency we just spoke of, to apply methodical procedures elaborated in the study of modern texts to the criticism of ancient texts, has its counterpart in the linguistics of the late nineteenth and twentieth centuries, which started out from the study of Neo-Latin origins or even living languages (and not, like Bopp and Schleicher, from Sanskrit), and modified the earlier concep-

---

46. See, e.g., Pasquali 1952a (1934): xvii, 160 (on which cf. above, pp. 86f.), and 472; 1952b [1933]: 133, 135, 136–39 = Pasquali 1968: 1.104, 106, 107–9 (acute observations on the parallelism between linguistics and paleography, though here and there they are a bit flawed by Idealistic influences in linguistics); Pasquali 1932b. The fact that the analogy between the two disciplines is still capable of being further developed and continues to allow fruitful exchanges of experiences is demonstrated by many of the communications at the Congress of Italian Philology collected in *Studi e problemi di critica testuale* 1961; see esp. Folena 1961. Out of this volume later arose a periodical on the subject of textual criticism.

tion of the kinship relations among the Indo-European languages on the basis of these data.

All this might make one conclude that Pasquali's book merely systematizes Schwartz's ideas, supplies them with many examples, and lends them further emphasis in certain points. Indeed, many felt that it did just this. Above all in Italy, in an atmosphere saturated with Idealism, and hence with the indiscriminate polemics against any classification and "mechanicism" to which I pointed earlier, the work of Pasquali seemed to be an invitation to neglect altogether the greater or lesser authority of the manuscripts, to abandon any effort at genealogical classification, to put *recentiores* and *vetustiores* on an equal footing, and to constitute the text solely on the basis of internal criteria.[47] The hypothesis of authorial variants, which is legitimate only as a last resort,[48] was invoked to explain obvious banalizations or even graphic corruptions. Pasquali himself, in his preface to the reprint of 1952, wrote, "I fear that in this regard my work has done even more harm than good, and I feel the duty to warn beginners, even older beginners, ὀψιμαθεῖς [late learners] in that kind of philology, to be cautious."[49]

But in reality, even in the first edition, Pasquali had been very far from proclaiming a pure and simple return to subjective *iudicium*. In this regard, indeed, a difference in mentality and orientation that had existed from the very beginning between Pasquali and one of the teachers he loved most, Girolamo Vitelli, became clearer. It was to Vitelli, next to Schwartz, that Pasquali had dedicated his *Storia della tradizione*. But for Vitelli, just as for

---

47. In fact, this happened not only in the years immediately following the appearance of Pasquali's book, and not only in Italy. See Dawe 1964, acute and learned, but too "angry" and destructive; the author learned of Pasquali's book after he had already begun his research and reacted to it with enthusiasm (157n*), but he ended up agreeing more with Schwartz than with Pasquali (160).

48. Already in the first edition (1934: 419–20), Pasquali showed himself more prudent than other scholars, although he sometimes exaggerated in hypothesizing authorial variants, and he warned, "'Authorial variants' are the last resort of textual criticism, and it is not legitimate to have recourse to them so long as the divergences can be explained in any other way."

49. Pasquali 1952a (1934): xxii; and already Pasquali 1942: 237 = Pasquali 1968: 2.166, and 1947: 261. This caution ended up becoming excessive, also because of the polemic, often acute, but not devoid of quibbles, that Günther Jachmann directed against the hypothesis of authorial variants. Scevola Mariotti, a scholar who at first had effectively and justly attacked some unmethodical hypotheses of authorial variants (S. Mariotti 1947: 303; 1950), later maintained that in certain cases the *probability* of authorial variants must be indicated, even if absolute certainty is unattainable, as is almost always the case in ancient texts (S. Mariotti 1954; 1952: 218). Cf. the methodologically rigorous analysis in Nardo 1967: 321–82.

Gottfried Hermann, *ars critica* was identical with the perfect knowledge of the style: although Vitelli was an extremely expert paleographer and investigator of manuscripts, nevertheless he did not admit that external considerations based on the authority of the witnesses had a significant weight in the choice of readings, and he felt distrust and even dislike for research into the history of tradition and the genealogy of manuscripts.[ll] So one can understand that he did not fully appreciate the value of a book on methodology, even if the methodology was as devoid of precepts as Pasquali's was.[mm] Commemorating his deceased teacher a few years later, Pasquali referred with restrained bitterness to that lack of understanding: "In these last years, in which I knew him better, I sometimes even suspected that he condemned systematic disquisitions on the relations among the various manuscripts of an author as useless and found them distasteful [. . .]. Certainly, even a few months before his death, he claimed the right to constitute the text of a verse of Aeschylus according to his own taste without submitting to canons that he found mechanical; I have not succeeded in convincing myself that he was right, either in that particular case or in general."[50]

Even Pasquali's great admiration for Schwartz did not prevent him from noticing the exaggerations in certain methodological pronouncements by the editor of Eusebius to which we have already referred. Reread pages 136–41 of Pasquali's book, and you will see that his agreement with Schwartz is accompanied by reservations: "I consider exaggerated only the first of these words, which attack the concept of archetype" (1952a [1934]: 136); "It would be mistaken to derive a presumption against the existence of an archetype from the number and quality of the variants" (137); "Not even here is everything right [. . .]. If it is true that errors can be transmitted by collation just as much as genuine readings can [. . .], nonetheless it is certain that the transmission of the text, the 'tradition,' occurs on principle in a vertical 'direction,' as is only natural" (140). Pasquali also rejected Leo's opinion that the whole manuscript tradition of Plautus goes back directly to an edition by Valerius Probus, and considered it indispensable to return to the hypothesis of an archetype—even if not a medieval archetype, but one of the

50. Pasquali 1936: 9–10 = Pasquali 1942: 300 = Pasquali 1968: 2.207. But see already Pasquali 1964 (1920): 77. I can add an oral testimony. Pasquali told me once (and he certainly will have told others as well) that Vitelli, after having read or skimmed the book—which was dedicated to him, with words full of admiration and affection which concluded, "In him I revere the greatest expert on Greek poetry among all living men"— said to him, with forthright frankness but also with a total lack of understanding, "You would have done better to write a book about an ancient author instead of a book on methodology."

third century AD (1952a [1934]: 339); and point 11 of the "Decalogue of 12 Articles" in his preface (1952a [1934]: xix–xx) proves that he considered this hypothesis valid for other authors too.[nn] In any case, the polemic against Lachmannism in Pasquali's book is never divorced from a recognition not only of its historical function but also of the value it still maintains in the present when we have to deal with mechanical[oo] recensions.

Certainly, the criteria of *lectio difficilior* and *usus scribendi* acquire primary importance in nonmechanical[pp] recensions.[51] But Pasquali's discussion of these two criteria (1952a [1934]: 122–24) aims precisely to free them from the dominion of pure subjective taste (or from that of an abstract rationalism, no less subjective even if it deludes itself that it is "universal") and to demonstrate that knowledge of the history of the tradition is necessary if they are to be applied well. "Easy and difficult are not absolute terms, and what is difficult, that is unaccustomed, for us could have been easy for people of other periods. Judgment regarding the ease or difficulty of a reading will be all the more secure, the better the judge knows the customs of language and thought of the periods that transmitted it and that might have coined it. The best critic of a Greek text with a Byzantine tradition will be the one who is not only a perfect Hellenist but also a perfect Byzantinist. The best editor of a Latin author transmitted in medieval or postmedieval manuscripts will be the one who knows the Middle Ages and Humanism just as well as he knows his author and his author's language and times and the language of his times. A critic of this sort is an ideal that no one can incarnate perfectly in himself, but toward which everyone has the duty to try to come as near as possible."[52]

But Pasquali did not even abandon external criteria altogether for nonmechanical[qq] recensions. He never completely resigned himself to Paul

---

51. I avoid Pasquali's terms *closed recension* and *open recension,* despite their popularity in Italy and abroad, because Alberti 1979: 1–18 has demonstrated that Pasquali already uses both terms, but especially the second one, in too many different senses. This takes nothing away from the fact that in Pasquali's time these two expressions were significant and effective in the polemic against orthodox Lachmannism.

52. See also the discussion with K. Ziegler about clausulas in the *Somnium Scipionis* (Pasquali 1952a [1934]: 117–18): Pasquali maintains rightly that a text cannot be constituted on the sole basis of *numerus* without taking the documentary authority of the various readings into account. Later, Ronconi and Castiglioni took up the problem of the divergences in the collocation of words in the *Somnium* once again and gave two different explanations for it (cf. now Ronconi 1961: 40, 61). My own view is that Ronconi was right, at least in most cases, and I think he should have defended his hypothesis more decisively against Castiglioni's. In any case Pasquali's requirement for the constitution of the text remains valid.

Maas's aphorism, "No specific has yet been discovered against contamination" (Maas 1958 [1927]: 49).[53] A good part of the fifth chapter of his book is dedicated to the search for new "objective criteria," ones more sophisticated than Lachmann's and capable of "resolving disagreements in the case of an open recension" (1952a [1934]: 160). Pasquali indicates one such criterion in the norm of lateral areas, which we have already had occasion to mention,[54] and another in Ulrich Knoche's attempt to classify contaminated manuscripts of poetic texts genealogically on the basis of lacunas that impair the meter (1952a [1934]: 180–83). If there is a defect in this part of Pasquali's book, rich in erudition as it is, it consists in his excessive faith that these criteria could be fruitful "not only for the history of the text, but for the text itself" (1952a [1934]: 177n1). The impression remains that when the history of a text is very complicated, it is not very useful for textual criticism, but otherwise has a value in itself, that it belongs to the history of culture, to the *Fortleben* [survival] of the Classics. And the practical exigency remains that certain critical editions not be postponed forever for the sake of studying the history of the tradition in all its smallest details, that scholars not bury themselves so deeply in the study of medieval and Humanist culture that they forget to return to textual criticism. Nonetheless, although in more recent works the separation between history of the tradition and textual criticism has now taken place and been codified,[55] in Pasquali's book the two disciplines are still conjoined. Pasquali's interest in the vicissitudes of Classical texts in the medieval and Humanist periods, lively as it was, never makes him forget his job as textual critic and interpreter. It is in this combination of a broad perspective on cultural history[rr] with an acute philological intelligence directed to the individual passage of an ancient author that the unmistakable character of Pasquali's work resides.

53. Cf. the preface to Maas 1958 [1927]: viii–ix.

54. See above, pp. 86–87.

55. See, e.g., Hunger et al. 1961–64, which even introduces a further distinction between *Textgeschichte* [history of the text] and *Textüberlieferung* [transmission of the text], and supports it with a certain doctrinaire ostentatiousness. Against this distinction cf. also S. Mariotti 1966: 236. In the last few years there has been a salutary reaction: more and more philologists first treat the manuscript tradition of a text in a monograph, making ample use of the assistance of codicology and cultural history, and then go on to do a critical edition of it with the same success. Other scholars, on the other hand, in textual criticism as in many other disciplines, have preferred the easy path of terminological exhibitionism to which no genuine conceptual progress corresponds; one of the worst examples of this tendency—it is useless to fool ourselves: it will certainly find admirers and followers—is the interdisciplinary seminar published as *Del testo* 1979.

Lachmann's First Attempt at a Mechanical *Recensio* in 1817

In July 1817 Lachmann published a long review of Friedrich Heinrich von der Hagen's edition of *Der Nibelungen Lied* (Hagen 1816) and Georg Friedrich Benecke's edition of Bonerius's *Der Edel Stein* (Benecke 1816).[1] Lachmann distinguished two redactions in the manuscript tradition of the *Nibelungen Lied:* a shorter and more genuine one contained in the manuscript he called *B;* and another, longer and heavily interpolated one, represented by the manuscripts *GEM.*[2] According to Lachmann, both redactions have reached us disfigured by corruptions and secondary interpolations, but while the first one cannot be reconstructed in its original form until another manuscript, a brother of *B,* is discovered, the second one can be reconstructed by comparing *GEM.*

According to Lachmann, such a comparison reveals that the ancestor of *GEM* was still fairly free of interpolations in the text written by the first hand but that a second hand inflicted many changes and arbitrary additions upon the original text. Each copyist of *GEM* reproduced now the reading of the first hand, now that of the second hand, and also interpolated on his own. So in order to make Lachmann's thought easier to understand we could trace out the following stemma:

1. Lachmann 1817. I warmly thank the director of the university library at Jena for sending me a photograph of this review. The review is republished in Lachmann 1876: 1.81–114.

2. *B* [now designated conventionally as *A*: Munich, Bayerische Staatsbibliothek, cod. germ. 34] and *M* [= *D*: Munich, Bayerische Staatsbibliothek, cod. germ. 31] are in Munich, *E* [= *C*: Karlsruhe, cod. Donaueschigen 63] in Donaueschingen [now in Karlsruhe], *G* [= *B*: St. Gallen, Stifstsbibliothek MS 857] at Sankt Gallen. Lachmann 1876: 1.84n indicates the correspondences between Lachmann's symbols and those that von der Hagen had used and which Lachmann himself went on to adopt in his own edition of the *Nibelungen Lied.* Nowadays, in contrast with Lachmann's view, scholars generally believe that the shorter redaction is the more recent one.

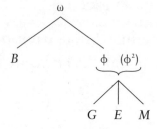

where ω would indicate the oldest redaction, φ the first hand of the ancestor of *GEM*, and $φ^2$ the interpolations by the second hand in the same
manuscript.

Lachmann adds that the editor's task is to identify the interpolations in
the ancestor of *GEM*: that is, as we would put it, to reconstruct the readings
of $φ^2$.[3] To achieve this purpose he provides the following rules, in which the
signs > and < signify, respectively, "better than" and "worse than," just as
in mathematics they signify "greater than" and "less than":

1. Three manuscripts out of our four outvote one every time.
2. When any two agree, then $BG < EM$ (i.e., where *B* agrees with *G*, the
   unanimous reading of *E* and *M* is to be preferred), $GE > BM, GM > BE$.
3. Where there are three readings, then $BG > E–M$ (the reading shared
   by *B* and *G* is preferable [to] the two others in *E* and *M*), $GE > B–M$,
   $GM > B–E$; on the other hand, $EM = B–G$ (the agreement of *E* and *M*
   leads to no secure decision against the two readings of *B* and *G*), $BM =
   G–E, BE = G–M$.
4. When all four disagree, the original reading is just as uncertain.
   (Lachmann 1817: 117–18 = Lachmann 1876: 1.86–87)

We have reproduced the passage from Lachmann 1817. The reprinted
version in Lachmann 1876 reads "then $BG < E–M$" in the third rule.

Aside from this variant, the text of Lachmann 1876 is identical to that of
Lachmann 1817. The eminent Germanist Karl[a] Müllenhoff, who edited this
first volume of his teacher's *Kleinere Schriften* (Lachmann 1876), did not
add any notes to these rules, as though they were perfectly clear. But in fact
they are a real brain-twister.

The first rule already seems to be unacceptable. Let us suppose that in ω

---

3. Lachmann 1817: 118 = Lachmann 1876: 1.87: "The editor's task is to discover
these changes, which now this copyist, now that one overlooked, and every one increased
with new changes." Antonio La Penna has helped me understand the task Lachmann set
himself.

there was a reading x, that it was reproduced faithfully by B and ϕ, and that ϕ^2 added a variant y in the margin. Let us also suppose that the copyists of G and E reproduced the reading of the first hand (x) and the copyist of M that of the second hand (y). In that case the agreement of three manuscripts (BGE) against one (M) would give us not ϕ^2 but ϕ.

The same thing may be said in case the reading x was reproduced by GM and y by E, or x by EM and y by G. Obviously the agreement of BGM (or of BEM) would give us ϕ and not ϕ^2.

In reality, in contrast with Lachmann's rule, the agreement of three manuscripts against one gives us with certainty the reading of ϕ (and of ω), *if one of the three that agree is B*. Only if none of the three that agree is B—that is, only if GEM agree against B—is it possible that the three preserve the reading of ϕ^2. For one can suppose that ϕ has the same reading as B (and as ω), and that GEM have all three reproduced the variant of ϕ^2. Such a hypothesis is not improbable, especially if we admit the possibility that the scribe of ϕ^2 did not limit himself to adding the variant in the margin or above the line, but also deleted the reading of the first hand. In any case this is only *one* of the possible hypotheses: the agreement of GEM against B could also be explained on the supposition that ϕ (not ϕ^2) had innovated with respect to ω and that its innovation had been reproduced by its three apographs, or else that B had innovated[4] and that the reading of ω had been reproduced by ϕ and hence by GEM. So the probability that the agreement of GEM against B represents ϕ^2 is not very high.

The second rule, on the other hand, is correct. When there are two readings, each one attested by two manuscripts, it is certain that the reading attested by B and by one apograph of ϕ was already found in ϕ and ω, while the other two apographs of ϕ reproduce the variant of the second hand (ϕ^2).

So too the fourth rule is correct (and obvious).

But the third one presents real absurdities in the form in which it is printed in Lachmann 1817. The agreement of BG against isolated readings of E and M certainly gives us ϕ (and ω), not ϕ^2, and hence it cannot be "preferable" in trying to reconstruct ϕ^2. The agreement of GE against isolated readings of B and M, or of GM against isolated readings of B and E, *can* represent ϕ^2, but can also represent ϕ. No less erroneous are the formulas $BM = G-E$ and $BE = G-M$ in the second part of the same rule: this time too the agreement of B with an apograph of ϕ gives us with certainty ϕ and not

4. Although Lachmann considered B to be the best manuscript, he still maintained that it was not free from corruptions and interpolations: "since it must be expected that neither the older recension in B nor the more recent one in G will have been transmitted to us without errors and arbitrary changes, partly negligent and partly intentional, on the part of the copyists" (Lachmann 1817: 117 = Lachmann 1876: 1.86).

ϕ^2: hence for reconstructing ϕ^2 such an agreement is "worse" and not "equivalent" compared to the isolated readings of the other two apographs of ϕ.

Such serious inconsistencies (to which must be added the syntactical absurdity of the parenthetic expression "the reading . . . is preferable [to] the two others") suggest that the genuine text of the rule has been distorted by typographical errors. Fritz Bornmann has made a very acute and persuasive attempt at correcting it in an article dedicated to this problem,[b,5] in which he has proposed that the third rule should read as follows:

> 3. Where there are three readings, then $BG < E-M$ (against the reading shared by B and G, the two others in E and M are preferable), $G-E > BM$, $G-M > BE$; on the other hand, $EM = B-G$ (the agreement of E and M leads to no secure decision against the two readings of B and G), $B-M = GE$, $B-E = GM$.

In the first formula, Bornmann evidently accepts Müllenhoff's correction in Lachmann 1876, already cited. But while Müllenhoff had limited himself to this single change, which is not enough to restore sense to the whole passage, Bornmann gives us for the first time a coherent text (except for the first rule, of which I have already spoken and to which I shall return)[c] and obtains this by means of relatively minor corrections: indeed, his restitution of the text requires changing not the letters but only the mathematical signs, which are often subject to displacement and confusion by typesetters, especially in difficult contexts.[6]

If we accept Bornmann's text—and I believe we must—then Lachmann's third rule can be paraphrased as follows: the agreement of one of the three apographs of ϕ with B gives us the certainty that that is the reading of ϕ, not of ϕ^2, while the isolated readings of the other two apographs *can* both reproduce ϕ^2; on the other hand, the agreement of two apographs of ϕ against isolated readings of the third apograph and of B does not give us any guarantee of reproducing the reading of ϕ^2, which might have been preserved by the third apograph. Strictly speaking, the formulation of the second part of the rule (starting with "on the other hand") is not very felicitous, because it might suggest that the readings of B and of the third apograph might both reproduce ϕ^2, like the shared reading of the other two apographs—while for

5. Bornmann 1962. In a first version of this study of mine, I had accepted a different attempt at correction, proposed to me by Eugenio Grassi and Antonio La Penna; although that attempt too was very astute, it does not now seem to me easy to defend it against the objections of Bornmann 1962: 48–49.

6. For a detailed reconstruction of the origin of the errors, see the observations of Bornmann 1962: 50.

B this is impossible. But in reality, as the parenthetic explanation ("the agreement . . .") also makes clear, the rule must be understood to mean that the shared reading of two apographs of φ and the *different* reading of the third apograph of *B* have an equal probability of reproducing φ².[7]

Thus there is perfect agreement between the second and third rules: both rules mean in substance that a reading attested by one or two apographs of φ can represent φ² as long as such a reading is not found in *B* too. As Bornmann notes, the two rules are parallel formally: in both cases Lachmann begins with a negative formulation ("such a reading is to be refused in favor of such another one") and then goes on to expound the second and third cases in a positive form ("such a reading is to be preferred to such another one").

All the same a striking contrast remains between these two rules and the first one, which we discussed above (pp. 140f.). In this case we cannot hypothesize a typographical error: the incoherence was in Lachmann's mind. Bornmann acutely detects the reason for this incoherence in the "superposition of two criteria, one purely recensional, aiming to identify mechanically the interpolated readings of φ, and the other, which I would call editorial, of reconstructing a text as close as possible to the original (which, however, is supposed to be capable of being reconstructed only in the class of manuscripts derived from φ)." An examination of the concrete examples that follow the formulation of the four rules in Lachmann's article seems to confirm Bornmann's hypothesis.[8] In fact there is something paradoxical about this whole complicated attempt to reconstruct φ² (a series of interpolations!) when Lachmann could have even reconstructed the first source of the whole tradition, ω, with much less effort and much greater profit. For the agreement of *B* with one of the apographs of φ gives us with certainty the reading of φ and of ω. It is perfectly natural that although Lachmann had set himself the difficult and all in all not very useful goal of reconstructing φ², he then tended more or less unconsciously to reconstruct ω. But it must be added that the first rule is erroneous not only from the point of view of reconstructing φ² but also, and just as much, from the point of view of reconstructing φ and ω: the agreement of *GEM* ("three manuscripts out of our four") against *B* can represent ω, but it can just as well reproduce an innovation of φ or even of φ². At this point Lachmann seems still to have been a victim of the false criterion of the majority, from which he will free himself only in his edition of the New Testament (see above, p. 85).

7. Cf. Bornmann 1962: 49n2: "The meaning [of *EM = B–G*] is: the coincidence of the two readings in *E* and *M* does not lead to a secure decision in comparison with *G* when *G* differs from *B,* that is, it does not permit us to reject *G.*"

8. Cf. Bornmann 1962: 50–53, and 47n5.

Three years later, in a review of a new edition of the *Nibelungen Lied* by the same von der Hagen, Lachmann reconfirmed the value of his rules, though he admitted the possibility that they could be rendered more precise.[9] Had he therefore not noticed that the rules were almost useless, at least in the form in which he had published them in Lachmann 1817?

Finally Lachmann published a critical edition of the *Nibelungen Lied* himself in 1826.[10] But this time he did not try to reconstruct the longer and (according to him) interpolated redaction and adhered fundamentally to the manuscript that he had called *B* and for which he now adopted von der Hagen's designation, *A*.[11]

9. Lachmann 1820a: Ergänzungsblätter 70–76 = Lachmann 1876: 1.216.

10. Lachmann 1851 (1826).

11. For an attempt to demonstrate the correctness of Lachmann's rules without having recourse to corrections of this sort, cf. Lutz-Hensel 1971 and 1975: 228–39. Lutz-Hensel's interpretation, which Bornmann and I do not consider to be at all persuasive, will soon be discussed by Bornmann in *Zeitschrift für Deutsche Philologie*. In any case this eminent scholar's book, praiseworthy as it is for its rich and detailed information, is ruined by its nebulousness and captiousness. Cf. now also Cecchini 1982, an intelligent article, which however does not resolve the question once and for all in my view. But Fritz Bornmann will deal with all this in the article whose appearance I announce in this note.[d]

Determining the Script of Lost Manuscripts

We have seen how Scaliger already tried to determine the script of the archetype of Catullus on the basis of some characteristic errors that appear in his manuscripts, and how Lachmann did the same thing for Lucretius (above, pp. 51–52, 107–8).

Attempts of this sort have a good chance of hitting the mark if they are performed with a rigorous method, and they are useful both for the history of tradition in itself and for textual criticism: for example, if one succeeds in demonstrating that the archetype was in capital script, conjectures that presuppose a confusion between minuscule letters become less probable, and so forth.

But if we wish to avoid getting lost in unfounded hypotheses, we must rely above all on a *large* number of readings that are certainly erroneous and cannot be explained otherwise than by the similarity between certain letters in a certain script. Errors that can be attributed to other causes too (that is, to confusions between graphic signs in other scripts, or to nongraphic reasons)[a] have no probative value. For example, confusions between *c* and *g*, or between *e* and *i*, might indeed be due to erroneous reading of a model written in capitals; but, at least in many cases,[b] they might also be phonetic vulgarisms (the confusions *c–g* might also provide an indication of a model in uncials, and an even better one),[c] and hence it will certainly be better to neglect them. Matters become even worse if we rely on readings that might be correct, or that could be corrected just as well (or better)[d] in a different way too.[e]

Once a large number of really probative errors has been collected, we must bear in mind the following points: (1) if each of the apographs of a lost manuscript α presents errors of its own due to misunderstanding a given script, then that was the script of manuscript α; (2) if the apographs of α present *shared* errors due to misunderstanding of a given script, then that was the script not of α but of the model from which α was directly or indirectly copied—for in that case the errors shared by the apographs *were already found in* α, and hence they were due to misunderstanding the script of a preceding manuscript.

Neither of these criteria is immune to objections. Against the former it can be noted that an error already found in α might have been reproduced by a copyist A and corrected conjecturally by a copyist B: in this case we would be attributing to α the script that was instead that of α's model. Against the latter it can be noted that various copyists might have misunderstood the same graphic sign of the model α independently of one another (for example, in pre-Caroline minuscule they might all have mistaken for a *u* an "open *a*," since this letter was particularly subject to being misread in that script): in this case we would be attributing erroneously to the model of α the script which was instead that of α.

If the examples on which we base our conclusions are few, these objections doubtless have a considerable weight; but in the face of a large number of examples, it becomes quite improbable that various copyists might independently have made a mistake every time at the same point, or that now one copyist, now another, might have made a felicitous conjecture, especially if there are not only two apographs of α but three or more.

Giovan Battista Alberti has called my attention to another possible objection against the *former* criterion: mistakes due to misunderstanding a given script which are found in the individual apographs of α might indicate the script not of α but of lost apographs intermediate between α and each of the extant manuscripts. This objection is valid above all when our data are few or contradictory, as in the case of Lucretius (see below). But if the graphical errors in the individual apographs *A, B,* etc. are numerous and they all derive from misunderstanding minuscule letters, then it is highly probable that they reflect the script of α and not of hypothetical intermediate links, since it would seem strange if no trace of misunderstanding of the script of α had survived. Furthermore, if the graphical errors of the individual manuscripts are all derived from misunderstanding majuscules, it is even more improbable that the common model α was not in majuscules: otherwise we would have to suppose a passage from an ancestor in minuscules to various descendants in majuscules—something not impossible, to be sure (especially now that we know that as a rule the first *ancient* copies of our Latin classics were not written in capitals: see below, p. 152 and n. 16), but difficult to postulate when all the manuscripts descend from a medieval archetype, and virtually impossible for Greek texts.[f]

The two criteria enunciated above are not to be found formulated explicitly in the manuals of textual criticism or paleography I have seen, but they do not represent a real novelty.[g] Giorgio Pasquali knew them well,[h] as some passages in his *Storia della tradizione* make clear,[1] even if a few other passages show some uncertainty.[i] And yet especially the second criterion has often been neglected. For example, W. V. Clausen quoted a large number of corruptions common to the two manuscripts of Persius *A* (Montepessulanus 212) and *B* (Vat. tabularii basilicae H 36) in his edition[j] of that poet in order to demonstrate that they were both derived from a model in minuscules (Clausen 1956: vii–viii). But no: those corruptions demonstrate that what was in minuscule was the manuscript from which the model of *AB* was copied. Certainly, this makes it likely that the model of *AB* too was in minuscule, even without going in search of minuscule corruptions characteristic of *A* alone and of *B* alone—but only as a secondary inference.[2]

For the same reason, even if the examples of corruptions of *scriptura Langobardica* (in the sense of pre-Caroline minuscule) that Scaliger collected in the whole tradition of Catullus he knew of had been numerous enough and had all been certain enough,[k,3] they would have served to dem-

---

1. Pasquali 1952a (1934): 149 and esp. 194–95. This question has also been well treated by Fabre 1947 (1936): lvi–lvii; Andrieu 1954: lxivn2; Pfeiffer 1949–53: 2.lxxxiv; K. Müller 1954: 785–97. See also the beginning of the following note. We shall discuss Lachmann and Duvau shortly.

2. Later, Clausen himself made this point quite well: Clausen 1963: 255. On the ancestor of the Palatine manuscripts of Plautus, see also O. Seyfferth's correct objection (Seyfferth 1896: 1551) against Lindsay, quoted and confirmed by Questa 1963: 218. In his edition of Caesar's *Bellum civile*, Klotz (1950: v) erroneously cites examples of errors due to misunderstanding of abbreviations in order to demonstrate that "the man who made the archetype of the manuscripts used many abbreviations, some of them rare ones," even though in the meantime the problem had been discussed in the right terms by Fabre (1947 [1936]: lvi–lvii): since those errors are found in all our manuscripts, the abbreviations that gave rise to them must have been found in a pre-archetype, not in the archetype. An analogous mistake is to be found in Klotz's preface to Statius's *Thebaid*, a preface that, in other regards, remains fundamental even today: he cites many examples of errors of minuscules (insular and perhaps, more generally, pre-Caroline ones?) in *individual* manuscripts of the ω class and concludes on this basis that between them and their ancestor there were intermediate exemplars in insular script (Klotz 1908: lvii–lix). In theory this is possible (see Alberti's observation cited above, p. 146); but precisely the large number of examples—which, as Klotz himself says, represent only a selection—provides a sufficient demonstration that already ω was written in insular script or in pre-Caroline minuscule: the "intermediaries" are neither a necessary nor a demonstrable hypothesis, one suggested, I suspect, by the preconception that the archetype necessarily had to be in capitals. The minuscule errors shared by all the descendants of ω which Klotz cites at 1908: lx serve to demonstrate that not ω but one of its ancestors was written in minuscules as well.

3. Grafton 1975: 171n58 cites from Scaliger's *Castigationes* five examples of the confusion *a–u*, three of *i–l*, seven of *c–t*, one of *c–g*. But the confusions *i–l* and *c–g* can oc-

onstrate that a manuscript earlier than the archetype was in pre-Caroline minuscule, but not the archetype itself.[4]

Considerable confusion reigns on this subject in many editions of Lucretius. To read the prefaces, one would think that Lachmann relied on corruptions shared by the whole tradition in order to maintain that the archetype was written in rustic capitals, and that Louis Duvau later demonstrated on the same basis that the archetype was in insular minuscule, copied in its turn from an archetype in capitals.[5] If this were correct, then both Lachmann and Duvau would have fallen victim to the same error that we have just now noted in Scaliger and in some recent Classical scholars. But in fact Lachmann limits himself in his preface to stating, "Many indications prove that the script of that manuscript [sc. the archetype] was in rather thin capital letters, not in uncials" (1850a: 1.3); in the commentary, unless I am mistaken, he notes explicitly only one of these indications, the reading *homofomerian* of the first hand of the Oblongus at 1.830, where the Quadratus and the Schedae have the correct reading *homoeomerian*.[6] He would certainly have done well to cite other examples to confirm his thesis, for that single case is not enough, as we shall soon see more clearly. But it cannot be said that in itself it was chosen poorly: Lachmann deduced the script of the archetype not from a corruption shared by the whole tradition but by a corruption in a single apograph, in conformity with the former of the two criteria we enunciated earlier. Nor can there be any doubt that the confusion between *e* and *f* presupposes a model in capital letters.

In an article of exemplary clarity and rigor,[7] Louis Duvau collected many

---

cur with other scripts too, and among the other confusions only very few indeed are probative: most are connected to completely fanciful conjectures on the part of Scaliger and collapse together with those conjectures.

4. There is also the possibility that some minuscule errors in Catullus's text, as in other authors', go back to a much earlier phase, that of "ancient minuscule": cf. Brunhölzl 1971: 21–22, and below, pp. 152–53 and nn. 16, 18.

5. See, e.g., Diels 1923–24: vii, xxiii; Ernout 1948 (1920): xvi–xvii; Leonard-Smith 1942: 107, 115; Bailey 1922 (1901): 1.37–38; Büchner 1956: 201 = Büchner 1964: 121. Brunhölzl too (1962: 98) rightly doubts the insular origin of the archetype and pre-archetype (cf. Reynolds-Wilson 1991 [1968]: 261) but incorrectly attributes to Duvau the opinion that the script of the archetype can be ascertained on the basis of the corruptions shared by the whole tradition. Martin 1969 (1934): viii reports Duvau's real opinion correctly, even if a bit too briefly, and without distinguishing between the Quadratus and the subarchetype common to the Quadratus and the Schedae.

6. Lachmann 1850b: 2.57 on 1.830: "The first hand of the Oblongus does not have *homoiomeriam,* as Havercamp reports, but *homofomerian,* from which we can tell what kind of script the archetype was written in."

7. Duvau 1888.

certain examples of corruptions due to misunderstanding of minuscule script;[8] but in fact, despite the claims of those who cite him without having read him with a minimum of attention, he derived from them the inference not that the archetype was in minuscules, but rather that what was in minuscules was the pre-archetype: "If all our manuscripts present shared errors deriving from a resemblance between certain letters that exists in minuscule script, and exists only in this script, then it follows: (1) that since these errors are shared by all our manuscripts, they were found in their archetype; (2) that the origin of these errors, that is, the minuscule script, was found in the manuscript to which this archetype goes back directly or indirectly" (Duvau 1888: 34). His judgment regarding corruptions due to the misunderstanding of abbreviations was just as precise: "Since they are found in all our manuscripts, they were made at the latest by the copyist of their archetype: hence their cause, that is, the use of abbreviations, was found in a manuscript earlier than this archetype itself" (1888: 33).

According to him, the archetype too was in minuscule script.[9] He did not give a positive demonstration of this claim; the fact that the pre-archetype was in minuscule script must have seemed sufficient to him to demonstrate that the same thing was true *a fortiori* for the archetype. Against the Lachmannian hypothesis of an archetype in capitals he observed. "I seek in vain for the reasons Lachmann thought he was obliged to believe that the original of the Oblongus was in capital script. The fact that no doubt led him to conceive this idea, the frequent confusion of letters that resemble one another only in capital script (for example, *i, e, l, t*), seems to me to prove exactly the opposite. For these errors are not committed separately by each of the copyists of the Oblongus, the Quadratus, and the Schedae: the same words are altered in the same way in all our manuscripts [. . .]. The conclusion is obvious: these errors existed in the archetype, either because the copyist of this manuscript introduced them himself when he copied an original in capitals or—and this is the hypothesis that must be accepted [. . .]— because they already existed in the manuscript that he was copying" (Duvau 1888: 34). Hence this was an archetype in minuscules, copied from a manuscript in minuscules too, that in its turn was derived directly or indirectly from a manuscript in capitals.

Now, there is no doubt that Duvau was perfectly correct in explaining

---

8. Duvau 1888: 35–36; some examples are repeated in Ernout 1948 (1920): xvii.

9. Duvau 1888: 33–34: "I believe that not only this direct original of the Oblongus [i.e., the archetype] was in minuscule script, but so too was the lost original of this manuscript." Purmann (1846: 14) had thought of an archetype or pre-archetype in *scriptura Langobardica* (i.e., Beneventan? or rather here too pre-Caroline minuscule, as in the passages from Scaliger we cited above, at chap. 1, n. 20?), but without adducing any proofs.

the capital errors *shared by the whole tradition* as errors inherited from a very ancient phase. But he was mistaken in supposing that Lachmann relied on *these* errors for his hypothesis concerning the archetype: we have already seen that Lachmann relied on a corruption in the Oblongus alone. Evidently Duvau did not notice this passage in the commentary to 1.830, and so he attributed to Lachmann the very same error of method that the editors of Lucretius would later attribute just as unfairly to himself.

In fact, although there can be no doubt concerning the existence of one pre-archetype in capitals and another one in minuscules, as we have seen just now, the indications regarding the script of the archetype are not unambiguous. *And, as far as I have been able to determine, this is a situation that occurs quite[l] frequently: it is much[m] easier to determine the script of manuscripts earlier than the archetype than the script of the archetype itself.*

In support of an archetype in capitals, there are other indications besides the *homofomerian* of the Oblongus at 1.830 noted by Lachmann (to which we shall return shortly): only O has *iam* for *tam* at 2.1088 and 5.902, *veniorum* for *ventorum* at 5.1230; Q and the Schedae (but not O) have *antfacta* for *anteacta* at 1.233 and *tinguntque* for *finguntque* at 3.90;[n] only Q has *eacies* for *facies* at 4.733, *forum* for *eorum* at 5.1337[10]—all[o] corruptions that do not seem to be explicable otherwise than by a model in capitals. Less certain is *reficit* for *reiicit* in O at 1.34: this could be a semiconscious banalization, since *reficit* seems to yield good sense, and the erroneous prosody *rē-* could have been influenced by apparently analogous cases like *rēligio* (aside from the fact that unmetrical readings are anything but rare in the manuscripts of Lucretius).[p]

Important indications in favor of an archetype in pre-Caroline minuscule are 1.282, where Q and the Schedae have *uuget* for *auget* (and hence so too did the subarchetype from which they descend), 413 (*meos aiauis* for *meo suauis*), 506 (*purumque* for *puramque*)[q]—all confusions between *u* and "open *a*."[11] So too, *parcis* for *partis* in O at 5.354 is quite probably an error of minuscules, certainly not one of capitals—if anything, then of uncials, even if the confusion is not between words of generally similar phonic and graphic appearance but instead between individual letters.[r] I would rely

10. In these last two passages the testimony of the Schedae is lacking; but nonetheless these cannot possibly be errors committed by the copyist of the Quadratus in the course of transcribing the archetype, since the subarchetype was certainly in pre-Caroline minuscule (see below, n. 13). So these must be errors committed by the copyist of the subarchetype in the course of transcribing the archetype.

11. David A. West has drawn my attention to some of these errors of minuscule. At 1.282 the second hand of the Oblongus has *urget,* preferred by Woltjer and Diels. Most editors prefer *auget,* rightly, I believe; in any case there is no doubt that this was the reading of the archetype.

with less confidence on 2.685 (*noscat* for *noscas* in Q and the Schedae) and 2.839 (*remotu* for *remota* in O): the first case may be a substitution of the more common third person for the second, while *remotu* may be the result of attraction from the preceding *sonitu*.[12] In the parts of the poem where the Schedae are lacking, the Quadratus presents some evident errors of pre-Caroline minuscule: 5.374 *aequori fundis* for *aequoris undis*, 482 *gurgites ossas* for *gurgite fossas*, 1147 *lusa* for *iura* (the Oblongus has *lura*); but since the subarchetype was certainly in pre-Caroline minuscule,[13] these errors may be peculiar to the Quadratus, so that we cannot make any inferences from them concerning the script of the archetype.

Thus the indications we have are few[s,14] and, what is worse, contradictory. Anyone who wishes to keep believing in the hypothesis of an archetype in minuscules will have to suppose that the capital corruptions of the Oblongus alone, or of the Quadratus + Schedae[t] alone, were already found in the archetype and were corrected conjecturally by the copyist of one of the two apographs. This is certainly possible for banal errors like *eacies* for *facies*; and even the sole error that, taken in isolation, might seem difficult to correct conjecturally, that is, the *homofomerian* at 1.830 upon which Lachmann insisted, could have been healed by the copyist of the Quadratus (or of the subarchetype from which the Quadratus and the Schedae descend) by comparison with 1.834, where the whole tradition has the correct reading *homoeomerian* (as has been correctly pointed out to me by E. J. Kenney[15]).

On the other hand, anyone who wanted to exclude the hypothesis of con-

---

12. At 2.833 (where the Oblongus has *discedunt*, the Quadratus and the Schedae have *disceduant*, and the correct reading is *discedant*, as Marullo saw), it is possible that the archetype already had a double reading, *discedunt* with an *a* added above the line: cf. Lachmann 1850a: 2.123.

13. See, e.g., 1.424 *referentes* G, *se ferentes* Q; 2.206 *volantes* Q, *voluntas* G; 2.891 *sedus* Q, *fedus* V; 6.1106 *brittanis* Q, *britunis* U; 6.1175 *mersans* O (correctly), *messans* U, *inerrans* Q; 6.1268 *videres* Q, *videses* U.

14. Some others can no doubt be found; but most of the corruptions peculiar to one of the two branches of the tradition consist in vulgarisms or elementary psychological errors (attraction of endings, etc.).

15. As Kenney reminds me, "The Middle Ages knew the word *homoios* from theological disputes." I add that Dr. E. Hulshoff Pol of the university library of Leiden, whom I asked to confirm the reading *homofomerian* of the first hand of the Oblongus, kindly warns me that that reading is not at all certain: "The *e* of *homoeomerian* in line 830 is written with a darker ink over an erasure. But I do not venture to say that what the first hand wrote was an *f*. Even under the infrared lamp no trace remains. The only thing that can be affirmed is that the erasure has more or less this form [the form of a right-angled triangle with the right angle at the top left] extending to the left and not to the right under the *e*." All the same, Lachmann's reading remains highly probable given the form of the erasure, and it has been accepted by all subsequent editors.

jectural interventions in both branches of the tradition would have to take recourse to a more complicated stemma: a pre-archetype in *ancient* minuscules (which would have caused the minuscule corruptions shared by the whole tradition), followed by another pre-archetype in capitals (which would have caused the capital corruptions shared by the whole tradition) and by the archetype likewise in capitals ("Lachmann's archetype," which would have caused the capital corruptions peculiar to each of the two branches);[u] an intermediate apograph in pre-Caroline minuscule (which would have caused the minuscule corruptions peculiar to each of the two branches) between the archetype and the Oblongus, and also between the archetype and the model of the Quadratus and the Schedae:

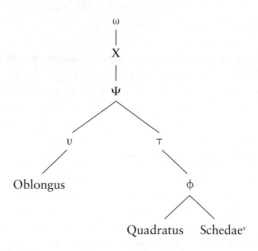

The phase in "ancient minuscule" (ω)[w] would not constitute any difficulty at all. One need only think of the studies of Jean Mallon and Robert Marichal and their followers,[x] who have demonstrated the early diffusion of this kind of script, and also of the fact that the Virgil manuscripts in capitals of the fourth and fifth centuries present many corruptions that can be explained only in terms of misunderstanding of minuscule letters.[16] This is

16. Out of Ribbeck's long and not entirely certain list (1866: 235–38) I select some particularly significant examples, which I have checked with the apparatus of M. Geymonat's edition of Virgil (Geymonat 1972): the first hand of the Mediceus has *monte* for *morte* (*Georg.* 3.518), *oriori* for *Orion* (*Aen.* 4.52), *arnam* for *Annam* (4.634), *ta* for *tu* (11.384); Fulvio Orsini's *Schedae Vaticanae* have *fluctur* for *fluctus* (*Aen.* 3.665); the Palatinus has *fecundut* for *fecundat* (*Georg.* 4.291), *ventas* for *ventus* (*Aen.* 5.777), *cyprism* for *cyprum* (u > i + s, *Aen.* 1.622),[y] *miseretcimus* (2.145), *nitu* for *nisu* (5.437), *tarnus* for *Sarnus* (7.738), *ulta* for *alta* (10.197). Ribbeck attributed these errors to cursive majuscules (he was thinking of "Pompeian" script, as was only natural at the time), but there is no doubt that these are errors of minuscule. Cf. also the following example, which I ran

what I wrote already in 1960 (Timpanaro 1960: 62 and n. 1). Since then, there have been great steps forward in this field. On the one hand, scholars have studied in greater depth the paleographical and cultural aspects of the "common script" in antiquity and of its various later (or sometimes contemporary) canonizations.[17] On the other hand, especially Franz Brunhölzl's examination of the minuscule corruptions already present in the most ancient surviving manuscripts in capitals (or in the manuscripts considered to be direct descendants of such manuscripts which have been lost), performed in conjunction with the examination of the most ancient Latin papyri, has led to the conclusion that the most ancient literary manuscripts of the Republican and Imperial ages did not resemble the Palatinus or Mediceus manuscripts of Virgil (Vatican, Pal. lat. 1631; Florence, Laur. 39. 1 + Vatican lat. 3225, fol. 76) but were *volumina* of semicursive script, minuscule or rich in minuscule aspects.[z,18]

Even if these recent studies seem capable of confirming the stemma I have proposed now,[aa] all in all the first hypothesis (an archetype in minuscules) continues to seem preferable[bb] to me, now that Kenney has overcome what had seemed to me the only serious obstacle, as I indicated above. Of course this does not in the least exclude the possibility that the corruptions due to ancient minuscule might in part go back to copies much older than the archetype.[cc,19]

---

into by accident (others can no doubt be found): Cicero, *de re p.* 2.39, where the first hand of the Vatican palimpsest has *certamine* for *centuriae*. The phrase "Kursiver-Kapitalis" [cursive capital], used by Brunhölzl precisely with regard to certain corruptions of the manuscripts of Lucretius (1971: 16–17, 21), does not seem appropriate. Brunhölzl (1971: 16n2) cites the first edition of this book of mine and even the earlier version (Timpanaro 1959, 1960), but he does not seem to have read them; and although he cites interesting examples of corruptions in Virgil (1971: 23–24), he does not refer to Ribbeck, who at an early time made a precious collection of material, even if it is in need of classification, and who had certainly understood that many errors of the oldest extant manuscripts of Virgil presupposed a script earlier than book-hand capitals.

17. I do not intend to burden my exposition with long bibliographical lists, which in any case would be inadequate. I only wish to recall the studies of E. Casamassima because of the novelty of their own contributions, and in particular Casamassima-Staraz 1977.

18. Brunhölzl 1971 (conclusions at 29–31). See also the following note. Cf. Cavallo 1975 for the general aspects (script, *volumen* and codex, Christian influences, the rise of a *new* type of luxury manuscripts in Late Antiquity, including pagan ones); see also the other essays collected in this volume and the final bibliography.

19. On this point, with regard to Lucretius, Brunhölzl 1971: 21 is right to correct himself with respect to Brunhölzl 1962. In my opinion, Brunhölzl's study, which he presents in any case only as a first version of a fuller work, has not only many virtues but also three defects: (1) for each text, the exemplification is too skimpy; (2) this skimpiness is wors-

Naturally this whole discussion can be neglected by an editor of Lucretius, since the only thing that matters for the practical purposes of constituting the text is to know that there are errors both of capitals and of minuscules in the tradition of Lucretius. It can be neglected; but it should not be explained in a confused and erroneous manner, as almost all the editors have done hitherto.[20]

*   *   *

Finally, there is one field of textual criticism in which the examination of graphic corruptions can render a useful service: *eliminatio codicum descriptorum.*

As is well known, this operation is particularly difficult when a manuscript presents not only a large number of corruptions in common with another older manuscript, but also a number of certainly or probably correct readings in passages in which the older manuscript is corrupt. This raises the following problem: *can* these readings be the fruit of conjecture, or are they such that they could not have been excogitated conjecturally in any way whatsoever? In the latter case, the more recent manuscript is a brother of the older one, not its son, and therefore must not be eliminated; in the former case (which unfortunately occurs quite frequently), the more recent manuscript *can* be a copy of the older one, but there is no certainty that this is how matters really stand.

Hence it is a great piece of luck to be able to find positive proofs that one manuscript is derived from another, consisting in material damage to the older manuscript (displacement of leaves or fascicles, "windows," etc.) to which transpositions or lacunas in the more recent manuscript correspond.[21] But it is just as useful to find proofs of *nonderivation,* which let us assert with certainty that the more recent manuscript is not a copy of another sur-

---

ened by the fact that the author is too sure that he can explain as being due to graphic confusions errors that could be psychological; (3) when late ancient manuscripts in capitals are not preserved but are reconstructed from Caroline copies, one must never forget the alternative hypothesis of errors of pre-Caroline minuscule: cf. Timpanaro 1970: 288. In the case of Lucretius this hypothesis becomes a certainty when what is involved are the errors of the common model of the Quadratus and the Schedae, cf. above, n. 13.

20. In his edition of Lucretius, K. Müller provides a far better stemma than those of earlier editions, even if it too is not free of "doubtful passages" (upon which I shall not insist, since my doubts can easily be inferred from what I have said until now): K. Müller 1975: 297–300. I am disregarding, of course, the problem of the "Italici," to which I have already referred (above, pp. 108–9, 111–12).

21. See above, pp. 47f., 99–101; and the magisterial chap. 3 of Pasquali 1952a (1934): 25–40.

viving manuscript and that in consequence the correct readings that it contains may represent tradition and not conjecture.

Now, one good proof of nonderivation can be provided by certain graphic substitutions. If, for example, a manuscript that is suspected of being derived from another surviving manuscript in Caroline script presents a certain number of corruptions typical of pre-Caroline minuscule, then we can conclude with certainty that that suspicion was groundless and that this manuscript must not be eliminated.

Pasquali warns quite correctly against hasty eliminations based on "graphic signs that lend themselves to being confused with one another" and observes, "When someone maintains that A is derived from B because A has misread a case ending in B which was expressed by an abbreviation 'by suspension' that can be resolved in more ways than one, or by a letter drawn so poorly that it can be confused with another one, then it is legitimate to observe that any manuscript of the same scriptorium, or even of more or less the same period as B, used or could have used the same abbreviation, which could easily be confused with another one every time it was not written impeccably" (1952a [1934]: 35). But although these corruptions due to misunderstanding of graphic signs count little or nothing for the purposes of the elimination of a manuscript, they can be decisive for the purposes of its nonelimination. Whereas five or six certain confusions between s and r do not at all serve to demonstrate that a manuscript A was copied from an extant[dd] manuscript B in insular script, inasmuch as any other insular model would have lent itself to analogous misunderstandings, they serve perfectly well to demonstrate instead that A was *not* derived from a manuscript C in Caroline script, even if by chance the two manuscripts present many coincidences in corruption.

Hence Maas's formulation, "If a witness, J, exhibits all the errors of another surviving witness, F, and in addition at least one error of its own ('peculiar error'), then J must be assumed to derive from F" (1958 [1927]: p. 4, sec. 8 [a]), is not only open to the more general objections that can be raised against such a rule;[22] what is more, one must in any case specify: "and in

22. What is more, this rule is presented by Maas himself as a deduction from a presupposition that need not correspond to reality: cf. Maas 1958 (1927): pp. 8–9, sec. 11; and Pasquali 1952a (1934): 30n3 (but Pasquali displays a certain reluctance to discuss directly with Maas and minimizes the difference between Maas's position and his own analysis of the problem of *eliminatio descriptorum*). In any case, a manuscript that had the characteristics of J, even if it had not been copied from F, would have to be eliminated anyway because it would be completely useless for constituting the text. The interesting (and difficult) case is not this one, which Maas considers "typical," but another one, in which J presents good readings that are not found in F and that can (but need not) be the fruit of conjecture; and in this case Maas always inclines toward elimination, not in his theoreti-

addition at least one error of its own that does not presuppose a script (or even a context) different from that of *F*."

In fact, Pasquali already indicated a specification of this sort when he wrote, "When, after collating a more recent manuscript in its entirety with an older one, one has found no probative indications of dependence, but neither has one discovered better readings or individual divergences, and *not even corruptions* that *cannot derive from the older manuscript* but raise the suspicion of a tradition that may be extremely disfigured but is still different—in that case, and in that case alone, one can be satisfied with the 'presumption' that the more recent MS is a copy of the older one" (1952a [1934]: 35, our emphasis). All the same, as is clear from the words "but raise the suspicion of a tradition that may be extremely disfigured but is still different," Pasquali was not thinking so much of graphic errors that can be explained by one determinate script and not by another, but rather of larger corruptions such as presuppose at their origin a different reading from that of the presumed model. And this too is a possible case; but I believe that the examination of purely graphic corruptions as well will be able to rescue from elimination manuscripts that have been unjustly suspected hitherto, if care is taken to collect a considerable number of certain examples.

---

cal pronouncements, but in his scanty exemplification: cf. 1958 (1927): pp. 26–27, sec. 27; cf. Maas 1960: 32. But I intend to return elsewhere to the problem of the *descripti*.

Bipartite Stemmas and Disturbances
of the Manuscript Tradition

In the last fifty[a] years (though often with long intervals, as is only natural),[b] the scholarly discussion regarding the extraordinary frequency of bipartite stemmas[c] has given rise to the most varied positions and to results of considerable methodological interest. Until about twenty years ago,[d] Classical philologists often displayed no knowledge of the contributions of their colleagues in Romance languages (sometimes the opposite occurred too, but less often); more recently the field of Greek and Latin studies too has witnessed a reawakening of interest in this problem, which is less marginal and less strictly technical than might be supposed. The first version of this appendix, in the 1963 edition of the present volume, may perhaps have made some contribution to this state of affairs. The second version, which I present here, does not differ substantially from the first one, but without aspiring to what would necessarily be a confusing bibliographic completeness it does take account of those works that have appeared since then, some of which are very important; and it aims to draw attention more decisively to what, in my opinion, has always been the central point of the whole controversy.[e,1]

In his brilliant and paradoxical article on the manuscript tradition of the *Lai de l'Ombre*, which we have already had occasion to cite more than once,[2] Joseph Bédier observed that in the overwhelming majority of cases the manuscript stemmas traced out by the editors of medieval texts had only two branches: even if the extant manuscripts were very numerous, they were almost always made to derive not directly from the archetype, but through two and only two subarchetypes; and even when preparatory works on the

---

1. Besides the studies I shall cite in the course of the following pages, see the copious bibliographical indications in Frank 1955: 463n1 (brought to my attention by Alfredo Stussi). Cf. also Balduino 1979: 237–41.

2. See above, pp. 44, 80n23. Bédier had already presented the same ideas in his preface to Renart 1913: xxv–xli, but less fully and with less polemical verve.

manuscripts of a given text had hypothesized the existence of three or more families, the scholar who finally set about to do the critical edition had reduced the number of families to two.

So, Bédier observed, it would appear that by a very singular chance almost all archetypes had possessed a direct progeny consisting of only two apographs, or, at least, that it was from only two apographs that all the extant copies had been derived. "The flora of philology knows only trees of a single kind: the trunk always divides into two dominant branches, and only into two. . . . A bifid tree is not at all strange, but a clump of bifid trees, a grove, a forest? *Silva portentosa* [a wondrous forest]." Bédier observed an analogous frequency of bipartite stemmas in the manuscript traditions of Classical texts as well, though he admitted that his research had been less extensive and profound in this field than for French medieval texts (1928: 171–72).

Bédier identified the cause of this strange phenomenon not in the objective conditions by which medieval manuscripts were produced but in the philologists' unconscious desire to maintain their freedom of choice when choosing variants. In fact, if the manuscript tradition has three or more branches, the reading of the archetype can almost always be established by a mechanical procedure, as long as the eventuality of contamination is excluded (see above, p. 109); but if it has only two branches, the mechanical method[f] can only serve to eliminate those innovations that have been produced in descendants of individual subarchetypes,[g] whereas the decision must be entrusted to internal criteria whenever the one subarchetype's reading is opposed to the other's.

Thus, according to Bédier, Lachmann's method, which had been elaborated precisely so as to expel subjective judgment from textual criticism, had been applied by philologists in such a way as to preserve the widest possible field of application for subjective judgment. If Bédier had noticed that Lachmann himself had unconsciously slipped from a tripartite classification of the manuscripts to a bipartite one in his preface to Lucretius (see above, pp. 108–11) and that Madvig had consciously changed his mind in an analogous way with regard to a group of Cicero's orations (see chap. 5, n. 19),[h] he would have seen in these facts the best possible confirmation of his thesis!

But following a suggestion of Mario Roques, Bédier also indicated another cause, this one subjective too, for the philologists' tendency to bipartitism, besides their unconfessed desire to preserve freedom of choice: their habit of always seeking new connections between groups of manuscripts, and thus of ascending to more and more encompassing[i] groupings, until they have reduced the fundamental regroupings to only two. According to Bédier, the Lachmannian textual critic feels "the persistent anxiety that, however far he has extended the criticism of variants, he has still not extended it far enough." And so, if a first phase of his research has led him to establish the existence of three families of manuscripts, that "anxiety" induces him to look for readings that unite two families against the third one, to convince himself that such readings are erroneous and hence to make these conjunctive errors go back to a shared subarchetype, from which the ancestors of the two families would have descended (instead of directly from the archetype). "It is not with impunity," Bédier concludes with ironic emphasis, "that he has accustomed himself to oppose the good reading to the bad one or ones, the rays of light to the darkness, Ormazd to Ahriman: once the dichotomic force has been aroused, it continues to act to the very end" (Bédier 1928: 176).

From this denunciation of Lachmannism, Bédier derived an exhortation to abandon any attempt at *recensio* and to adhere instead to a single manuscript. The illogicality of this exhortation has already been demonstrated too clearly for it still to be necessary for us to linger on this subject.[3] What interests us here, and what constitutes the only really interesting and acute part of Bédier's article, is the question of the frequency of bipartite stemmas.

On this point, two very different answers were given to Bédier, by Giorgio Pasquali on the one hand, and by Paul Maas and various Romance philologists[j] on the other. Pasquali, at least at first,[k] denied for Latin and Greek texts the datum from which Bédier had started out, namely, the extraordinary rarity of stemmas with more than two[l] branches: "I would like to ask Bédier to extend his inquiry to Classical texts; there he would find umpteen three-, four-, five-branched stemmas."[4]

Was this answer correct? To a certain extent it was, but to an entirely inadequate extent. There is no doubt that Bédier exaggerated the extreme rarity of stemmas with more than two branches when he performed his examination of the editions of medieval French texts: Arrigo Castellani redid that examination with great accuracy and precision and reached less radical con-

---

3. See the works cited above, chap. 3, n. 23. And setting aside, as always, the case in which each manuscript represents an independent "redaction," it should be noted that it is not at all true that the "lesser evil" is to follow a single manuscript when no stemma can be reconstructed. In these cases the lesser evil is to choose the variants according to internal criteria, without abandoning the attempt to provide a complete evaluation of the greater or lesser tendency of each manuscript's copyist to reproduce the model faithfully even where it is corrupt or on the other hand to "patch it up," to "prettify," to falsify. It is senseless to reject such a procedure as "eclectic." Every time more than one copyist transcribes a model, "eclecticism" is objectively created, inasmuch as they make different mistakes in different parts of the text, with rare exceptions. To this random and irrational eclecticism we must oppose our choice, which is based on rational argument and therefore is not eclectic in the pejorative sense.

4. Pasquali 1932a: 130–31.

clusions. And yet he had to admit that Bédier's accusation remained substantially valid. As he writes, "Bifid trees are about 75–76 percent; they are 82–83 percent if the uncertain trees are not included in the total. Even if their predominance is not as overwhelming as in Bédier's statistics, it still remains quite remarkable. Four bifid stemmas for every multifid one: that is a ratio which does indeed seem 'surprising.'" As for Greek and Latin texts, in 1932 Pasquali was still able to collect a respectable number of stemmas with more than two branches on the basis of the most authoritative editions; he himself cited some of them two years later in his *Storia della tradizione* (e.g., 1952a [1934]: 149, 195, 270, 303). And yet it is not by chance that his brash phrase about the "umpteen" multipartite stemmas is no longer to be found in that book; it is not by chance that Pasquali later returned to attacking Bédier rightly for his demand that editions should be based on a single manuscript but never again breathed a word regarding the question of stemmas with more than two branches. Those very same passages of his *Storia della tradizione* that we have cited just now, and others which could also be cited, demonstrate that even when Pasquali accepts a multipartite stemma as a starting point for his discussion about the tradition of an author, he almost always ends up observing later that the distinction into "branches" or families is far less clear than is customarily believed, or even making such branches (it matters little whether they are two or more in number) go back to stages earlier than the archetype, to ancient editions compared with which the medieval archetype, even if it is still hypothesized, is conceived as a "collecting basin" for different traditions, or else as a true Lachmannian archetype, but one whose descendants have received by collation the contribution of other streams of ancient tradition, now lost (on this possibility see below, p. 183 and n. 51).

   Thus Pasquali already admitted implicitly that there were only a few true tripartite stemmas, and later studies have reduced their number rather than increasing it. In Classical philology the same phenomenon has occurred that Bédier observed in his own field of studies (and that anyway had already begun with Lachmann and Madvig, as has been seen): manuscript traditions that had first been considered tripartite were later reduced to only two initial subarchetypes. This has happened, for example, for Plato's fourth tetralogy and for Macrobius's *Saturnalia*.[5] And just now Giovan Battista Alberti has performed a strict examination that leaves very few stemmas with more than two branches intact (Alberti 1979). In certain cases this exami-

---

   5. For Plato see the introduction to Carlini 1963; other Platonic tetralogies or individual dialogues cannot be traced back to medieval archetypes, so that the problem that interests us here does not even arise. For Macrobius, Willis 1957: 156–57 against a tripartite stemma proposed earlier by A. La Penna.

nation may have been too strict: I still incline to believe that the stemma of Calpurnius's eclogues is tripartite, because I do not believe that a subarchetype can be postulated on the basis of a single shared corruption, aside from coincidences in hardly significant innovations: if there really had been such a subarchetype, it would have left greater and less ambiguous traces.[6] But Alberti's arguments are incontrovertible in the vast majority of the eighty or so Greek and Latin manuscript traditions that he examines.[7] The path which we saw that Pasquali temporarily chose, to deny the very existence of the fact observed by Bédier, must be abandoned.[n]

Maas tried another path. He fully admitted the overwhelming prevalence of stemmas with two branches, but sought its explanation[o] above all in considerations of a statistical nature: "First of all we must remind ourselves that of the twenty-two types of stemma possible where three witnesses exist, only one has three branches [. . .]. Furthermore it is in the very nature of the medieval tradition that in the case of little-read texts three copies were only rarely taken from the same archetype; more rarely still have all these copies, or descendants from each of them, survived; on the other hand, where texts were much read there is a tendency for contamination to creep in, and where contamination exists the science of stemmatics in the strict sense breaks down. In the later subbranches it would certainly have been easier to presuppose the existence, and survival, of three copies from the same archetype; but in these cases the editors were often able, without doing any

---

6. Cf. Alberti 1979: 67–68, who discusses the tripartite stemma proposed by Castagna 1976: 181–243. Apart from three other passages, which Alberti too admits are not decisive, the only conjunctive error between two of the three branches traced out by Castagna is *altera* for *arida* at Calpurnius Siculus 2.48. The error belongs to the category of confusions between words of similar graphical or phonic "total appearance," on which cf. Timpanaro 1976: 64–71, 97, with further bibliographical references; it may already have been present in the archetype, and the correct reading may be the fruit either of conjecture or of collation with another manuscript unknown to us (extra-stemmatic contamination: cf. below, p. 179). Alberti declares that he is skeptical with regard to the former possibility but he does not consider the latter one. But I repeat that the price that must be paid in order to obtain a bipartite stemma is a subarchetype whose copyist committed only one serious error. On the tradition of Calpurnius Siculus see also below, p. 175. One problem I would like to reexamine sometime is that of Cicero's *Catilinarians* (Alberti 1979: 61–67). On the tradition of the lesser Latin bucolic poets, see now, after Castagna 1976, Reeve 1978. I have not yet had the time to reexamine this problem with the attention it deserves.[m]

7. As we shall see, such arguments only rarely induce Alberti to construct bipartite stemmas (cf. below, p. 182); in substance his conclusions coincide with my own regarding the role played by contamination. Alberti is always or almost always right in his opposition to hypothesized stemmas with more than two branches which permit a mechanical recension.

harm, to avoid adducing more than two of these copies in order to reconstruct a hyparchetype of no stemmatic importance."[8]

Objections against this[p] statistical argument have been raised correctly,
if a bit too briefly, by Jean Irigoin, Arrigo Castellani, and István Frank;[9] and
more recently, after the first edition of the present study, Alexander Kleinlogel has expressed even more radical objections, as we shall see shortly.[q]
But since Maas (an exceptional philologist, but entirely impervious to other
people's objections, entirely unable to understand from others anything that
he did not understand from himself)[r] always continued to believe in the validity of that absurd argument,[s] and later as well, and[t] even recently has received the approval of scholars who are excellent but too inclined to *iurare
in verba magistri* [to swear upon their teacher's words],[u,10] it will not be useless to return to this question in a rather detailed way, even at the cost of
causing the reader some fatigue.[v]

According to Maas (1937: 287–89 = 1958 [1927] 44–47), with three
witnesses there are twenty-two possible stemmatic types. More precisely,
there are six combinations in which from a first manuscript a second one derives, and from this latter a third one; three combinations in which from one
of the three manuscripts derive the other two; three combinations in which
two manuscripts derive from the third by means of a lost intermediary; three
combinations in which a lost archetype has produced on the one hand one
of the surviving manuscripts and on the other a lost manuscript from which
in turn the other two surviving ones derive; six combinations in which a lost
archetype has given rise to two surviving manuscripts, from one of which
the third surviving one is then derived; and finally one combination in which
each of the three surviving manuscripts is derived independently from a lost
archetype. This last combination is the only tripartite one, while none of the

---

8. Maas 1937: 289–91 = Maas 1958 (1927): 48–49.

9. Irigoin 1954; Castellani 1980 (1957) (an excellent treatment: Castellani gives a particularly detailed refutation of J. Fourquet's arguments, cf. below, p. 165 and n. 13, but his
refutation is also valid against Maas, to whom he replies briefly at p. 170n5); Frank 1955:
465 (correct, but a bit too general).

10. Roncaglia 1952: 281–82; Erbse 1959: 97; Hering 1967. Hering's article is an attempt to develop Maas's argument further by correcting it in some secondary points but
leaving its substance intact; it is worth reading for some acute observations on individual
points and for its author's full knowledge of manuscript traditions, but Hering does not invalidate the basic objections that had already been raised against Maas by myself and others; indeed I would go so far as to say that he has not even understood them, even though
they are not difficult. Even more recently, in a valuable anthology of writings on philological method, Bruno Basile selected from Maas precisely that wretched passage on stemmatic types and on the rarity of stemmas with more than two branches (Basile 1975: 59–
64)! Cf. Belloni 1976: 507.

other twenty-one is tripartite. Here is an outline of the various species of stemmas (the Greek letters indicate lost manuscripts):

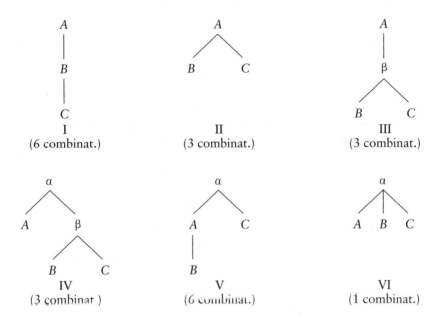

But to combine all these possibilities under the common label of "types of stemma possible where three witnesses exist" means to lump together things that ought to remain quite distinct for the purposes of the calculation of probabilities. For in the stemmas of the first and second species there was an original total of three manuscripts, all three preserved; in the stemmas of the third, fifth, and sixth species there was an original total of four manuscripts, of which one has been lost and three are preserved; in the fourth species finally the lost manuscripts are two, that is, the original total was five manuscripts. The only element common to the twenty-two types listed by Maas is the fact that the *surviving* manuscripts are always three. But the number of genealogical combinations of three surviving manuscripts *out of an undefined number of originally existing manuscripts* is not twenty-two but infinite. Maas's list does not include, for example, stemmas like these:

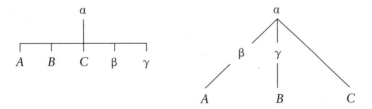

and like all the others that can be traced out by multiplying the number of lost manuscripts at will.

It will be objected that from the point of view of *recensio* these infinite stemmas can be reduced in every case to one of the twenty-two listed by Maas. The stemma that the textual critic ends up tracing out on the basis of the indications furnished by the shared corruptions is in fact a greatly simplified one, as has long since been made clear:[11] the method of shared corruptions allows one to establish that two manuscripts *AB* both descend from a lost manuscript α, but except in rare cases it does not allow one to identify possible intermediate copies between α and *A* and between α and *B*. If it were possible to trace out the genealogical tree of all the manuscripts of a given text that really existed (what Fourquet and Castellani call "the real tree"), then this would almost always turn out to be much richer than the stemma that we end up reconstructing on the basis of shared corruptions.[12] For the purposes of *recensio,* this causes no problems: our simplified stemmas function just as well for reconstructing the reading of the archetype as they would if we were able to trace out the "real stemmas." But when the point is to calculate the probability that three manuscripts belong either to a bipartite stemma or to a tripartite one, then it is not legitimate to neglect the real stemmas as Maas does and simply to assign an *equal* probability to each simplified stemma.

Let us consider, for example, these four stemmas:

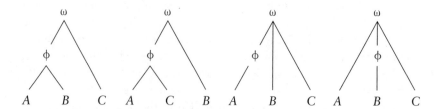

For the purposes of *recensio,* the first two have the right to an autonomous existence, but the third and fourth do not, since even if the existence of an intermediate member φ between ω and *A* or between ω and *B* could be demonstrated, this would in any case be irrelevant for reconstructing the archetype's readings. But when we calculate the probabilities, it falsifies everything if we take account of the first and second type, attributing an equal probability to each one, and then eliminate the third and fourth ones by re-

---

11. Cf. Seel 1936: 19, and more recently, Fourquet 1946: 4–5.

12. One way of approaching (but only approaching, though still remaining quite distant) the complexity of the "real tree" is to investigate the scripts of lost manuscripts of which we would otherwise have no trace, as we have indicated in the preceding Appendix B.

ducing them to the *only* tripartite stemma traced out by Maas and attributing *only an equal* probability to this stemma, which includes within it those others as well.

So if we ask ourselves: "Given three surviving manuscripts out of an undefined number of originally existing manuscripts, what is the probability that those manuscripts belong to a bipartite stemma or to a tripartite one?" the answer must be that the problem is insoluble. The probability that three surviving manuscripts belong to two or to three different branches of the manuscript tradition is obviously quite different, depending on whether the original total in that tradition was four manuscripts or fifty, and depending on whether three different branches of tradition originally developed out of the archetype or ten.

If, on the other hand, we define not only the number of manuscripts that survive but also the number of the ones that originally existed, then a calculus of the probabilities is indeed possible, but it does not at all indicate the kind of preponderance of bipartitism over multipartitism imagined by Maas and, later, Jean Fourquet. Castellani has demonstrated that if the "real stemma" is rich enough, the chances are virtually equal that three surviving manuscripts will belong to a bipartite stemma or to a tripartite one.[13] Castellani's polemic is directed against Fourquet's arguments, but, as he himself indicates in a note, the same objections are also valid against Maas.[14]

Let us add that it cannot even be said, strictly speaking, that when Maas listed those "twenty-two types of stemma possible with three witnesses" of his he was restricting himself to types that are significant for the purposes of *recensio*. In fact, most of these Maasian stemmas present manuscripts that should be eliminated as *descripti:* in as many as eighteen cases out of twenty-two, one or even two of the three manuscripts are copies of a surviving manuscript, and hence either *recensio* does not take place (in the case of a unique manuscript) or else it is reduced to only two manuscripts, and then it is evident that even the possibility of a tripartite stemma cannot be conceived.[15]

13. Castellani 1980 (1957): 164–70. Castellani 1980 [1957]: 170n4 cites another refutation of Fourquet by Whitehead-Pickford 1951: I was able to see this thanks to Castellani himself, who kindly lent me an offprint. See now also Whitehead-Pickford 1973; but this article has too many gaps to provide a good summary of the whole discussion, nor does it seem to me to contain new contributions of any great importance.

14. Castellani 1980 (1957) 171n5: "Answer to Mr. Maas: the number of bifid stemmatic types that three manuscripts can form has no importance. What matters is the place occupied by these three manuscripts in the real tree."

15. This objection was already raised by Irigoin 1954: 212, but he still gave too much credit to Maas, inasmuch as he maintained that only the twelve cases in which a surviving manuscript is the source of the other two were to be eliminated from his list. But so too

But when Bédier noticed to his astonishment the great prevalence of bipartite stemmas over multipartite ones, he was referring to stemmas traced out after *eliminatio codicum descriptorum* had already been performed. So that while on the one hand Maas excludes from his list the infinite "real stemmas" to which three surviving manuscripts can belong, on the other hand he inflates the list illegitimately by including within it all the cases in which one or two of the three manuscripts ought to be eliminated.

In reality, the fundamental defect of all these probabilistic arguments is that they start "from the tail" instead of "from the head." People tend to forget that the real historical process is that a certain number of copies are derived from a model, and then a certain number of subcopies are derived from them, and so on. The inverse process, grouping together a certain number of copies so as to form different stemmatic figures, is purely abstract. Hence we should be trying not to see into how many bipartite or tripartite combinations a given number of manuscripts can be grouped together but to establish whether it is more probable that only two copies were initially derived from an archetype, or three, or more. Once we put the problem in this way, we immediately see that it cannot be resolved by means of a mere mathematical calculation. Whether a manuscript is copied only once, twice, or ten times depends on a complex set of cultural and economic conditions: the number of persons who wish to read that text, the number of copyists who are available for copying it, the cost of the writing materials, and so forth. And in the same way, the greater or lesser probability that all the copies of that text have been preserved or that they have been destroyed to a greater or lesser extent is determined by quite variable historical conditions.[16]

The defectiveness of Maas's reasoning is already clear from what has already been said, but Kleinlogel's arguments make it even more evident. He

---

where only two manuscripts remain, the problem of a tripartite stemma does not even arise: hence six other combinations must also be eliminated.

16. According to Greg 1930–31: 401–3, Andrieu 1943: 462, and Ullman 1956: 580, the preponderance of bipartite stemmas is precisely a consequence of the "decimation" undergone by most manuscript traditions. But Castellani 1980 (1957): 174 demonstrates that it is only in special cases that the decimation could have increased the number of bipartite stemmas (somewhat contradictorily, he later assigns greater importance to the decimation; 1980 [1957]: 181). Indeed, why must the decimation every time have been precisely so destructive as to let the descendants of exactly two subarchetypes survive and not of three? This is already unlikely from the point of view of an abstract calculation of probability; it becomes even more unlikely (and here Castellani perhaps did not go into the question deeply enough) if we consider that decimation too is a series of historical events that depend on accidental causes (fires, etc.) and degrees of "cultural depression" that are highly variable and cannot be calculated in the absence of detailed documentation.

demonstrates that Maas presupposes tacitly and unconsciously, and without the least experimental basis, that the different stemmatic types are to be considered as "equiprobable events" (Kleinlogel 1968: 66–68).[17] Quite correctly he objects: "In Maas's typology we neither have statistics which establish that each type is found with the same frequency nor have we any reason to assign them the same probability *a priori*. The structural differences that provide the only criterion for classifying the types imply nothing about their probability or frequency" (1968: 67). I myself am not capable of following Kleinlogel's argument in all its steps and details (he also availed himself of the advice of a mathematician, H. G. Kellerer; cf. Kleinlogel 1968: 63n1), but the conclusion is clear (1968: 74–75) and agrees with what others and I had already observed: it is not possible to solve the problem of the great prevalence of bipartite stemmas by merely deductive means, by an abstract calculation of probabilities unsupported by empirical data.[w]

The *second* of Maas's arguments that we reported above seems to lead us onto a genuinely historical and empirical terrain, and hence a much more concrete one:[x] "it is in the very nature of the medieval tradition that in the case of little-read texts three copies were only rarely taken from the same archetype; more rarely still have all these copies, or descendants from each of them, survived; on the other hand where texts were much read there is a tendency for contamination to creep in, and where contamination exists the science of stemmatics in the strict sense breaks down." And yet this argument too turns out to be fallacious if it is examined with a minimum of attention. Maas's reference to "little-read texts" can certainly explain well the lack of stemmas with ten or twenty branches, for example, but it does not at all suffice to explain the enormous divergence in frequency between stemmas with two branches and stemmas with three. We would obviously expect to find a *gradually decreasing* frequency of stemmas corresponding inversely with an equally gradual increase in the number of their branches: for example, given fifteen different manuscript traditions, five stemmas with two branches, four with three, three with four, two with five, one with six— obviously I have artificially regularized this example for the sake of expository convenience: in reality the decrease would turn out to be more "capricious." But what we cannot understand is such an abrupt "jump" between the number of bipartite stemmas and the number of tripartite ones. It seems that Maas and the many scholars who have found this argument of his convincing have forgotten that the difference between two and three is only one! To listen to them, one would think that the category of "poor traditions" is

17. Even before Kleinlogel's article, this was pointed out to me privately by my friends Giuseppe Torresin and Giampiero Zarri.

constituted only by traditions with a single branch (for which stemmatic problems do not exist) and by those with two branches; the domain of "rich traditions" would suddenly begin starting with three branches. This is not at all "in the very nature of the medieval tradition," and it is not even in the nature of common sense: just because a tripartite tradition *is only richer by a very little bit* than a bipartite one, it ought to have occurred fairly often even in the case of little-read texts.[18] Such a "jump" between bipartite stemmas and tripartite ones could only be explained if some regulation or inveterate habit in the Middle Ages were known that ensured that every ancient manuscript was copied not more than two times and was then destroyed. But obviously we do not have the slightest indication of such a regulation, and it is entirely improbable. Among other considerations (but I realize that I am discussing absurdities at too great a length), how are we to imagine such a regulation remaining in effect just as much in the Latin and Romance and Germanic West as in the Byzantine East, in different cultural environments, in very different periods?

As we shall see later, the only thing that is really correct in that passage from Maas is his appeal to contamination. But Maas uses this too in a distorted way, exonerating the bipartite traditions from contamination (so that "stemmatic rigor" would rule in them) and postulating a contamination, beginning with tripartite traditions, so intense as to cancel out any genealogical relation. Since all traditions (including those with two branches: cf. above, chap. 6, n. 18; and below, pp. 182f.) are more or less contaminated, and since richer traditions as a rule are more contaminated, one wonders why there should not have been numerous intermediate cases of traditions not so contaminated as to be irreducible to any stemma but on the other hand not so meager as to be limited to only two branches.

Setting aside Maas's pseudo-explanations, we can still wonder whether the conditions of the transmission of medieval texts were such as to explain this stubborn preponderance of bipartite stemmas. Various hypotheses have been put forward in this regard. For example, Castellani has acutely observed that[y] the widespread diffusion of a text and a stemma with many branches need not be connected with one another (1980 [1957]: 175–82). Anyone who wants to obtain a certain number of copies from a manuscript in the shortest time possible should not have the model copied successively as many times as he wants there to be copies of it but rather should first have

18. As for the improbability, asserted by Maas, that "all these copies [. . .] survived," see what I have already observed in n. 16 about "decimation." Once again we return to the improbable "leap" in frequency between tripartite stemmas and bipartite ones. And it is ridiculous to describe just three copies as "*all* these copies."

the model copied, then have the model and the first copy copied simultaneously by two different copyists, and so on. By means of this procedure, which Castellani calls "production maximum," three copies can be obtained in two units of time, seven copies in three units of time, fifteen copies in four units of time. And whereas with the method of successive copies the production of seven copies results in a stemma with seven branches, the production of fifteen copies results in a stemma with fifteen branches, and so on, in the case of "production maximum" the production of seven copies results in a stemma with three branches, the production of fifteen copies results in a stemma of four branches, and so on:

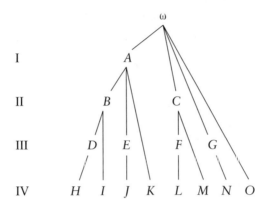

Thus this type of diffusion leads to a considerable reduction in the initial ramification of the stemma, compared with the method of successive copies from a single model. But only to a considerable reduction: not necessarily to bipartite stemmas, unless other factors (nonproductivity of certain copies, rapid withdrawal or rapid destruction of the initial model, etc.) intervene that may in fact have operated in many cases but whose operation has no character of necessity at all and is in any case independent of the mechanism of "production maximum" as such.[19] It also remains to be seen how far such a mechanism, which concentrates the production of many copies into a relatively brief time, corresponds to what we know about the transmission of *Classical* texts in the Middle Ages. It seems likely that copies of a given Classical text were not produced intensely but were staggered in time, at least in many cases: a manuscript of a work of Cicero, preserved in a monastery, will have been copied once or twice, and the copies will have been

19. Perhaps Castellani 1980 (1957): 177–81 insists a bit too much on these additional factors. And in any case these do serve to explain a further reduction in the number of branches but not their almost constant reduction to only two.

sent elsewhere; then a third copy will have been made of that same manuscript years later, and so on. The model of "production maximum" is much better suited to the "publication" of a new work by a medieval author (in fact Castellani, a Romance philologist, was thinking of cases of this type) than to the medieval transmission of an ancient text.[20] But even with these reservations, such a scheme remains valid to a certain extent for Classical texts too and can at least make some contribution toward explaining the rarity of stemmas with *many* branches. The most difficult fact to explain still remains the rarity of stemmas with three or four branches—I hope the reader will forgive my insistence, which may seem a bit obsessive but is, I believe, justified.

Another hypothesis has been proposed by D'Arco Silvio Avalle:[21] the bipartitism of so many stemmas would depend on a procedure of "embryonic *pecia*," by means of which the model was divided into two parts and each of two copyists copied one half and then exchanged their parts; in this way two transcriptions could be performed in the same time in which a single copyist would have performed a single transcription; then the two branches of the stemma originated from these two copies once the model had been lost or destroyed. I shall not repeat here at length the objections that I have expressed more fully elsewhere[22] but shall confine myself to a single point. It seems hard to believe (alas, I must return to the leitmotif of all my objections!) that exactly two copies were derived from the model with such consistency and that each time the model was not transcribed again before being lost. In the real system of *pecia*, which became widespread in the thirteenth and fourteenth centuries for the use of the students of the great medieval universities, each copyist transcribed a fascicle, not a half manuscript;[23] and this would lead to highly ramified stemmas. An analogous procedure of transcription divided up among various copyists was in use in the Hu-

20. Cf. also Balduino 1979: 238–41 on the usefulness of Castellani's hypothesis with regard to the edition of medieval works; perhaps Brambilla Ageno 1975a: 158 is too quickly negative. On the fact that it is much less applicable to the transmission of ancient texts cf. also Kleinlogel 1968: 72 and n. 1. In any case it should be borne in mind that for Castellani the "production maximum" is not the most important cause of bipartitism; he subordinates it to other causes that more specifically concern brief medieval texts and are therefore not applicable to ancient ones (except for decimation, on which see above, n. 16; Castellani 1980 [1957]: 181).

21. Avalle 1961: 95–96 = Hunger et al. 1961–64: 2.297.

22. Timpanaro 1965: 394–95.

23. Destrez 1935 is still fundamental. Fink-Errera 1962 is more up-to-date and disagrees with Destrez on various points but, at least according to my impression, does so with a certain ostentation of novelty to which real progress sometimes does not correspond.

manist age.[24] None of this can be imagined in the conditions of slow textual transmission of the High Middle Ages,[25] when a limited number of copies seems in general to have been derived from one manuscript, often at intervals of time. Avalle's "embryonic *pecia*" seems an artificial expedient, an unattested *quid medium* [something in the middle] between two essentially different types of production of copies. It must also be added that Avalle himself seems to have abandoned this hypothesis, which he had originally proposed with caution.[z,26]

We shall now propose two other hypotheses that fit better with what is known about the transmission of Classical texts, even if they are only suited for explaining *certain* cases of bipartitism.[aa] In any case, a separate category is formed by those cases in which the bipartitism really consists of the opposition between a single manuscript (or, more rarely, very few manuscripts) of the High Middle Ages or even of Late Antiquity on the one hand, and a considerable number of more recent manuscripts on the other. Cases of this sort are often cited in Pasquali's work and in the first volume of the *Geschichte der Textüberlieferung* [History of text transmission; Hunger et al. 1961–64: vol. 1]: it should suffice to recall Aeschylus, Sophocles, Isocrates, and Theophrastus among Greek authors; Plautus, Terence, Seneca's tragedies, and Statius's *Thebaid* and *Achilleid* among Latin ones.[27] It is perfectly natural that the more recent manuscripts should be united by a certain number of banalizations and conjectural "improvements," or else by real corruptions, from which the oldest manuscript is immune: for they go back to an edition "revised" in the Carolingian period or even later[bb] that intro-

---

24. Rizzo 1973: 196 and n. 1, cf. 43. Rizzo too emphasizes the connection between *pecia* and these procedures of the Humanist age.

25. Some of the essays collected in Cavallo 1977 provide a clear idea regarding these conditions: see especially G. Cavallo's introduction and the essays by A. Petrucci and B. Bischoff. It goes without saying that I ought to cite many other recent and innovative works, many of them written by the same scholars I have mentioned now; but I cannot leave my subject too far behind. In any case, see the full bibliography in Cavallo 1977 and bear in mind that this research is still in full and rapid development.

26. He no longer mentions it in Avalle 1972; on p. 92 he speaks of *pecia* but without connecting it to the problem of bipartite stemmas.

27. Cf. Pasquali 1952a (1934): 25–30, 126, 175–80, 294, 331–48, 354–74; Hunger et al. 1961–64: 1.264–65, 274–75, 375–78, 404–6, 409 (this latter work must be used with caution). See in particular Pasquali's formulation at 1952a (1934) 126: "Like so many other texts, Seneca's tragedies are transmitted in an ancient manuscript that stands apart and in a large number of more recent manuscripts linked together by close kinship relations." For Isocrates the existence of an archetype can probably not even be demonstrated, as Dieter Irmer points out to me, referring to Seck 1965: 106–7.

duced those changes and from then on constituted a vulgate, but also, un-surprisingly, preserved correct readings that were corrupted in the oldest manuscript.[cc,28] In this case the bipartition is really caused by a chronological discrepancy—so long as we understand this expression to designate not a mere interval of years or centuries but a changed cultural environment, the arrival of those "medieval Renaissances" that occurred several times in western and central Europe, and even more in the Byzantine Empire. To this must be added the fact that the group of more recent manuscripts owes its homogeneity, at least in many cases, not only to medieval or even Humanist innovations but also to their shared derivation from an ancient edition that was different from the one of which a single witness remains.[dd] On the other hand, given that medieval manuscripts earlier than the ninth century are relatively rare and manuscripts going back to Late Antiquity are even rarer, it is not at all strange that for many texts only a single *codex vetustior* [more ancient manuscript] has been preserved, which then ends up constituting by itself a "first family" as opposed to the "second one" represented by the *recentiores*.[29] This was more or less how Marouzeau already explained the prevalence of bipartite stemmas in the Latin tradition; analogous considerations are applicable to Greek texts as well, but they cannot be applied to all Latin texts: Marouzeau apparently limited his hypothesis too much in one direction and extended it too far in the other.[ee,30]

28. An analogous but more complex case is constituted by the tradition of Hippocrates: see D. Irmer's interesting note to Timpanaro 1971: 131n286a.

29. In cases of this sort scholars have almost always proposed the hypothesis that the *recentiores* derived from the most ancient manuscript; this hypothesis is sometimes correct but more often erroneous (see above, pp. 100, 124; and chaps. 3 and 4 of Pasquali 1952a [1934]).

30. I say "apparently" because Marouzeau's thesis, which I have reformulated quite freely here, is known to us only from a brief reference in Dain 1975 (1949): 113: "He explains this bifidity by the fact that one part of the tradition came from the copy that had been transliterated around 800 while the other part was derived from pre-Carolingian copies antedating the transliteration." At the time of the first edition of this work of mine, Dain and Marouzeau were both still alive; but when I asked them, neither one could remember where this explanation had been formulated for the first time and more fully. "I am ninety-two years old, and I do not remember!" Marouzeau wrote to me with some sadness. Pasquali too speaks of a "Caroline vulgate" for Statius (Pasquali 1952a [1934]: 175). The formation of such a vulgate need not be connected in every case with the transliteration, conceived too simplistically as an operation performed once and for all. Such a conception has been shown to be fallacious for many Greek texts and is even less certain for Latin ones, for which indeed there was strictly speaking no transliteration in the "Byzantine" sense. Those vulgates were formed gradually by processes of contamination and convergence caused by shared cultural environments and hence by the intensification of contacts and exchanges (see also above, chap. 8, n. 31).

Dain has drawn attention to another possible reason for stemmatic bipartition.[31] Like any other manuscript, archetypes can undergo more or less serious alterations in the course of time: addition of interlinear or marginal variants, abrasion of earlier readings, substitution of new ones. If first an apograph *A* has been copied from an archetype, then two other copies *B* and *C* are copied from that same archetype after it has been greatly altered, the tradition really has three branches but the philologist will be led to attribute the innovations shared by *B* and *C* to an imaginary subarchetype and hence to trace out a bipartite stemma. Jean Irigoin has demonstrated that this possibility really happened in the descendants of the *Vaticanus graecus* 1 of Plato.[32] Erbse (1959: 97–98) has objected against Irigoin that none of this has any practical importance, since it matters little for the purposes of *recensio* whether the agreement *BC* represents a subarchetype or a "second stage" of the archetype. But Dain's observation, developed further by Irigoin, was aiming precisely at *explaining* the surprising frequency of bipartite stemmas; and for this purpose it is much more valid than Maas's mathematical considerations, in which Erbse still unreasonably believes (see above, p. 162n10). Moreover, the "alterations" to which an archetype is subject consist not only in corrections but also sometimes in mechanical damage, for example, the loss of leaves or the transposition of fascicles during re-binding.[33] If copy *A* has been derived from the archetype before the damage and copies *BC* after the damage, and if the philologist considers the lacuna or transposition to be a conjunctive error and therefore traces out a bipartite stemma instead of a tripartite one, this erroneous genealogical reconstruction can also have adverse consequences for the *recensio*: he will attribute the value of "one against one" to the agreement of *BC* against *A*

31. Dain 1932: 79–80; cf. Dain 1975 (1949): 112. Yet in 1964, the year in which the second edition of his *Manuscrits* appeared, Dain 1964:121 refused to accord any significance to the problem of bipartite or tripartite stemmas; but the example he adopts reveals that he was now thinking of traditions without a medieval archetype (however conceived), in which the various manuscripts or groups of manuscripts represent the continuation of different ancient editions. This is certainly the case in many traditions, especially Greek ones (cf. p. 182), but not in all. So in my view one cannot speak of a "false problem." On the contrary, as we shall see, the discussion of the rarity of multipartite stemmas makes an important contribution to the criticism of Lachmannism.

32. Irigoin 1954: 213–14. A "fluid archetype" is also hypothesized by Reynolds 1965: 56.

33. We have run into cases of this sort with regard to ancestors that are preserved and therefore allow the *descripti* to be eliminated (pp. 47f., 99; and many other examples could be cited). But entirely analogous damage might have occurred and did in fact occur to archetypes in the Madvigian-Lachmannian sense, that is, to lost manuscripts, beginning with Lucretius (see immediately below).

when in reality it is worth "two against one." [34] We have already drawn attention to this danger above (chap. 6, n. 13), and we have explained that major lacunas or transpositions that can be attributed to the loss or displacement of leaves or fascicles are not enough by themselves to define a subgroup.

With this hypothesis of the "mobile archetype" we have entered into the field of those manuscript traditions that have a bipartite *appearance*, although in reality they were tripartite or had even more than three branches. But this hypothesis, like Marouzeau's discussed just now, only explains a limited number of cases. It is not reasonable to suppose that between the first transcription and subsequent ones almost all archetypes underwent corrections so numerous and so extensive as to produce an "apparent subarchetype." Moreover, it is easy to identify the case of later material damage to the archetype, and most manuscript traditions are free of it. There must be other reasons for this "deception," which produces errors of classification and makes bipartite stemmas seem much more numerous than would seem probable. We shall go on now to examine them, beginning with the most banal and avoidable ones and finally arriving at the ones that are harder to avoid and all in all more frequent.[ff]

In my opinion, the old custom of classifying manuscripts not genealogically but axiologically by dividing them into the two categories of *meliores* and *deteriores* may have contributed toward increasing the number of bipartite stemmas beyond due measure. We have already seen how the young Lachmann still followed this custom, and how some of the first genealogical classifications (e.g., Madvig's of the manuscripts of *De finibus*) originated in earlier axiological classifications and inherited their bipartite structure.[35] It is likely that scholars often merely transferred into the genealogical domain the old bipartition based on a judgment of value, and therefore derived from the archetype two apographs, a "good" one (the work of a stupid and faithful copyist) and a "bad" one (the work of a deceitful interpolator), from which the two races of the *meliores* and the *deteriores* would have originated. The *deteriores* in particular will often have been considered too hastily to represent a single class from the genealogical viewpoint as well; it will be remembered that Moriz Haupt, like Lachmann, exhorted

34. I do not understand the reply of Kleinlogel 1968: 79n6 on this point. He objects against me that the two more recent apographs have the value of two against one "only [. . .] when the change of condition consisted in a purely mechanical corruption." But this is the very case I was considering above; and the fact that this is not a purely theoretical case is demonstrated by the example of Lucretius, discussed in chap. 6, n. 13.

35. See above, pp. 77–78, 92–93, 98.

scholars not to waste their time classifying Humanist manuscripts.[36] His exhortation was largely followed, not only because such manuscripts were distrusted but also precisely because they are more contaminated and therefore harder to classify than medieval ones. Sometimes the old editors added a third group of *mixti* alongside the two families of *meliores* and *deteriores;*[37] but tripartite classifications of this sort were destined to be short-lived, since later editors ended up either adding the *mixti* to the family of the *deteriores* or else noticing that almost all manuscripts are "mixed," that is, contaminated (we shall return to this point shortly).[gg]

Another[hh] cause of erroneous bipartite classifications is partially connected with the preceding one but is more strictly derived from a logical mistake:[ii] the tendency to identify one class of manuscripts α on the basis of shared characteristics and then to call β everything that in reality is merely "non-α." There is a danger of falling into a similar error not only in textual criticism but wherever classifications need to be made: Aristotle already fought against it in zoology.[38] If a certain number of shared corruptions defines a family of manuscripts, the lack of those corruptions does not define another family: so after having identified a family α it will be necessary to see whether the other manuscripts are connected by shared innovations in their turn, or whether instead they constitute different groups, or whether, as is also possible, they are so contaminated that their derivation from one or more subarchetypes cannot be detected. An error of this sort was committed by Heinrich Schenkl when he divided the V class of the manuscripts of Calpurnius's eclogues into two subclasses *v* and *w*. Cesare Giarratano (a Classical philologist who may not have had the gift of genius but was rigorous and scrupulous as few others) observed that *w* was a real family but *v* was a heap of manuscripts not united by particular affinities. Schenkl replied that he had indeed used the sign *v* in the sense of "V minus *w*," but even then he refused to recognize the illegitimacy of a stemma traced out according to such criteria.[39] The mistake Mario Casella committed in his attempt to classify the manuscripts of Dante's *Commedia* was analogous: the family α which he believed he could identify "is characterized in exclusively

36. Above, chap. 3, n. 15.

37. So, e.g., Goerenz 1809–13: vi; Nipperdey 1847–56: 1.46–47 (see above, p. 96 and n. 18); and Orelli 1826–38: 4.6.

38. *Topics* 6.6. 143b11–13; *On the Parts of Animals* 1.2–4; cf. Gomperz 1922–25: 4.213–14.

39. See Schenkl 1913: 265, and the correct reply in Giarratano 1943: vi–vii. Cf. Castagna 1976 on the tradition of Calpurnius Siculus 1–4.12 and on some defects of Giarratano's edition, which do not, however, invalidate his objection to Schenkl.

negative terms, as not β." [ii,40] Here Bédier would indeed have been right to point to Schenkl and Casella as two victims [kk] of the dichotomic aberration! Only, such an aberration is not without remedy. [ll]

But the most serious and insidious causes of "apparent bipartitism" are contamination ("horizontal transmission), the copyists' conjectural activity, and, even if to a lesser extent, polygenesis of innovations. For the sake of brevity I use the term *disturbances* to indicate all three of these phenomena, although I distinguish them whenever it is necessary to do so for my argument.

I intend to insist here not on the general difficulties that these phenomena cause the textual critic—I would merely be repeating what is to be found in every good manual of textual criticism, and Pasquali's book can be said to be a full critical examination of "disturbed" traditions, each with its own particular problems—but rather on the mechanism by which they lead scholars to interpose fictitious subarchetypes between the ancestor and its descendants and hence to confer a bipartite appearance upon manuscript traditions that in reality had three or more branches.

Let there be given a tripartite tradition: from an archetype ω let there be independently derived three copies that produced three streams of tradition αβγ by successive "vertical" transcriptions. If at a certain time a process of horizontal transmission intervenes, because of which a certain number of errors of β are transmitted to γ or vice versa, or else if a copyist of the α branch corrects a good number of errors of the archetype by felicitous conjectures, the shared errors of βγ (which in the former alternative had originally been errors of β alone or of γ alone and in the latter one were originally errors shared by the whole tradition) will be attributed to a subarchetype, and the tripartite tradition (fig. 1) will assume a deceptive bipartite appearance (fig. 2):

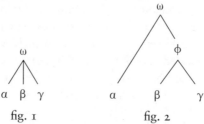

fig. 1   fig. 2

The two phenomena can also be associated with one another, and this will certainly have happened in many cases: given four branches of tradition

---

40. Quaglio 1965: 248; cf. Folena 1965: 75. Recently Waszink 1979: 84 has once again warned against this classificatory error. Cf. also Kenney 1974: 134.

αβγδ, a felicitous emendation of an error of the archetype performed by a copyist of the α branch can be transmitted by contamination to β, so that γδ seem to be connected by a conjunctive error and therefore to derive from a subarchetype that in reality never existed.

Castellani has already drawn attention to these two phenomena,[41] but has only assigned them a secondary importance, wrongly in my view. This underestimation derives from three causes: (1) Castellani believes that the greatest significance should be assigned to other "factors of dichotomy," at least for medieval lyrical texts (but as we have already seen, p. 170 and n. 20, such a significance cannot be defended for the transmission of ancient texts during the Middle Ages); (2) he asserts that "from the point of view of textual constitution, a scheme in which two contaminated families form only one functions just as well as the genetically correct scheme in which the two families go back to the original" (but this is not true in all cases: compare fig. 1 above, which represents the genetically correct scheme, with fig. 2, which represents the scheme altered by contamination, and it will be seen that in the former case a reading shared by βγ would have the value of "two against one" and hence would give us the reading of the archetype but in the latter case is demoted to "one against one" and hence must be entrusted to the editor's *iudicium*); (3) Castellani considers it relatively easy ("one need only pay attention"; Castellani 1980 [1957]: 182) to identify the corruptions that can be healed conjecturally, so that for these one must deny the possibility that the same errors, uncorrected in other manuscripts, might falsely appear to be conjunctive errors;[mm] and although he does not fail to recognize the deceptiveness of contamination, he recalls the well-known principle that some errors (lacunas, gross errors) cannot be attributed to horizontal transmission. We shall return to this point shortly.

More recently, Romance philologists and Germanists among others have excogitated more subtle "remedies against contamination," for the most part of a statistical character.[42] I have already expressed my position with regard to such methods: I acknowledge their acuity and, more importantly, their usefulness for disentangling to some extent, even if only approximately, the genealogy of those manuscript traditions in which genuine corruptions or mechanical lacunas are lacking or are too infrequent; but I have also discovered that such methods are obliged to ignore completely or al-

---

41. Castellani 1980 (1957): 181–82; these phenomena had already been mentioned in passing by Bédier and Fourquet, both cited by Castellani.

42. Cf. above all Segre 1961; Avalle 1961: 159–78 (Appendix 1, "On Some Remedies against Contamination"; more briefly Avalle 1972: 81); Okken 1970 (I owe to D. Irmer my knowledge of this work, which reexamines a text already edited by Lachmann).

most completely the distinction between coincidence in conservation (which in itself proves nothing) and coincidence in innovation;[nn,43] and I have already indicated the reasons why I think (and others agree) that clinging to Dom Quentin's method is a bad way of escaping the difficulties of Lachmann's method (see above, chap. 4, n. 18).

Another, much surer criterion was already enunciated a long time ago, was repeated with particular rigor by Ulrich Knoche and Pasquali,[44] has been reaffirmed, as we saw just now, by Castellani and in general by all those who have recently written treatises on textual criticism, and is recognized as fundamental by Avalle himself: corruptions and, even more, lacu-

43. Timpanaro 1965: 398 and n. 14.

44. See above, p. 137; and Pasquali 1952a (1934): xvii: "Also errors that would seem to us to be obvious ones often penetrate into manuscripts by collation. It is only the lacunas that, at least as a rule, are transmitted directly." This principle would seem to be formulated almost too restrictively. And yet some cases, naturally very rare ones, can apparently be documented in which even omissions that destroy the meaning have been transmitted by contamination: cf. Willis 1972: 22, who mentions the case of a copyist of Macrobius's *Saturnalia* (1.6.14), who "has performed the remarkable feat of interpolating an omission," deriving the omission itself from another family of manuscripts (the case is highly likely, even if not quite certain, since *matrimisque* preceded by *patrimis* and followed by *pronuntiantibus* runs a certain risk of being omitted independently by two different copyists). It would be worth developing further an interesting point made by La Penna 1964: 369: "The need for a critical apparatus, for a *recensio* must have existed *in nuce* in certain medieval compilers of variants, even before the Humanistic ones: sometimes they note for themselves not only variants which yield a plausible meaning, as is their custom, but also meaningless variants: to the variants that serve to correct the text, or that produce another acceptable text, and which could be called 'correction variants,' are sometimes added others that serve to show how the text is transmitted elsewhere, and which could be called 'apparatus variants.'" Well, let us suppose that an "apparatus variant," noted down by a learned copyist in a manuscript that is no longer extant, has been mistaken for a "correction variant" by a later, ignorant copyist who has introduced it into the text: the result will be an error of the sort that we are accustomed to attribute with certainty to vertical transmission, and that instead has been transmitted horizontally (there is a case of this kind, even if it is somewhat more complicated, in Timpanaro 1978: 408–10). Marginal and interlinear "apparatus variants" are also found in ancient manuscripts: see the case, cited by Pasquali 1952a (1934): 256, of P. Oxyrhynchus 1017 (a passage from Plato's *Phaedrus*) furnished with variants "that cannot be conjectures, because too often they make the text obviously worse." Papyrologists will be able to cite other examples; it is likely that some variants of this sort have insinuated themselves into the medieval tradition, or into one part of it.[oo] On the possibility of the horizontal transmission of evident errors, see also Pasquali 1952a (1934): 87. An extremely interesting example is furnished by the readings of the second hand in the Ambrosian-Vatican palimpsest of Fronto (Milan, Ambros. E.147 sup. + Vatican lat. 5750): cf. Zetzel 1980 (pp. 49–57 on Fronto: a precious collection of material, not always well interpreted).[pp]

nas that evidently impair the meaning, without, however, constituting a "copyist's trap"—jumps *du même au même,* similar beginnings or endings of words, letters or abbreviations that can easily be confused in a given script, words that can be confused with one another because of phonetic vulgarism, etc.—can almost certainly be attributed to vertical transmission and not to contamination or polygenesis; so too, the copyists' emendatory activity can be excluded when an error found in the rest of the tradition is greater than the conjectural capabilities of the copyists of a given period. Nonetheless these principles themselves[qq] are not always easy to apply. With regard to the second point, it is often difficult to set precise limits to the conjectural acumen of medieval copyists and "editors," especially if they lived in one of those periods of partial cultural "renaissance" that, as has been well known for a long time, interrupted the long depression of the Middle Ages.[45] And all the same this is still the lesser danger: there are correct readings at which no medieval copyist-philologist (in certain cases not even the best modern philologist) could arrive conjecturally. A more serious danger consists in the possibility that a copyist, for example, of the α branch (see fig. 1 on p. 176) might have healed errors or filled lacunas not by conjecture and not even by checking one of the other witnesses that have survived to our day, but by collating a manuscript of a completely different branch or tradition which was later lost. In his book Pasquali cites many cases in which one must have recourse to this hypothesis[46] even if he seems to have forgotten them when he discusses Knoche's criteria (Pasquali 1952a [1934]: 181–82). At Timpanaro 1965: 397 I suggested designating this phenomenon by the term *extra-stemmatic contamination* (that is, contamination deriving from manuscripts that do not form part of the tradition that has survived more or less completely) and to distinguish it from *intra-stemmatic contamination* (relations of collation between surviving manuscripts which form part of the stemma we can reconstruct).[47] Now, even extra-stemmatic contamination will have the effect of increasing the number

45. For Greek texts, see, after Maas 1935 and 1936, also Erbse 1959: 99–100. For Latin ones see, e.g., Munari 1970: xxii–xxiii; but Kenney's studies have demonstrated that more readings of the *recentiores* represent genuine tradition and should be preferred to the *vetustiores* than had been thought.

46. E.g., Pasquali 1952a (1934): 48, 49, 304–5, 318–26 (but on the tradition of Thucydides see the progress later achieved by Bartoletti, Alberti, and Kleinlogel, and briefly summarized in Alberti 1979: 10–11), 381–85, and elsewhere. Cf. also Andrieu 1943: 468; Di Benedetto 1965 (see the index under "contaminazione").

47. In German, the term *Fremdlesung* [foreign reading], coined by Fränkel 1964: 78 and n. 2, can be useful for indicating "a reading that derives from a line of tradition otherwise unknown to us."

of apparent bipartite stemmas:[rr] since the damage that goes back to the archetype has been corrected in α, such damage will be attributed to a subarchetype, and the stemma will once again take on the false appearance of figure 2 on page 176; and what is worse, if the error remaining in βγ is of the sort that cannot be healed conjecturally, it will all the more have the appearance of an unquestionably genuine conjunctive error.

And yet the difficulties we have reminded the reader of, serious as they are, do not always prevent the construction of a plausible stemma based on rigorous criteria, that is, solely on "significant errors," excluding all coincidences not only in correct readings but also in banalizations, in "errors with the semblance of truth" that can easily be transmitted by collation, and in errors that can be polygenetic, and taking account also of the possibility of conjectural activity on the part of the copyists. The possibility of "extrastemmatic contamination" will always remain, alongside less frequent risks like those indicated in note 44; but if this is limited to a few cases it will not completely alter the fundamental outlines of the stemma; whereas if it is systematic it will be recognized as another source of tradition that can be indicated with figures like this (which have already been used by a number of editors):

But it is here that the most insidious dangers begin. Let us suppose that a stemma with three branches has been produced on the basis of "significant errors" alone. What is to be done now with the coincidences in insignificant errors? We cannot either attribute them with certainty to vertical transmission or exclude the possibility that they might be the "residue" of errors already present in the archetype and corrected conjecturally in one branch of the stemma—this is precisely what their insignificance consists in. *But we cannot even exclude the possibility that such coincidences derive from vertical transmission,* that is, that they go back to a subarchetype. To put this point better: we can exclude this possibility only if it happens to *contradict* a stemma that has already been constructed on the basis of significant errors alone. If, for example, a manuscript A shares lacunas and other gross errors with B but only a few banalizations or "prettifications" or unimportant alterations with C, we will certainly attribute these latter to disturbances. But if A does not visibly share significant errors with B and shares only insignificant errors with C, or else if it shares more insignificant errors with C and fewer ones with *B*, we can neither affirm nor deny that *AC* are derived from a subarchetype.[55]

These are the cases in which the philologist who wishes to reduce the disturbances to a minimum and to present in a stemma as systematic as possible an image of the manuscript tradition will "verticalize" the insignificant errors too (or the largest group of them) and will postulate a new subarchetype, which *can* but *need not* ever have existed.

This is the criterion of the "most economical hypothesis" theorized by Avalle (with a certain ostentation of analogies with the physical and mathematical sciences) but already broadly followed in practice by Classical and Romance philologists.[48] Recently Irigoin too has reaffirmed the importance of reconstructing the skeleton of the vertical transmission as far as possible, in an important article that was inspired by the legitimate desire to react against Dawe's exasperatedly and exaggeratedly antistemmatic tendency.[49]

In itself, the criterion of the most economical hypothesis is probabilistic and entirely reasonable. Since, as Pasquali reminded Schwartz (see above, p. 136), vertical transmission is a constant fact, while disturbances are extremely frequent phenomena that exist in all or almost all manuscript traditions but are nonetheless always desultory and accidental, *every single coincidence in innovations (even in insignificant innovations) has a greater chance of deriving from a lost shared model than of being due to contamination or polygenesis or a copyist's corrective activity. But if we prefer the hypothesis of vertical transmission *every time,* the total picture of manu-

---

48. Cf. Avalle 1961: 172, 194 (and already 1957: 64); 1972: 82–86. In this last work Avalle (perhaps answering implicitly my objections in Timpanaro 1965: 397) vigorously asserts that the principle of the "most economical hypothesis" should not be followed to the detriment of stemmatic research performed with strict criteria, and in particular should not lead to an undue increase in the number of subarchetypes. An excellent warning: and yet I have the impression that in this way the principle itself is invalidated, and survives more as an "epistemological coquetry" than as an instrument that can be used for textual criticism.

49. Irigoin 1977; "Without permitting himself to be led astray by superficial and contradictory links, he [i.e., the textual critic] must try to discover underneath them the constants of the 'vertical' tradition with all the means available to his scholarship and to his native talent. It is at this price, and at this price alone, that he will be able to determine the reality, and perhaps also the extent, of a horizontal transmission" (243). There is nothing really erroneous in this formulation (but in fact there is: there is also the case of "total pre-traditional contamination");[tt] but anyone who sets out to do stemmatic work in this spirit will end up verticalizing everything that can be verticalized and admitting disturbances only as a last resort. And by multiplying the subarchetypes he will naturally obtain a bipartite stemma.

script traditions will certainly be distorted, because we have thereby *reduced to zero* an event that will have happened in a minority of cases but will none-theless almost certainly have happened, and in a rather large minority of cases. For example, instead of 60 percent of coincidences due to vertical transmission and 40 percent due to disturbances (percentages that obvi-ously are hypothetical and unfortunately cannot be tested, but all the same seem plausible), we shall obtain 100 percent of coincidences of the former sort—with an evident error. The main reason (not the only one, as we have seen) for the improbable prevalence of bipartite stemmas consists precisely in this paradox: if in every case of coincidence in innovation one prefers the more economical hypothesis, the majority becomes a totality, while the mi-nority is cancelled out. Naturally the paradox only persists because in tex-tual criticism, unlike other situations in which a statistical prediction can be tested empirically *post eventum,* no similar verification is possible: no one can tell us whether certain presumed lost subarchetypes really existed or not.[uu,50] And if we studied this question in greater depth, we would discover that this serious limit to the application of statistical methods is found in many other diachronic disciplines as well, in which it is not possible to per-form repeatable experiments and test their outcome.

These considerations of ours are substantially corroborated by the book of Alberti's I have already mentioned, even if, as I have indicated, Alberti dis-sents more than once from my earlier statements regarding stemmas that at the time I presumed to be multipartite. To a hasty reader (especially to one who does not read closely the book's brief but fundamental last chapter), Alberti's treatment might seem to confirm the thesis of "extreme bipartit-ism." Certainly, as we have seen (pp. 160f.), he demonstrates the fragility or improbability of most of the few multipartite stemmas that scholars of Greek and Latin manuscript traditions have hitherto hypothesized. But, as he himself takes care to emphasize (Alberti 1979: 93), only very rarely does he replace them with bipartite stemmas: instead he speaks for the most part of "probable contamination, which has rendered the relations among the various branches uncertain but without eliminating them" (1979: 93); in other cases he concludes that contamination has completely obscured the

50. It now seems to me so certain that errors of classification result in exaggerating the number of bipartite stemmas, at least in the overwhelming majority of cases, that I con-sider it useless to discuss once again the opposite thesis of Fourquet 1946 and then espe-cially Fourquet 1948, who thought that the philologist ran the risk of not noticing "hid-den subarchetypes" and hence of mistaking bipartite traditions to be multipartite. Anyone who still feels the need for a refutation of this thesis can read Timpanaro 1963a: 130 and especially my observations in Timpanaro 1965: 395–96.

genealogical relations; in still others, summarizing or developing further the conclusions of earlier scholars, he questions the very hypothesis that our witnesses are derived from a medieval archetype, a hypothesis that is *a priori* extremely improbable for texts that continued to be very widespread throughout the Middle Ages; and even in those cases in which such an archetype must have existed (as the presence of serious damage shared by all the extant tradition demonstrates), its descendents must have been enriched very early with contributions deriving from extra-stemmatic contamination, so that we are very far indeed from a Lachmannian model.[51]

Alberti adds (1979: 94) that an examination of the stemmas that were hitherto considered bipartite "would lead one to doubt many stemmas [. . .]

---

51. As is well known, the problem of the existence or nonexistence of a medieval (or late ancient) archetype is rendered difficult by the contradictory situation we find in many surviving texts: on the one hand, the existence of gross errors and above all lacunas, and sometimes also dislocations of whole passages, in all the extant manuscripts, which make it hard to exclude the existence of a single lost ancestor that exhibited that damage; on the other hand the fact that the ancient tradition (papyri, quotations in other authors, etc.) often agrees in inferior readings now with one part of the medieval tradition, now with another. Pasquali 1952 (1934) is full of examples of this sort, which have increased even further in the last decades. Against the hypothesis of the "archetype with variants" (to which Pasquali still granted too much), cf. esp. Di Benedetto 1965: 145–46, 149–52. It has been possible to demonstrate in many cases that the errors shared by our whole tradition were of a sort judged "tolerable" by ancient and Byzantine philologists (for Euripides, but with observations that can be applied to other manuscript traditions as well, see Di Benedetto 1965: 163–93; for Hesiod's *Theogony*, Arrighetti 1961: 266–79 has cast doubt on the existence of an archetype with good arguments). A loose conception of the archetype, not as a unique exemplar but as a "kind of text," as a proto-medieval vulgate already contaminated by horizontally transmitted errors, is proposed by West 1973: 41–42 and Waszink 1979: 79. In my opinion, the concept of archetype formulated by Dain and taken up again by Irigoin (also in Irigoin 1977) has not been very useful and has also caused terminological confusion. I am sorry to see how little the difficulties regarding the concept of archetype pointed out by Eugenio Grassi have been taken into consideration, except for Di Benedetto (cf. above, p. 38). In the face of so complicated a problem, which in many aspects concerns Romance texts as well, it seems strange how hastily a scholar as learned and competent as Franca Brambilla Ageno (1975b) peremptorily asserts that there always was an archetype, relying on arguments of statistical probability that unfortunately recall the ones Maas used when he tried to demonstrate the numerical prevalence of stemmas with two branches. Prof. Brambilla Ageno kindly informs me by letter that her ideas regarding the archetype only concern traditions of vernacular texts with specific characteristics: despite the title of her article and some formulations it contains, they are not intended to set forth a theory covering all cases. She also informs me that she intends to return to this subject with more detailed arguments.[vv]

not in the sense of making them become tripartite or multipartite, but rather in the sense of introducing elements of doubt, due above all to contamination."

So must we abandon altogether the attempt to trace out stemmas (cf. Munari)?[ww] No, except when the tradition is totally disturbed. Instead, above all, we must continue Alberti's work by examining many stemmas that are asserted to be certainly bipartite. I do not exclude[xx] the possibility that such an examination might sometimes correct earlier errors of classification and lead to the construction of multipartite stemmas still sufficiently solid despite some inevitable traces of disturbance;[52] in this regard I would be a bit more confident than Alberti. All the same I too believe that results of this sort will be quite rare. I think instead that in more cases those "elements of doubt" to which Alberti refers will induce us to propose two or three stemmas as equally probable or one as just a little more probable than the others[53] and in the prolegomena of the editions or in separate works to state clearly which subarchetypes can be postulated with almost absolute certainty, which ones with a good probability, which ones only with considerable uncertainty. Sometimes it will also be necessary to trace out stemmas of only one part of the tradition but to give up on them for another part that is too disturbed.[54] In this way the user of a critical edition will know for the practical purposes of constituting the text to what point the agreement of certain manuscripts invests a certain reading with "authority" (an authority that is always relative and in need of confirmation).[yy]

Finally, a last problem. In his notorious treatment of stemmas with two

52. Sometimes a "third branch" can be obtained by examining a series of corrections derived from a lost manuscript: cf. Nardo 1966. In other cases (as, for example, for Thucydides; see above, n. 46) an analogous technique, which for Greek texts can also take advantage of papyri, makes it possible to reconstruct lines of extra-stemmatic tradition, even if only partially.

53. This custom is already followed by some scholars (e.g., La Penna 1957: cxlvi), but in my opinion it should become more widespread: not so as to derive from it the purely skeptical and destructive consequences Bédier was aiming at when he had fun tracing out the ten possible stemmas of the *Lai de l'Ombre* (many of which, in fact, were unfounded: Castellani 1980 [1957]: 182–92), but in order to distinguish better the various possibilities and the various degrees of probability. Editors still have recourse too often to the two extreme solutions: either to trace out with excessive confidence a single stemma or to abstain from any discussion of the genealogy of the manuscripts.

54. This kind of solution, in my opinion, can be recommended, for example, for the *Ephemeris* of Dictys Cretensis (L. Septimius), where family γ can be reduced to a fairly rigorous stemma, while family ε is too highly disturbed: cf. Timpanaro 1978: 397–422, and now Eisenhut 1973, who partially takes account of my observations but does not abandon the attempt to trace out a complete stemma.

or more branches, at the end of the passage we cited on page 161, Maas wrote, "In the later subbranches it would certainly have been easier to presuppose the existence, and survival, of three copies from the same archetype;[55] but in these cases the editors were often able, without doing any harm, to avoid adducing more than two of these copies in order to reconstruct a hyparchetype of no stemmatic importance."

Two objections come to mind upon reading these words. Above all, it is curious that Maas envisioned the case of "later subbranches" only in a manuscript tradition that presents more ancient witnesses and ones sufficient for reconstructing the archetype. It did not occur to him that many traditions of Classical texts (those going back to a manuscript discovered in the Humanistic age, copied or even reproduced in print by scribes or philologists of that age, and then lost) consist *entirely* of "later subbranches," which scholars must of necessity not "avoid adducing," at least if they do not wish to give up reading those texts; it did not occur to him to investigate to find out whether such traditions too would turn out to be prevalently bipartite or not.[56] Second (and this was observed by La Penna 1964: 374), even investigations of recent manuscripts not useful for reconstructing the archetype are interesting for the question of bipartite stemmas, in order to determine whether the greater production of copies that began with the start of the Humanist age in fact produced an abundance of stemmas with more than two branches.[zz]

Now, Alberti draws attention to the fact that, among the few manuscript traditions that remain multipartite even after his strict examination, almost all "are represented by rather recent manuscripts";[57] so too, though he has not exhaustively studied the recent ramifications of traditions that also present older manuscripts, he does mention the "lower part" of the stemma of Aristotle's *Metaphysics*, in which Bernardinello's research indicates a filiation of as many as nine branches, and that of Cicero's *De legibus*, in which the extremely extensive stemma traced out by P. L. Schmidt presents "ramifications with eight, nine, eleven branches."[58]

55. "Easier," as the reader will recall, because of the absence of the medieval "poverty" of the manuscript tradition (cf. above, pp. 167–68).

56. It is superfluous to add that, in the case of traditions containing medieval manuscripts, Maas's contempt for "a hyparchetype of no stemmatic importance," although slightly moderated by his warning that editors can neglect them "often" (and not "always"), is excessive and reveals once again his prejudicial distrust for the *recentiores* (see above, chap. 5, n. 35).

57. Alberti 1979: 94–95 (cf. 57, 92, and n. 104).

58. Bernardinello 1970: 225; P. L. Schmidt 1974: stemma at the end of the volume. See also Irmer 1972: stemmas on pp. 116–17, 120.

To me it seems necessary to make a distinction here. Filiations as rich as those with eight or eleven branches do indicate that the production of copies in the Humanist age increased so conspicuously that not even disturbances have succeeded in reducing them to those holy two copies, even though disturbances doubtless became more frequent in that age, given that Renaissance copyist-editors conjectured more often and more felicitously and collated more than medieval amanuenses had done.[59] So here Maas's reference to "much-read texts" becomes valid—for the very first time. But none of the multipartite manuscript traditions, "all recent," that Alberti scrutinized presents more than three or four branches:[60] and in these cases, as Alberti himself recognizes (1979: 95 and n. 18), Maas's opposition between "poor" and "rich" traditions, once more, can have no validity, for the reason upon which we have already insisted too much (esp. p. 167). At least provisionally I would suggest a different explanation: these are traditions in which there has been a relatively brief interval of time, a relatively small number of intermediate links, between the archetype and the extant copies, so that although *ceteris paribus* disturbances acted with greater intensity in the Humanist age than in the Middle Ages, they ended up being a bit less intense than in traditions in which the archetype produced descendants for centuries and the first copies were already often subject to extra-stemmatic contamination. But let us not forget that to these few examples of tripartite or quadripartite Humanist traditions other traditions can be opposed, bipartite ones (think only of Catullus) and above all highly contaminated ones (think only of the *integri* of the *De oratore,* or of Tibullus). Fundamentally, if we disregard a few exceptions, not even the Humanist age represents a sudden break with regard to the multipartition of stemmas. Here too disturbances, and in the first instance contamination, have either created "ficti-

59. Naturally, without wishing at all to cast doubt on the seriousness of Bernardinello's work and, even more, of Schmidt's, it would not be a bad idea to see whether the "nine" and "eleven branches" really are free of coincidences in innovation among smaller groups of manuscripts, due to contamination or other disturbances. (As Schmidt himself points out to me, he does speak of contamination in the course of his book, 1974: 251, 343, 359, 386, etc.)

60. Four for Corycius's *Dialexeis* (or at least for one of them, studied by Perosa-Timpanaro 1956), four for Callimachus's *Hymns,* three for Galen's *On Diagnosis from Dreams,* three for most of Pausanias's *Description of Greece,* three for Sextus Empiricus's *Outlines of Pyrrhonism,* and three for Libanius's fifty-first oration (but where one of the manuscripts goes back to the tenth century). Alberti is inclined to hypothesize a multipartite stemma (but apparently one with few branches) for Cicero's *Brutus* (Alberti 1979: 74–75). In other cases, ones that are more uncertain or are limited to brief texts, the stemmas would always have three or four branches.

tious subarchetypes" or made it impossible to disentangle the manuscript traditions with absolute rigor.*,bbb

*I still believe substantially that my observations in this Appendix C are correct. But it is my duty to indicate that the discussion will continue, and that in particular Michael Weitzman will go on in the near future to use statistical arguments (much more sophisticated ones than Maas's, as is only obvious) in order to argue that there is nothing strange in the preponderance of bipartite stemmas. On this point and on others objections will also be made against me by M. D. Reeve, with whom I have had a fruitful epistolary exchange, and to whom I am indebted for corrections and suggestions, as I have already indicated at the end of the preface (but, at least for now, we are not in agreement on everything). With regard to what I interpret as Maas's failure to understand Pasquali, I had written that Maas "understood nothing of Pasquali's work and perhaps did not even have the desire and the patience to read it" (chap. 5, n. 35). Prof. Reeve informs me that he possesses a copy of Pasquali's book densely annotated by Maas: hence that hypothesis of mine was entirely unfounded. I do not know the character of Maas's annotations: corrections of mistakes? additions of further examples besides the ones Pasquali cited? objections on principle? In any case, I hope that Reeve will publish them soon. Naturally the most interesting ones would be the objections on principle. The fact that Maas did not make them public remains strange. For the present, on the basis of his "Retrospect 1956" I remain convinced that "Maas understood nothing of Pasquali's work," even though I recognize that I expressed myself with excessive severity (in any case it should be obvious that with the word *understood* I meant, and mean, "knew how to evaluate the criteria of the work and Pasquali's concept of the history of tradition," certainly not *understood* in the literal sense). I know well that Maas was a great philologist. His best work, in my view, is to be found in the notes on individual passages of ancient authors now collected in Maas 1973 and in the contributions he made, with equal acumen and modesty, to many editions of the *Bibliotheca Oxoniensis,* of which he was an invaluable proofreader. His contribution to Greek metrics is also of great importance, even if the rigor of his formulations is too often an end in itself and is sometimes more apparent than real. For me, the Maas of the *Textual Criticism* is the weakest one. But, as is obvious, the discussion on this point too is anything but concluded.aaa

Bibliography

Alberti 1979: G. B. Alberti, *Problemi di critica testuale*. Florence, 1979.

Andrieu 1943: J. Andrieu, *Principes et recherches en critique textuelle*. Paris, 1943.

Andrieu 1954: J. Andrieu, *César: Guerre d'Alexandrie*, ed. and trans. J. Andrieu. Paris, 1954.

Arrighetti 1961: G. Arrighetti, "Il testo della Teogonia di Esiodo," *Athenaeum* 39 (1961): 211–79.

Ast 1819: F. Ast, *Platonis opera*, vol. 1. Leipzig, 1819.

Avalle 1957: D. S. Avalle, "Una 'editio variorum' delle canzoni di P. Vidal," in *Studia Ghisleriana*, ser. 2: vol. 2, *Studi letterari per il duecento impumuunumo anno dalla nascita di C. Goldoni*, 57–78. Pavia, 1957.

Avalle 1961: D. S. Avalle, *La letteratura medievale in lingua d'oc nella sua tradizione manoscritta*. Turin, 1961.

Avalle 1972: D. S. Avalle, *Principi di critica testuale*. Padua, 1972.

Bailey 1947: *Titi Lucreti Cari De rerum natura libri sex*, 3 vols., ed. with prolegomena, translation, and commentary by C. Bailey. Oxford, 1947.

Baiter-Sauppe 1839–43: J. G. Baiter-H. Sauppe, *Oratores Attici*. Zurich, 1839–43.

Balduino 1979: A. Balduino, *Manuale di filologia italiana*. Florence, 1979.

Bartoli 1925: M. Bartoli, *Introduzione alla neolinguistica*. Geneva, 1925.

Bartoli 1943: M. Bartoli, "Una nuova riforma della lex Lachmann," *Studi Italiani di Filologia Classica*, n. s., 20 (1943): 59–77.

Basile 1975: B. Basile, *Letteratura e filologia*. Florence, 1975.

Bédier 1928: J. Bédier, "La tradition manuscrite du *Lai de l'Ombre*," *Romania* 54 (1928): 161–96.

Belger 1879: C. Belger, *M. Haupt als akademischer Lehrer*. Berlin, 1879.

Belloni 1976: G. Belloni, "Rassegna di studi e manuali filologici," *Lettere Italiane* 28 (1976): 482–514.

Benecke 1816: G. F. Benecke, *Der Edel Stein von Bonerius*. Berlin, 1816.

Bengel 1725: *Johanni Chrysostomi De sacerdotio libri sex*, ed. J. A. Bengel. Stuttgart, 1725.

Bengel 1734: J. A. Bengel, *Novum Testamentum Graecum*. Tübingen, 1734.

Bengel 1763a (1734): J. A. Bengel, *Apparatus criticus ad Novum Testamentum*. Tübingen, 1763 (the 1st ed. is included as an appendix in Bengel 1734).

Bengel 1763b (1742): J. A. Bengel, *Gnomon Novi Testamenti*. Ulm, 1763 (1st ed. Stuttgart, 1742).

Bentley 1711: R. Bentley, ed., *Q. Horatius Flaccus*, 2 vols. Cambridge, 1711.

Bentley 1713: R. Bentley, *Remarks upon a Late Discourse of Free-Thinking*. London, 1713 (= Bentley 1836–38: 3.287–368).

Bentley 1721: R. Bentley, *Proposals of Printing a New Edition of the Greek Testament*. London, 1721 (= Bentley 1836–38: 3.477–86).

Bentley 1836–38: R. Bentley, *Works*, 3 vols., ed. A. Dyce. London, 1836–38.

Bernardinello 1970: S. Bernardinello, *Eliminatio codicum della Metafisica di Aristotele*. Padua, 1970.

Bernays 1847: J. Bernays, "De emendatione Lucretii," *Rheinisches Museum* 5 (1847): 533–87.

Bernays 1852: *Titi Lucretii Cari De rerum natura*, ed. J. Bernays. Leipzig, 1852.

Bernays 1855: J. Bernays, *J. J. Scaliger*. Berlin, 1855.

Bernays 1885: J. Bernays, *Gesammelte Abhandlungen*, 2 vols. Berlin, 1885.

Bertheau 1908: C. Bertheau, "Wettstein, Johann Jakob, gest. 1754," *Realencyklopädie für protestantische Theologie und Kirche*, 3rd ed. (1908), 21.198–203.

Birt 1913: T. Birt, *Kritik und Hermeneutik*. Munich, 1913.

Blass 1892 (1886): F. Blass, "Hermeneutik und Kritik," in *Handbuch der Altertumswissenschaft*, 2nd ed., ed. I. Müller, 1.149–295. Munich, 1892 (1st ed. Nördlingen, 1886).

Blok 1949: F. F. Blok, *N. Heinsius in Dienst van Christina van Zweden*. Delft, 1949.

Blume-Lachmann-Rudorff 1848–52: F. Blume, K. Lachmann, and A. Rudorff, *Die Schriften der römischen Feldmesser*: vol. 1, *Texte und Zeichnungen;* and vol. 2, *Erläuterungen und Indices*. Berlin, 1848–52.

Boeckh 1886: A. Boeckh, *Encyklopädie und Methodologie der philologischen Wissenschaften*. Leipzig, 1886.

Bornmann 1962: F. Bornmann, "Sui criteri di 'recensio' meccanica enunciati da Lachmann nel 1817," *Rivista di Letterature Moderne e Comparate* 15 (1962): 46–53.

Brambilla Ageno 1975a: F. Brambilla Ageno, *L'edizione critica dei testi volgari*. Padua, 1975.

Brambilla Ageno 1975b: F. Brambilla Ageno, "Ci fu sempre un archetipo?" *Lettere Italiane* 27 (1975): 308–9.

Branca 1973: V. Branca, "Mercanti e librai fra Italia e Ungheria," in *Venezia e Ungheria nel Rinascimento*, ed. V. Branca, 335–52. Florence, 1973.

Bremi 1798: *Marci Tullii Ciceronis De finibus bonorum et malorum*, ed. J. H. Bremi. Zurich, 1798.

Brink 1978: C. O. Brink, "Studi classici e critica testuale in Inghilterra," *Annali della Scuola Normale Superiore di Pisa*, ser. 3, 8, no. 3 (1978): 1071–1228.

Bröcker 1885: L. O. Bröcker, "Die Methoden Galens in der literarischen Kritik," *Rheinisches Museum* 40 (1885): 415–38.

Bruhn 1887: E. Bruhn, "Lucubrationum Euripidearum capita selecta," *Jahrbücher für classische Philologie,* Suppl. 15 (1887): 227–324.

Brunhölzl 1962: F. Brunhölzl, "Zur Überlieferung des Lukrez," *Hermes* 90 (1962): 97–104.

Brunhölzl 1971: F. Brunhölzl, "Zu den sogenannten codices archetypi der römischen Literatur," in *Festschrift B. Bischoff zu seinem 65. Geburtstag*, ed. J. Autenrieth-F. Brunhölzl, 16–31. Stuttgart, 1971.

Büchner 1956: K. Büchner, "Präludien zu einer Lucrezausgabe," *Hermes* 84 (1956): 198–233.

Büchner 1964: K. Büchner, *Studien zur römischen Literatur,* 2 vols. Wiesbaden, 1964.

Canfora 1964: L. Canfora, review of S. Timpanaro, *La genesi del metodo del Lachmann* (Florence, 1963), *Belfagor* 19 (1964): 611–15.

Canfora 1968: L. Canfora, "Critica textualis in caelum revocata," *Belfagor* 23 (1968): 361–4.

Canfora 1982: L. Canfora, "Origine della 'stemmatica' di Paul Maas," *Rivista di Filologia e Istruzione Classica* 110 (1982): 362–79.

Caprioli 1969: S. Caprioli, *Indagini sul Bolognini: Giurisprudenza e filologia nel Quattrocento italiano.* Rome, 1969.

Carlini 1963: *Plato: Alcibiades I, Alcibiades II, Hipparchus, Anterastae,* ed. with an introduction, translation, and notes by A. Carlini. Turin, 1963.

Carlini 1967: A. Carlini, "L'attività filologica di F. Robortello," *Atti Accad. di Udine,* ser. 7, 7 (1967): 53–84.

Carlsson 1926: G. Carlsson, *Die Überlieferung der Seneca-Tragödien.* Lund, 1926.

Casamassima 1964: E. Casamassima, "Per una storia delle dottrine paleografiche dall'Umanesimo a Jean Mabillon," *Studi Medievali,* ser. 3, 5 (1964): 525–78.

Casamassima-Staraz 1977: E. Casamassima-E. Staraz, "Varianti e cambio grafico nella scrittura dei papiri latini: Note paleografiche," *Scrittura e Civiltà* 1 (1977): 9–110.

Castagna 1976: L. Castagna, *I Bucolici latini minori.* Florence, 1976.

Castellani 1980: A. Castellani, *Saggi di linguistica italiana e romanza,* 3 vols, Rome, 1980.

Castellani 1980 (1957): A. Castellani, *Bédier avait-il raison? La méthode de Lachmann dans les éditions de textes du Moyen Age.* Fribourg, 1957 (= Castellani 1980: 3.161–200).

Castiglioni 1937: L. Castiglioni, review of T. Lucreti Cari, *De rerum natura libri sex,* ed. J. Martin (Leipzig, 1934), *Gnomon* 13 (1937): 558–65.

Cavallo 1975: G. Cavallo, "Libro e pubblico alla fine del mondo antico," in *Libri, editori e pubblico nel mondo antico,* 81–132. Bari, 1975.

Cavallo 1977: G. Cavallo, *Libri e lettori nel Medioevo.* Bari, 1977.

Cecchini 1982: E. Cecchini, "Sulle 'quattro regole' di Lachmann," *Orpheus,* n. s., 3 (1982): 133–39.

Chatelain 1908: E. Chatelain, *Lucr. Cod. Voss. Oblongus phototypice editus.* Leiden, 1908.

Chatelain 1925: E. Chatelain, "Louis Havet," *Revue des Études Latines* 3 (1925): 22–24.

Chiari 1924: A. Chiari, "A proposito di una nuova edizione di Lucrezio," *Rivista di Filologia e Istruzione Classica* 52 (1924): 233–45 (= Chiari 1961: 1–27).

Chiari 1961: A. Chiari, *Indagini e letture.* Florence, 1961.

Cini 1976: G. Cini, "La posizione degli 'Italici' nello stemma lucreziano," *Atti e Memorie della Società Colombaria* 41 (1976): 116–76.

Citroni 1975: M. Citroni, ed., *Martialis: Epigrammaton liber I.* Florence, 1975.

Clausen 1956: A. Persi Flacci et D. Iuni Iuvenalis Saturae, ed. W. V. Clausen. Oxford, 1956.

Clausen 1963: W. Clausen, "Sabinus' MS of Persius," *Hermes* 91 (1963): 252–56.

Cobet 1847: C. G. Cobet, *Oratio de arte interpretandi grammatices et critices fundamentis innixa primario philologi officio.* Leiden, 1847.

Collins-Schlyter 1827: D. H. S. Collins and D. C. J. Schlyter, eds., *Corpus iuris Sueo-Gothorum antiqui.* Stockholm, 1827.

Contini 1942: G. Contini, *Un anno di letteratura*. Florence, 1942.

Contini 1955: G. Contini, "Ancora sulla canzone 'S'eo trovasse pietanza,'" *Syculorum Gymnasium* 8 (1955): 122–38.

Corti 1961: M. Corti, "Note sui rapporti fra localizzazione dei MSS e 'recensio,'" in *Studi e problemi di critica testuale*, 85–92. Bologna, 1961.

Courtney 1968: E. Courtney, "The Textual Transmission of the Appendix Vergiliana," *Bulletin of the Institute of Classical Studies* (London) 15 (1968): 133–41.

Curtius 1858–62: G. Curtius, *Grundzüge der griechischen Etymologie*, 2 vols. Leipzig, 1858–62.

Curtius 1862: G. Curtius, *Philologie und Sprachwissenschaft*. Leipzig, 1862.

Dain 1932: A. Dain, "Edition des textes classiques: Théories et méthodes," in *Assoc. G. Budé, Congrès de Nîmes 1932, Actes du Congrès*, 61–88. Paris, 1932.

Dain 1949: A. Dain, *Les manuscrits*. Paris, 1949.

Dain 1964: A. Dain, "À propos de la 'méthode' de Lachmann," *Bulletin de l'Association Guillaume Budé*, ser. 4, no. 1 (1964): 116–22.

Dain 1975 (1949): A. Dain, *Les manuscrits,* 3rd ed. Paris, 1975 (1st ed. Paris, 1949).

Dawe 1964: R. D. Dawe, *The Collation and Investigation of MSS of Aeschylus*. Cambridge, 1964.

Dawe 1973: R. D. Dawe, *Studies on the Text of Sophocles*. Leiden, 1973.

de Jonge 1978: H. J. de Jonge, "Jeremias Hoelzlin, Editor of the *Textus receptus* printed by the Elzeviers, Leiden 1633," in *Miscellanea Neotestamentica*, 1.105–28. Leiden, 1978.

de Jonge 1984: H. J. de Jonge, "Novum Testamentum a nobis versum: The Essence of Erasmus' Edition of the New Testament," *Journal of Theological Studies*, n. s., 35 (1984): 395–413.

Del testo 1979: *Del testo: Seminario interdisciplinare sulla costituzione del testo*. Naples, 1979.

Destrez 1935: J. Destrez, *La pecia dans les manuscrits universitaires*. Paris, 1935.

Devoto 1958: G. Devoto, *Scritti minori*, 3 vols. Florence, 1958.

Di Benedetto 1965: V. Di Benedetto, *La tradizione manoscritta euripidea*. Padua, 1965.

Diels 1923–24: *T. Lucretius Carus De Rerum Natura*, ed. and trans. H. Diels. Berlin, 1923–24.

Dindorf 1870: W. Dindorf, "Über die Venetianische Handschrift des Athenäus und deren Abschriften," *Philologus* 30 (1870): 73–115.

Dindorf 1876: W. Dindorf, *Lexicon Aeschyleum*. Leipzig, 1876.

Duvau 1888: L. Duvau, "Lucretiana," *Revue de Philologie* 12 (1888): 30–37.

Eisenhut 1973: *Dictys Cretensis Ephemeridos belli Troiani libri a Lucio Septimio ex Greco in Latinum sermonem translati*, ed. W. Eisenhut. Leipzig, 1973.

Ellis 1862: A. A. Ellis, *Bentleii critica sacra*. Cambridge, 1862.

Ellis 1878 (1867): *Catulli Veronensis liber,* 2nd ed., ed. R. Ellis. Oxford, 1878 (1st ed. Oxford, 1867).

Elmsley 1810: P. Elmsley, review of C. J. Blomfield, ed., *Aeschyli Prometheus Vinctus* (Cambridge, 1810), *Edinburgh Review* 33 (1810): 211–42.

Erasmus 1538 (1500): Erasmus, *Adagiorum Chiliades*. Basel, 1538 (1st ed. Paris, 1500).

Erbse 1959: H. Erbse, review of P. Maas, *Textkritik* (Leipzig, 1957), *Gnomon* 31 (1959): 97–103.

Ernesti 1761: *Callimachi hymnos, epigrammata et fragmenta cum notis variorum,* ed. J. A. Ernesti. Leiden, 1761.

Ernesti 1801 (1772): *Taciti opera,* vol. 1, ed. J. A. Ernesti, rev. J. J. Oberlin. Leipzig, 1801 (1st ed. Leipzig, 1772).

Ernout 1926: A. Ernout, "À la mémoire de L. Havet," *Revue des Études Latines* 4 (1926): 20–26.

Ernout 1948 (1920): *Lucrèce: De la nature,* 2 vols., ed. and trans. A. Ernout. Paris, 1948 (1st ed. Paris, 1920).

Fabre 1947 (1936): *César: La guerre civile,* 2 vols., ed. and trans. P. Fabre. Paris, 1947 (1st ed. Paris, 1936).

Fink-Errera 1962: G. Fink-Errera, "Une institution du monde médiéval: la pecia," *Revue Philosophique de Louvain* 60 (1962): 187–210, 216–43 (= Cavallo 1977: 131–66).

Flora 1937: *Tutte le opere di G. Leopardi,* ed. F. Flora: vol. 1, *Zibaldone di pensieri.* Milan, 1937.

Flores 1978: E. Flores, "Ecdotica e tradizione manoscritta lucreziana," *Vichiana,* n. s., 8 (1978): 21–37.

Folena 1961: G. Folena, "Filologia testuale e storia linguistica," in *Studi e problemi di critica testuale,* 17–34. Bologna, 1961.

Folena 1965: G. Folena, "La tradizione delle opere di Dante Alighieri," in *Atti del Congresso internazionale di studi danteschi,* 1.1–78. Florence, 1965.

Fourquet 1946: J. Fourquet, "Le paradoxe de Bédier," *Mélanges 1945, II: Études Littéraires* (Publications de la Faculté des Lettres, Strasbourg): 1–16.

Fourquet 1948: J. Fourquet, "Fautes communes ou innovations communes?" *Romania* 70 (1948): 85–95.

Fox 1954: A. Fox, *J. Mill and R. Bentley.* Oxford, 1954.

Fraenkel 1926: E. Fraenkel, "Anzeige von Lucani Bellum Civile ed. A. E. Housman," *Gnomon* 2 (1926): 497–532 (= Fraenkel 1964, 2.267–308).

Fraenkel 1950: E. Fraenkel, *Aeschylus Agamemnon.* Oxford, 1950.

Fraenkel 1964: E. Fraenkel, *Kleine Beiträge,* 2 vols. Rome, 1964.

Frank 1955: I. Frank, "De l'art d'éditer les textes lyriques," in *Recueil de travaux offert à C. Brunel,* 1.463–75. Memoires et documents publiés par la Société de l'École des Chartes. Paris, 1955.

Fränkel 1964: H. Fränkel, *Einleitung zur kritischen Ausgabe der Argonautika des Apollonios.* Göttingen, 1964.

Freté 1926: A. Freté, "À la mémoire de L. Havet," *Revue des Études Latines* 4 (1926): 20–26.

Froger 1968: J. Froger, *La critique des textes et son automatisation.* Paris, 1968.

Fröhner 1862: W. Fröhner, ed., *Aviani fabulae.* Leipzig, 1862.

Gamberale 1975: L. Gamberale, "Note sulla tradizione di Gellio: In margine alla più recente edizione delle *Noctes Atticae,*" *Rivista di Filologia e Istruzione Classica* 103 (1975): 35–55.

Geymonat 1972: *P. Vergili Maronis Opera,* ed. R. Sabbadini and A. Castiglioni, rev. M. Geymonat. Turin, 1972.

Giarratano 1943: C. Giarratano, ed., *Calpurnii et Nemesiani Bucolica,* 2nd ed. Turin, 1943 (1st ed. Naples, 1910).

Giarratano 1951: C. Giarratano, "La critica del testo," in *Introduzione alla filologia classica,* 73–132. Milan, 1951.

Goebel-Goebel 1857: A. Goebel-E. Goebel, "Die Schedae Vindobonenses und der Codex Victorianus des Lucrez," *Rheinisches Museum* 12 (1857): 449–56.

Goerenz 1809–13: J. A. Goerenz, ed., *Ciceronis philosophica omnia,* 3 vols. Leipzig, 1809–13.

Gomperz 1905: T. Gomperz, *Essays und Erinnerungen.* Stuttgart, 1905.

Gomperz 1922–25: T. Gomperz, *Griechische Denker,* 4 vols. Berlin and Leipzig, 1922–25.

Goold 1958: G. P. Goold, "A Lost Manuscript of Lucretius," *Acta Classica* 1 (1958): 21–30.

Goold 1963: G. P. Goold, "Richard Bentley: A Tercentary Commemoration," *Harvard Studies in Classical Philology* 67 (1963): 285–302.

Grafton 1975: A. T. Grafton, "J. Scaliger's Edition of Catullus (1577) and the Traditions of Textual Criticism in the Renaissance," *Journal of the Warburg and Courtauld Institutes* 38 (1975): 155–81.

Grafton 1977a: A. T. Grafton, "On the Scholarship of Politian and Its Context," *Journal of the Warburg and Courtauld Institutes* 40 (1977): 150–88.

Grafton 1977b: A. T. Grafton, "From Politian to Pasquali," *Journal of Roman Studies* 67 (1977): 171–76.

Grafton 1983: A. T. Grafton, *Joseph Scaliger: A Study in the History of Classical Scholarship:* vol. 1, *Textual Criticism and Exegesis.* Oxford, 1983.

Grassi 1961: E. Grassi, "Inediti di Eugenio Grassi (a cura di V. Bartoletti, F. Bornmann, M. Manfredi, S. Timpanaro)," *Atene e Roma* 6 (1961): 129–65.

Greg 1930–31: W. W. Greg, "Recent Theories of Textual Criticism," *Modern Philology* 28, no. 4 (1930–31): 401–4.

Gregory 1900–1909: C. R. Gregory, *Textkritik des Neuen Testamentes,* 3 vols. Leipzig, 1900 (vol. 1), 1902 (2), and 1909 (3).

Griesbach 1796 (1774): *Novum Testamentum Graece,* 2 vols., 2nd ed., ed. J. J. Griesbach. Halle, 1796 (1st ed. Halle, 1774).

Grimm 1864–71: J. L. Grimm, *Kleine Schriften,* 5 vols. Berlin, 1864–71.

Hagen 1816: F. H. von der Hagen, ed., *Der Nibelungen Lied,* 2nd ed. Breslau, 1816.

Hagen 1879: H. Hagen, *Gradus ad criticen.* Leipzig, 1879.

Haupt 1836: M. Haupt, *Quaestiones Catullianae.* Leipzig, 1836 (= Haupt 1875–76: 1.1–72).

Haupt 1875–76: M. Haupt, *Opuscula,* 3 vols. Leipzig, 1875–76.

Haupt 1911 (1854): M. Haupt, "De Lachmanno critico (Rede 1854)," *Neue Jahrbücher für das klassische Altertum* 27 (1911): 529–38.

Havet 1884: L. Havet, "Les fautes issues de corrections dans les mss. de Nonius," *Mélanges Graux,* 803–14. Paris, 1884.

Havet 1911: L. Havet, *Manuel de critique verbale.* Paris, 1911.

Heinsius 1661: N. Heinsius, ed., *Publii Ovidii Nasonis opera omnia.* Amsterdam, 1661.

Hemmerdinger 1977: B. Hemmerdinger, "Philologues de jadis (Bentley, Wolf, Boeckh, Cobet)," *Belfagor* 32 (1977): 485–522.

Hering 1967: W. Hering, "Zweispaltige Stemmata: Zur Theorie der textkritischen Methode," *Philologus* 111 (1967): 170–85.

Hermann 1827–77: G. Hermann, *Opuscula,* 8 vols. Leipzig, 1827–77.

Hermann 1842: G. Hermann, "De hymnis Dionysii et Mesomedis." (= Hermann 1827–77: 8.343–52).

Hertz 1851: M. Hertz, K. *Lachmann: Eine Biographie.* Berlin, 1851.

Heyne 1817 (1755): C. G. Heyne, ed., *Tibulli carmina,* 4th ed., rev. C. F. Wunderlich, vol. 1. Leipzig, 1817 (1st ed. Leipzig, 1755).

Hoenigswald 1963: H. Hoenigswald, "On the History of the Comparative Method," *Anthropological Linguistics* 5, no. 1 (1963): 1–11.

Holm 1972: G. Holm, *Carl Johan Schlyter and Textual Scholarship.* Uppsala, 1972.

Housman 1927 (1926): M. *Annaei Lucani: De bello civili,* ed. A. E. Housman. Oxford, 1927 (1st ed. Oxford, 1926).

Housman 1931: D. *Iunii Iuvenalis,* ed. A. E. Housman. Cambridge, 1931.

Housman 1937 (1903): M. *Manilii Astronomicon,* book 1, 2nd ed., ed. A. E. Housman. Cambridge, 1937 (1st ed. Cambridge, 1903).

Housman 1972: *The Classical Papers of A. E. Housman,* 3 vols., collected and ed. J. Diggle and F. R. D. Goodyear. Cambridge, 1972.

Humboldt 1903–20: W. Von Humboldt, *Gesammelte Schriften,* 15 vols., ed. A. Leitzmann, B. Gebhardt, S. Kähler, and E. Spränger. Berlin, 1903–20.

Hunger et al. 1961–64: H. Hunger et al., *Geschichte der Textüberlieferung,* 2 vols. Zurich, 1961–64.

Irigoin 1954: J. Irigoin, "Stemmas bifides et états de manuscrits," *Revue de Philologie* 80 (1954): 211–17.

Irigoin 1977: J. Irigoin, "Quelques réflexions sur le concept d'archétype," *Revue d'Histoire des Textes* 7 (1977): 235–45.

Irmer 1972: D. Irmer, *Zur Genealogie der jüngeren Demostheneshandschriften.* Hamburg, 1972.

Jahn 1843: A. *Persii Flacci saturarum libri cum scholiis antiquis,* ed. O. Jahn. Leipzig, 1843.

Jahn 1849: O. Jahn, *G. Hermann.* Leipzig, 1849.

Jahn 1851: *Auli Persii Flacci saturarum libri,* ed. O. Jahn (smaller ed.). Leipzig, 1851.

Jebb 1889: R. C. Jebb, *Bentley.* London, 1889.

Jebb 1900 (1886): R. C. Jebb, *Sophocles: The Plays:* vol. 2, *The Oedipus Coloneus,* 3rd ed. Cambridge, 1900 (1st ed. Cambridge, 1886).

Jocelyn 1984: H. D. Jocelyn, review of A. Grafton, *Joseph Scaliger: A Study in the History of Classical Scholarship:* vol. 1, *Textual Criticism and Exegesis* (Oxford, 1983), *Liverpool Classical Monthly* 9 (1984): 55–61.

Kaibel 1887–90: *Athenaei Naucratitae Deipnosophistarum libri XV,* 3 vols., ed. G. Kaibel. Leipzig, 1887.

Kämmel 1879: H. J. Kämmel, "J. A. Goerenz," *Allgemeine Deutsche Biographie* 9 (1879): 373.

Kantorowicz 1921: H. Kantorowicz, *Einführung in die Textkritik.* Leipzig, 1921.

Kenney 1974: E. J. Kenney, *The Classical Text: Aspects of Editing in the Age of the Printed Book.* Berkeley, Los Angeles, and London, 1974.

Kenney 1980: E. J. Kenney, "A Rejoinder," *Giornale Italiano di Filologia* 32 (1980): 321–23.

Kirner 1901: G. Kirner, "Contributo alla critica del testo delle *Epistolae ad Familiares* di Cicerone," *Studi Italiani di Filologia Classica* 9 (1901): 369–433.

Klaproth 1823: J. Klaproth, *Asia polyglotta.* Paris, 1823.

Kleinlogel 1968: A. Kleinlogel, "Das Stemmaproblem," *Philologus* 112 (1968): 63–82.

Klotz 1908: P. *Papinius Status: Thebais,* ed. A. Klotz. Leipzig, 1908.

Klotz 1923: M. *Tullius Cicero: In Verrem actionis secundae libri I–III,* ed. A. Klotz. Leipzig, 1923.

Klotz 1950: C. I. *Caesar: Commentarii Belli Civilis libri,* ed. A. Klotz. Leipzig, 1950.

Koerte 1833: W. Koerte, *Leben und Studien F. A. Wolfs,* 2 vols. Essen, 1833.

Kramer 1844–52: *Strabonis Geographica,* 3 vols., ed. with critical commentary by G. Kramer. Berlin, 1844–52.

Kretschmer 1896: P. Kretschmer, *Einleitung in die Geschichte der griechischen Sprache.* Göttingen, 1896.

Kretschmer 1927: P. Kretschmer, "Sprache," in *Einleitung in die Altertumswissenschaft,* 3rd ed., ed. A. Gercke-E. Norden, 1.1–121. Leipzig and Berlin, 1927.

Küster 1710: L. Küster, ed., *Novum Testamentum Graecum.* Rotterdam, 1710.

La Penna 1957: A. La Penna, *Publius Ovidius Naso Ibis,* ed. with a commentary by A. La Penna. Florence, 1957.

La Penna 1964: A. La Penna, review of S. Timpanaro, *La genesi del metodo del Lachmann* (Florence, 1963), *Critica Storica* 3 (1964): 369–74.

Lachmann 1816: *Sextus Aurelius Propertius: Carmina,* ed. with notes by Karl Lachmann. Leipzig, 1816.

Lachmann 1817: K. Lachmann, review of F. H. von der Hagen, *Der Nibelungen Lied* (Breslau, 1816), and of G. F. Benecke, *Der Edel Stein von Bonerius* (Berlin, 1816), *Jenaische Allgemeine Literatur Zeitung* (1817): 114–42 (= Lachmann 1876, 1.81–114).

Lachmann 1818: K. Lachmann, "Über G. Hermann's Ausgabe von Sophokles' Ajax," *Jenaische Allgemeine Literatur Zeitung* 203–4, no. 4 (1818): 249–63 (= Lachmann 1876: 2.1–17).

Lachmann 1820a: K. Lachmann, review of *Der Nibelungen Noth und der Nibelungen Lied,* ed. F. H. von der Hagen (Breslau, 1820), *Jenaische Allgemeine Literatur Zeitung* 1820, Ergänzungsblätter 70–76 (= Lachmann 1876: 1.206–77).

Lachmann 1820b: K. Lachmann, *Auswahl aus den hochdeutschen Dichtern.* Berlin, 1820.

Lachmann 1826: K. Lachmann, *Über Vossens Tibull und einige andere Tibull-Übersetzungen, Jenaische Allgemeine Literatur Zeitung* 63–67, no. 2 (1826): 113–52 (= Lachmann 1876: 2.102–45).

Lachmann 1829: K. Lachmann, ed., *Albii Tibulli carmina.* Berlin, 1829.

Lachmann 1830: K. Lachmann, "Rechenschaft über Lachmanns Ausgabe des Neuen Testaments," *Theologische Studien und Kritiken* 3, no. 2 (1830): 817–45 (= Lachmann 1876: 2.250–72).

Lachmann 1831: K. Lachmann, ed., *Novum Testamentum Graece.* Berlin, 1831.

Lachmann 1836: K. Lachmann, "Über Dissen's Tibull," *Hallische Allgemeine Literatur-Zeitung* 109–10, no. 2 (1836): 250–63 (= Lachmann 1876: 2.145–60).

Lachmann 1842–50: K. Lachmann, ed., *Novum Testamentum Graece et Latine,* 2 vols. Berlin, 1842 (vol. 1), 1850 (2).

Lachmann 1850a: K. Lachmann, ed., *Lucretii de rerum natura libri VI.* Berlin, 1850.

Lachmann 1850b: K. Lachmann, *In Lucretii de rerum natura libros commentarius.* Berlin, 1850.

Lachmann 1851 (1826): K. Lachmann, ed., *Der Nibelungen Not mit der Klage,* 3rd ed. Berlin, 1851 (1st ed. Berlin, 1826).

Lachmann 1876: K. Lachmann, *Kleinere Schriften*, 2 vols. Berlin, 1876.

Lachmann 1879 (1833): *Wolfram von Eschenbach*, ed. K. Lachmann. Berlin, 1879 (1st ed. Berlin, 1833).

Lachmann 1892: K. *Lachmann's Briefe an Moriz Haupt*, ed. J. Vahlen. Berlin, 1892.

Le Clerc 1730 (1697): J. Le Clerc, *Ars critica*, 5th ed. Amsterdam, 1730 (1st ed. Amsterdam, 1697).

Lefmann 1891: S. Lefmann, *Franz Bopp*, 2 vols. Berlin, 1891.

Lehrs 1882: K. Lehrs, *De Aristarchi studiis Homericis*. Leipzig, 1882.

Leo 1893: F. Leo, *Rede zur Saecularfeier K. Lachmanns*. Göttingen, 1893 (= Leo 1960: 2.415–31).

Leo 1960: F. Leo, *Ausgewälte Kleine Schriften*, 2 vols., ed. E. Fraenkel. Rome, 1960.

Leonard-Smith 1942: *Titi Lucretii Cari De rerum natura*, ed. W. E. Leonard and S. B. Smith. Madison, 1942.

Leumann 1977: M. Leumann, *Lat. Laut-und Formenlehre*. Munich, 1977.

Leutsch 1851: *Corpus Paroemiographorum Graecorum*, vol. 2, ed. E. L. Leutsch. Göttingen, 1851 (reprint: Hildesheim, 1965).

Lindsay 1902: W. M. Lindsay, *The Ancient Editions of Martial*. Oxford, 1902.

Lindsay 1903: M. *Valerii Martialis Epigrammata*, ed. W. M. Lindsay. Oxford, 1903.

Lobeck 1853: C. A. Lobeck, *Pathologiae Graeci sermonis elementa*, 2 vols. Königsberg, 1853.

Ludwich 1885: A. Ludwich, *Aristarchs Homerische Textkritik*, vol. 2. Leipzig, 1885.

Lutz-Hensel 1971: M. Lutz-Hensel, "Lachmanns textkritische Wahrscheinlichkeitsregeln," *Zeitschrift fur Deutsche Philologie* 90 (1971): 394–408.

Lutz-Hensel 1975: M. Lutz-Hensel, *Prinzipien der ersten textkritischen Editionen mittelhochdeutscher Dichtung: Brüder Grimm, Benecke, Lachmann*. Berlin, 1975.

Maas 1935: P. Maas, "Eustathios als Konjekturalkritiker, I," *Byzantinische Zeitschrift* 35 (1935): 299–307.

Maas 1936: P. Maas, "Eustathios als Konjekturalkritiker, II," *Byzantinische Zeitschrift* 36 (1936): 27–31.

Maas 1937: P. Maas, "Leitfehler und stemmatische Typen," *Byzantinische Zeitschrift* 37 (1937): 289–94.

Maas 1958 (1927): P. Maas, *Textual Criticism*, trans. B. Flower. Oxford, 1958 (= *Textkritik*, 3rd ed. Leipzig, 1957; 1st ed. Leipzig, 1927).

Maas 1960: P. Maas, *Textkritik*, 4th ed. Leipzig, 1960.

Maas 1973: P. Maas, *Kleine Schriften*. Munich, 1973.

[Mace] 1729: [D. Mace], ed., *The New Testament in Greek and English*. London, 1729.

Madvig 1828: J. N. Madvig, *Ad virum celeberrimum Io. Casp. Orellium epistola critica de orationum Verrinarum libris II extremis emendandis*. Copenhagen, 1828.

Madvig 1832: J. N. Madvig, *De aliquot lacunis codicum Lucretii*. Copenhagen, 1832 (= Madvig 1887: 248–62).

Madvig 1833: J. N. Madvig, *De emendandis Ciceronis orationibus pro P. Sestio et in P. Vatinium*. Copenhagen, 1833 (= Madvig 1887: 333–407).

Madvig 1834: J. N. Madvig, *Opuscula academica*. Copenhagen, 1834.

Madvig 1842: J. N. Madvig, *Opuscula academica altera*. Copenhagen, 1842.

Madvig 1869 (1839): M. *Tullii Ciceronis De finibus bonorum et malorum*, 2nd corrected ed., ed. J. N. Madvig. Copenhagen, 1869 (1st ed. Copenhagen, 1839).

Madvig 1871: J. N. Madvig, *Adversaria critica*, 2 vols. Copenhagen, 1871.

Madvig 1887: J. N. Madvig, *Opuscula academica ab ipso iterum collecta, emendata, aucta*. Copenhagen, 1887.

Maher 1966: J. P. Maher, "More on the History of the Comparative Method: The Tradition of Darwinism in August Schleicher's Work," *Anthropological Linguistics* 8, no. 3 (1966): 1–12.

Malcovati 1938: *L. Annaei Flori quae extant*, ed. E. Malcovati. Rome, 1938.

Mälzer 1970: G. Mälzer, *J. A. Bengel: Leben und Werk*. Stuttgart, 1970.

Marichal 1961: R. Marichal, *La critique des textes*. Paris, 1961.

I. Mariotti 1947: I. Mariotti, "Un passo di Sallustio falsamente attribuito a Cicerone," *Studi Italiani di Filologia Classica* 22 (1947): 257.

S. Mariotti 1947: S. Mariotti, "Varianti d'autore nella tradizione diretta dell'Eneide?" *Paideia* 2 (1947): 303.

S. Mariotti 1950: S. Mariotti, "Ancora su varianti d'autore," *Paideia* 5 (1950): 26–28.

S. Mariotti 1952: S. Mariotti, "Rileggendo la storia della tradizione," *Atene e Roma* 11 (1952): 212–19.

S. Mariotti 1954: S. Mariotti, "Probabili varianti d'autore in Ennio, Cicerone, Sinesio," *La Parola del Passato* 9 (1954): 368–75.

S. Mariotti 1966: S. Mariotti, "Qua ratione quave via huius saeculi philologi veterum opera edenda curaverint," in *Acta omnium gentium ac nationum conventus lat. Litteris linguaeque fovendis*. Rome, 1966.

S. Mariotti 1971: S. Mariotti, "'Codex unicus' e editori sfortunati," *Studi Urbinati*, ser. B, 45 (1971): 837–40.

Marshall 1977: P. Marshall, *The Manuscript Tradition of Cornelius Nepos*. London, 1977.

Martin 1969 (1934): *T. Lucretii Cari De rerum natura libri sex*, 6th ed., ed. J. Martin. Leipzig, 1969 (1st ed. Leipzig, 1934).

Mastricht 1711: G. von Mastricht, ed., *Novum Testamentum*. Amsterdam, 1711.

McLachlan 1938–39: H. McLachlan, "An Almost Forgotten Pioneer in New Testament Criticism," *Hibbert Journal* 37, no. 4 (1938–39): 617–25.

Meillet-Vendryes 1963: A. Meillet-J. Vendryes, *Traité de grammaire comparée des langues classiques*. Paris, 1963.

Merrill 1913: W. A. Merrill, "The Archetype of Lucretius," *University of California Publications in Classical Philology* 2, no. 10 (1913): 227–35.

Metzger 1968 (1964): B. M. Metzger, *The Text of the New Testament: Its Transmission, Corruption, and Restoration*, 2nd ed. Oxford, 1968 (1st ed. Oxford, 1964).

Migne 1845: *Patrologiae cursus completus*, ed. J. P. Migne, vol. 22: *S. Eusebii Hieronymi opera omnia*, pt. 1. Paris, 1845.

Migne 1846: *Patrologiae cursus completus*, ed. J. P. Migne: vol. 29, *S. Eusebii Hieronymi opera omnia*, pt. 10. Paris, 1846.

Momigliano 1974: A. Momigliano, review of A. E. Housman, *The Collected Papers*, collected and ed. J. Diggle and F. R. D. Goodyear III (Cambridge, 1972), *Athenaeum* 52 (1974): 368–71.

Momigliano 1975: A. Momigliano, *Quinto contributo alla storia degli studi classici e del mondo antico*, 2 vols. Rome, 1975.

Morel 1766: J. B. Morel, *Eléments de critique*. Paris, 1766.

Moricca 1946–47: *L. Annaei Senecae Tragoediae*, 2 vols., 2nd ed., ed. U. Moricca. Turin 1946–47.

Morpurgo Davies 1975: A. Morpurgo Davies, "Language Classification in the Nineteenth Century," in *Current Trends in Linguistics*, ed. T. A. Sebeok, 13.607–716. The Hague-Paris, 1975.

G. Müller 1958: G. Müller, "Die Problematik des Lucreztextes seit Lachmann, I," *Philologus* 102 (1958): 247–83.

G. Müller 1959: G. Müller, "Die Problematik des Lucreztextes seit Lachmann, II," *Philologus* 103 (1959): 53–86.

K. Müller 1954: *Q. Curtius Rufus: Geschichte Alexanders des Grossen*, ed. K. Müller and H. Schönfeld. Munich, 1954.

K. Müller 1973: K. Müller, "De codicum Lucretii Italicorum origine," *Museum Helveticum* 30 (1973): 166–78.

K. Müller 1975: K. Müller, ed., *Titus Lucretius Carus: De rerum natura*. Zurich, 1975.

L. Müller 1869: L. Müller, *Geschichte der klassischen Philologie in den Niederlanden*. Leipzig, 1869.

Munari 1950: F. Munari, "Codici heinsiani degli *Amores*," *Studi Italiani di Filologia Classica*, n. s., 24 (1950): 161–65.

Munari 1957: F. Munari, "Manoscritti ovidiani di N. Heinsius," *Studi Italiani di Filologia Classica*, n. s., 29 (1957): 98–114.

Munari 1970: *P. Ovidii Nasonis Amores*, ed. with an introduction, translation, and notes by F. Munari. Florence, 1970.

Munro 1886: *Titi Lucretii Cari De rerum natura libri sex*, ed. H. A. J. Munro. Cambridge, 1886.

Murgia 1980: C. E. Murgia, "A Problem in the Transmission of Quintilian's *Institutio Oratoria*," *Classical Philology* 75 (1980): 312–20.

Mynors 1964: *Panegyrici Latini*, ed. R. A. B. Mynors. Oxford, 1964.

Nardo 1966: D. Nardo, "Le correzioni nei due codici Medicei 49, 7 e 49, 9 delle 'Familiares' di Cicerone (una terza tradizione diretta?)," *Atti Istituto Veneto di Scienze e Lettere*, "Scienze Morali" 124 (1966): 337–97.

Nardo 1967: D. Nardo, "Varianti e tradizione manoscritta in Ausonio," *Atti Istituto Veneto di Scienze e Lettere*, "Scienze Morali" 125 (1967): 321–82.

Nardo 1970: D. Nardo, *Il Commentariolum petitionis*. Padua, 1970.

Nardo 1981: D. Nardo, "Scienza e filosofia nel primo Settecento padovano: Gli studi classici di G. B. Morgagni, G. Poleni, G. Pontedera, L. Targa," *Quaderni per la Storia dell'Università di Padova* 14 (1981): 1–40.

Nencioni 1946: G. Nencioni, *Idealismo e realismo nella scienza del linguaggio*. Florence, 1946.

Nestle 1893: E. Nestle, "Bengel als Gelehrter: Ein Bild für unsere Tage," in *Marginalien und Materialen*, 2.1–143. Tübingen, 1893.

Nipperdey 1847–56: *Caesaris Commentarii*, 2 vols., ed. C. Nipperdey. Leipzig, 1847–56.

Nolte 1913: F. Nolte, *J. A. Bengel*. Gütersloh, 1913.

Nouvelle biographie générale 1855: "J. Boivin," in *Nouvelle biographie générale*, 5.479–80. 1855.

Okken 1970: L. Okken, *Ein Beitrag zur Entwirrung einer kontaminierten Manuskripttradition: Studien zur Überlieferung von Hartmann von Aue "Iwein."* Utrecht, 1970.

Orelli 1826–38: J. C. Orelli, ed., *Ciceronis Opera quae supersunt omnia,* 5 vols. Zurich, 1826–38.

Orelli 1827: J. C. Orelli, review of H. Meyer, *Ciceronis Orator* (Leipzig, 1827), *Jahrbücher für Philologie und Paedagogik,* ser. 3, 4 (1827): 84–91.

Orelli 1832: J. C. Orelli, *De provinciis consularibus.* Zurich, 1832.

Orelli 1835: J. C. Orelli, *Interrogatio in Vatinium.* Zurich, 1835.

Orelli 1837: J. C. Orelli, *Aratea.* Zurich, 1837.

Orelli-Beier 1830: J. C. Orelli and K. Beier, eds., *Ciceronis Orator Brutus Topica De optimo genere oratorum.* Zurich, 1830.

Pascal 1918: C. Pascal, "Emendare," *Athenaeum* 6 (1918): 209–16.

Pasquali 1929: G. Pasquali, review of P. Maas, *Textkritik* (Leipzig, 1927), *Gnomon* 5 (1929): 417–35, 498–521.

Pasquali 1931: G. Pasquali, "Teologi protestanti predecessori del Lachmann," *Studi Italiani di Filologia Classica,* n. s., 9 (1931): 243–54.

Pasquali 1932a: G. Pasquali, review of P. Collomp, *La critique des textes* (Paris, 1931), *Gnomon* 8 (1932): 128–34.

Pasquali 1932b: G. Pasquali, "Edizione critica," in *Enciclopedia Italiana,* vol. 13, cols. 477–80. Milan, 1932.

Pasquali 1934: G. Pasquali, *Storia della tradizione e critica del testo.* Florence, 1934.

Pasquali 1935: G. Pasquali, *Pagine meno stravaganti.* Florence, 1935.

Pasquali 1936: G. Pasquali, "Ricordo di Girolamo Vitelli," in *In memoria di G. Vitelli,* 7–20. Florence, 1936 (= Pasquali 1942: 297–312 = Pasquali 1968: 2.205–15).

Pasquali 1942: G. Pasquali, *Terze pagine stravaganti.* Florence, 1942.

Pasquali 1947: G. Pasquali, "Preghiera," *Studi Italiani di Filologia Classica* 22 (1947): 261.

Pasquali 1951a: G. Pasquali, *Stravaganze quarte e supreme.* Venice, 1951.

Pasquali 1951b: G. Pasquali, review of A. Dain, *Le manuscrits* (Paris, 1949), *Gnomon* 23 (1951): 233–43.

Pasquali 1952a (1934): G. Pasquali, *Storia della tradizione e critica del testo.* Florence, 1952 (1st ed. Florence, 1934).

Pasquali 1952b (1933): G. Pasquali, *Vecchie e nuove pagine stravaganti di un filologo.* Florence, 1952.

Pasquali 1959 (1925): G. Pasquali, *Gregorii Nysseni epistulae.* Leiden, 1959 (1st ed. Berlin, 1925).

Pasquali 1964 (1920): G. Pasquali, *Filologia e storia.* Florence, 1964 (1st ed. Berlin, 1920).

Pasquali 1968: G. Pasquali, *Pagine stravaganti,* 2 vols. Florence, 1968.

Pasquali 1986: G. Pasquali, *Rapsodia sul classico: Contributi all'Enciclopedia italiana di G. Pasquali,* ed. F. Bornmann, G. Pascucci, and S. Timpanaro. Rome, 1986.

Perazzini 1775: B. Perazzini, "Correctiones et adnotationes in Dantis Comoediam," in *In editionem tractatuum vel sermonum S. Zenonis,* 55–86. Verona, 1775.

Peri 1967: V. Peri, "Nicola Maniacutia: Un testimone della filologia romana del XII secolo," *Aevum* 41 (1967): 67–90.

Peri 1977: V. Peri, " 'Correctores immo corruptores': Un saggio di critica testuale nella Roma del XII secolo," *Italia Medievale e Umanistica* 20 (1977): 19–126.

Perosa 1955: A. Perosa, *Mostra del Poliziano nella Biblioteca Medicea Laurenziana.* Florence, 1955.

Perosa-Timpanaro 1956: A. Perosa and S. Timpanaro, "Libanio (o Coricio?): Poliziano e Leopardi," *Studi Italiani di Filologia Classica,* n. s., 27–28 (1956): 411–25.

Per Sebastiano Timpanaro 2001: M. Feo and M. Rossi, eds., *Per Sebastiano Timpanaro, Il Ponte* 57, nos. 10–11 (October–November 2001).

Petitmengin 1966: P. Petitmengin, "À propos des éditions patristiques de la Contre-Réforme," *Recherches Augustiniennes* 4 (1966): 199–251.

Pfeiffer 1949–53: *Callimachus,* 2 vols., ed. R. Pfeiffer. Oxford, 1949–53.

Pfeiffer 1968: R. Pfeiffer, *History of Classical Scholarship from the Beginning to the End of the Hellenistic Age.* Oxford, 1968.

Pfeiffer 1976: R. Pfeiffer, *History of Classical Scholarship from 1300 to 1850.* Oxford, 1976.

Pighi 1973: P. *Ovidii Nasonis Fastorum libri,* ed. G. B. Pighi. Turin, 1973.

Pizzani 1959: U. Pizzani, *Il problema del testo e della composizione del "De rerum natura."* Rome, 1959.

Politian 1972: A. Poliziano, *Miscellaneorum centuria seconda,* ed. V. Branca and M. Pastore Stocchi. Florence, 1972.

Politian 1978: A. Poliziano, *Commento alle Silve di Stazio,* ed. L. Cesarini Martinelli. Florence, 1978.

Pontedera 1740: J. Pontedera, *Antiquitatum Latinarum Graecarumque enarrationes atque emendationes.* Padua, 1740.

Purmann 1846: H. Purmann, *Quaestionum Lucretianarum specimen.* Bratislava, 1846.

Quaglio 1965: A. Quaglio, "Sulla cronologia e il testo della *Divina Commedia,*" *Cultura e Scuola* 13–14 (1965): 241–53.

Quantin 1846: M. Quantin, *Dictionnaire raisonné de diplomatique chrétienne.* Paris, 1846.

Quentin 1926: H. Quentin, *Essais de critique textuelle.* Paris, 1926.

Questa 1963: C. Questa, "Per un'edizione delle Bacchides, I: I manoscritti," *Rivista di Cultura Classica e Medievale* 5 (1963): 215–54.

Reeve 1974: M. D. Reeve, "Heinsius's Manuscripts of Ovid," *Rheinisches Museum* 117 (1974): 133–66.

Reeve 1976: M. D. Reeve, "Heinsius's Manuscripts of Ovid: A Supplement," *Rheinisches Museum* 119 (1976): 65–78.

Reeve 1978: M. D. Reeve, "The Textual Tradition of Calpurnius and Nemesianus," *Classical Quarterly* 72 (1978): 223–38.

Reeve 1986: M. D. Reeve, "Stemmatic Method: 'Qualcosa che non funziona?'" in *The Role of the Book in Medieval Culture: Proceedings of the Oxford International Symposium,* 26 September–10 October, ed. P. Ganz, *Bibliologia* 3 (1986): 57–69.

Reiske 1770: J. J. Reiske, ed., *Oratorum Graecorum . . . quae supersunt,* vol. 1. Leipzig, 1770.

Renart 1913: J. Renart, ed., *Le lai de l'Ombre.* Paris, 1913.

Reynolds 1965: L. D. Reynolds, *The Medieval Tradition of Seneca's Letters.* Oxford, 1965.

Reynolds 1983: L. D. Reynolds, ed., *Text and Transmission: A Survey of the Latin Classics.* Oxford, 1983.

Reynolds-Wilson 1991 (1968) : L. D. Reynolds and N. G. Wilson, *Scribes and Scholars.* Oxford, 1991 (1st ed. Oxford, 1968).

Ribbeck 1866: O. Ribbeck, *Prolegomena critica ad Vergilii opera maiora.* Leipzig, 1866.

Ribbeck 1879: O. Ribbeck, *F. W. Ritschl*, 2 vols. Leipzig, 1879.

Ritschl 1832: *Thomae Magistri sive Theoduli Monachi Ecloga vocum Atticarum*, ed. F. Ritschl. Halle, 1832.

Ritschl 1835: F. Ritschl, "Über die Kritik des Plautus," *Rheinisches Museum* 4 (1835): 153–216, 486–570 (= Ritschl 1866–68: 2.1–165).

Ritschl 1838: F. Ritschl, *De emendandis Antiquitatum libris Dionysii Halicarnassensis commentatio duplex*. Breslau, 1838 (= Ritschl 1866–68: 1.471–515).

Ritschl 1845: F. Ritschl, *Parerga zu Plautus und Terenz*. Berlin, 1845.

Ritschl 1847: F. Ritschl, *De codice Urbinate Dionysii Halicarnassensis*. Bonn, 1847 (= Ritschl 1866–68: 1.516–40).

Ritschl 1849–54: *T. Macci Plauti Comoediae*, 3 vols., ed. F. Ritschl. Elberfeld, 1849–54.

Ritschl 1866–68: F. Ritschl, *Opuscula*, 5 vols. Leipzig, 1866–68.

Rizzo 1973: S. Rizzo, *Il lessico filologico degli umanisti*. Rome, 1973.

Rizzo 1977: S. Rizzo, review of S. Timpanaro, *Il lapsus freudiano: Psicanalisi e critica testuale* (Florence, 1974), *Rivista di Filologia e Istruzione Classica* 105 (1977): 102–5.

Robortello 1557: F. Robortello, *De arte sive ratione corrigendi antiquos libros disputatio*. Padua, 1557.

Roncaglia 1952: A. Roncaglia, "Critica testuale," *Cultura Neolatina* 12 (1952): 281–83.

Ronconi 1961: *Ciceronis Somnium Scipionis*, ed. with an introduction and commentary by A. Ronconi. Florence, 1961.

Rostagni 1947: *Anonimo Del Sublime*, ed. A. Rostagni. Milan, 1947.

Ruhnken 1875 (1789): D. Ruhnken, *Elogium Tiberii Hemsterhusii*, ed. J. Frey. Leipzig, 1875 (1st ed., 1789).

Sabbadini 1920: R. Sabbadini, *Il metodo degli umanisti*. Florence, 1920.

Salemme 1981: C. Salemme, review of S. Timpanaro, *La genesi del metodo del Lachmann* (Padua, 1981), *Bollettino di Studi Latini* 11 (1981): 288–91.

Santoli 1961: V. Santoli, "La critica dei testi popolari," in *Studi e problemi di critica testuale*, 111–18. Bologna, 1961.

Sauppe 1841: H. Sauppe, *Epistola critica ad Godofredum Hermannum*. Leipzig, 1841 (= Sauppe 1896: 80–177).

Sauppe 1870: H. Sauppe, "De arte critica in Flori bellis recte facienda," *Index Scholarum Hibernarum* (Göttingen) 1870: 3–21 (= Sauppe 1896: 608–28).

Sauppe 1896: H. Sauppe, *Ausgewählte Schriften*. Berlin, 1896.

Savile 1612: *Johannis Chrysostomi Opera*, ed. H. Savile, vol. 8. Eton, 1612.

Scaliger 1582 (1577): *Iosephi Scaligeri Catulli Tibulli Propertii nova editio cum castigationibus in Catullum, Tibullum, Propertium*. Antwerp, 1582 (1st ed. Paris, 1577).

Scaliger 1600 (1579): J. J. Scaliger, ed., *M. Manilii Astronomicon Libri quinque*. Leiden, 1600 (1st ed. Strasburg, 1579).

Scaliger 1627: *Iosephi Scaligeri Epistolae*. Leiden, 1627.

Schenkl 1913: H. Schenkl, review of *Calpurnii et Nemesiani Bucolica*, ed. C. Giarratano (Naples, 1910), *Berliner Philologische Wochenschrift* (1913): cols. 264–69.

Schiche 1915: *Ciceronis De finibus bonorum et malorum libri quinque, Tusculanae Disputationes*, ed. T. Schiche. Leipzig, 1915.

Schleicher 1863: A. Schleicher, *Die Darwinische Theorie und die Sprachwissenschaft*. Weimar, 1863.

Schleicher 1874: A. Schleicher, *Die deutsche Sprache*. Stuttgart, 1874.

Schmid 1967: W. Schmid, review of K. Büchner, *Studien zur römischen Literatur I* (Wiesbaden, 1964), *Gnomon* 39, no. 2 (1967): 468–78.

Schmid 1968: W. Schmid, "F. Ritschl und J. Bernays," in *Bonner Gelehrte, Beiträge zur Geschichte der Wissenschaften in Bonn, Philosophie und Altertumswissenschaften,* 127–43. Bonn, 1968.

J. Schmidt 1872: J. Schmidt, *Die Verwantschaftsverhältnisse der indogermanischen Sprachen.* Weimar, 1872.

P. L. Schmidt 1974: P.L. Schmidt, *Die Überlieferung von Ciceros Schrift "De legibus" im Mittelalter und Renaissance.* Munich, 1974.

Schneider 1794–96: J. G. Schneider, *Epistulae ac dissertationes,* 4 vols. Leipzig, 1794–96.

Schneidewin 1842: M. *Valerii Martialis epigrammaton libri,* ed. F. G. Schneidewin. Grimmen, 1842.

Schuchardt 1866–68: H. Schuchardt, *Der Vokalismus des Vulgärlateins,* 2 vols. Leipzig, 1866–68.

Schwartz 1909: E. Schwartz, ed.; Eusebius, *Kirchengeschichte.* Leipzig, 1909.

Schweighäuser 1798: J. Schweighäuser, ed., *Epicteti Manuale et Cebetis Tabula.* Leipzig, 1798.

Schweighäuser 1801–7: J. Schweighäuser, ed., *Athenaei Naucratitae Deipnosophistarum libri quindecim.* Strasburg, 1801–7.

Scivoletto 1961: *A. Persius Flaccus: Saturae,* ed. with a commentary by N. Scivoletto. Florence, 1961.

Seck 1965: F. Seck, *Untersuchungen zum Isokratestext.* Hamburg, 1965.

Seel 1936: O. Seel, review of G. Pasquali, *Storia della tradizione e critica del testo* (Florence, 1934), *Gnomon* 12 (1936): 16–30.

Segre 1961: C. Segre, "Appunti sul problema delle contaminazioni dei testi in prosa," in *Studi e problemi di critica testuale,* 63–68. Bologna, 1961.

Semler 1765: J. S. Semler, *Hermeneutische Vorbereitung,* vol. 3, pt. 1. Halle, 1765.

Seyfferth 1896: O. Seyfferth, review of W. M. Lindsay, *The Palatine Text of Plautus* (Oxford, 1896), *Berliner Philologische Wochenschrift* (1896): cols. 1549–51.

Shackleton Bailey 1963: D. R. Shackleton Bailey, "Bentley and Horace," *Proceedings of the Leeds Philosophical Society* 10, no. 3 (1963): 105–15.

Siebelis 1844: J. Siebelis, "Beiträge zur Kritik und Erklärung des Lucretius," *Zeitschrift für die Altertumswissenschaft* 2 (1844): 99–101, cols. 785–92, 793–800, 801–7.

Simon 1689: R. Simon, *Histoire critique du texte du Nouveau Testament.* Rotterdam, 1689.

Skutsch 1960: O. Skutsch, *A. E. Housman.* London, 1960.

Sparnaay 1948: H. Sparnaay, *K. Lachmann als Germanist.* Bern, 1948.

Stackmann 1964: K. Stackmann, "Mittelalterliche Texte als Aufgabe," in *Festschrift für J. Trier,* 240–67. Graz and Cologne, 1964.

Studi e problemi di critica testuale 1961: *Studi e problemi di critica testuale,* Atti del Convegno di studi di filologia italiana nel centenario della Commissione per i testi di lingua (Bologna, 1960). Bologna, 1961.

Timpanaro 1955: S. Timpanaro, review of *Niccolò Perotti's Version of the Enchiridion of Epictetus,* ed. with an introduction and a list of Perotti's writings by R. P. Oliver (Urbana 1954), *La Parola del Passato* 10 (1955): 67–70.

Timpanaro 1959: S. Timpanaro, "La genesi del metodo del Lachmann, I," *Studi Italiani di Filologia Classica* 31 (1959): 182–228.

Timpanaro 1960: S. Timpanaro, "La genesi del metodo del Lachmann, II," *Studi Italiani di Filologia Classica* 32 (1960): 38–63.

Timpanaro 1963a: S. Timpanaro, *La genesi del metodo del Lachmann.* Florence, 1963.

Timpanaro 1963b: S. Timpanaro, "Per la critica testuale dell'*Ephemeris* di Ditti Settimio," in *Lanx Satura Nicolao Terzaghi oblata,* 325–42. Genoa, 1963.

Timpanaro 1964: S. Timpanaro, review of *Ambrosii Theodosii Macrobii Saturnalia,* ed. J. Willis, vols. 1–2 (Leipzig, 1963), *Gnomon* 36 (1964): 784–92.

Timpanaro 1965: S. Timpanaro, "Ancora su stemmi bipartiti e contaminazione," *Maia* 17 (1965): 392–99.

Timpanaro 1970: S. Timpanaro, "Due introduzioni alla critica del testo," *Maia* 22 (1970): 285–90.

Timpanaro 1971: S. Timpanaro, *Die Entstehung der Lachmannschen Methode.* Hamburg, 1971.

Timpanaro 1972: S. Timpanaro, "Friedrich Schlegel e gli inizi della linguistica indoeuropea in Germania," *Critica Storica* 9 (1972): 72–105.

Timpanaro 1973: S. Timpanaro, "Il contrasto tra i fratelli Schlegel e Franz Bopp sulla struttura e la genesi delle lingue indoeuropee," *Critica Storica* 10 (1973): 553–90.

Timpanaro 1975: S. Timpanaro, *Sul materialismo.* Pisa, 1975.

Timpanaro 1976: S. Timpanaro, *The Freudian Slip: Psychoanalysis and Textual Criticism,* trans. from the original (*Il lapsus freudiano: Psicanalisi e critica del testo* [Turin, 1974]) by K. Soper. London, 1976.

Timpanaro 1978: S. Timpanaro, *Contributi di filologia e storia della lingua latina,* vol. 1. Rome, 1978.

Timpanaro 1979: S. Timpanaro, "Giacomo Lignana e i rapporti tra filologia, filosofia, linguistica e darwinismo nell'Italia del secondo ottocento," *Critica Storica* 16 (1979): 406–503.

Timpanaro 1980: S. Timpanaro, *Aspetti e figure della cultura ottocentesca.* Pisa, 1980.

Timpanaro 1985a: S. Timpanaro, "Recentiores e deteriores, codices descripti e codices inutiles," *Filologia e Critica* 10 (1985): 164–92.

Timpanaro 1985b: S. Timpanaro, "Appunti per un futuro editore del *Liber Proverbiorum* di L. Lippi," in *Tradizione classica e letteratura umanistica: Per A. Perosa,* ed. R. Cardini, E. Garin, L. Cesarini Martinelli, and G. Pascucci, 2.391–435. Rome, 1985.

Timpanaro 1997 (1955): S. Timpanaro, *La filologia di G. Leopardi,* 3rd rev. ed. with addenda. Bari, 1997 (1st ed., 1955).

Tischendorf-Gebhardt 1897: L. F. C. F. von Tischendorf and O. von Gebhardt, "Bibeltext des NT," in *Realencyclopädie für protestantische Theologie und Kirche,* ed. A. Hauck, 2.713–73. Leipzig, 1897.

Traube 1895: L. Traube, "Zur lateinischen Anthologie," *Philologus* 54 (1895): 124–34 (= Traube 1909–20: 3.51–59).

Traube 1909–20: L. Traube, *Vorlesungen und Abhandlungen,* 3 vols., ed. S. Brandt. Munich 1920.

Troje 1971: H. E. Troje, *Graeca leguntur.* Cologne and Vienna, 1971.

Ullman 1956: B. L. Ullman, "The Transmission of Latin Texts," *Studi Italiani di Filologia Classica,* n. s., 27–28 (1956): 578–87.

Usener 1902: H. Usener, "Bernays," *Allgemeine Deutsche Biographie* 46 (1902): 393–404.

Vahlen 1876: *Lucilii fragmenta*, ed. J. Vahlen. Berlin, 1876.

Vahlen 1883: *Marci Tullii Ciceronis De finibus bonorum et malorum*, ed. J. Vahlen. Berlin, 1883.

Vahlen 1893: J. Vahlen, "Öffentliche Sitzung zur Feier des Leibnizischen Gedächtnisstages: Ansprache," *Sitzungsberichte der Königlich Preussischen Akademie der Wissenschaften zu Berlin*, no. 2 (1893): 615–23.

Vallarsi 1766 (1734): *Sancti Eusebii Hieronymi Opera*, 11 vols., ed. D. Vallarsi. Verona, 1766 (1st ed., 1734).

Venturi 1959: F. Venturi, "Contributi ad un dizionario storico 1: Was ist Aufklärung? Sapere aude," *Rivista Storica Italiana* 71 (1959): 119–28.

Vettori 1540: *Petri Victorii Explicationes suarum in Ciceronem castigationum*. Leiden, 1540.

Vettori 1569: *Petri Victorii Variarum lectionum XIII novi libri*. Florence, 1569.

Vettori 1571: *Ciceronis Epistulae ad Atticum*, ed. P. Victorius. Florence, 1571.

Vettori 1586 (1558): *Ciceronis Epistulae ad Familiares*, ed. P. Victorius. Florence, 1586 (1st ed., 1558).

Vieillefond 1970: J.-R. Vieillefond, *Les "Cestes" de Julius Africanus*. Florence and Paris, 1970.

Vitelli 1962: G. Vitelli, *Filologia classica . . . e romantica*, ed. T. Lodi, with a preface by U. E. Paoli. Florence, 1962.

Voemel 1857: J. T. Voemel, ed., *Demosthenis Contiones*. Halle, 1857.

Waszink 1975: J. H. Waszink, "Osservazioni sui fondamenti della critica testuale," *Quaderni Urbinati di Cultura Classica* 19 (1975): 7–24 (= Waszink 1979: 71–88).

Waszink 1979: J. H. Waszink, *Opuscula selecta*. Leiden, 1979.

Weitzman 1982: M. Weitzman, "Computer Simulation of the Development of Manuscript Traditions," *Bulletin of the Association for Literary and Linguistic Computing* 10 (1982): 55–59.

Weitzman 1985: M. Weitzman, "The Analysis of Open Traditions," *Studies in Bibliography* 38 (1985): 82–120.

West 1973: M. L. West, *Textual Criticism and Editorial Technique*. Stuttgart, 1973.

Wettstein 1730: J. J. Wettstein, *Prolegomena ad Novi Testamenti Graeci editionem accuratissimam*. Amsterdam, 1730.

Wettstein 1734: J. J. Wettstein, review of J.A. Bengel, ed., *Novum Testamentum Graecum* (Tübingen, 1734), *Bibliothèque Raisonnée des Ouvrages des Savans de l'Europe* 13, no. 1 (1734): 203–28.

Wettstein 1751–52: *Novum Testamentum Graecum*, ed. J. J. Wettstein, 2 vols. Amsterdam, 1751–52.

Wetzer-Welte 1882–1903: *Kirchenlexicon*, 13 vols., 2nd ed., ed. H. J. Wetzer and B. Welte. Freiburg, 1882–1903.

Whitehead-Pickford 1951: F. Whitehead and C. E. Pickford, "The Two-Branch Stemma," in *Bulletin Bibliographique de la Societé Internationale Arthurienne* 3 (1951): 83–90.

Whitehead-Pickford 1973: F. Whitehead and C. E. Pickford, "The Introduction to the *Lai de l'Ombre*: Sixty Years Later," *Romania* 94 (1973): 145–56.

Wilamowitz 1894: U. von Wilamowitz-Moellendorff, "Gedächtnisrede auf Hermann

Sauppe," *Nachrichten von der Gesellschaft der Wissenschaften zu Göttingen* (official reports), 1 (1894): 36–48.

Wilamowitz 1914: U. von Wilamowitz-Moellendorff, ed., *Aeschyli Tragoediae*. Berlin, 1914.

Wilamowitz 1927: U. von Wilamowitz-Moellendorff, "Geschichte der Philologie," in *Einleitung in die Altertumswissenschaft*, 3rd ed., ed. A. A. Gercke and E. Norden, 1.1–80. Leipzig and Berlin, 1927.

Wilamowitz 1982 (1921): U. von Wilamowitz-Moellendorff, *History of Classical Scholarship*, trans. from the German by A. Harris, ed. with an introduction and notes by H. Lloyd-Jones. London, 1982 (= *Geschichte der Philologie*, Leipzig and Berlin, 1921; rev. ed., 1927).

Willis 1957: J. Willis, "De codicibus aliquot manuscriptis Macrobii Saturnalia continentibus," *Rheinisches Museum* 100 (1957): 152–64.

Willis 1972: J. Willis, *Latin Textual Criticism*. Chicago, 1972.

Winterbottom 1979: M. Winterbottom, review of *Panegyrici Latini*, ed. V. Paladini and P. Fedeli (Rome, 1976), *Classical Review* 93 (1979): 234–35.

F. A. Wolf 1782: F. A. Wolf, "Vorrede zu Platons Gastmahl," preface to *Platonis Symposium*, ed. F. A. Wolf. Ilfeld, 1782 (= Wolf 1869: 1.130–57).

F. A. Wolf 1804: *Homeri et Homeridarum opera et reliquiae*, vol. 1, ed. F. A. Wolf. Leipzig, 1804.

F. A. Wolf 1807: F. A. Wolf, "Darstellung der Altertumswissenschaft," in *Museum der Altertums-Wissenschaft*, ed. F. A. Wolf and P. Buttmann, 1.1–145. 1807 (= Wolf 1869: 1.808–95).

F. A. Wolf 1869: F. A. Wolf, *Kleine Schriften*, 2 vols. Halle, 1869.

F. A. Wolf 1985 (1795): F. A. Wolf, *Prolegomena to Homer*, trans. with an introduction and notes by A. Grafton, G. W. Most, and J. E. G. Zetzel. Princeton, 1985 (= *Prolegomena ad Homerum*, Halle, 1795).

H. Wolf 1572: H. Wolf, ed., *Demosthenis opera*. Basel, 1572.

Zarri 1969: G. P. Zarri, "Il metodo per la 'recensio' di Dom Quentin esaminato criticamente mediante la sua traduzione in un algoritmo," *Lingua e Stile* 4 (1969): 161–82.

Zarri 1979: G. P. Zarri, "Une méthode de dérivation quentinienne pour la constitution semi-automatique de généalogies de manuscrits: Premier bilan," in *La pratique des ordinateurs dans la critique des textes*, Colloque International du CNRS (Paris, 29–31 March 1978), 121–42. Paris, 1979.

Zetzel 1980: J. E. G. Zetzel, "The Subscriptions in the MSS of Livy and Fronto and the Meaning of Emendatio," *Classical Philology* 75 (1980): 38–59.

Ziebahrt 1910: E. Ziebahrt, "Sauppe," *Allgemeine Deutsche Biographie*, suppl., 55 (1910): 146–58.

Ziegler 1950: K. Ziegler, ed., *Ciceronis De legibus*. Heidelberg, 1950.

A. W. Zumpt 1851: A. W. Zumpt, *De Caroli Timothei Zumptii vita et studiis*. Berlin, 1851.

C. G. Zumpt 1826: *Curtii Rufi De rebus gestis Alexandri*, ed. C. G. Zumpt. Berlin, 1826.

C. G. Zumpt 1831: *Verrinarum libri septem*, 2 vols., ed. and with notes by C. G. Zumpt. Berlin, 1831.

[Final Remarks on Bipartite Stemmas] *

Being refuted inflicts a wound, to be sure, on that petty personal vanity which almost all scholars possess and which I too possess. But on the other hand it also produces a sense of joy when the refutation is rigorous, lucid, based on vast scholarship and lively intelligence, and, at the same time, is free from personal rancor, indeed leaves a friendship intact. So, after having read and reread attentively the refutation that M. D. Reeve has written (Reeve 1986) about the third appendix [i.e., Appendix C, "Bipartite Stemmas and Disturbances of the Manuscript Tradition"] of my too often revised and reprinted *Genesis of Lachmann's Method,* I said to myself, "Well then! That appendix may well have persuaded even some notable philologists, but Reeve has finally cut it to shreds by all the rules of our craft." If I could have read Reeve's article before the recent [1985] reprint of my little volume, I would have prevented that reprint; if that little volume—which continues to

---

* This text was found among Timpanaro's papers at his death and has not previously been published; I am grateful to his widow, Maria Augusta Timpanaro, for making it available to me and permitting its publication. It represents a further stage in Timpanaro's reflections on bipartite stemmas beyond the point reached in 1985 in the last published form of Appendix C of the present book; although the manuscript is undated, the similarities in argument and language to a letter written by Timpanaro to Paolo Mari on 10 October 1986 (published in *Per Sebastiano Timpanaro* 2001: 176–83) and the fact that Timpanaro wrote this essay in part upon page proofs of Pasquali 1986, which he coedited, indicate 1986 as the likeliest date for its composition. Given the interest and importance of this text, it is appended to the present translation of this book, even though it was never published by Timpanaro himself and clearly expresses his firm intention not to permit the book's republication. The manuscript did not receive Timpanaro's final revisions for publication and is sometimes little more than a sketch or outline; in a number of passages it can be deciphered only with great difficulty, and in others hardly at all. Material in square brackets has been supplied by myself where the text is unreadable or lacunose but the meaning is fairly clear; when in such cases the meaning is not clear at all I have used the indication [. . .]. For the sake of convenience I have supplied the text with a title that corresponds to its contents.

sell copies, I believe, only because friends of mine who teach at universities often suggest it to their students—should happen ever to be sold out again, then I will do what I should have already done, since a reprint in which the third appendix was suppressed (or with a third appendix revised to the tune of self-criticisms and of *mea maxima culpa* [I confess my grievous fault]) would be extremely strange. My little volume has now fulfilled its purpose, it has also revealed its flaws (and not only in the third appendix), and now is the moment in which *requiescat in pace* [may it rest in peace].

I fear lest those readers who up to this point have appreciated my so-called eloquence (though in fact there is little to appreciate, since what is involved is my clear duty) will feel some consternation when they discover that the present article continues for a number of pages instead of stopping right here. They will suspect that I have made an insincere ostentation of scholarly rectitude and then wish to even the score by resorting to sophisms and to demonstrate that, all in all, that notorious third appendix is not as mistaken as Reeve thinks. But this is not the case. I remain convinced that that appendix, in the form in which I wrote it, is full of contradictions and of genuine, serious errors (even more in the last, more ambitious version than in the earlier ones, as Reeve himself has noticed, cf., e.g., Reeve 1986: 68n35). But I would like to explain what I meant to say subsequently, and to say it as briefly as possible in a more correct form. This will not save that text of mine from *damnatio* [being convicted]; but it might be useful for others (including, obviously, Reeve himself) who will wish to continue to work on the question of bipartite stemmas. As for me, I swear by the Styx that after these few pages I shall never work on it again, at least not as a general problem of methodology.

A first problem: In the critical editions of Classical and modern texts and in studies of manuscript traditions, does that overwhelming majority or even totality of bipartite stemmas that Bédier denounced really exist? In a first reaction to Bédier's essay, Pasquali 1932a: 130–31 wrote that if Bédier had extended his investigation to the traditions of Classical texts, he would have found "umpteen" [in Hülle und Fülle] tripartite, quadripartite, quinquepartite stemmas. Reeve writes that in 1963 Timpanaro had declared that Pasquali's assertion was exaggerated, but "now, under the influence of Giovan Battista Alberti's book *Problemi di critica testuale*, published at Florence in 1979, he has convinced himself that pluripartite stemmata are even rarer than he believed in 1963"; he [i.e., Timpanaro] has not noticed that Alberti's principal purpose was to determine the number of (lost) archetypes that can be reconstructed mechanically, and hence that from his own viewpoint Alberti was justified in neglecting those cases in which the "archetype" (understood here by Reeve simply as the single ancestor of all the surviving manuscripts) is preserved (Reeve 1986: 59). Reeve has also explored traditions in which the ancestor is preserved, making use of a book on which he collaborated himself, Reynolds 1983. He has discovered that out of eighteen traditions in which a preserved ancestor has produced copies that are preserved as well, six have a multipartite stemma (mostly with three branches), while for the time being the other twelve cannot be reduced to a precise stemma. Reeve also writes that "Alberti ignores, and consequently Timpanaro ignores, a number of lost archetypes that gave rise to pluripartite stemmas" (Reeve 1986: 60): Cornelius Nepos (tripartite stemma, according to Marshall 1977, an exemplary investigation), Valerius Maximus (a tripartite stemma, which Marshall brought to Reeve's attention as well; cf. Reeve 1986: 61), the *Notitia dignitatum* (six Renaissance copies made independently of one another from a lost medieval ancestor; cf. Reeve in Reynolds 1983: 253–57), and finally Cicero's *De optimo genere oratorum*, in the tradition of which Reeve has recognized three independent groups, which might also be six (Reeve 1986: 61; cf. Reeve in Reynolds 1983: 100–102). Reeve expects that further research will uncover other stemmas with more than two branches; all the same, he admits (Reeve 1986: 61), "I still incline to agree with Timpanaro that Pasquali exaggerated" (sc. in the phrase cited above).

Now, I was fully aware that because of his principal goal Alberti had limited his investigation to traditions with a lost ancestor. But since Alberti (on the basis of his own studies and other scholars') has demonstrated that various traditions that I mentioned in 1963 as being multipartite are in fact bipartite, it seems to me that I had every right to *make use* of Alberti's results in order to reach the conclusion that there are fewer multipartite stemmas than I had believed. Indeed, Alberti asserts what his theme is and repeats it in many passages too. Moreover, I took account (rightly, I believe) of the fact that Pasquali himself, before Alberti and Reeve and myself, had implicitly considered that that energetically anti-Bédierian statement of his was exaggerated. In fact, in Pasquali 1952a (1934) and in other writings of his later than Pasquali 1932a in which he polemicizes against Bédier, the "umpteen" [in Hülle und Fülle] multipartite stemmas of up to even five branches have vanished. I myself wrote this (p. 160), and perhaps Reeve should have recalled it. From my friend Alberti I have learned an enormous amount. Pasquali 1952a (1934) examines many traditions that can be reduced to stemmas: only very few indeed have more than two branches (check this). Besides, already in 1963, before Alberti, I had observed that tripartite stemmas have been transformed into bipartite ones. If Reynolds 1983 indicates the existence of multipartite traditions with a preserved stemma, I am very pleased, but I could not know this in 1980, nor had I received from Marshall the information about Cornelius Nepos and Valerius Maximus which Reeve has received (be careful about Marshall! Gamberale 1975 disagrees with Marshall about Aulus Gellius).

On the other hand, the fact I too am sure that multipartite stemmas can be recognized in cases in which scholars hitherto believed they saw bipartite stemmas is demonstrated by my continuing even in the last edition of my text to issue warnings against the dangers of apparently bipartite stemmas caused by erroneous classification on the part of philologists (definition of a class α which really exists and the error of calling β everything which is merely "non-α," pp. 175–76; genealogical classifications that may be a bad inheritance from axiological classifications, p. 175). And so, if Reeve, who cites three examples of bipartite stemmas in which considerations deriving solely from the examination of conjunctive errors are reinforced by historical and geographical data, declares that he is "curious" to know whether I will refuse to agree that these are bipartite stemmas (Reeve 1986: 64), I can answer that his curiosity is a bit curious. Not only have I never denied the existence of bipartite stemmas, but I have always maintained that it is likely that bipartite stemmas are the majority in what Maas called "poor traditions" (Maas 1937: 293–94). On the other hand, what I considered unlikely was that the majority was *so strong,* that what separated bipartite stemmas and tripartite ones was not a slight discrepancy but rather a very steep "step," given that the latter too are typical of a poor tradition. And this "step" continues to be very large even after the many examples of tripartite or multipartite stemmas Reeve mentions (note on the Humanist age), and the same applies for decimation (Reeve 1986: 61–64), except for Castellani 1980 (1957). I find no answer to this observation in Reeve's article. Weitzman 1982 considers the observation to be unfounded for statistical reasons ("mathematical" ones, to use Reeve's terminology). But Reeve himself admits, together with Whitehead-Pickford 1951 (and with me), even if in a form that is not entirely clear-cut (cf. also Weitzman 1985), that the purely mathematical method does not resolve the question of the predominance of bipartite stemmas, and that Weitzman has inserted into his computer "historical information," some of which is open to question (Reeve 1986: 62). So it is better, he says, to leave the computers aside and to deal directly with historical (and geographical) observations (Reeve 1986: 62–63).

With regard to historical and geographical observations, Reeve observes, "Strangely for a pupil of Pasquali, Timpanaro says little about history and even less about geography, which nowhere appears in his appendix" (Reeve 1986: 63). I recognize that this criticism is fundamentally justified, not only with regard to the third appendix (and to my little volume on Lachmann as a whole), but also with regard to all my activity as a Classical philologist. I have concerned myself very little, too little, with manuscript tradition in the empirical sense of cultural history that goes from Traube to Pasquali and on to codicology, a branch of scholarship that Pasquali lived just long enough to see institutionalized but that has made extraordinary progress since the Second World War. What is more, I have concerned myself too little with something else that is more basic, namely, with studies on individual manuscript traditions performed with the "old" method as well. My philological production consists almost entirely of *adversaria*, of textual and exegetical discussions of individual passages. This is also because very often Classical philology has become for me "a second matrix of study" in comparison with the cultural and political history of the nineteenth century, with excursions toward the eighteenth and twentieth centuries—but this obviously provides no excuse for my ignorance. It is symptomatic that I have never prepared a full critical edition of a text, and that even without the stimulus of a critical edition I have concerned myself with genealogies of manuscript traditions only two or three times. In comparison with me, Reeve has an incontrovertible superiority in this field, since it is precisely to this field that he has dedicated what is perhaps the best part of his activity.

But it is not true that I have failed to recognize the importance of historical and geographical investigations directed toward the genealogy of manuscripts. I myself have indicated, and I believe that Reeve agrees, that one essential reason for the inadequacy of the "mathematical criterion" resides precisely in the great variety of historical and geographical conditions (citations).

Let us go on to what Reeve calls a "methodological argument" (Reeve 1986: 64–69). I do not repudiate the phrase which I wrote to Reeve in a private letter, and I assure my friend Reeve that he has in no way "infringed scholarly courtesies" by citing it without asking my permission (cf. Reeve 1986: 64–65)—I believe that courtesy among scholars does not consist in such formalities. But Reeve distorts my thought considerably when he writes that "Timpanaro has now come close to saying that the application of stemmatic method is in itself an editorial misjudgment" (Reeve 1986: 65)—when, that is, he attributes to me the position of Dawe 1964 or Dawe 1973 (check whether I have cited it) or a very similar position.

I maintain that [. . .] stemmas are always disturbed, even Lucretius. So I maintain, in agreement with what various scholars have done in practice, that in the choice of readings [we must evaluate every reading on its own merits and not dismiss a reading too hastily as a mere conjecture] (cf. the example of *licenda* from Kenney 1974: 144–45). Murgia 1980: 318 traces out a stemma and then says that two [manuscripts] do not count against one. *Eliminatio lectionum singularium* is useful in the case in which there is no substantial difference between variant readings; but like Waszink 1975: 23 = Waszink 1979: 87 I am convinced that such readings are less [frequent than is sometimes thought]. I too in my article "G[. . .]" [made the same argument] as Waszink. Many other times *eliminatio lectionum singularium* serves to eliminate what is clearly corrupt even without it (Lucretius).

Nonetheless, all these doubts do not signify a repudiation of stemmatics on my part (on "norm" and "exception," cf. Timpanaro 1985a). It is strange that Reeve denies (1986: 65) that nonetheless there are cases (many ones, as Pasquali already saw) in which contamination and interpolation have acted so extensively and so early as to make it impossible to trace out any stemma at all (those cases in which Pasquali, referring only to contamination, speaks of "total pretraditional contamination"; 1952a [1934] 146–55, 177–80). Would he be able to trace out a stemma of the manuscripts of the New Testament, of the *Iliad,* of the *Odyssey,* of the *Metamorphoses,* of many Patristic texts, of the works of Virgil, to name only a few of the most well known and, I believe, indisputable cases? In any case, I believe that his statement is erroneous or ambiguous. Or else, if the stemma turns out to be so complicated by "dotted lines" (indicating contamination or interpolation) as to preclude any certain *eliminatio lectionum singularium* (cf. Ovid's *Fasti,* e.g., Pighi 1973: lxxxviii), does he believe that it is worth the trouble to dedicate years of work to tracing it out? Certainly, a stemmatics with value only in terms of cultural history is legitimate as the schematization of the later reception of an author's work; but it will be necessary to recognize that in this case, even if its utility is hardly diminished, the scholars who believe that contamination and interpolation are so extensive as to preclude tracing stemmas "are biting the hand that fed them, because unless one can actually see scribes contaminating and interpolating under one's nose it is only by applying stemmatic method that one can detect contamination and interpolation" (Reeve 1986: 65). Let us suppose with Maas 1958 (1927) that [. . .]. If Reeve calls "applying stemmatic method" this consecration of its failure too, then he is right but he is saying something that is sophistical and useless. If, on the other hand, he believes (as his citation of Irigoin 1977 at Reeve 1986: 65n28 would lead one to suppose) that it is only possible to recognize the "violations of the stemma" after the "vertical" tradition has been represented in a stemma and if he refers indifferently to interpolation and contamination, then he is mistaken, for he does not consider the aforementioned case, in which contamination and interpolation are revealed precisely by the impossibility of tracing any stemma at all. Irigoin's observation is correct in its first part ("[an editor] must try to discover . . . the constants of the 'vertical' tradition with all the means available to his scholarship and to his native talent"; Irigoin 1977: 243) as an admonition not to abandon the field too early, not to refuse to recognize that agreements, for example, in lacunas or in highly significant errors, should be attributed with high probability to the vertical tradition (note: this too with some reserves, see below). But it is no longer correct in its second part ("It is at this price, and at this price alone, that he will be able to determine the reality, and perhaps also the extent, of a horizontal transmission"; Irigoin 1977: 243), for the reasons that we have already indicated. On the other hand, Reeve himself, a little later, writes, "My general impression of contamination, and I believe Alberti's too, is that it has the effect not of falsifying stemmata but of frustrating attempts at drawing them up; and where it does falsify stemmata, as in Timpanaro's example, it falsifies them in a way that may mislead editors but will not alter the total of bipartite stemmata" (Reeve 1986: 67). So according to him too there exist cases in which contamination reveals itself not as a secondary fact after the stemma has been traced out, but as a fact that precludes any attempt to trace out the stemma. Since Reeve is a powerful reasoner and only with difficulty contradicts himself, there is quite probably something in his argument that I have not understood well, and I would be grateful to him if he would explain it to me.

Let us return to bipartite stemmas. Here the level of Reeve's polemic rises again after the observations that we have discussed just now, and that frankly seem to me erroneous; and I must recognize (though with reservations, which I shall explain) the incisiveness and correctness of his distinction between contamination and interpolation with regard to stemmas that are probably bipartite. Here I must recognize that I did not explain with sufficient clarity what I mean by *extra-stemmatic contamination*—or, to put it better, I had explained my meaning better the first time. Reeve distinguishes two cases: contamination "below the level of the archetype" and contamination in the archetype itself; in this latter case, on which I shall not linger for reasons of brevity, he admits that contamination can produce stemmas that are only apparently bipartite, but only in very rare cases (Reeve 1986: 67), and I agree with him (but at Reeve 1986: 67n30 he would have done better to cite Irigoin 1977: 242–45 rather than Marichal 1961: 1284). But what I mean is *outside of the archetype;* see Herman Fränkel's concept of *Fremdlesung* [foreign reading] (Fränkel 1964: 78n2). I do not intend here to discuss once again the question of whether there was always an archetype. I am referring to the cases, which I believe are frequent, in which there was indeed an archetype; [some scholars speak of] "éclectisme des papyrus" [see Dain 1975 (1949): 111], but in reality the eclecticism occurs lower down. In this case figure 2 at Reeve 1986: 66 does not need to be completed, and my not completing it myself was not intended as a "device" in order [to conceal the fact that the stemma is really tripartite and to make it seem bipartite instead], but instead precisely because I believed that the dotted line [produces nothing other than] an extra-archetypal line. Here Reeve has been handicapped by only working on Latin texts, for which papyri are rare; but here too see [the case of] Sallust [*Cat.* 6.2, also transmitted by

P. Oxy. 884, cf. I.] Mariotti [1947: 257; for another example, see] Timpanaro 1985b: 424–35.

Finally Reeve 1986: 68 [criticizes pp. 180–81 of the present work]. In the
form in which it appears in the last edition of my little volume, the argument
pertained to the pitfalls of the tendency to "verticalize." My argument: (*a*) it
is valid for successive bipartitions; (*b*) *Appendix Vergiliana*, Dictys Cretensis [cf. Timpanaro 1963b = Timpanaro 1978a: 397–422]. [My reference
to] "insignificant errors" merits Reeve's contemptuous dismissal. It is true
that I had expressed myself better in the 1971 edition, and I add that it is
also true that even back then I did not express myself very well. Here too it
would be useful, for my partial exculpation, to go read the first formulation
of that argument which is found in Timpanaro 1965. It is clear from there
that what I wanted to warn against was not so much initial bipartitions of
the stemma as rather "infinite bipartitions," to use a jocular phrase. In my
view, stemmas that have the following configuration are very suspect, and
unfortunately very frequent:

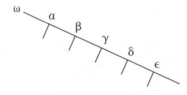

Now, the multiplication of subarchetypes [is produced] very often, by the
work of excellent philologists too, on the basis of variants of little significance or of none whatsoever (cf. Winterbottom 1979: 234–35). (Sometimes
one arrives at the archetype too; Reeve 1986: 69n36; cf. Watt, whom I then
did not name; Dictys.) As Reeve notes, I never did write that article criticizing the stemmas of the Oxford edition of the *Appendix Vergiliana,* which I
had once promised [in Timpanaro 1971: 148]. I did not write it because of
the appearance in the meantime of Courtney 1968, which, even if it does not
satisfy me in every detail, says in substance a large part of what I would have
wished to say and other things that did not occur to me. But let me cite a
single example: [. . .] Dictys.

Toward the end of his article, before summarizing his objections, Reeve
writes courteously, "The new version [of Timpanaro's Appendix C, even
more than the old, should be read and digested by anyone who proposes to
edit a text, because there is no better warning against the pitfalls that may
occur in classifying manuscripts]" (Reeve 1986: 69). I too believe that, *for
the present,* a more detailed treatment of the pitfalls *etc.* is lacking; but that
appendix has revealed itself to be too full of ambiguities and errors, and
hence—after having responded to certain objections of Reeve's that seemed

to me rather strained—I feel the duty to warn anyone who will make use of this third appendix even more than Reeve does. And I hope that someday, after a further enlargement of studies on manuscript traditions, and not only on Latin ones, my discussion will be replaced by another one, more rigorous and more reliable.

Differences among the Various Editions

This appendix lists textual differences among the various editions of Timpanaro's *The Genesis of Lachmann's Method*.

The basis for the present translation was provided by Timpanaro's own copy of the last edition printed during his lifetime:

La genesi del metodo del Lachmann, first corrected reprint with some additions (Padua: Liviana Editrice, 1985): indicated in the apparatus as *1985*. The addenda to this edition have been added to the main body of this translation as footnotes signaled by one or more asterisks and are indicated in the apparatus as *1985 Addenda;* Timpanaro's marginal annotations on this copy are integrated into the text and notes of this translation and are indicated in the apparatus as *MS 1985*.

Differences between this edition and the following ones are signaled in the text of the translation by superscript letters and are recorded in this apparatus:

La genesi del metodo del Lachmann (Florence: Felice Le Monnier, 1963): indicated in the apparatus as *1963*.
Die Entstehung der Lachmannschen Methode, 2nd enlarged and revised edition, authorized translation from the Italian by Dieter Irmer (Hamburg: Helmut Buske Verlag 1971): indicated in the apparatus as *1971*. The postscriptum of this edition is indicated in the apparatus as *1971 Postscriptum*.
La genesi del metodo del Lachmann, new edition, revised and enlarged (Padua: Liviana Editrice, 1981): indicated in the apparatus as *1981*. Timpanaro's marginal annotations on this copy are indicated as *MS 1981*.

Only divergences in the body of the text, not in the footnotes, are recorded here: given Timpanaro's habit of scrupulously bringing his bibliographic references up to date in each new edition, any attempt to indicate all the differences in the notes among his various editions would have ended up submerging the important and interesting developments of his thought under a mass of trivial and largely futile data. The only exceptions are provided by Timpanaro's own marginalia to *1981* and *1985* when these refer to the notes. And among the divergences in the body of the text, only those are recorded that are not purely stylistic in character.

The first version of Timpanaro's monograph appeared in the form of two long articles:

"La genesi del metodo del Lachmann, pt. 1," *Studi Italiani di Filologia Classica* 31 (1959): 182–228; and
"La genesi del metodo del Lachmann, pt. 2," *Studi Italiani di Filologia Classica* 32 (1960): 38–63.

The differences between these two articles on the one hand and the book in its various editions, despite their obvious similarities, are so great that it would not have been useful to integrate all the discrepancies into this textual apparatus on the same footing as those among the editions. Instead, the differences between the articles and the book are briefly summarized here.

The articles already present the same structural organization in eight chapters which is found in all editions of the book; they also include the first two appendices but not Appendix C on bipartite stemmas. The transformation of the articles into the book involved numerous revisions of both content and form and considerable expansions. Some of the more significant changes are the following:

In chapter 5 ("Contributions of Lachmann's Contemporaries," *SIFC* 31 [1959]: 212–18), Timpanaro at first attributed the elaboration of the earliest *stemma codicum* to Ritschl in his 1832 edition of Thomas Magister's Ἐκλογὴ ὀνομάτων καὶ ῥημάτων Ἀττικῶν (213); in *1963* the merit of this invention is assigned instead to Zumpt for his 1831 edition of Cicero's Verrine orations (*1963:* 45–47); in *1981* Timpanaro records and justifies this change (*1981:* 51–52). In this same chapter, Timpanaro at first devoted only a few lines to Orelli after his discussion of Ritschl (216); in later versions Orelli is treated much more fully in the first two pages of the chapter as the first contemporary of Lachmann's who made important contributions to the method of textual criticism (*1963:* 43; *1981:* 49). So too the treatment of Madvig is much briefer in the first version (216–17).

In chapter 8 ("Textual Criticism and Linguistics, and Their Crisis at the End of the Nineteenth and in the Twentieth Century"), the sections on L. Havet (*1963:* 85–86; *1981:* 93–94) and G. Vitelli (*1963:* 88–89; *1981:* 99–100) are entirely lacking in the first version.

In Appendix A ("Lachmann's First Attempt at a Mechanical *Recensio* in 1817," *SIFC* 32 [1960]: 52–56), Timpanaro at first adopted a suggestion of Antonio La Penna and Eugenio Grassi and so corrected Lachmann's third stemmatic rule of 1817 in the following way: "3. Where there are three readings, then $EM > B-G$ (the reading shared by E and M is preferable [to] the two others in B and G), $GE > B-M$, $GM > B-E$; on the other hand, $BG = E-M$ (the agreement of B and G leads to no secure decision against the two readings of E and M), $BM = G-E$, $BE = G-M$" (p. 55). In later versions he preferred Fritz Bornmann's emendation and adopted the following text of Lachmann's rule: "3. Where there are three readings, then $BG < E-M$ (against the reading shared by B and G, the two others in E and M are preferable), $G-E > BM$, $G-M > BE$; on the other hand, $EM = B-G$ (the agreement of E and M leads to no secure decision against the two readings of B and G), $B-M = GE$, $B-E = GM$" (*1963: 107–8; 1981: 107–8*).

In Appendix B ("Determining the Script of Lost Manuscripts," *SIFC* 32 [1960]: 57–63), Timpanaro at first wrote, "It is not so easy to believe that the *homofomerian* of [Lucretius] 1.830 was healed conjecturally by the copyist of the Quadratus or of the subarchetype, given the rarity of the word and the very low cultural level of the medieval copyists of Lucretius" (p. 62). After E. J. Kenney brought to Timpanaro's attention the fact that the scribe could well have made the correction by comparison with 1.834, where the whole tradition has the correct reading *homoeomerian*, Timpanaro abandoned his skepticism (*1963: 106–7; 1981: 116–17*). Timpanaro notes his change of opinion at *1963: 97n1* and *1981: 108n5*. In 1960 this appendix concluded with the following sentence: "If in that first review of von der Hagen he [i.e., Lachmann] had set himself the goal of reconstructing not ϕ^2, but ϕ and ω (as would have been more natural), he would have ended up formulating a rule analogous to the one he will later devise for the New Testament (see part I, p. 208): the agreement of B with one of the apographs of ϕ gives us with certainty the reading of ϕ and ω" (p. 63). In its place a discussion of the practice of *eliminatio codicum descriptorum* is found in later versions (*1963: 108–11; 1981: 119–21*).

Preface to the Second Edition

a.   N. *: On Pontedera see now Nardo 1981... others will follow. *added 1985 Addenda*
b.   This edition ... new ideas to it. *added 1985*

Introduction

a.   (this was ... authors) *added 1981*
b.   divinatory talent is *1981*: divinatory talent and sense of style are *1963, 1971*

c.   or a Bentley *added 1981*
d.   at all *added 1981*

Chapter 1. *Emendatio ope codicum* from the Humanists to Bentley

a.   evaluating . . . exaggerated *added 1981*
b.   first and second *added 1981*
c.   corrupt *1981:* interpolated *1963, 1971*
d.   compositional structure *1981:* compositional structure and style *1963, 1971*
e.   (sometimes . . . believable!) *added 1981*
f.   Later . . . majority. *1981:* In certain cases, to be sure, one has the impression that this *eliminatio codicum descriptorum* is merely affirmed rather than being actually demonstrated. A manuscript of remarkable antiquity on one side, a mass of *recentiores* on the other naturally suggested the idea that the latter were derived from the former: the hypothesis that both the one and the others were derived from a lost common model was less obvious. Thus too in the genealogy of the Indo-European languages, the hypothesis that first suggested itself as the most natural one was derivation from one of the historically attested languages, be it Greek or Celtic or German, or later Sanskrit; only at a later time, and not without dissent, did scholars come to postulate a lost mother-language. And yet Politian was also capable of performing an *eliminatio codicum descriptorum* based upon solid evidence. *1963, 1971*
g.   He eliminated . . . prove. *added 1981*
h.   venerates *1981:* respects *1963, 1971*
i.   What is more . . . occasionally. *added 1971* (he had a full . . . apply it *added 1981* | Pliny *1981:* Varro *1971*)
j.   copyist-interpolators *1981:* Humanist interpolators *1963, 1971*
k.   belittle *1981:* eliminate *1963, 1971*
l.   with clarity *added 1981*
m.   the use of *added 1981*
n.   We must linger . . . traditions. *added 1981:* Here the word *archetypum* does not yet denote the medieval ancestor of the manuscript tradition, as it does later in Madvig. Instead, as already in Cicero (*ad Att.* 16.3.1) and often in the Humanist period, it indicates the first official text, from which all the other copies are derived. This is the only way we can explain that limiting qualification, "so long as it has some specious appearance of the truth," which is illegitimate if one thinks of a medieval archetype (in which quite mechanical and crude errors could be found), but is justified in the case of an ancient "archetype," written under the supervision of the author and revised and corrected by himself or by someone he trusted: in such a manuscript only insidious errors, ones with an appearance of truth, could remain undiscovered. In any case, Erasmus enunciated in this way the concept of a lost ancestor of all the manuscripts that have reached us; this permitted him to explain the existence of errors common to the entire manuscript tradition. *1963, 1971*
o.   we shall . . . Lachmann. *1981:* this contrast can be noted already in Scaliger; we shall find it again in Bentley and also in Lachmann. *1963, 1971*
p.   N. *: On Scaliger, A. T. Grafton . . . Jocelyn 1984: 60. *added 1985 Addenda*
q.   From his . . . collations. *added 1981*

r.   and not only . . . obsolete. *added 1981*

s.   Later he worked . . . requirements. *added 1981*

t.   and printed editions *added 1971, 1981*

u.   With only a few . . . numerous *added 1981*

v.   cf. now Nardo 1981 *added 1985 Addenda*

w.   and one . . . times, *added 1981*

x.   repeated . . . scholars *added 1981*

y.   even if it runs . . . former. *added 1981*

z.   (just . . . Manilius) *added 1981*

aa.   vigorous *added 1981*

bb.   accepting the transmitted reading or choosing between variants does *1981:* choosing
       between attested variants does, for the scholar engaged in this activity can all too eas-
       ily be led to overvalue the first reading that some manuscript happens to offer him
       1963, 1971

cc.   Against a lazy . . . degrees. *1981:* Against an eclectic *recensio,* such as was the fash-
       ion among the Dutch, Bentley's reasoning had a certain degree of truth; but it also
       opened the way to conjectural excesses, since it did not establish any difference be-
       tween what is transmitted and what is not. A brake to this tendency was constituted
       by the *ars critica* of J. Le Clerc, which argued for an intelligently conservative ap-
       proach. *1963, 1971*

dd.   The English Classical philologists . . . textual criticism *1981:* The English Classical
       philologists who were the successors of Bentley (Porson, Elmsley, Dobree) did not ne-
       glect the manuscripts, but they too were primarily oriented toward conjectural criti-
       cism, based on a perfect knowledge of linguistic and metrical usage, especially re-
       garding the recitative parts of Greek tragedy and comedy. *1963, 1971*

Chapter 2. The Need for a Systematic *Recensio* in the Eighteenth Century

a.   N. *: On the *textus receptus* . . . no need. *added 1985 Addenda*

b.   just like . . . isolated *added 1981*

c.   so that in Italy that *1981:* And in philologically marginal areas, for example in Italy,
       this *1963, 1971*

d.   but the very spirit of the Reformation encouraged *1981:* but the very spirit of the Ref-
       ormation, especially in the rationalistic developments of certain currents, such as So-
       cinianism and Arminianism, encouraged *1963, 1971*

e.   He understood that those principles . . . Methodists. *added 1981*

f.   In comparison, *added 1981*

g.   except . . . Simon *added 1981*

h.   We have named . . . criticism. *added 1981*

i.   But history follows . . . task. *1981:* Bentley was the first to plan an edition of the
       Greek New Testament based exclusively on the comparison of the oldest Greek man-
       uscripts with the Latin Vulgata. He recognized that *recensio* had to take precedence
       over conjectural criticism in the case of a textual tradition that was so rich and an-
       cient. But his project, though inspired by a thoroughly unrevolutionary concern to
       defend the authority of the biblical text against the destructive criticism of Anthony
       Collins, encountered the opposition of the theologians who, as we said above, iden-

tified the tradition with the *receptus*. And Bentley, also because he was committed to other projects, ended up giving up this plan, which, in this form, was to be fulfilled only by Lachmann. *1963, 1971*

j.   There were certainly more practicable ways . . . questions. *added 1981*

k.   Each felt *1981:* Of the two greatest New Testament critics of the eighteenth century, Johann Albrecht Bengel and Johann Jacob Wettstein, each felt *1963, 1971*

l.   —an infelicitous expression . . . a better one *added 1981*

m.   (which in fact . . . immediately) *added 1981*

n.   and other Englishmen *added 1981*

o.   (accusations that he was aiming . . . Amsterdam) *added 1981*

p.   N. ** On Wettstein . . . particularly committed. *added 1985 Addenda*

q.   ended up adhering . . . criteria. *added 1981:* ended up abandoning internal criteria and adhering to the erroneous criterion of the majority of manuscripts alone. *1963, 1971*

r.   with such clarity *1981:* with such great methodological clarity *1963, 1971*

s.   did not free himself from it courageously enough *1981:* continued to take it as the basis for his own text *1963, 1971*

t.   N. ***: In the 1981 edition . . . unpublished documents. *added 1985 Addenda*

u.   of the Attic orators and of Atticists like Libanius *1981:* of Demosthenes and of other Greek prose authors *1963, 1971*

v.   But Wolf's recognition of the need . . . directly). *added 1981*

Chapter 3. The First Phase of Lachmann's Activity as a Textual Critic

a.   not only one aspect . . . century. *1981:* one aspect of that antihistoricism which prevented him from understanding the new Classical philology of Wolf and Boeckh. *1963, 1971*

b.   , sometimes . . . caution, *added 1981*

c.   and all . . . circle." *added 1981*

d.   and other Classical philologists who followed him *added 1981*

e.   populist *1981:* popular *1963, 1971*

Addendum to Chapter 3

a.   Addendum *added 1981*

Chapter 4. Lachmann as an Editor of the New Testament

a.   Gaius (1841) . . . Lachmann *1981:* Gaius (1842) *1963, 1971*

b.   persistent acquiescence in *1981:* acquiescence in *1963,* rigorous adherence to *1971*

c.   times had changed and *added 1981*

d.   included *1981:* implied *1963, 1971*

e.   sociocultural *1981:* cultural *1963, 1971*

f.   or no *added 1981*

g.   (that is, to polygenesis of innovations) *added 1981*

Chapter 5. Contributions of Lachmann's Contemporaries

a.   an intelligent follower of Pestalozzi's ideas *1981:* full of the spirit of Pestalozzi *1963, 1971*

b.   revision *1981: recognitio 1963, 1971*

c.   Is this the first *stemma codicum* . . . in Schlyter. *1981:* As far as we know hitherto, this is the first *stemma codicum* that was ever actually drawn up, and not only planned like Bengel's *tabula genealogica. 1963, 1971*

d.   In the field . . . Goerenz *1981:* Certainly, already Johann August Goerenz *1963, 1971*

e.   than Schlyter *added 1981*

f.   and so far as we know *added 1981*

g.   —from this point of view . . . later *added 1981*

h.   But when the disarray . . . stemma! *added 1981*

i.   "mechanical recension" *1981:* "closed recension," to use Pasquali's terminology *1963, 1971*

j.   the fourth one in time after those of Schlyter (Collins-Schlyter 1827), Zumpt (1831), and Ritschl (Ritschl 1832) *1981:* the third one in time after those of Zumpt (1831) and Ritschl (Ritschl 1832) *1963, 1971*

k.   he considers this fact to be "strange" but nonetheless undeniable *added 1981*

l.   some of the principles of *recensio* and *emendatio 1981:* the principles of the genealogy of manuscripts *1963, 1971*

m.   *descriptorum.* . . . century *1981: descriptorum,* a procedure that had already been practiced, as we saw, by Politian, but had been entirely neglected by Bekker and by Lachmann himself *1963, 1971*

n.   Later, Jean Boivin . . . stopgaps *added 1981*

o.   These *eliminationes* follow one another . . . indicated *added 1981*

p.   He also gave an excellent application, *1981:* Sauppe gave a splendid example of this procedure *1963, 1971*

q.   A little later . . . *Criticism added 1981*

r.   Pasquali's work. *1985:* Pasquali's work and perhaps did not even have the desire and the patience to read it. *1981*

s.   and we shall see that with regard to Lucretius it is also true of Jacob Bernays *added 1981*

t.   N. *: Cf. n. ** in chap. 2. *added 1985 Addenda*

Chapter 6. Studies on the Text of Lucretius

a.   perhaps *added 1981*

b.   (but today . . . probable*) added 1981*

c.   usage. *1971, 1981:* But when it was a matter of staging an easy polemic against some mediocre Classical philologist, for example, against the wretched Forbiger, then any fear of burdening his readers with too frequent quotations vanished all at once from Lachmann's mind. *1963*

d.   proposed several shrewd conjectures but, *added 1981*

e.   much *added 1981*

f.   as is well known *1981:* as we shall indicate *1963:* as we shall see *1971*

g.   Until the first version of this study of mine, everyone attributed *1981:* Today every-
     one attributes *1963, 1971*

h.   It would certainly be unjustified . . . it. *added 1971*

i.   this question was controversial for a long time and probably will never be finally re-
     solved *1981:* this question is still uncertain *1963:* this question is still unresolved *1971*

j.   scholars have disagreed—and they will continue to disagree—about whether *1981:*
     despite many studies and discussions, scholars have not yet succeeded in clarifying
     definitively whether *1963, 1971*

k.   as now seems almost certain *1981:* as is perhaps more likely *1963, 1971*

l.   But just one page later . . . tradition *added 1981*

m.   For the moment . . . archetype *1981:* But a little later, enunciating the rules for re-
     constructing the readings of the archetype *1963, 1971*

n.   Without saying so and, apparently, without *1981:* Without *1963, 1971*

o.   even if they were independent of the Oblongus, as now seems entirely excluded,
     added 1981

p.   in any case *added 1981*

q.   And another peculiarity . . . *deteriores! added 1981*

r.   The very contradictions we have noted in the course of our exposition make such a
     "didactic" quality very doubtful! *added 1981*

s.   texts in which all the manuscripts agree in errors and lacunas *1981:* cases in which
     the derivation from an archetype is certain *1963, 1971*

t.   — on the contrary, the commentary is superior to the preface if we do not wish to as-
     sume as a criterion of judgment only the "method" but to consider instead its results
     added 1981

Chapter 7. What Really Belongs to Lachmann

a.   even if in that same field . . . century *added 1981*

b.   (much reduced . . . Lucretius) *added 1981*

c.   an *1971, 1981:* the *1963*

d.   very limited and uncertain *1981:* almost nothing *1963:* very small *1971*

e.   Schlyter (in a field different from Classical philology), *added 1981*

f.   or late ancient *added MS 1985*

g.   Boivin, Schweighäuser, *added 1981*

h.   *Homerum. 1981: Homerum.* The only time Lachmann ever set forth a genealogical
     classification of manuscripts, in his preface to Lucretius, he did nothing more than
     follow in Bernays's footsteps, and did so, as we have seen, in a rather confused way.
     1963, 1971

i.   most genuine *1981:* real original *1963:* real individual *1971*

j.   and, nearer in time, to Madvig *added 1981*

k.   It might be objected that we have committed a sophism . . . pages. *1981:* The third
     and fourth points (genealogy of the manuscripts and mechanical reconstruction of
     the archetype) seem to us, and are in reality, united by a particularly strict connec-
     tion: one cannot perform *eliminatio lectionum singularium* unless one has first made
     oneself a stemma. And yet we have found that the two requirements were fulfilled for
     the first time by different scholars. Ritschl, who showed better than anyone else how

to disentangle a manuscript tradition genealogically, did not make use of this work for the constitution of the text (the same may be said of Zumpt and Bernays). Lachmann knew how to use genealogies traced out by others for the purposes of textual criticism; he possessed neither the patience nor, fundamentally, the aptitude for tracing them out himself. Among the founders of the new method, the most "complete" and balanced one was Madvig (even if he was not, perhaps, the most original one). *1963, 1971*

l.   as a textual critic *added 1981*

m.   But there were also more serious and fundamental reasons for this development. Whereas *1981:* But it must also be borne in mind that, whereas *1963:* But there are also quite important and essential reasons for this development. Whereas *1971*

n.   —a limit, as we have said, but also a strength *added 1981*

o.   (a requirement that other . . . effective) *added 1981*

p.   and although he tended more toward a certain dogmatism than they did *added 1981*

Chapter 8. Textual Criticism and Linguistics, and Their Crisis at the End of the Nineteenth and in the Twentieth Century

a.   not for a mere ostentation of interdisciplinarity . . . itself *added 1981*

b.   On the other hand . . . another. *added 1981*

c.   or as a banalization that constitutes a deterioration too, *added MS 1985*

d.   Schlyter, Zumpt, and Ritschl, *1981:* Ritschl *1963:* Zumpt and Ritschl *1971*

e.   (or better, of a somewhat earlier one: Jones, F. Schlegel) *added MS 1985*

f.   These analogies authorize us to ask . . . criticism. *1981:* These analogies might in themselves make one think of a direct relation: one might hypothesize that comparative linguistics, which arose between the end of the eighteenth Century and the beginning of the nineteenth, supplied Lachmann, or better still Ritschl, with a model for textual criticism. *1963, 1971*

g.   However, this hypothesis does not withstand closer examination. *1981:* However, I do not believe in a direct connection of this sort. *1963, 1971*

h.   At first the inverse hypothesis . . . emphasize. *1981:* The inverse hypothesis, that Schleicher had been influenced by the model of textual criticism, would be more probable from a chronological point of view, and yet this does not seem probable to me either: his gaze was directed at the natural sciences, not at Classical philology: as is well known, he saw an abyss between philology and linguistics. *1963, 1971*

i.   But beyond this direct connection (which, I repeat, is probable, but still only hypothetical) one might think *1981:* At most one can think with a certain probability *1963, 1971*

j.   What is certain is that the similarity . . . on the other. *1981:* But even if Indo-European linguistics and "Lachmann's method" originally had no direct relation, at a certain moment the adherents of the two disciplines became aware of the similarity in their research methods. *1963, 1971*

k.   who *1981:* who, unlike Schleicher, *1963, 1971*

l.   In Romance philology too . . . Rajna. *added 1981*

m.   and leave out of consideration certain cases of contamination among the Oblongus, Quadratus, and Schedae as well *added MS 1985*

n. (too many) *added 1981*

o. even Leo . . . (Florence, Laur. 37.13) *added 1981*

p. and the innovations introduced by copyists and ancient and medieval "editors" *added 1981*

q. (or if it was, then only with many precautions and reservations) *added 1981*

r. a return to principles . . . contamination) *added 1981*

s. (which is already . . . seen) *added 1981*

t. In the specific case of Persius . . . Lachmann. *added 1981*

u. —and with undeniable exaggerations—*added 1981*

v. ; or, at least, that expression contained a certain ambiguity *added 1981*

w. which rarely is the *sole* cause . . . others *added 1981*

x. prevalent *1981:* prevalent by far *1963, 1971*

y. We must also remind ourselves . . . Probability"]). *added 1981*

z. since it was linked . . . reworkings *added 1981*

aa. : the study of the genealogy . . . corruptions *added 1981*

bb. Here, certainly, he went too far . . . the "inferior" correction. *1981:* The danger here was that of forgetting the close relation of reciprocity between textual criticism and interpretation. *1963, 1971*

cc. without their always being rigorous in fact *added 1981*

dd. See now Canfora 1982 and Timpanaro 1985a. *added 1985 Addenda*

ee. 471). *1981:* 471). It was only in Pasquali's last years that with interest and sympathy he approached the French school, which had independently achieved at least partly analogous results. *1963, 1971*

ff. Other approaches that were akin to his own . . . hitherto. *added 1981*

gg. Let us return to Pasquali. *added 1981*

hh. against prejudiced and hasty condemnations *added 1981*

ii. the Wilamowitzian and Schwartzian inspiration of his work *1981:* this inspiration *1963, 1971*

jj. , especially following . . . Barbi *added 1981*

kk. —and, what is more, not Structuralism either—*added 1981*

ll. , and he felt distrust . . . manuscripts *added 1981*

mm. , even if the methodology was as devoid of precepts as Pasquali's was *added 1981*

nn. Pasquali also rejected Leo's opinion . . . too. *added 1971*

oo. mechanical *1981:* closed *1963, 1971*

pp. nonmechanical *1981:* open *1963, 1971*

qq. nonmechanical *1981:* open *1963, 1971*

rr. a broad perspective on cultural history *1981:* historicism with a broad horizon *1963, 1971*

Appendix A. Lachmann's First Attempt at a Mechanical *Recensio* in 1817

a. The eminent Germanist Karl *added 1981*

b. an article dedicated to this problem *1981:* a recent article *1963, 1971*

c. (except . . . return) *added 1981*

d. Cf. now also Cecchini 1982 . . . this note. *added 1985 Addenda (Bornmann's article never appeared)*

Appendix B. Determining the Script of Lost Manuscripts

a.   (that is . . . reasons) *added 1981*

b.   at least in many cases, *added 1981*

c.   (the confusions . . . one) *added 1981*

d.   just as well (or better) *added 1981*

e.   way too. *1981:* way too, just as Scaliger did for Catullus. *1963, 1971*

f.   Giovan Battista Alberti . . . texts. *added 1971*

g.   novelty. *1981:* novelty; many editors have already applied them correctly. *1963, 1971*

h.   well *1981:* very well indeed *1963, 1971*

i.   even if a few other passages show some uncertainty *added 1981*

j.   his edition *1981:* his recent and, all in all, valuable edition *1963:* his excellent edition *1971*

k.   For the same reason . . . enough *1981:* For the same reason, even if the examples of corruptions in the text of Catullus cited by Scaliger had been probative—and we have already seen that they were not—*1963, 1971*

l.   *quite 1981:* rather *1963, 1971*

m.   *much added 1981*

n.   Q and the Schedae . . . 3.90 *added 1971*

o.   all *1981:* absolutely mechanical *1963, 1971*

p.   Less certain . . . Lucretius). *added 1981*

q.   413 (*meos aiauis* for *meo suauis*), 506 (*purumque* for *puramque*) *added 1971*

r.   even if the confusion . . . letters. *added 1981*

s.   few *1981:* very few *1963, 1971*

t.   + Schedae *added 1981*

u.   a pre-archetype in *ancient* minuscules . . . branches) *1981:* an archetype in capitals (as Lachmann had supposed); a pre-archetype in ancient minuscules (which would have caused the minuscule corruptions shared by the whole tradition), preceded or else followed by another pre-archetype in capitals (which would have caused the capital corruptions peculiar to each of the two branches) *1963, 1971*

v.   *1981:*

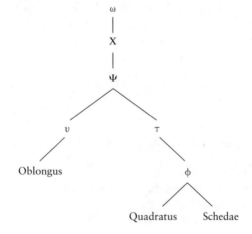

1963, 1971

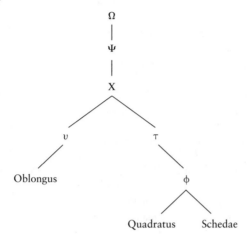

w.   (ω) *1981:* (ψ) *1963, 1971*

x.   and Robert Marichal and their followers, *added 1981*

y.   *cyprism* for *cyprum* (u > i + s, *Aen.* 1.622), *added MS 1985*

z.   This is what I wrote . . . aspects. *added 1981*

aa. Even if these recent studies   now, *1981:* Nonetheless, *1963, 1971*

bb. preferable *1981:* preferable because of its greater simplicity *1963, 1971*

cc. Of course this does not in the least exclude . . . the archetype. *added 1981*

dd. extant *added 1981*

Appendix C. Bipartite Stemmas and Disturbances of the Manuscript Tradition

a.   fifty *1981:* thirty *1963, 1971*

b.   (though often with long intervals, as is only natural) *added 1981*

c.   the extraordinary frequency of bipartite stemmas *1981:* bipartite stemmas and their frequency *1963, 1971*

d.   Until about twenty years ago, *1981:* But *1963, 1971*

e.   more recently the field of Greek . . . controversy *1981:* Hence it will not be useless if I provide a brief panorama of the discussion, adding some observations on those points that in my view have hitherto been treated too hastily. *1963, 1971*

f.   the mechanical method *1981:* the mechanical method excogitated by Bengel and formulated with greater precision by Lachmann *1963, 1971*

g.   of individual subarchetypes *1981:* of one subarchetype or another *1963, 1971*

h.   and that Madvig . . . (see chap. 5, n. 19) *added 1981*

i.   encompassing *1981:* vast *1963, 1971*

j.   and various Romance philologists *added 1981*

k.   at least at first *added 1981*

l.   two *1971, 1981:* three *1963*

m. On the tradition of the lesser . . . the attention it deserves. *added 1985 Addenda*

n. Was this answer correct? . . . abandoned. *added 1981*

o. Maas tried . . . its explanation *1981:* Maas, on the other hand, fully admitted the truth of the fact Bédier had pointed out, and not only for the Latin and Romance traditions but also for the Greek one; but he sought its explanation *1963, 1971*

p. this *1981:* this first *1963, 1971*

q. and more recently . . . shortly. *added 1981*

r. (an exceptional philologist . . . himself) *added 1981*

s. always continued to believe in the validity of that absurd argument *1981:* has not abandoned that argument even in the fourth edition of his *Textkritik 1963, 1971*

t. later as well, and *added 1981*

u. scholars who are excellent . . . words] *1981:* some scholars *1963, 1971*

v. in a rather detailed way, even at the cost of causing the reader some fatigue *1981:* in a slightly less hasty way than that of the critics just cited *1963, 1971*

w. The defectiveness of Maas's reasoning . . . empirical data. *added 1971 Postscriptum*

x. seems to lead us onto a genuinely historical and empirical terrain, and hence a much more concrete one *1981:* leads us onto this terrain, a much more concrete one *1963, 1971*

y. And yet this argument too. . . . For example, Castellani has acutely observed that *1981:* But enunciated in this way the argument still gives rise to serious doubts. To be sure, the limited diffusion of culture in the Middle Ages may well make it seem probable, in very general terms, that a considerable number of archetypes could have produced a line of descent of only two copies, a smaller number of archetypes could have produced three lines of descent, an even smaller number four lines of descent, and so forth. But this would not explain so great a preponderance of bipartite traditions over tripartite ones as the one which was pointed out by Bédier and accepted by Maas and most scholars. In this way it could certainly be understood why stemmas with very many branches were so rare, but stemmas with three branches ought not to be so much rarer than those with two branches. What is certainly correct (and we shall see this more clearly in what follows) is the reference to contamination; but when Maas contrasts "little-read" texts (those with a tradition that is almost always bipartite) to "much-read" ones (in which contamination makes a stemma impossible), one wonders why there ought not to have existed numerous intermediate cases, those of a tradition not so rich and entangled as to be irreducible to a stemma but not so poor as to be limited to only two branches. A tripartite tradition is a little bit richer than a bipartite one, and hence ought to have been produced fairly easily even in the case of little-read texts. It is true that, as Castellani has acutely observed, *1963:* Maas's reference to "little-read texts" . . . the number of tripartite ones *added 1971 Postscriptum:* Such a "jump" . . . in very different periods? *added 1971 Postscriptum*

z. Another hypothesis . . . with caution. *1981:* At this point we ought to wonder whether tripartite or multipartite stemmas really are as rare as Bédier, Maas, and many other scholars maintain. With laudable precision and self-denial, Castellani has reexamined those editions of medieval French texts from which Bédier had derived his conviction of the extreme rarity of stemmas with more than two branches, and he has arrived at conclusions that are much less radical, but not such as to refute altogether the existence of the phenomenon Bédier pointed out. As Castellani puts it, "Bifid trees are about 75–76 percent; they are 82–83 percent if the uncertain trees are not included in the total. Even if their predominance is not as overwhelming as in Bédier's statistics, it still remains quite remarkable. Four bifid stemmas for every multifid one: that is a ratio which does indeed seem 'surprising.'" I think that it would be even more difficult to come up with reliable statistics for Greek and Latin texts, given the vast size of the field and the enormous number of cases which are still the subject of discussion. I myself have not even tried to do this. But I think that even a quite partial and superficial exploration would suffice to demonstrate two points which agree in substance with the results of Castellani's investigation: (1) Stemmas with three or more branches are in fact not as rare as would be required by the "probability calculus" of Maas and Fourquet (and this confirms that that calculus is erroneous). Some examples: according to the results accepted by the most recent editors, the manuscript traditions of Cicero's *Catilinarians,* his speech *Pro imperio Cn. Pompei,* Catullus's poems, Calpurnius's and Nemesianus's eclogues, Martial's epigrams, Quintilian's *Institutio,* the younger Pliny's letters, and Isidore's *Origines* are all tripartite. Cicero's *Tusculan Disputations*—as well as his *Brutus,* where, however, only Humanist manuscripts are involved—and Lactantius's *Divinae Institutiones* have traditions with more than three branches. With regard to Greek literature, we must not forget that many of the great Classic authors (beginning with Homer and Hesiod) have traditions that cannot be reduced at all to Lachmannian schemas: traditions in which an archetype never existed, or at least must be conceived as a canonical edition, Alexandrian or Byzantine, rather than as a single manuscript. In any case, here too tripartite stemmas are not lacking: Aristotle, Demosthenes, Plato (at least in part), Apollonius Rhodius, the second half of Procopius's *Histories,* at least a group of Corycius's *Dialexeis.* . . . So Pasquali's answer to Bédier, which we cited above, was based on real facts. (2) Despite all of this, bipartite stemmas remain the very great majority for Greek and Latin texts too. And in Classical philology too we find that phenomenon which Bédier observed in his own field of study: manuscript traditions that at first were considered tripartite are reduced to only two subarchetypes. We have already spoken of Lachmann's wavering concerning Lucretius, of Madvig's change of mind (due to Halm's objections) concerning a group of Ciceronian speeches. But even much more recently a similar transition from a tripartite stemma to a bipartite one has taken place, for example, for the fourth tetralogy of Plato and for Macrobius's *Saturnalia.* *1963:* Another hypothesis . . . lost or destroyed. *added 1971 Postscriptum*

aa.   We shall now propose . . . *certain* cases of bipartitism. *1981:* This leads us to consider other possible causes of such a strong prevalence of stemmas with two branches. *1963, 1971*

bb.   in the Carolingian period or even later *added 1981*

cc.   but also, unsurprisingly, preserved correct readings that were corrupted in the oldest manuscript *added 1981*

dd.   —so long as we understand this expression . . . of which a single witness remains *added 1981*

ee.   but they cannot be applied to all Latin texts . . . extended it too far in the other *added 1981*

ff.   With this hypothesis . . . more frequent. *1981:* But contamination and the copyists'
conjectural activity constitute far more serious and frequent causes of "apparent bipartitism." If these two phenomena occur to a very great extent, affecting the whole
range of the manuscript tradition, the philologist must even abandon any form of genealogical reconstruction, and in that case one no longer speaks of stemmas, either
bipartite ones or tripartite ones: it is to this extreme case that Maas is referring when
he says that stemmatic rigor is lacking in the case of "much-read texts." But often
contamination or the scribes' conjectural activity has the effect not of totally obscuring the manuscripts' genealogy but of falsifying it. Let there be given a tripartite
tradition: A, B, C, derived independently from the archetype. If the copyist of A successfully corrects a certain number of errors of the archetype, or if a certain number
of errors of B are transmitted by collation to C or vice versa, the tradition will take
on a deceptively bipartite appearance: the shared errors of BC will be attributed by
the textual critic to a subarchetype. Castellani has foreseen these two possibilities
more clearly than his predecessors and observes that there are methods for detecting
this kind of error of reconstruction, or at least for suspecting it and adopting in consequence a position of prudent skepticism. It will be enough to attribute the value of
conjunctive errors only to those corruptions which cannot be healed by conjecture
and which, on the other hand, constitute so evident an error that they cannot be the
object of a horizontal transmission: in fact, only errors with a semblance of truth
(that is, for the most part, banalizations) are transmitted by collation, not obvious
errors. These warnings, which are well known and are universally recommended in
theoretical terms, are not always easy to apply in practice, because it is difficult to set
precise limits to the conjectural skill of copyists and medieval philologists. Furthermore, the danger always remains that the copyist of A might have healed errors not
by conjecture but by checking a manuscript of an entirely different tradition which
later was lost. But those criteria have often been neglected even when applying them
did not present particular difficulties. If we read through the prefaces of critical editions and studies of textual criticism written even by first-rate philologists, it is easy
to run into genealogical groupings based only on a few coincidences in banalizations
and even in correct readings! Hence we must suppose that a careful reexamination
would lead to the conclusion that some presumed bipartite stemmas are more probably multipartite stemmas in which contamination has produced phenomena of
"convergence" between certain branches or in which a certain number of corruptions
that go back to the archetype have been corrected in one part of the tradition and
have only remained in another part, thereby creating the impression that this whole
part is derived from a shared subarchetype. In short, in many cases we shall have to
go backward along the path followed until now by editors who, as Bédier observed
(and his observation of the phenomenon was correct, even if the explanations he provided were unfounded), have gradually multiplied the subarchetypes until they reduced the principal branches of the tradition to only two. Certainly, in the majority of
cases this laborious reexamination will not lead to establishing with certainty multipartite stemmas in place of bipartite ones, but rather to rendering our conclusions
more cautious. We shall often remain uncertain whether particular agreements in innovation must be attributed to a shared model or to horizontal transmission. This is
the element of truth contained in Fourquet's paradoxical statement that every multi-

partite stemma might be an unrecognizable bipartite stemma, so that "a scrupulous editor will establish a bipartite stemma, or no stemma at all." Certainly, in purely theoretical terms, one can even do as Fourquet does and go to the extreme of suspecting that two branches of the tradition which are not connected by any conjunctive error go back nonetheless to a shared subarchetype free of any peculiar corruptions of its own; but in practice this hidden subarchetype could be entirely neglected, precisely because it would have been a perfect reproduction of the archetype. In fact, quite serious corruptions are not lacking where the tradition is mostly mechanical (that is, where it is the work of ignorant copyists), and so the possible derivation of certain manuscripts from a subarchetype is not likely to pass unobserved; where the tradition is not mechanical, the most worrisome pitfalls are posed not by the "hidden subarchetype" (and hence by traditions that appear to be multipartite but in reality are bipartite) but instead by contamination (and hence by traditions that appear to be bipartite but in reality are multipartite). In any case it should not be forgotten that Fourquet was starting out from the premise that multipartite stemmas had to be extremely rare for the calculation of the probabilities: the few stemmas with more than two branches that are found in critical editions seemed to him to still be too frequent, and so he suspected that they had arisen in error. We are convinced, on the contrary, that what are too frequent are the bipartite stemmas. But between the case in which contamination has produced "unifications by convergence" of certain families, and the case in which it has made the genealogical relations entirely unrecognizable, there is another, intermediate case, a very frequent one, in which it has spread irregularly, creating numerous "anomalous constellations" without entirely canceling out every distinction among the families. So it is often possible to establish with sufficient certainty some genealogical groupings on the basis of lacunas or shared serious corruptions, but then there are also coincidences in innovations, in one place between α and β, in another between β and γ, somewhere else between α and γ, etc. In these cases, the correct method would be for the philologist to attribute all the irregular constellations to contamination (or, perhaps, to the copyists' conjectural activity). But the philologist, who legitimately desires that his stemma serve to explain at least the maximum number of constellations of variants, if not all of them, is led as a last resort to attribute as many variants as he can to horizontal transmission alone. For this reason, if among the numerous irregular constellations it is above all the ones shared, for example, by α and β that strike him (either because they really are more numerous and important than the others, or because for whatever reason his attention has been drawn more to them), he will "regularize" these coincidences by making them go back to a subarchetype ϕ from which α and β would have derived, and only in the case of the other constellations (β-γ, α-γ) will he resign himself to admitting horizontal transmission. In this way a contaminated tripartite stemma will be transformed into a bipartite one. There is no doubt that if certain coincidences between two groups of manuscripts really are exceptionally numerous and, what matters more, exceptionally significant (coincidences in lacunas, nonobvious dittographies, etc.), one has every right to attribute them to the vertical transmission and not to contamination. But often the coincidences that are "verticalized" in preference to others are simply the ones that by purest chance first presented themselves to the philologist's eyes: let us not forget that scholars almost always begin to trace stemmas on the basis of samples and not of complete collations; and once a stemma has been outlined—even if only as a simple working hypothesis—it is not easy to resist its appeal. Just now, while reexamining Werner Eisenhut's valuable critical edition of Dictys Cretensis, I noticed that the editor had hypothesized the existence of a lost manuscript π, the shared model of the manuscripts P and V, on the basis of only a few insignificant innovations, ones much less numerous and significant than the ones that unite both of the manuscripts P and V to other manuscripts and that Eisenhut rightly attributes to contamination. In this specific case what is involved is only a secondary branch, not the initial one: the stemma of Dictys Cretensis remains fundamentally bipartite, just as Eisenhut has traced it. But in other cases this kind of classificatory error, which can happen quite easily psychologically, can have more serious consequences. And if in cases like this one many editors distinguish the vertical transmission from the horizontal one by indicating the former with continuous lines in their stemma and the latter with dotted ones, it will be necessary here too to see whether this distinction has always been based in fact upon a clear difference in the number and significance of the coincidences in innovation. Whenever this difference does not exist, it is preferable to indicate various stemmas as equally possible, or to give up the schematization of the stemma and to content oneself with indicating various affinities. *1963, 1971*

gg.   (we shall return to this point shortly) *added 1981*

hh.   Another *1981:* Lastly, a final *1963, 1971*

ii.   is partially connected with the preceding one but is more strictly derived from a logical mistake *added 1981*

jj.   The mistake Mario Casella committed . . . not β." *added 1971*

kk.   Schenkl and Casella as two victims *1971:* Schenkl as a victim *1963*

ll.   not without remedy. To summarize: in all probability, manuscript traditions that are really bipartite are only slightly more numerous than those with three or four branches. If in our editions bipartite stemmas are present in very slight prevalence (in any case not in as overwhelming a prevalence as other scholars have believed), this is due in part to objective causes that led to the fusion of branches of the manuscript tradition that originally were distinct (and among these causes contamination and the scribes' conjectural activity have the first place), and in part to errors of classification or to the refusal to investigate very intricate manuscript traditions more deeply. A careful reexamination of many bipartite stemmas will in some cases lead to replacing them with multipartite stemmas, more often to recognizing that the genealogical relations among the manuscripts are far less linear than what has hitherto been supposed. Often the reexamination will have to go on beyond the ramifications of the archetype and will end up putting into doubt the existence of the archetype itself— but not so that one dogmatism will have to be replaced by another dogmatism, the faith in the archetype by its *a priori* denial. This is the direction in which studies have already been moving for some time now, but much still remains to be done; and this is where the problem of bipartite and multipartite stemmas will find its proper place. *1963 (Appendix C ends at this point in 1963; all that follows is added for the first time in 1981, with the following exceptions.)*

mm.   conjunctive errors peculiar to a single branch of the tradition *added MS 1981*

nn.   I have already expressed . . . in innovation *1971 Postscriptum*

oo. it. For "apparatus variants" in Latin manuscripts, the Ambrosian-Vatican manuscript of Fronto (which I hope to discuss soon in this connection) is especially interesting. *added MS 1981*

pp. On the possibility . . . not always well interpreted). *added 1985 Addenda*

qq. themselves (even leaving out of consideration the cases to which we have referred in note 41) *added MS 1981*

rr. Now, even extra-stemmatic contamination . . . apparent bipartite stemmas *1971 Postscriptum*

ss. What is to be done . . . a subarchetype. *1971 Postscriptum*

tt. (but in fact there is: there is also the case of "total pretraditional contamination") *added MS 1985*

uu. Since, as Pasquali reminded Schwartz . . . really existed or not. *1971 Postscriptum*

vv. Prof. Brambilla Ageno . . . more detailed arguments. *added 1985 Addenda*

ww. (cf. Munari) *added MS 1985*

xx. I do not exclude *1985:* I would still not completely exclude *added MS 1981*

yy. So must we abandon altogether . . . confirmation). *1971 Postscriptum*

zz. Second (and this . . . more than two branches. *1971 Postscriptum*

aaa. N. *: I still believe . . . concluded. *added 1985 Addenda*

bbb. Postscript. For the present reprint the author has made some slight alterations to the text. The author knows of forthcoming studies by excellent English scholars in which the almost absolute preponderance of bipartite stemmas will be explained once again by means of statistical considerations, this time far more sophisticated than Maas's. The author confesses that he awaits these studies (of which he has kindly received anticipations in letters) with a certain skepticism, nonetheless he feels the duty to indicate that the discussion will have further developments. For the rest, the present text, in many essential points, already intends to pose problems rather than to resolve them. *added MS 1981*

Recent Bibliography

Chapter 1

On the Philological Method of the Humanists, especially Politian, Scaliger, and Erasmus
G. Avezzù, "Pier Vettori editore di testi greci: 'La Poetica' e altre ricognizioni preliminari,"
Atti e Memorie Accademia Patavina 100 (1987–88): 95–107; A. Cottrell, "Renaissance
Codicology: Poliziano's Early Practice of a Modern Discipline," *Manuscripta* 41 (1997):
110–26; J. F. D'Amico, *Theory and Practice in Renaissance Textual Criticism: Beatus
Rhenanus between Conjecture and History* (Berkeley and London, 1988); A. Daneloni,
"Niccolò Niccoli, Angelo Poliziano ed il Laur. Plut. 49, 7," *Rinascimento* 35 (1995): 327–
42; V. Fera, "Polemiche filologiche intorno allo Svetonio di Beroaldo," in *The Uses of
Greek and Latin: Historical Essays,* ed. A. C. Dionisotti, A. Grafton, and J. Kraye (London, 1988), 85–87; idem, "Problemi e percorsi della ricezione umanistica," in *Lo spazio
letterario di Roma antica,* vol. 3: *La ricezione del testo* (Rome, 1990): 513–43; idem, "Tra
Poliziano e Beroaldo: L'ultimo scritto filologico di Giorgio Merula," *Studi umanistici* 2
(1991): 7–88; J. H. Gaisser, *Catullus and His Renaissance Readers* (Oxford, 1993), 178–
92 (on Scaliger); A. Grafton, *Defenders of the Text: The Traditions of Scholarship in an
Age of Science (1450–1800)* (Cambridge, MA and London, 1991); idem, *Joseph Scaliger:
A Study in the History of Classical Scholarship,* vol. 2: *Historical Chronology* (Oxford,
1993); idem, "*Correctores corruptores?* Notes on the Social History of Editing," in *Editing Texts: Texte edieren,* ed. G. W. Most (Göttingen, 1998), 54–76; A. Grafton and L. Jardine, *From Humanism to the Humanities* (London, 1986); A. Grafton and G. W. Most,
"Philologie und Bildung seit der Renaissance," in *Einleitung in die Lateinische Philologie,*
ed. F. Graf (Stuttgart and Leipzig, 1997), 35–43; V. Juren, "Les notes de Politien sur les
lettres de Ciceron à Brutus, Quintus et Atticus," *Rinascimento* 28 (1988): 235–56; F. Lo
Monaco, "Poliziano e Beroaldo: Le 'In Annotationes Beroaldi' del Poliziano," *Rinascimento* 32 (1992): 103–65; A. Maranini, "Nel laboratorio filologico degli umanisti e
nell'officina moderna: Storia e problemi della tradizione di Manil. 5, 126," *Schede umanistiche* 1 (1988): 7–71; W. McCuaig, *Carlo Sigonio* (Princeton, 1989); U. Pizzani, "Angelo Poliziano e i primordi della filologia lucreziana," in *Poliziano nel suo tempo: Atti del
VI convegno internazionale (Chianciano-Montepulciano 18–21 luglio 1994),* ed. L. Secchi Tarugi (Florence, 1996), 343–55; C. Pyle, "Philological Method in Angelo Poliziano
and Method in Science: Practice and Theory," in *Poliziano nel suo tempo,* 371–86; M. D.
Reeve, "Classical Scholarship," in *The Cambridge Companion to Renaissance Human-*

ism, ed. J. Kraye (Cambridge, 1996), 20–46; idem, "John Wallis, Editor of Greek Mathematical Texts," in Most, *Editing Texts*, 77–93; E. Rummel, *Erasmus' Annotations on the New Testament: From Philologist to Theologian* (Toronto, 1986).

On Bentley C. O. Brink, *English Classical Scholarship: Historical Reflections on Bentley, Porson and Housman* (Cambridge and New York, 1985).

Chapter 2

On Wolf S. Cerasuolo, ed., *Friedrich August Wolf e le scienze dell'antichità* (Naples, 1997); R. Di Donato, "Storia della tradizione come storia della cultura: Filologia e storia nei *Prolegomena* di F. A. Wolf," *Annali della Scuola Normale Superiore di Pisa* 16 (1986): 127–39; S. Fornaro, "Lo studio degli antichi (1793–1807)," *Quaderni di Storia* 43 (1996): 109–55; A. Grafton, *Defenders of the Text*, 214–43; R. S. Leventhal, "The Emergence of Philological Discourse in the German States, 1770–1810," *Isis* 77 (1986): 243–60; R. Markner and G. Veltri, eds., *Friedrich August Wolf: Studien, Dokumente, Bibliographie* (Stuttgart, 1999); G. W. Most, "Homer between Poets and Philologists," in *A New History of German Literature*, ed. D. Wellbery (Cambridge, MA, 2005); idem, "How Many Homers?" in *The Multiple Author* (Pisa, 2005); A. Neschke-Hentschke, "Friedrich August Wolf et la science de l'humanité antique: Contributions à l'histoire des sciences humaines," *Antike und Abendland* 44 (1998): 177–190; M. Riedel, "Die Erfindung des Philologen: Friedrich August Wolf und Friedrich Nietzsche," *Antike und Abendland* 42 (1996): 119–36.

On Heyne H. Berthold, "Bewunderung und Kritik: Zur Bedeutung der Mittlerstellung Christian Gottlob Heynes," in *Winckelmanns Wirkung auf seine Zeit: Lessing-Herder-Heyne*, 161–70 (Stendal, 1988); F. Graf, "Die Entstehung des Mythosbegriffs bei Christian Gottlob Heyne," in *Mythos in mythenloser Gesellschaft: Das Paradigma Roms*, ed. F. Graf (Stuttgart and Leipzig, 1993), 284–94; Grafton and Most, "Philologie und Bildung," 43–48; M. Vöhler, "Christian Gottlob Heyne und das Studium des Altertums in Deutschland," in *Disciplining Classics: Altertumswissenschaft als Beruf*, ed. G. W. Most (Göttingen, 2002), 39–54.

Chapters 3 and 4

On Lachmann J. N. Birdsall, "The Recent History of New Testament Textual Criticism (from Westcott and Hort, 1881, to the Present)," in *Aufstieg und Niedergang der römischen Welt*, pt. 2, vol. 26.1: *Religion*, ed. W. Haase (Berlin and New York, 1992), 99–197; J. Bumke, *Die vier Fassungen der "Niebelungenklage": Untersuchungen zur Überlieferungsgeschichte und Textkritik der höfischen Epik im 13. Jahrh.* (Berlin and New York, 1996); C. Cormeau, "Zur textkritischen Revision von Lachmanns Ausgabe der Lieder Walthers von der Vogelweide: Überlegungen zur Neubearbeitung am Beispiel von MF214, 34/L120, 16," in *Textkritik und Interpretation: Festschrift Karl K. Polheim*, ed. H. Reinitzer (Bern and Frankfurt, 1987), 53–94; idem, "Überlegungen zur Revision von Lachmanns Walther-Ausgabe," in *Methoden und Probleme der Edition mittelalterlicher deutscher Texte,* ed. R. Bergmann and K. Gärtner, 32–39 (Tübingen, 1993); M. Deck, *Die Nibelungenklage in der Forschung: Bericht und Kritik* (Frankfurt, 1996); P. Fedeli, "Il Properzio del Lachmann," in *Commentatori e traduttori di Properzio dall'Umanesimo al Lachmann,* ed. G. Catanzaro and F. Santucci (Assisi, 1996), 355–78; G. Fiesoli, *La genesi del lachmannismo* (Florence, 2000); E. Grunewald, *Friedrich H. von der Hagen (1780– 1856): Ein Beitrag zur Frühgeschichte der Germanistik* (Berlin and New York, 1988); U. Hennig, "Karl Lachmann," in *Berlinische Lebensbilder,* vol. 4: *Geisteswissenschaftler,* ed. M. Erbe (Berlin, 1989), 73–86; U. Meves, "Die Anfänge des Faches Deutsche Sprache und Literatur an der Universität Königsberg: Von K. Lachmann bis zu J. Zacher," *Zeitschrift für deutsche Philologie* 114 (1995): 376–412; O. Nikitinski, "Recentiores, non deteriores auf dem Arbeitstisch Karl Lachmanns," *Philologus* 143 (1999): 362–64; G. Orlandi, "Perché non possiamo non dirci lachmanniani," *Filologia Mediolatina* 2 (1995): 1–42; P. L. Schmidt, "Lachmann's Method: On the History of a Misunderstanding," in *The Uses of Greek and Latin,* ed. A. C. Dionisotti, A. Grafton, and J. Kraye (London, 1988), 227–36; W. Schröder, "Bumke contra Lachmann oder: Wie die 'Neue Philologie' die mittelhochdeutschen Dichter enteignet," *Mittellateinisches Jahrbuch* 33 (1998): 171– 83; H. Weigel, *"Nur was du nie gesehn wird ewig dauern." Karl Lachmann und die Entstehung der wissenschaftlichen Edition* (Freiburg, 1989).

Textual Criticism on the New Testament   Birdsall, "Recent History of New Testament Textual Criticism"; M. E. Boismard, W. R. Farmer, and F. Neirynck, *The Interrelations of the Gospels: A Symposium* (Leuven, 1990); G. D. Fee, "The Use of Greek Patristic Citations in New Testament Textual Criticism: The State of the Question," in *Aufstieg und Niedergang der römischen Welt,* pt. 2, vol. 26.1: *Religion,* ed. W. Haase (Berlin and New York, 1992), 246–65; Fiesoli, *Genesi del lachmannismo,* 107–68; O. Merk, "Anfänge neutestamentlicher Wissenschaft im 18. Jahr. Von Jean-Alphonse Turretini zu Johann Jakob Wettstein," in *Wissenschaftsgeschichte und Exegese: Gesammelte Aufsätze,* ed. R. Gebauer, M. Karrer, and M. Meiser (Berlin and New York, 1998), 1–23, 47–70; F. Neirynck, *Evangelica,* vol. 1: *Gospel Studies;* vol. 2.: *Collected Essays* (Leuven, 1990–91).

On Boeckh   G. Cambiano, "Filologia e storia delle scienze in August Boeckh," in *L'antichità nell'Ottocento in Italia e Germania,* ed. A. Momigliano and K. Christ (Bologna and Berlin, 1988), 77–98; A. Garzya, introduction to A. Boeckh, *La filologia come scienza storica: Enciclopedia e metodologia delle scienze filologiche,* ed. A. Garzya, trans. R. Masullo (Naples, 1987), 8–21; A. Horstmann, "L'herméneutique théorie générale ou organon des sciences philologiques chez A. Boeckh?" in *La naissance du paradigme herméneutique: Schleiermacher, Humboldt, Boeckh, Droysen,* ed. A. Laks and A. Neschke (Lille, 1990), 327–47; idem, *Antike Theoria und moderne Wissenschaft: August Boeckhs Konzeption der Philologie* (Frankfurt and New York, 1992); C. Lehmann, "Sach- und Wortphilologie in der deutschen klassischen Altertumswissenschaft des 19 Jhs.," *Wissenschaftliche Zeitschrift der Humboldt-Universität Berlin* 36 (1987): 15–19; H. Schneider, "August Boeckh," in *Berlinische Lebensbilder,* vol. 4: *Geisteswissenschaftler,* ed. M. Erbe (Berlin, 1989), 37–54.

On Hermann   I. Benecke-Deltaglia and E. G. Schmidt, "Zum 150. Todestag von Gottfried Hermann: Stücke aus dem Nachlass," *Philologus* 142 (1999): 335–58; E. Degani, "Filologia e storia," *Eikasmos* 10 (1999): 279–314 ; G. W. Most, "Karl Otfried Müller's

Edition of Aeschylus' *Eumenides,*" in *Zwischen Rationalismus und Romantik: Karl Otfried Müller und die antike Kultur,* ed. W. M. Calder III, R. Schleiser, and S. Gödde (Hildesheim, 1998), 349–73; W. Nippel, "Philologenstreit und Schulpolitik: Zur Kontroverse zwischen Gottfried Hermann und August Boeckh," in *Geschichtsdiskurs,* vol. 3: *Die Epoche der Historisierung,* ed. W. Küttler et al. (Frankfurt, 1997), 244–53.

Chapter 5

On Ritschl H. L. Barth, "Friedrich Ritschl und Otto Jahn," *Gymnasium* 97 (1990): 104–16.

On Cobet A. Carlini, "Recentiores non deteriores," "Comburendi non conferendi," in Μοῦσα: *Scritti in onore di G. Morelli* (Bologna, 1997), 2–9; J. H. Waszink, "Greek and Latin Philology: Netherlands," in *La filologia greca e latina nel secolo XX* (Pisa, 1989), 1.47–9, 53–54, 62.

Chapter 6

On Bernays *Jacob Bernays: Un philologue juif,* ed. J. Glucker and A. Laks, with help from Véronique Barré, (Villeneuve d'Ascq [Nord], 1996); among the papers of this volume, see esp. M. Bollack, "Jacob Bernays ou l'abandon du commentaire," 31–44; and J. Glucker, "'Lachmann's Method': Bernays, Madvig, Lachmann and Others," 45–56.

Chapter 8

Relationships between Philological Method and Linguistics E. E. Campanile, "Recentiores, non deteriores," *Studi Classici e Orientali* 42 (1992): 31–42; A. Morpurgo Davies, *La linguistica dell'Ottocento* (Bologna, 1996) = G. Lepschy, ed., *History of Linguistics,* vol. 4 (London, 1998); M. D. Reeve, "Shared Innovations, Dichotomies, and Evolution," in *Filologia classica e filologia romanza: Esperienze ecdotiche a confronto,* ed. A. Ferrari (Spoleto, 1988), 445–505; H. Röllecke, "Jacob Grimms handschriftliche Nachträge zu seiner Gedenkrede auf Lachmann," *Brüder-Grimm-Gedenken* 5 (1985): 1–20.

Appendix C

Bédier and Bipartite Stemmas A. Castellani, "J. Bédier et l'édition critique de textes médiévaux," in *Menschen und Werke: Hundert Jahre wissenschaftlicher Forschung an der Universität Freiburg Schweiz/Les hommes et les oeuvres de l'Université: Cent ans de recherche scientifique à l'Université de Fribourg Suisse* (Fribourg/Friburg, 1991), 119–31; A. Corbellari, *Joseph Bédier écrivain et philologue* (Geneva, 1997); C. Flight, "How Many Stemmata?" *Manuscripta* 34 (1990): 122–28; idem, "Stemmatic Theory and the Analysis of Complicated Traditions," *Manuscripta* 36 (1992): 20–46; J. Grier, "Lachmann, Bédier and the Bipartite Stemma: Towards a Responsible Application of the Common-Error Method," *Revue d'Histoire des Textes* 18 (1988): 263–77; J. B. Hall, "Why Are the Stemmata of So Many Manuscript Traditions Bipartite?" *Liverpool Classical Monthly* 17

(1992): 31–32; W. Lapini, "Contaminazione e codices descripti," *Giornale Italiano di Filologia* 46 (1994): 103–22; R. Howard Bloch, "The Siege of the Manuscripts: Military Philology between the Franco-Prussian and the First World War," in *Historicization/Historisierung*, ed. G. W. Most (Göttingen, 2001), 259–73; E. Montanari, "Meliores e deteriores," *Invigilata lucernis* 21 (1999): 257–62; idem, "Il paradosso di Bédier," in *Per Sebastiano Timpanaro*, ed. M. Feo and M. Rossi, *Il Ponte* 57, nos. 10–11 (October–November 2001): 144–57; M. D. Reeve, "Archetypes," in *Miscellanea in onore di A. Barigazzi, Sileno* 11 (1985): 193–201; idem, " 'Eliminatio codicum descriptorum': A Methodological Problem," in *Editing Greek and Latin Texts,* ed. J. N. Grant (New York, 1989), 1–35.

On Maas   E. Montanari, *La critica del testo secondo P. Maas: Testo e commento* (Florence, 2003).

On Pasquali   F. Bornmann, ed., *Giorgio Pasquali e la filologia classica del Novecento* (Florence, 1988), esp. J. Irigoin, "Giorgio Pasquali, storico e critico del testo," 101–12, and C. J. Classen, "L'influsso di G. Pasquali sulla filologia classica in Germania," 135–58; E. Degani, in *La filologia greca e latina nel secolo XX* (Pisa, 1989), 2.1128–34; M. Cagnetta, "Croce vs Pasquali: Quale storicismo?" *Quaderni di Storia* 48 (1998): 5–32.

Recent Works on the Theory of Text Edition   G. Bornstein and R. G. Williams. eds., *Palimpsest: Editorial Theory in the Humanities* (Ann Arbor, 1993); B. Cerquiglini, *Éloge de la variante: Histoire critique de la philologie* (Paris, 1989); P. Cohen, ed., *Devils and Angels: Textual Editing and Literary Theory* (Charlottesville, 1991); P. d'Iorio, "L'edizione elettronica," *Annali della Scuola Normale Superiore di Pisa,* ser. 4, no. 1 (1998): 253–75; A. Ferrari, ed., *Filologia classica e filologia romanza: Esperienze ecdotiche a confronto* (Spoleto, 1998), cf. A. Gostoli, "Problemi di critica del testo tra Filologia classica e Filologia romanza," *Quaderni Urbinati di Cultura Classica* 75, no. 3 (2003): 133–37; E. Flores, *Elementi critici di critica del testo* (Naples, 1998); D. Greetham, *Textual Scholarship: An Introduction* (New York, 1994); idem, *Scholarly Editing: A Guide to Research* (New York, 1995); idem, *The Margins of the Text* (Ann Arbor, 1997); idem, *Textual Transgressions: Essays toward the Construction of a Biobibliography* (New York, 1998); J. Hamesse, *Les problèmes posés par l'édition critique des textes anciens et médiévaux* (Louvain, 1992); D. F. Hult, "Reading It Right: The Ideology of Text Editing," *Romanic Review* 79 (1988): 74–88; K. Kanzog, *Einführung in die Editionsphilologie der neueren deutschen Literatur* (Berlin, 1991); T. W. Machan, *Textual Criticism and Middle English Texts* (Charlottesville, 1994); J. McGann, *Textual Criticism and Literary Interpretation* (Chicago, 1985); idem, *The Textual Condition* (Princeton, 1991); idem, *A Critique of Modern Textual Criticism* (2nd ed. Charlottesville, 1992; 1st ed. Chicago, 1983); H. Meyer, *Edition und Ausgabentypologie: Eine Untersuchung der editionswissenschaftlichen Literatur des 20. Jahrhunderts* (Bern, 1992); G. W. Most, *Editing Texts/Texte edieren* (Göttingen, 1998); L. Mundt et al., eds., *Probleme der Edition von Texten der frühen Neuzeit: Beiträge zur Arbeitstagung der Kommission für die Edition von Texten der frühen Neuzeit* (Tübingen, 1992); D. Oliphant and R. Bradford, eds., *New Directions in Textual Studies* (Austin, TX, 1990); G. Orlandi, "Recensio e apparato critico," *Filologia Mediolatina* 4 (1997): 1–42; M. D. Reeve, "Cuius in usum? Recent and Future Editing," *Journal of Roman Studies* 90 (2000): 196–205; L. D. Reynolds, "Experiences of an Editor of Classical

Latin Texts," *Revue d'Histoire des Textes* 30 (2000): 1–16; P. M. Robinson, "'Collate': A Program for Interactive Collation of Large Textual Traditions," *Research in Humanities Computing* 3 (1995): 32–45; idem, "Redefining Critical Editions," in *The Digital Word: Text-Based Computing in the Humanities*, ed. G. P. Landow and P. Delany (Cambridge, MA, 1993), 271–91; P. L. Schillingsburg, *Scholarly Editing in the Computer Age: Theory and Practice* (Athens, OH, 1986); C. Segre, "Ermeneutica e critica testuale," in *Ermeneutica e critica,* Atti dei Convegni Lincei, 135 (Rome, 1998), 241–62; N. Spadaccini and J. Talens, eds., *The Politics of Editing* (Minneapolis, 1992).

On the History of Classical Scholarship For a general introduction and recent bibliography for many important individuals in the history of Classical scholarship, see W. W. Briggs-W. M. Calder III, eds., *Classical Scholarship: A Biographical Encyclopedia* (New York-London, 1990). See also H. J. Apel and S. Bittner, *Humanistische Schulbildung 1890–1945: Anspruch und Wirklichkeit der altertumskundlichen Unterrichtsfächer* (Cologne-Weimar-Vienna, 1994); M. Landfester, *Humanismus und Gesellschaft im 19. Jahrhundert: Untersuchungen zur politischen und gesellschaftlichen Bedeutung der humanistischen Bildung in Deutschland* (Darmstadt, 1988); M. Weissenberger, "Geschichte der Klassischen Philologie," in *Einführung in das Studium der Latinistik,* by P. Riemer, M. Weissenberger, and B. Zimmermann (Munich, 1998), 12–41.

On Timpanaro A complete list of his works can be found in "L'opera di S. Timpanaro," ed. M. Feo, *Il Ponte* 57, nos. 10–11 (October–November 2001): (= R. Di Donato, ed., *Il filologo materialista: Studi per S. Timpanaro* [Pisa, 2003], 191–293, with revisions and refinements). Among the works related to the topics he dealt with in the *Genesis,* see: *Per la storia della filologia virgiliana antica* (Rome, 1986); "La filologia e il postmoderno," interview with P. Cataldi, *Allegoria* 3, no. 8 (1991): 95–108; *Virgilianisti antichi e tradizione indiretta* (Florence, 2001), reviewed by J. E. G. Zetzel, *Bryn Mawr Classical Review,* 9 February 2002, http://ccat.sas.upenn.edu/bmcr/2002/2002-02-09.html; *Stemmi tripartiti e lapsus (antichi e moderni),* four letters addressed to G. Magnaldi, in *Per Sebastiano Timpanaro, Il Ponte* 57, nos. 10–11 (October–November 2001): 323–30.

On Timpanaro's Life, Intellectual Activity, and Scholarship R. Williams, *Problems of Materialism and Culture* (London, 1980), 104–22; H. Lloyd-Jones, *Blood for the Ghosts: Classical Influences in the Nineteenth and Twentieth Centuries* (Baltimore, 1982), 105–8; R. S. Dombroski, "Timpanaro's Materialism: An Introduction," *Journal of the History of Ideas* 44 (1983): 311–26; G. Steiner, "New Movements in European Culture," *Times Literary Supplement* 77, no. 4422 (1–7 January 1988): 22; P. Anderson, "On Sebastiano Timpanaro," *London Review of Books* 23, no. 9 (10 May 2001): 8–12; *Per Sebastiano Timpanaro,* ed. M. Feo and M. Rossi, *Il Ponte,* 57, nos. 10–11 (October–November 2001); *Per Sebastiano Timpanaro,* with contributions by U. Carpi, R. Luperini, R. Castellana, G. Corlito, P. Cristofolini, A.T. Drago and P. Totaro, A. G. Drago, and R. Dombroski, *Allegoria* 13 (September–December 2001); *Il filologo materialista: Studi per S. Timpanaro,* ed. R. Di Donato, with contributions by V. Di Benedetto, T. De Mauro, L. Blasucci, U. Carpi, G. M. Cazzaniga, P. Anderson, and M. Feo (Pisa, 2003); E. Ghidetti and A. Pagnini, eds., *Sebastiano Timpanaro e la cultura europea del secondo Ottocento* (Rome, 2003).

Index of Names

Index of Topics

Index of Manuscripts Discussed